Laurence O'Toole has written book reviews for the *New Statesman*, *Independent* and *Daily Telegraph*. He lives in London and travelled widely in the UK and the USA to research *Pornocopia*, his first book.

Praise for *Pornocopia*

'No shortage of books . . . about the porn industry, but Laurence O'Toole is head and shoulders above them for research, felicity of phrase, and liberal attitude . . . Excellent' *Time Out*

'*Pornocopia* is a highly readable, sane and non-judgemental tour of the entire landscape of the modern porn industry. Drawing refreshingly upon interviews with actors, producers and consumers, O'Toole delivers a humane indictment of the state's passion, especially strong in the UK, for censorship and overregulation' Andrew Ross

'Brilliantly argued' *Sight & Sound*

'For decades, the intellectual argument about the porn business has tended to be one-sided. It's always been hard to find anyone willing not just to stand up for porn on principle but to positively identify themselves as a fan. Well, take a bow Mr Laurence O'Toole, a man unafraid to speak up for the charms of *The Devil in Miss Jones* and *Buttman's Inferno*. *Pornocopia* is both an excellent history of mass-market hardcore porn from the Sixties to the Nineties and a well-argued case for the need for less rather than more censorship' *GQ*

'This overview of the state of porn combines good, hard journalism with critical analysis. O'Toole wants to overturn the tired cliches of the porn debate. . . . This is a timely, witty look at the world's biggest, least discussed industry' *Esquire*

Pornocopia

porn, sex, technology and desire

Laurence O'Toole

To Marion

Library of Congress Catalog Card Number 97–061913

A complete catalogue record for this book can be obtained from the British Library on request

The right of Laurence O'Toole to be acknowledged as the author of his work has been asserted by him in accordance with the Copyright, Patents and Designs Act 1988

First published in 1998 by Serpent's Tail
4 Blackstock Mews, London N4

Web site: http://www.serpentstail.com

Phototypeset in 10.5/13.5pt Plantin by Intype London Ltd
Printed in Great Britain by Mackays of Chatham, plc

10 9 8 7 6 5 4 3 2

Contents

'Everybody knows there is no fineness or accuracy of supression; if you hold down one thing you hold down the adjoining.'

(Saul Bellow, *The Adventures of Augie March*)

'There are no places for people like me to go to, to meet and be accepted, so it has to be kept under wraps . . . I live alone and porn is part of my life: without it, would be like leaving off my shoes and going around barefooted.'

(Anonymous gay farmer from the west of Ireland)

'Why has no one cracked this before?'

(Alfred C Kinsey, sex researcher)

Acknowledgements

To research and write this book meant calling upon the generosity and patience of a lot of people who offered their time, knowledge, information and help. I am indebted to so many, a lot of whom, because of the subject, feel a need either to remain anonymous or pseudonymous or to go without any acknowledgement whatsoever.

I would like to thank the couple of hundred people who wrote or emailed me about their views as porn fans. Of those I can cite, a special thank you to 'Nicholas White', 'Jonathan Martin', 'Kate', Geoff Williams, 'Burkman', 'Shamenero', Andrew, Jeff Faria, Kevin Haynor, 'bbyabo', 'dander', 'knife', 'Wazza T', 'Donovan', 'starrz', 'Anita-M', John, 'Mace', 'Suzi', Amy, Jeff Pruett, 'Chaotic Sojourner', 'Thumper', 'Ace', J Zunti, 'thunder', 'SAcks', 'Demaret', 'Tresman', 'der Mouse', 'Mr Freep', 'Wildchild', Julie, Julia, Steve, Ben, 'Barlow', Mandy, 'Arcadian', 'billp', 'Gaetan', 'Zippy', 'Zennor', 'Imperator', the other countless people and never-ending discussion threads at alt.sex.movies and rec.arts.movies.erotica. In Britain and the United States I met, interviewed and learned from numerous people. Again, many thanks are offered specifically to Tuppy Owens, Zak Keir, Avedon Carol, Spencer Woodcock, Sam Shad, David Kastens, Brandy Alexandre, Vivid Video, John Stagliano, Jenteal, Paul Thomas, Henri Pachard, Jacquie Martine, Isabelle, Gaby, Nicola, 'Angel', Melanie, 'Syd', Catherine, Chasey Lain, Julie Rage, Christy Canyon, Cindy Cox, Woody Long, Michael Rose, Lesley Anne

Sharrock, Peter Webb, Rosie Gunn, Kerri Sharp, Ted Goodman of the Campaign Against Censorship, David Webb of the National Campaign for the Reform of the Obscene Publications Act, the Area Clubs And Vice Unit of the Metropolitan Police, Nicky Akehurst, and Stephen J. King.

Gratitude also goes to Pascal Cariss, Mark Slater, Joseph O'Neill, Dave and Alison, Emma Waghorn, Pete Ayrton and Peter Dyer. Also Kathy B, and Kathy Thorpe, who read parts of the text at a pivotal moment, offering the right combination of critical abuse and constructive insight.

Without the intellectual and emotional input from Marion Steel this book wouldn't have been written. Over three years her supply of thoughts, ideas, support and encouragement didn't once flag. I owe her a great deal.

Prologue

In *Manhattan*, Woody Allen's film of 1979, a character suggests that 'gossip is the new pornography'. Ironically, in mainstream coverage of porn in Britain and America much that is said isn't particularly accurate; it is more fuelled by hearsay, guesswork and fabrication than anything particularly factual – pure gossip, in other words. *Pornocopia* is an attempt to deal more truthfully with leading aspects of porn in Britain and the USA. Rather than treat porn as simply a problem, the book tries to look on it as an industry, a legal event, a film genre and a viewing experience.

Key scenes from this book include a first-hand account of the making of an American porn film. In Los Angeles, on the set of a high-cost hard-core feature film, a porn actress dressed like a futuristic warrior out of the *Mad Max* films explains why she left her job in the US Army to make porn films instead. Despite various rumours to the contrary, as will be demonstrated, women and men are working in porn voluntarily, happily and successfully.

Away from California, cut to a scene in Britain in the late nineties, to a North London courtroom, where a porn-smuggling operation faces prosecution. Any consideration of porn in the UK inevitably becomes intertwined with issues of censorship. Hard-core porn is virtually illegal in Britain. In the main, 'hard core' means unambiguous depictions of sexual conduct – erections, penetration, oral sex – while soft core tends to offer simulated or euphemistic versions of sex, or just nudity. If a couple of Martians visiting Earth landed in the London of the eighties or nineties, an examination of the legal pornographic videos on general release would lead them to wonder how Earthlings manage to procreate without genital contact. If the Martians were to go looking for something a little more realistic (while also hoping not to be ripped off), then they might find themselves, like I did, searching for hard core in a temporary, hole-in-the-wall porn shop in London's East End. Such an experience exists in sharp contrast to watching a porn film at a regular multiplex cinema in West Hollywood, or buying a video from a swish retail outlet in San Francisco or Florida.

On the question of how the porn fan gets hold of the goods, *Pornocopia* also considers the complex, evolving relationship between porn and the new information technologies. Covering the unstoppable rise of cyberporn not only finds me scrolling through rude pictures on the internet, courtesy of assorted cyberporners, but sharing a digital orgasm with a pair of screen lovers who, though physically hundreds of miles apart, are having sex online, using hard-core porn for arousal.

Although the opening chapters of this book will seek to engage with some of the familiar issues that tend to arise with porn – like how to make a definition that works, or the flare-ups over porn within the feminist movement – *Pornocopia* will mostly attempt to move things forward, opening up what has previously proved a closed subject. One way of doing this is by looking at porn as a viewing experience. It is a curious thing that when porn is up for discussion the many people who make use of porn are rarely consulted. 'Porn is sex without secrecy, out in the open,' suggests Bernard Arcand, the French-Canadian anthropologist, 'but its users are secret.'[1] This silence leaves the porn debate much the poorer. A British opinion poll of 1991 suggested that out of 800 middle-class Englishmen, 75 per cent had seen soft-core porn at some time in their life, and 50 per cent hard-core porn.[2] But porn is no longer just a guilty secret of heterosexual males. It is a leisure activity pursued by considerable numbers of gay men, heterosexual and lesbian women, fetishists, sex therapists, pensioners, etc., and one that is occurring both inside and outside sexual relationships, with or without a partner.

The last chapter of *Pornocopia* features excerpts from numerous interviews with porn users. It also includes observations drawn from a wide-ranging survey that I conducted through letters and via the internet, which garnered responses from hundreds of men and women – both gay and straight – from North America, Scandinavia, Australia, and the British Isles. According to the majority of porn users, and contrary to the usual gossip on porn, most people seem to find their time with porn pleasurable rather than sad, demeaning, addictive or harmful.

These things are best seen against the backdrop of an increased sexualisation of British and American society during the nineties, where sex seems to be everywhere in the media and in commerce, selling every type of commodity and lifestyle. At the same time, anxiety over AIDS, and maybe also the state of social and family cohesion, finds recent sex surveys in Britain and the USA reporting an apparent decline in sexual promiscuity, where the main romantic goal for the majority of adults is a long-term, monogamous relationship. Within such a conflictual social context, porn features not only as short-term sex therapy for some, but also as a fantasy fling, a vicarious sexual adventure, and possibly, therefore, a relationship saver.

In researching this book I became increasingly aware of the need to raise new and different questions – if not necessarily expecting to answer them all, or to answer them to everybody's satisfaction – in order to think differently on porn. For instance, despite the mainstream presentation of porn as bad for women, as well as the traditional social exclusion of women from access to such materials, in actuality many women are now using porn. This growing trend leaves the view that porn is intrinsically sexist open to doubt. Indeed, to brand porn simply as offensive to women not only tends to halt any conversation on the matter before it has really begun but also stops some women from trying out something they may enjoy.

Two or more decades of debate in the sphere of cultural politics, of thoroughgoing media-content analysis, have shown how difficult it is to find common ground, let alone agreement, on what a sexist image might look like. As no two people are likely to take the same thing from an image, to brand all porn 'sexist', and thus beyond the pale, is neither valid nor particularly helpful. In reality, porn is a multifaceted phenomenon in itself, made more diffuse and complex by the way different people experience and interpret porn as viewers. The more I found out about the diverse reactions of different people to porn, the more I had to recognise that not only is the content of porn frequently transgressive of the dominant cultural attitudes on sex, morality and, arguably, gender, but the very experience of using porn (like sex) will often be tumultuous, even dislocating. Knowing this makes it hard to accept any characterisation of porn as this hidden place within the culture where matters of sexuality are neatly resolved, or where gender inequalities are unconditionally reaffirmed.

Another way of thinking differently on porn comes by closely observing the actual thing itself. *Pornocopia* takes a good, long look at porn films, a briefer look at porn magazines, and none at all at erotic novels. This particular focus is partly due to limitations of space. Also, as books are afforded far more cultural weight and respect, these days they are rarely a target for censorship. Therefore, to look at erotic fiction would necessarily become an exercise in literary evaluation, and so the subject of a whole other book. The porn magazine, meanwhile, has become a rather stagnant form, whose chief function for many, it would seem, is providing a portable, more discrete stand-in, or back-up, to the porn video.

At the end of the nineties, many of the more interesting developments in popular porn are occurring on film. *Pornocopia* will treat porn films like regular films. In wishing to make sense of porn classics of the seventies like *Devil in Miss Jones* or *The Opening of Misty Beethoven*, or the new high-gloss porn of the nineties – *Hidden Obsessions, Companion* or *Latex* – I have tried, in part, to consider porn as just another cinematic genre. This approach is also a useful way of guiding readers through some of the complex workings of porn – which explains the extended film reviews, and the rather unorthodox shape of the brief, potted history of mainly motion-picture porn in Chapter 3.

To write, as I have, with an enthusiasm for something so loathed in certain quarters is maybe asking for trouble. (Indeed, through some eyes simply to choose porn as a subject for a book is enough to impeach the author.) However, the risk of becoming a social outcast, simply for recognising the potential in porn for arousal, was weighed up against the need to open readers' eyes to this very same possibility: of the need to get it across to the uninitiated that they, too, could actually get to like porn, and be aroused by it.

Finally, the clear bias towards heterosexual porn in Britain and the USA in this book is down both to my own sexuality and to an Englishman's difficulties with foreign languages, which prevent me from fully engaging with such materials. It also needs to be said that European porn is not so deeply locked in with issues of law and regulation, and therefore the European porn story is quite different from the porn stories of Britain and the USA. Restrictions of language, as well as budget, also explain why this book has not covered the global porn scene. Such a project is probably beyond a single writer anyway. No matter how fast or sophisticated communication systems have become, no matter how much reference is made to a 'globalised' culture at the end of the twentieth century, any attempt to cover porn on a world level would need a drastic abridgement of the cultural differences that continue to exist between disparate communities and societies. This would also mean an equally drastic foreshortening of the book's insight or value. Such an account of porn would inevitably come to rely upon assorted unreliable forms of knowledge, like guesswork and hearsay. It would become, therefore, another work of gossip.

It is, in fact, one of the most common, most repeated myths about porn – the one that says that porn has always been with us, is as old as history itself – that will serve as a jumping-off point for the opening chapter of this book, in a discussion of the many ways of defining pornography.

1
Definitions

Pornography, as we understand it, is a modern phenomenon. Porn is not timeless, has not always been with us. It is only in 1857 that 'pornography' receives its definition in the *Oxford English Dictionary*. We don't mean just the word, however, but the thing itself, or the series of things. If by porn we mean regulated, explicit depictions of bodies, sex organs and sexual activity specifically designed to sexually arouse (or the fetish-ised stand-in: image of a stiletto on a white shiny plate, a submissive male licking a woman's ankle-length boot, a fleece-quilted sleeping bag immersed in a steamy bath), if this is what we take porn to be, and surely we do, then pornography only came into being at the close of the eighteenth century, attaining widespread circulation and attention from the middle of the last century.

Previously, throughout early modern European history, 'pornography' was used chiefly to satirise, criticise, to tilt at the Church, the state, the monarchy. This was political porn: product of the birth of print culture and the beginning of an urban market society where increasing numbers of people, partly distanced from laws of kinship, met to trade ideas, as well as commodities, and inevitably to question the values of traditional authorities who they now rivalled in the power game. Porn was controlled during this period not because it was obscene but because it was seditious, blasphemous or defamatory. From Pietro Aretino through to the Marquis de Sade, and shortly thereafter, the motivation for drawing lewd, for talking dirty, was being anti-authority and anti-tradition. Porn was an oppositional form for freethinkers, libertines, sensualists and democrats. Writers would use brazen and graphic characters from the bordello also as a philosophical appeal for unhindered straight talk and truth-telling. The prostitute Antonia in Aretino's *Ragionamenti* calls for the ditching of euphemism: 'Speak plainly, and say "fuck", "prick", "cunt" and "arse".'[1]

Porn also changed depending upon who saw it, and how readily available it became. High-class 'hot' texts were without public controversy when not widely circulated. John Cleland's *Fanny Hill* is a case in point. This tale of élitists, libertines and Greek revivalism (originally called *Memoirs of a Woman of Pleasure*) caused not the merest legal flutter on publication in 1748. And this is how things remained during the rest of the eighteenth century. Though thoroughly rude, there was no political sin intrinsic to Fanny, who, since she was also only available to a highly restricted readership, was seen to pose no threat. This was a time before mass literacy, or before the purely sexual offence had been dreamed up by the censor. Problems started once it became possible for the book to be read at large, and during a period when the Victorians started to close in on sex for closer supervision, at which stage the élite classes felt an urgent need to keep such exotic fancies out of the grubby reach of the lower orders, and beyond the delicate gaze of the fairer gender. The previously unimpeachable Fanny was now in trouble, and in court. 'By overvaluing both sex and representations,' writes Kendrick, 'the nineteenth century created a category which had not existed, or only in rudimentary form, in any past age.'[2]

Modern porn is partly about democracy, about sharing out the treats. Many celebrated painters of the eighteenth and nineteenth centuries turned out spots of rude art on the quiet. Today, two hundred years later, these salacious items remain, according to Bernard Arcand, hidden away as part of the closet collections of discrete collectors, while images of Pamela Anderson or David Duchovny adorn the global teenager's bedroom wall. Provocative representations for dirty little minds are no longer the exclusive pleasures of the privileged. Modern porn is more open, Arcand argues: 'Just as music composed for the private enjoyment of a king can now be heard by anyone owning a Walkman, so any member of the proletariat can contemplate the most spectacular bodies.'[3]

Porn, in the form of regulated materials designed for sexual arousal, emerged partly as a consequence of the decline in religion, and partly through the separating of sex from procreation, coupled with views from the Enlightenment that sex might actually make a person happy. Locked in with these ideological shifts were the new theories of gender difference in the West, figuring women as fairer, gentler, rather innocent creatures ideally secluded in domesticity. The new-fashioned porn was at loggerheads with gender separation.[4] Hence its status as a troublemaker. 'As new biological and moral standards for sexual difference evolved,' writes the historian Lynn Hunt, 'pornography seemed to become even more exotic and dangerous. It had to be stamped out.'[5]

The start of the specialised pornographic era we are still living through in the West duly followed after the close of the earlier political pornographic tradition, which reached its climactic end with the antics of the French revolution. The political pornographer's range reached its full extension 'and then some' – as hard-core film-maker Patrick Collins might put it – with the imaginative extremes of the Marquis de Sade. Henceforth the political, subversive content of porn started to dry up in Europe and North America, as an era began in which commercial, sexually arousing porn was suppressed on moral and social grounds.

Political pornography did survive into the twentieth century in Mexico. After the revolution, the victorious generals appropriated Hollywood cameras and film stock to capture some live footage of the ongoing cultural and sexual upheavals, commissioning the production of short porn films – 'stag' movies. These stag movies of the twenties often featured priests pursuing the carnal desires they so piously urged their congregation to renounce, and were designed to undermine the social influence of the Catholic church, which had supported the previous regime. Mexican stag endeavoured to show sex as good and liberating, promoting sexual experimentation and excess, and an end to all constricting pruderies. Political revolution and sexual freedom were seen as profoundly enmeshed. The Russian film-maker Sergei Eisenstein visited to film *Viva Mexico* and drew several sketches, still unpublished, depicting the revolutionary spirit combining bullets with ejaculate. Not just land and freedom, but the porn of plenty too. Modern Mexican porn – what there is of it – now principally concerns itself with sexual arousal. There may be additional sub-textualities, but it's the horn that's the thing.[6]

In nineties Italy, Joe D'Amato's period porn movie *Stella d'Italienne* features a priest and some landowners in turn-of-the-century Italy. Our handsome, virile cleric visits the film's wealthy lead couple at their opulent Tuscan palazzo to offer succour during a rocky patch in their marriage. They all drink wine at dusk on the terrazzo with its *merveilloso* view of the hills, the fields and the woods. Later, in his bedchamber, the priest is visited by the sexually unhappy wife. He is wearing only his shirt and smalls. She tells him she thinks her husband doesn't find her sexually attractive. The priest insists she's a real looker, which he then confirms by having sex with her. Though still a churchgoing nation, the pluralist culture of modern Italy characterises D'Amato's movie, with the priest's hard-core participation little to do with any residual anti-clericalism and much more about the generous spirit of pornocopia, the porn of plenty, where everybody shares in the carnal abandon.

Modern porn is about fantasy and arousal. Anything else, be it revolutionary, educational or philosophical, is strictly secondary. And should it ever start to be more than that, it's most likely getting in the way, and then it's probably no longer porn we're talking about. It's a very rare day in pornland that the content of a new video includes a political rant. There are exceptions. There's *Infamous Crimes Against Nature*, a porn film about the Las Vegas eleven (and pretty much starring the Las Vegas eleven), the porn actresses arrested for lewd lesbian conduct at a private gathering in Las Vegas in 1993.[7] There is also *The Trial,* a porn fantasy from the early nineties, featuring the real-life obscenity prosecution of Vivid Video, with rural Mississippi as narrative backdrop. To say that porn is no longer working to bring the system to its knees (though performers spend a fair part of an average adult movie in such a position) is not to suggest that politics is no longer in attendance. As a phenomenon, porn is saturated with political meanings concerning sexual practices, morality, pleasure, private liberties and individual rights. Likewise the continued regulation of porn is a very political matter.

Knowing the elephant
(on defining porn as a legal hunt)

To make sense of modern porn, and of how it might be defined, one needs to follow the law. There's a near absence of porn history in the US government's Meese Commission report on pornography (1986). Far more space is devoted to the history of the regulation of porn. 'This disproportion between the history of the practice and the history of its regulation is significant,' writes Hunt, 'since pornography has always been defined in part by the efforts undertaken to regulate it.'[8] The history of the legal definitions of pornography has seen the hunt after a lewd thing that can be decoupled from the rest of art and expression and labelled as obscene. In the realm of law, modern times have witnessed an endless struggle between producers and regulators over nuances of words and definitions – hence Kendrick's assertion that porn is not a thing, more an argument.[9] This argument has witnessed the repeated dismissal of cases of alleged obscenity as social values have shifted and the acceptable levels of sexual frankness extended. Meanwhile, as the courts were happily declaring what wasn't pornographic (thereby widening the category of the non-obscene to accommodate the sex-counselling work of Marie Stopes, *Ulysses,* D.H. Lawrence, *Inside Linda Lovelace* and so on), the often unstated conviction that there is such a thing that is definitely obscene, unequivocally porn, has persisted. It was just a matter of tracking the little sucker down.[10]

Despite all the talk and trials over porn, any attempt to fix upon a satisfactory, abiding definition has failed. Though the word is hurled around as if everybody knows for sure what's being referred to, porn itself – a thing so explicitly self-advertising and so vehemently reviled – remains partly unknown. Perhaps the much ridiculed US Supreme Court judge, Potter Stewart, came as close to definition as any when in 1964 he declared that though he might not be able to aptly phrase it, 'I know it when I see it'. This is what Bernard Arcand refers to as the Sophism of the Elephant: 'The belief that there are things in the world that, like the elephant, are impossible to describe but are, nonetheless, instantly recognisable.'[11]

The word 'pornography' doesn't actually feature much on the statute books. The term is more a social and political designation. Likewise with 'erotica'. These days erotica serves as the acceptable level of sexual expression, defining itself in contrast to porn, which represents the unacceptable. In an email to the author, a porn fan disputes the separation. 'The distinction between porn and erotica is a totally false, political distinction; basically, if I like it, it's wonderful, life-affirming erotica; if you like it and I don't, it's cheap, sleazy porn.'[12] This false distinction is partly a class issue, a matter of taste, and gender politics too. Here, an alleged rift finds women's erotica on one side and male porn on the other, the suggestion being that female sexuality innately leans towards sensitive erotica, something wholly different to the hard, phallic, male porn. But when sex campaigner and therapist Tuppy Owens takes a camera and photographs herself floating down the river in Oxford 'with a stick of rhubarb up my cunt'; when the performer and movie producer Tianna Collins puts a vibrator inside another actress's vagina; when a dominatrix gives some chained-up bloke a hiding; and when Carol Leigh films a session of hand-balling, with a woman anally fisting a man – is this female erotica or male porn? How do we keep them apart?[13]

Most of what passes for erotica today would previously have done time as porn. It's just that the line has got shifted. 'What is erotica,' wonders critic Charlotte Raven, 'if not pornography wearing a veil?' The term 'erotica' could be about women finding their own desiring space in the culture, but is possibly also a way of 'protecting' women from their lustier selves. In considering the burgeoning genre of women's erotic fiction, Raven spots the real difference: 'Female erotica is pornography that's ashamed of itself.'[14] There's a thing called the Davis Conundrum, named after a wine test at the University of California at Davis, and described as 'information that may call into question a tenet that is central to a system of belief'. Apparently, wine experts in blindfolds often struggle to tell their red wine from their white.[15] Lay out the constituent parts of an erotic novel and those of a Paul Thomas hard-core movie, in some kind of blind test, and see if the distinction of forms still holds. It won't.

Like erotica and porn, 'obscenity' and 'indecency' depend upon subjective evaluation for definition. The difference is that both obscenity and indecency are 'bad objects', which the law seeks to locate for juridical attention. In Britain, 'indecency' is mostly a lesser crime. Indecency creates a feeling of disgust where one really oughtn't to be exposed to it – on the television, at the newsagent's, on a streetside advertising billboard, 'something an ordinary decent man or woman would find to be shocking, disgusting or revolting' (Lord Denning, 1976). Whereas obscenity more seriously threatens to 'deprave and corrupt' (Lord Justice Cockburn, 1888).[16] Obscenity, it is suggested, has the potential to change the way someone behaves, even make a monster of him or her, and so it shouldn't be allowed. What obscenity might actually look like is pretty much determined by what the customs or police officer, censor, prosecutor, judge or jury sees in a text or an image, and what they choose to object to. It is vital to remember this. When Canada altered its laws in 1992 to accommodate a more anti-porn, so-called 'feminist' position, it was heterosexual male customs officers who deemed lesbian, feminist-produced 'erotica' to be pornographic – since these kinds of material were not to their subjective liking (see Chapter 2, 'Porn Wars').

In the USA the legal situation of pornography is complicated. Although free speech is protected under the First Amendment to the United States Constitution, a landmark case in 1957, known as *Roth* v. *United States*, held that 'obscenity' was not to be accorded such protection. At the time, obscenity was described as anything utterly lacking redeeming qualities. The word 'utterly' was significant. If defendants could summon up the briefest glimpse of something redeeming in their salacious piece of goods, then chances were they left court with a smile on their face. Rather than tighten the situation by making clear what was considered prurient or otherwise in any representation of sex, the word 'utterly' opened things up. Not only were James Joyce and other 'true' artists free from allegations of obscenity simply for exploring the matter of sex, but so too was Russ Meyer. He and a hatful of other smart operators in the fringe world of nudie and so-called 'sexploitation' films were able to hide behind the redemptive fig leaf of a plot, a story, a psychological angle, or the noble cause of documentary, education, or whichever alibi was likely to float.[17]

After *Roth* v. *United States* the hunt for the obscene was on, taking America all the way through the sixties and into the early seventies, during an era of profound social and sexual change, and bringing it to 1972, to the New World Theater, New York, and the full-on, big-screen entertainments and hard-core largesse of *Deep Throat* – the whole sex show, and plenty of pervy trimmings, the groans, moans, the sucking and fucking, the 'attack' of the ten-foot penises. Clearly 'utterly' hadn't achieved what it was supposed to. It was time to go back to the Supreme Court and get a new ruling on the matter. The 1973 case of *Miller* v. *California* established a stricter test of obscenity: that a work was obscene if it were 'utterly' without redeeming social worth, *and* if it lacked 'serious' literary, artistic, political or scientific value. And this was to be judged according to contemporary community standards. The 'serious' part was meant to rid the land of the trash hard core. But, since 'community standards' in many parts of America had liberalised, in the main 'serious' didn't really do the trick.

It didn't take a legal genius to spot that the so-called Miller Test wasn't much of a definition. Miller was part dodge, part delegation, passing the job of definition down the line to the local level. This time round the key words were 'community standards', which continue to haunt the American hard-core industry into the late nineties. Celebrating a legal victory in Las Vegas in 1996, *Adult Video News* (*AVN*), the industry trade magazine, picks up on an off-hand remark made by the defeated prosecutor: "'This is one jury. If we had 12 other people, it might [be different]'" – meaning that another prosecution could be brought, any time, anywhere, alleging that a video or magazine is obscene, and it all depends on what the jury decide. In theory you could win in forty-nine states, with forty-nine different juries, and then be brought to trial in the fiftieth state and lose and face three to five years in jail. 'The point is,' *AVN* continues, 'one of the bedrocks of the law in this country is supposed to be that the *law* tells you what you can and can't do, and if you've got any questions about it, you just go to the statutes and get the answer. A guy who walks into a bank, pulls a gun and says "Gimme all your money" is a bank robber, pure and simple. No jury of "12 good men and true" could find otherwise.' However, that's not the case with pornography. 'The law no longer tells you whether you're breaking "the law" or not. Now, you have to spend thousands of bucks on attorneys who try to convince 12 good ol' boys in Pig's Knuckle, Nebraska that they'll "tolerate" your product.'[18]

A significant consequence of the 'community standards' definition is that the range and availability of pornography in America varies enormously. In the South, there are towns that are totally porn free and others that will only stock *Playboy*. Several southern states of the Union are effectively no-go areas for hard core – 'taboo' states, as the adult industry knows them. The greatest availability is in the urban spaces. Cities like Boston, San Francisco and Los Angeles will take a lot of materials, and traditionally New York's liberal community standard takes the most. There have been things for sale in New York – for example, tapes and magazines on watersports (urination), and certain kinds of bondage, on import from Continental Europe and Asia – that are to be found almost nowhere else. (Child pornography is illegal in terms of production, distribution and possession, anywhere in the USA.)[19]

Where the Miller Test was wrong, as far as the American porn industry is concerned, was in failing to clearly separate porn from obscenity. The two continue to be linked together both legally and culturally. Hence some people who make what is effectively hard-core porn – known to all by its explicit quality, its depiction of erections, penetration, oral–genital contact, ejaculation – prefer to use another word to describe their product: 'adult entertainment', 'erotic entertainment', 'adult erotica'. This is not really a case of euphemism, more of pragmatism. If US pornographers have one common goal, apart from making dollar fortunes, it is to achieve First Amendment protection for what they do, so that porn would become protected as free speech through being defined as not obscene. Until that happens – and it's probably still a long way off – the ascription 'porno' is, for some, untenable.

This separation of sexually explicit materials from 'obscenity' already exists with literature, where effectively a novel can be 'pornographic' and yet not obscene. In recent times the porn story has not really concerned texts. At the American trial of *Ulysses* in 1933, the presiding judge was a literary buff who was prepared to read this difficult modernist text and who determined that the book was many things but it wasn't obscene. This was a turning point in America, marking the beginning of the end of times spent looking for censorable porn in prose. A similar landmark would be reached some thirty years later in the UK with the trial of *Lady Chatterley's Lover*.

During the previous hundred and fifty years the novel did its time as a public menace, threatening to turn readers into nutters. Outraged spokespersons bemoaned the fearful collision of racy prose and a new kind of massed, urbanised public. 'The only acquaintance which the writer of this article has with Zola's novels is from two pages of one of the most notorious of them,' declared an appalled Reverend Sanger. 'The matter was of such a leprous character that it would be impossible for any young man who had not learned the divine secret of self control to have read it without committing some form of outward sin within 24 hours after.'[20] It is a familiar call for restraint. Sanger is not only a prude and a killjoy, he is also a paternalist who 'knows best' without viewing the offending material properly. He is one of those archetypes of censorship that have appeared repeatedly over the last few centuries, like the English Catholic cardinal who warns his flock not to see the film *The Last Temptation of Christ* but hasn't watched it himself, or the Christian anti-drugs campaigner on British television who urges that the movie *Trainspotting* be banned because its 'pro-drugs' message will cause addiction levels to go through the roof – although she's yet to see it, she mutters.

Occasionally, fires are still started over the content of books – *Naked Lunch* and *Last Exit to Brooklyn* in the sixties and *Inside Linda Lovelace* during the seventies featuring as notorious examples. *American Psycho*, *The Satanic Verses*, *Lord Horror* and *The Anarchist's Cookbook* are more recent kerfuffles or acts of state intervention in the field of text. Broadly speaking, however, books haven't been the site of the real porn action since the midpoint of the century. Graphic fictions from authors as diverse as Samuel Delaney, Helen Zahavi, Anaïs Ninn, Will Self – featuring paedophilic lusts, gun-toting femme annihilators, women raping women with penknives, and torso-less heads employed in the service of fellatio – do rear up from time to time, but will most likely find their way to the local bookstores unhindered. If they achieve controversy the heat doesn't lead to prosecution, merely newspaper thought pieces or equivocal notices in the literary review pages. Books have gradually ceased to function in public demonology as dangerous cultural packages. Familiarity with the novel, combined with the rapid extension of visual media like cinema, television, video and computers, has mainly seen it venerated as a safe haven for the reader. A more deeply sedimented dread of the power of the image, its perceived force of impact, perhaps ensured that the porn wars were destined to revolve around pictures. Furthermore, as the elephant hunt gradually became a search for the visual obscenity, it equally became, as we shall see, a search for the visceral obscenity, a hunt for something that moves the body, something that isn't 'art'.

Pornography versus art

(on defining porn as not art)

Close to the heart of the porn-definitions argument is an ongoing dispute between art and porn, the valuable versus the worthless. At times science has been brought in as an expert witness for the defence against accusations of obscenity, notably in the early years of the century with Havelock Ellis and his pioneering publications in the field of sexology. However, the use of artistic licence as a defence is longer-standing. This is not just a case of searching for an alibi – though this certainly goes on – but also a process of fixing a marker along the continuum, to clearly establish how far 'art' can go before it slips beneath the 'pulp line' and into pure sleaze.[21]

The continuum goes like this. You start with Michelangelo's David, you do Ingres, Lautrec, Alma-Tadema, Lawrence, Fellini, Roeg, Aragon and Bataille, you go past Verhoeven and then, by current community standards, you start to get twitchy. But where exactly does the guillotine fall? Do you stop at 'art' movies by Oshima, Andy Warhol, Walerian Borowczyk or Curt McDowell, the high-style fashion plates of Helmut Newton, Joel Peter Witkin's corporeal horrors? Will the camp scatology of early John Waters or the cultish gore of Jess Franco not be redeemed. Or do you let all of these people in, but stop at Andrew Blake – effectively Helmut Newton but in the video hard-core format. Some porners argue that their product should be placed with the arts, on the sunny side of the continuum. But not Larry Flynt of *Hustler* magazine. 'I never tried to justify what I was doing by wrapping it in art,' he says. 'But Hugh Hefner and Bob Guccione, they try to masquerade their pornography as art ... *Hustler* [is] about sex, and from that point of view we see ourselves apart by being an entertainment magazine.'[22]

With the continuum model there needs to be a way to make the cut-off point logically defensible. This is mainly achieved either by arguing for an offence to common sensibilities (of the man on the Clapham omnibus, or the equally elusive Joe

Sixpack), or by asserting that the material, while it might be art to some poor fools, could nevertheless cause them harm – that it is corrupting. Not corrupting of you or me, of course, but someone else. *We* can view the material and not be depraved; it is always somebody else who ought to be kept from seeing obscenity. An anonymous porn fan shares this fear: 'Whilst I think it's okay for myself and others in a privileged, educated clique to consume all kinds of material within the context of sophisticated, caring friendships, there are many different types of people looking at porn and I guess there are many variables. What effect does it have on, say, a racist BNP supporter living in Canning Town?'[23]

In arguments over porn and corruption and harm that embrace the platonic ideal of art as something that affects behaviour, people rarely point to the platonic ideal working in the opposite direction, where all art needs to make good.[24] This is more than just an abstract philosophical point; it touches on the politics of cultural hierarchies. In part they rarely point to a positive visceral response because art is argued to be non-visceral; it's supposed to make you lofty, not horny – it is the very opposite of porn. Beyond the continuum there exists within the 'art' argument an attempt to construct a kind of antipodean conflict, where art and porn aren't slyly linked, or dangerously adjoining, but are polar opposites. However, no valid separation can be offered, certainly not at the receiver's end. Plainly it all depends on your point of view, and what does it for you. Both art and porn have the potential to sexually excite. Surrealist art, a Nabokov novel, the films of David Lynch, even the Bible, may provoke a pornographic response, causing arousal. Erotic stimulation is also sought in advertising – arresting billboard posters, slick seductive commercials, magazine come-ons. The difference is that porn directly focuses upon causing arousal. This is porn's genre specificity. Though arousal might occur any time, any place, in any genre, it is porn's one-track mind that gets it into trouble.

But this doesn't make porn anti-art. It is the assertion of this book that porn is as much art as is any other kind of expression. Although it is not necessarily desirable in and of itself that porn be elevated from out of the sleaze category and into the art canon, there are good reasons why it would be better if it were treated with more respect. Criticism tends to help genres grow. Consider the once-marginal thriller, or science-fiction novel. It is hard to think of two genres more culturally happening these days. Porn may well benefit from closer critical appraisal, while also gaining through artistic recognition a protected status that may enable legal reforms to occur.

In late 1996 the film *Crash* was under threat of censorship in Britain. The liberal intelligentsia was mortified: an art house director's freedom of expression risked being curtailed by the forces of cultural darkness. A group of critics went on a day trip to Brussels for BBC television's *Late Review* programme to see *Crash*, then to return and defend it from censorship. Mostly, it is only when the liberal intelligentsia finds its privileges under fire that it goes to war. The critics could have gone to Brussels and watched porn movies. They might then have debated the glaring anomaly of two similar Western nations with very different laws on censorship, and the social acceptability of the continued restrictions on freedom of expression in Britain. They didn't, and they probably won't so long as porn continues to be deemed as having no cultural or artistic weight, but is seen merely as wankers' fodder of no critical interest.

It is from the rejection of porn as art that many pejorative views concerning the genre derive. Porn is silly, boring, coarsening, soulless, demeaning; it makes you unhappy. Apart from anything else, such defamation speaks of porn as though it were one thing. However, porn is not a single image infinitely duplicated, it's a whole series of images, a particular entity that branches out into many subgenres, ranging from the computer-generated flash of Michael Ninn to the carry-on carnivalesque of the British porn magazine *Razzle*, from the DIY amateur video in grainy black and white to John Leslie's high-gloss porn noir.

If it makes someone feel aroused, at some level, we still seem to think that that is all we need to know. This is peculiar, as we recognise from within ourselves, as well as from what we see about us as we travel through the nineties, that sexualities are numerous and multi-flavoured. We become aware that, as with hunger, this supposedly simple Neanderthal impulse is actually very complicated, causing a complex mishmash of cuisines and recipes to evolve. The voluminous review section for *AVN* kicks off every month with an explanation of its complex ratings system of porn subgenres. Broadly speaking, it reads like this: there are film and video 'features', there's 'gonzo', 'wall-to-wall', gay, lesbian, and then there's the very busy realm of 'specialty', the whole range that is legally permissible in America – fetish, bondage, girl–girl, domination, foot fanciers, fat ladies, pensioner porn, pregnant tapes, wrestling, corsetry, spanking, lesbians who smoke ... then there's amateur, pro-am, and assorted themed compilations.

It is not possible to take such a diverse entity and call it a singular thing, available to be read in a singular way, and always resulting in a negative experience. Not only is porn a genre made of many subgenres, but it elicits an endless variety of viewer responses. The pornographic image may be received in a thousand different ways by a thousand different people. Traditionally theories of mass culture – film, TV, magazines, pop music, video games – tend to depict viewers as brainwashed drudges straight out of Aldous Huxley. The mass-cultural artefact is said to carry a pre-programmed response where the viewer has no choice: he *will* do what the singular media message requires of him; I shall obey.[25] Recent reappraisals of the way we are with culture – from Eco to Bordieu – try to take the viewer's autonomy into account. It is actually possible that recipients have a say in what the mass media 'means' to them – have input, in fact, through filtering and rearranging the cultural signals, even subverting them for themselves, in a way that makes sense to them. Jennifer Wicke suggests that we 'accept that people transform the mass-cultural objects that come before them in a variety of ways'.[26]

A key point, one that runs throughout this book, is that porn is too easily dismissed because it isn't properly understood. Although porn is a direct address to the body, it requires as much, if not more, cerebral effort from the viewer than other art forms in order for it to work. It's what the hard-core director Henri Pachard calls the '80/20 rule': 'The producer provides the 80, and for the product to work, the user has to make up the missing 20 from themselves.' Arguably, the proportion of effort required of the porn consumer can be a lot more than 20 per cent. In itself porn is a 'small', compressed parcel of data, which is in need of decompression through the addition of the viewer's own erotic potentiality, their cerebral activity, their art-work. In this respect porn is less a wicked demon and more like a Pot Noodle, or a sprinkling of instant coffee granules in a coffee cup, waiting on the viewer's contribution of hot water in order for things to go off.[27] Porn will upset and offend some, and may not work for all, as proportions of sales in deregulated markets indicate, but the notion of porn as a powerful presence likely to overwhelm the defenceless viewer with greater knowledge becomes hard to trust. Porn is actually relatively small. It is the viewer who makes it big.

This art-work inherent in porn mostly goes unrecognised in mainstream culture. A lack of familiarity with the genre causes its summary dismissal as mind-numbingly repetitive. It's true that the stray, infrequent glimpse towards the top shelf would suggest the same old porn imagery. This is partly because magazine porn is not the most aggressively innovative medium in the world, but it is also because porn has a different aesthetic purpose: first and foremost, porn is about arousal. As Carol Clover writes, 'Pornography's shame lies in the fact that it has one simple, unequivocal intention: to excite its consumer.'[28] This is the vital porn component. Other expressive forms may privilege newness. A modish twist to your porn diet might be fine, but what's the point if it doesn't arouse you. Not every porn number need be wildly different from the last for it to work; it just has to be good. The critic George Steiner once characterised porn as a vice of repetition. To which Kenneth Tynan replied, 'he contends that, since the number of sexual positions and combinations is limited, porn is doomed to ultimate monotony. To which one replies that dawn and sunset are likewise limited, but that only a limited man would find them monotonous.'[29]

Porn is the straightforward depiction of sexual fantasy, using an image system that has little room for working things out analogously or metaphorically. The fantasies may be complex, but they are nearly always full on. 'Art' works quite differently – it is about deferral, the sublimation of bodily needs to higher planes of detachment. Thus 'art' is said to be improving while porn is mechanical waste. Plainly this denial of porn's complexity, the denigration of art that works on the body, is part of a larger political process. Art removing itself from porn's clutches is also a class act. The arts represent the escape from the useful, but also from the manual, the arduous, lowly, sweaty, grubby, proletarian. The middle classes used to distinguish themselves from their 'inferiors' by wearing suits and ties, by not having suntans, callused hands, or dirty fingernails. A further distancing was achieved through choosing art over sheer, raw pleasure – the vulgar, the impure, bawdy and rambunctious. The mind gains hold over the body; the sublime evacuates the base. Art is not porn because it sublimates desire. Erotica is not porn, 'because they drink wine and the women have smaller breasts'.[30] So not only does art make us better, it shows we are better than someone else. 'At stake in maintaining the absolute discursive distinction between art and pornography,' writes Laura Kipnis, 'are the class divisions that a distinctively high art works to maintain.' Art, it might be argued, cannot therefore be really revolutionary if all it does is assure the bourgeois of their status as distanced from 'the materiality of everyday life'.[31] Porn, on the other hand, might still pack a punch. Which is one reason porn is political. Doesn't matter how many times they say you're just a tosser.[32]

The naked city
(on defining porn as a minority opinion)

In 1970, the US presidential commission on pornography suggested that, since all porn did was release the sexual in people, it should therefore be constitutionally protected speech. Richard Nixon did not agree. He was furious. This could not happen, and since he was president at the time, he was able to

ensure that it didn't. Nixon believed that permission leads
to disorder, that if you unloose one thing you unloose others.
Typically the Cold War warrior saw a line of dominoes sent
tumbling, with sheer anarchy up ahead.

Several decades earlier, around the turn of the century,
Anthony Comstock was a high-ranking postal official who
wished to keep the US mail safe from harm. Comstock is
another one of censorship's archetypes who, like Thomas
Bowdler, became a synonym for restraint. An American of
uncommon censorial zeal, Comstock once boasted about how
he had pulped or torched 160 tons of 'obscene literature' and
convicted 'persons enough to fill a passenger train of 61
coaches'.[33] Like Nixon, Comstock considered permission and
the uncontrolled distribution of information a threat to the
social hierarchy and public order. Comstock especially wished
for all sexual information to be banned. He intercepted and
destroyed dirty novels, lewd line drawings, and early photographic precursors of *Playboy* magazine – including the 1896
'Tenderloin' issue of *Broadway* magazine, where, if the punter
removed the lampblack on certain pages by rubbing it with a
piece of bread, he would find several naked females reclining
on chaise longues.[34] In 1994, the first legal porn magazine in
the post-apartheid era in South Africa was a similarly discrete
fancy. A blonde beauty posed naked as nature intended –
except, that is, for her sex, which needed rubbing with the edge
of a coin for the viewer to gain the full view. Scratch-card porn
aside, Comstock also impounded and burned every last scrap
of sex-education materials on pregnancy, family planning,
health care – anything that might enable women to gain greater
control over their bodies, and hence their lives.

Comstock had no doubts regarding the work he was doing,
and the forcefully repressive way he went about it. In late twentieth-century Britain both the political left and right are eager
to speak of reducing state involvement in people's lives, while
continuing to support sexual censorship. There are many who
oppose homophobia, who would defend the arts – for Jarman
and Greenaway they will put their reputations on the line – and
yet with adult hetero hard core they reach for the scissors. This

is when the expression is not to their liking. The dilemma for those who would regulate is locating good reasons to prohibit the cultural expression they don't agree with. With Comstockery, the position is straightforward: you don't like it, you block it; you think it's bad, then ban it. These days, now that we live in diverse, plural democracies, those who argue for extended censorship often need to negotiate the line between continuing to appear tolerant and free while arguing for anti-democratic measures.

In a pluralist society, different religions, races, cultures, ethnicities, classes, tastes, sexualities, moralities and ideas are trying to get along.[35] Pluralism is the acceptance, or toleration, of different outlooks and minority opinions. Porn is political in that it proposes an alternative to the previously dominant version of sexuality: expressing the fantasy of sexual license, of variegated, multi-partnered promiscuity without guilt or social consequence. In hard core, people have sex with each other and they do not suffer for this, and they do not extend the bloodline. Such a vision is alleged to threaten the sanctity of marriage, the family, procreation, romance. Porn is a transgressive idea, a hotly contested point of view. In strictly proportional terms, porn is also a minority opinion and marginal taste. Pluralism and porn ought to be happy bedfellows, therefore, but they are not. The rise of pluralism has conversely seen the stiffening of a resolve to find those things beyond the pale, to cast out what pluralism will not accept. This is what defining porn is partly about, removing over time all that is acceptable, while reaching after the hard core that cannot be tolerated.[36] Porn is a form of cultural expression that often struggles not to be one of pluralism's outcasts. And, of course, porn also gains an extra vitality precisely because it is so reviled.

Having been singled out, porn – like action movies, horror movies, video games or heavy metal – is then readily available for being blamed should things ever go wrong. In the midst of economic and social anxiety, in these times of so-called 'panic culture', and during an era of endism and millennial anxiety, the intermittent urge for binding 'murderous certainties' will nearly always require the expulsion or victimisation of someone, something, or some minority.[37] Also with such expulsion there lurks the beginnings of an opportunity for fixing upon a simple solution to a tricky problem. An attendant worry that comes with the profusion of pluralism is the absence of easy, ready-made answers to events that have complex causes. There are times, however, when nobody wishes to know that it is not easy to explain or to establish why a man commits rape – people would much rather be advised that porn has done it. 'Women don't come into shelters saying, "This is pornography that is doing this to me",' declares Colleen Cobel, executive director of the Missouri Coalition Against Domestic Violence. 'They don't call rape crisis lines saying, "If he just wouldn't have read that magazine I don't think I would have been assaulted on my date." '[38] In such instances of slickly, quickly placing the blame, we find yet another definition of pornography: that is, of porn as the social and legal scapegoat, porn the fall guy.

Porn free
(on defining porn as more than what the censor says it is)

Historically, the relationship between porn and the law has been tight, casting a long shadow over attempts to make a definition. But is porn really to be defined as merely an argument about what's censored, and what is let be? Porn is not just the history of censorship, suggests Bernard Arcand, because, 'In some countries pornography is no longer a criminal offence.'[39] This rebuttal, however, is not entirely convincing. Regulation, censorship and freedom are constantly in flux. Just because pornography has been legal in a country for a while, that doesn't mean it no longer fears for its long-term security. For good reason, as during the nineties there are often murmurings about the recriminalisation of hard core in parts of Continental Europe. Though possibly little more than murmurings, they do rather underscore porn's deep-rooted connection with censorship.

The nature of censorship may change, however, as can be

seen in the context of the efforts of certain feminists to place further restraints on explicit materials. Even if the actual censor remains an old Etonian patriarch, or a blue-collar male heterosexual customs officer, he may now be using the language of a version of radical feminism in order to justify impounding a consignment of lesbian porn magazines. It is interesting to reflect on the fact that a hundred years ago the patriarchal Anthony Comstock wished to regulate women's access to sexual information in defence of the male élite. Ironically, in the eighties and nineties, feminists such as Catherine Mac-Kinnon have sought to work the exact same tools of the traditional male élite to block access for men and women to porn materials that they define as representative of, and fundamental to, the functioning of patriarchy.

But although MacKinnon and her associates try to use the conventional means of censorship, as women 'under patriarchy' it is hard to characterise their actions as just another case of the privileged few pulling the power levers in order to veto explicit materials for the many. Therefore, to argue that porn only gains definition through the actions of the controlling élite lacks some plausibility. If we took all the laws away, closed the courts, allowed people freedom of speech, we know that porn would continue to exist. If the censor retired tomorrow, or went on a long fishing trip, porn wouldn't suddenly find itself bereft of a state of being. This is not meant to be a contradiction of the argument given earlier that porn, as we know it, is a relatively recent phenomenon shaped by power and discourse. For a pornography made outside the modern legal dimension would look very different from how it does now; it wouldn't be the same porn as the one we're seeking to define.

Porn, nevertheless, is partly in the eye of the beholder, and not just what the censor saw. The potential for arousal by non-graphic materials is demonstrated with fetish imagery. There are magazines on sale in porn shops that involve images of people rolling in mud or having a food fight. An amateur video may simply feature various scenes of women trying on shoes. This will push all the right buttons for the foot fetishist, but would, in most communities, be of little interest to the police.

In the porn shops in North Beach, San Francisco, you can find shelves of video compilations of excerpts recovered from the mainstream and remade as porn. There's Eugene Bernard's series of classic corporal punishment clips from cinema and television, full of scenes of cowgirls being spanked by cowboys and of tanned, muscular male leads being strung up and whipped in biblical epics, on the high seas or in the Sheriff of Nottingham's dungeon.

And then there are other ways porn makes a life for itself away from the censor's beady eye. A couple may record their lovemaking on video. If this record remains unseen by the law, it can nonetheless be pornographic in that it is a representation able to cause arousal – for the couple themselves, or in the eyes of the house guest who, late one night after the hosts have gone to bed, is looking for something to watch on the VCR. There are also the self-made images privately exchanged in cyberspace. When a lover sends a playmate his or her scanned-in dirty picture downline, modem-to-modem, a pornographic transaction is occurring that cannot be fully characterised within the confines of the law.

The real thing
(on defining porn as an endless quest for the sexual 'truth')

When defining pornography proves so taxing, it's tempting just to settle for the industrial definition: that porn is whatever is being commercially produced as porn – produced, marketed, sold into shops, mailing catalogues, downline, as video, film, magazines, CD-ROM, books, net porn. It is a definition that is extending to include home-made amateur materials sold on, traded or distributed.

This will still, of course, be a product deeply affected by legal restrictions. Yet the form remains very open. A sex movie's style and tone can vary considerably – from the low-end, all-sex 'wall-to-wallers' to the 'high-end' fantasy with a proper story line as well as the sex – suggesting that porn has some autonomy from the law. Moving from an industrial definition of porn, to porn as the definitive fantasy, the range of hard-core dreams stretches from sunny Californian, with sports cars, palm trees, yachts and other aspirational trappings, to indoors and intense in New York, featuring method porners and wallpaper that sweats, or a period Italian porn hierarchy of sexually deprived contessas and studly farm hands. In *Other Victorians*, Steven Marcus describes porn as fantasy, purely and simply an escapist genre 'whose governing tendency in fact is toward the elimination of external or social reality'.[40] This dream realm he calls 'pornutopia', a Shangri-La of everlasting concupiscence, where 'time and space measure nothing but sexual encounters'.[41] There's an otherworldly quality with porn, unlike anybody's reality. The pornutopian fantasy offers sex now and without complication or issue; there's no headache, no limitations of size, stamina, performance or desirability, and the stresses of work, childcare, or what have you, don't impinge. In pornland the mood's always the right mood for good loving, where things just click and people always get off.

There are some who criticise porn for not showing real-life problems, such as floppy dick, or premature ejaculation. Interviewing former British porn star Linzi Drew, the photographer Mick Cooper wonders why pornography isn't more like 'normal life', featuring men with anxieties. 'You certainly don't get many men in porn mags expressing their insecurities,' he says to Drew. 'Or taking their socks off . . .' she replies. 'But we gloss over the socks, like we gloss over the insecurities. Otherwise it gets boring.'[42] The criticism rather misses the escapist purpose of porn, where the fantasist temporarily evades the limitations of the real. Where's the porn in a scenario with a character who's got a headache tonight? A porn fan writes, 'It's like someone saying, "I don't like musicals because people don't break into song on the street in real life." That's true – but I like musicals "because" they're not real life.'[43]

At the same time, Marcus is wrong to entirely eliminate the real from his 'pornutopia'. For instance, American porn is clearly prepossessed of the blow job, because, it is said, oral sex is considered problematic for a lot of Americans in real life. Also an American cultural preoccupation with youth and virility finds the average hard-core scene lasting longer than its

European counterpart. Meanwhile the current leading fantasy in French porn – where about a third of the hard-core releases see a good girl turning bad, from ingénue to hooker – suggests a very particular national spin on transgressive sex.

Other kinds of porn realism find instances of safer and regular partnered sex on the rise in contemporary hard core. Larger American companies now offer the condom option, while star performers like Racquel Darrian have elected to have sex onscreen only with their real-life partners. There are problems with this: the real-life partners of star performers might not be any good; they might be ugly or lack presence, or their repeated appearances on screen might reduce the viewing pleasure for those who don't appreciate their fantasy materials reminding them of the real-life constraints of monogamy or AIDS.[44] The kind of realism fans are more likely to ask of porn is that the fantasy's internal logic stays true. 'Women like matching sheets,' says Steffani Martin, 'and if our disbelief is going to be suspended, it's gotta be pretty good. If a woman is going to walk in off the street in a porn movie, jump into bed and her shoes are clean on the bottom, all of a sudden I'm not turned on any more.'[45] A contributor to the porn 'zine *Batteries Not Included* urges that actors remain in character: 'For example, a virginal cheerleader type being seduced for the very first time . . . the whole fantasy takes a nosedive when the cheerleader has a three foot serpent tattoo, with a tongue pointing towards her crotch, and pierced nipples . . . This quickly turns the high school sweetheart into the biker chick from hell (not that I'm complaining – I'm flexible, but let's stick to one fantasy at a time).[46]

To define porn requires working through many complex, often conflicting arguments, without even necessarily reaching a settlement. Additionally, it requires speaking of concepts of 'the real'. Some theorists consider porn as part of the culture's ongoing search for the 'truth' of sex. Specifically, heterosexual hard core tries to 'know' the mysteries of the female orgasm. Modern technologies like photography and film offer tools for a closer scrutiny of the body. In the twenties, Walter Benjamin linked Freud and film as changing the way the world is seen:

'*The Psychopathology of Everyday Life* made analysable things which had heretofore floated around unnoticed in the broad stream of perception . . . the film has brought about a similar deepening of apperception.'[47]

In *Hard Core*, Linda Williams tells of the early history of moving pictures and cinema, and how in the pioneering filmic works of artists like Eadweard Muybridge the new instruments of visual record rapidly switched from being merely 'observational' as the production of the 'real' became a highly choreographed affair. The point being that to speak of porn, even to part-define it, as concerned with the truth of sex requires also clearly recognising how porn is, at the very least, a performed version of the real. Hard core is the staging of sex. Firstly, it didn't just happen. They got a call from the producer, they drove to work, or at least they set the video camera on top of the tripod in their bedroom, and then they started 'doing it'. 'Sex in porn isn't like real sex,' confesses the director Steve Perry. 'It's like a fight in a Stallone movie, which isn't a real fight . . . In porn you have to stop and do it again for different angles. You can't have real sex in a porno movie because it has to be a certain length and take a predicted form.'[48]

Porn is also staged because it can't demonstrate the whole reality of pleasure. It's not just the psychological, spiritual, emotional and metaphysical verities that are missing; not even the whole physical reality can be captured. For one thing, the female orgasm lacks a definite visibility or materiality. Such absences of the 'real' are covered for in commercial porn by way of assorted conventionalised stand-ins, the groans, the moans and the external male ejaculation – known as pop shot, come shot, or money shot. The invisibility of the female orgasm, according to Linda Williams, is hard core's great irresolvable dilemma, which the genre seeks to overcome partly through the fetishisation of the female body. Which brings us, finally, to another of the many definitions of porn – as the objectification of women – and to the subject of the next chapter.

2
The porn wars

There are two main wings to the anti-porn argument, the Christian, moral authoritarian, and the feminist anti-porn position. The former, the 'moraltarians', object to explicit representations of sex as the morally unacceptable removal of sex from its 'proper' context of procreation, marriage, romantic love, monogamy and non-perverse sexual activities. Pornography, according to this view, fosters sexual licence; it poses a threat to the family and to traditional social and religious values, seriously coarsening the moral outlook and fibre of the community. The anti-porn feminist arguments, meanwhile, deem pornography to be sexist and misogynous in content, abusive at the stage of its production, and functioning as an incitement to men who come into contact with its noxious messages to commit crimes of sexual violence against women.

This book will mainly leave the first set of porn objections aside. Although the outspoken protestations of assorted characters from Jesse Helms to Mary Whitehouse represent a powerful lobby in our societies, it is possible to expose the moraltarians' ideological position as unacceptable to most people. Furthermore, their doctrine is refutable if you decide that you don't want to live in a theocratic state, or a one-morality culture. The actions of the moraltarians against porn are part of a larger campaign to achieve this backward step. Although the anti-porn feminists also represent a moral viewpoint, they have succeeded in appearing as something different – not offering an argument against porn as such, but the untreated truth on the matter. Although much aired, their arguments remain underexamined within mainstream culture; for this reason we will primarily address the anti-porn feminist position.

Raised in Minnesota
(on when certain feminists came to loathe porn)

At the start of the seventies, during the early stages of the century's second wave of feminism, porn did not loom large in the struggle for women's rights. From mid-decade, however, the work of writers such as Susan Brownmiller, Robin Morgan and most famously of all, Andrea Dworkin, started to offer porn as a pressing concern. In Dworkin's *Pornography: Men Possessing Women* (1981), still the most mentioned, most revered, most central text in the anti-porn feminist's library, porn is defined in many ways, including, 'Dachau brought into the bedroom and celebrated'.[1]

Such high-temperature language has been an abiding feature of anti-porn feminism (with comparisons not only to the holocaust, but also slavery and the Soviet Gulag prison camps). The fact that adult porn is actually produced by consenting adults free from any coercion, and is not violent in content, and that it is not possible to demonstrate how watching porn causes harm to occur (all of which will be discussed) explains perhaps why the feminist anti-porn position has become so focused on rhetoric. Indeed, pumping up the language so high it threatens almost to self-destruct is arguably indicative of a lobby group that is unconfident of finding evidence to support it.

Beyond the deployment of controversial analogies with genocide and the like, some of the key terms associated with the anti-porn feminists' critique of porn is that it is 'sexist', 'degrading', that porn 'objectifies' women. There are many problems with such words, not least being their lack of groundedness. These are very subjective meanings. Once a discussion on such matters gets started most often it becomes clear that very few people share the exact same point of view as to what an 'objectifying' image might look like.

In the cultural field, the last few decades have seen a greater recognition of how hard it is to establish a singular, unambiguous meaning for an image, a film, a book or a piece of music. In spite of so much media theory and analysis, and so much debate, the likelihood of fixing upon a universally held definition of what makes an image 'sexist' has actually greatly receded. Anti-porn feminists argue that a porn image is 'sexist' in the face of other women who simply don't agree, who make or watch porn for themselves, and have other ideas as to what makes a cultural representation objectionable (as will also be discussed). It becomes increasingly difficult to argue, therefore, that such hotly contested rhetoric is in itself sufficient justification for having porn banned.

Indeed, broadly speaking the second wave of feminism started out opposing censorship, and did not seek to legally forbid porn. Instead, a criticism of porn, a counter-argument to what some considered its sexist messages, was proposed. However, into the eighties, certain anti-porn feminists intensified their actions by formulating a proposed legal solution to this 'problem' of porn. The Minneapolis Ordinances of 1983 were the first attempt to bring into American law a new, 'feminist' definition of pornography. Written by legal scholar Catherine MacKinnon as well as Andrea Dworkin, the Ordinances define porn as a thing, not an interpretation, but a concrete entity that shall be recognised as 'a form of discrimination on the basis of sex' made up of images or words that present women as 'dehumanized sexual objects . . .'[2] Although an expert mix of legalese and rousing language, the Ordinances do not represent a solution to the formidable problem of defining porn (as discussed in the previous chapter). As the feminist critic Wendy McElroy says, 'This is not a definition, it is a conclusion . . . offered without argument or evidence.'[3]

The city of Minneapolis adopted the Ordinances as law – for a while. Over the next couple of years, several other cities and counties in America also considered doing the same, including Suffolk County, New York; Madison, Wisconsin; and Los Angeles County, California. Each time, the Ordinances arrived in the locality with some level of hullabaloo, and a heated campaign would ensue. In the case of Indianapolis, Indiana, the local Christian lobbyists and out-of-town anti-porn feminists fixed up an unofficial short-term alliance to work together on the legislative proposal. Local feminist groups, including the Indiana chapter of the National Organization for Women, vigorously opposed the ordinances, but they were disregarded. In Suffolk County, the bill was proposed by Michael D'Andre, a moral conservative whose stated aim was to save women, to 'restore them to what ladies used to be'.[4]

The feminist anti-porn position has at times been deeply intertwined with the moraltarians. This marks a dramatic shift from previous terms of engagement in American and British society, which used to pit sexual liberals, including women's rights advocates, against the common foe of the patriarchal state. Now porn was the common foe for moraltarians and certain feminists to join battle against. 'There has been this incredible alliance between the feminists, the Catholic schools and the far right,' suggests Camille Paglia. 'As a result, something very bad has happened.'[5]

Although the feminist anti-porners may lack the social and political power of the moraltarians, over time their arguments have achieved a considerable cultural sway, with a profound influence upon the language of censorship, which finds anti-porn feminist terms such as 'objectifying', 'dehumanizing' and 'degrading' tripping off the tongue of patriarchs and old-style moral guardians.[6] Feminist anti-porners have contributed not only a new semantic vigour to the culture of censorship in Britain and the US, but also a fresh impetus for a level of policing of visual material that would be considered extreme if ventured by the moraltarians. 'If two Baptist ministers from Oklahoma came up with their arguments,' suggests the novelist Anne Rice, in reference to Dworkin and MacKinnon, 'they would have been immediately laughed out of the public arena. They got away with their nonsensical arguments because they were feminists, and because they confused well-meaning liberals everywhere.'[7]

The spread of the Ordinances in the USA came to an end in the state of Indiana when a test case was brought to court and the judges failed to find the anti-porners' arguments convincing. These were female as well as male judges who didn't agree that porn was intrinsically discriminatory, or the kind of speech that demonstrably causes injury. The state judges would be supported by the American Supreme Court in 1986 when it declined a petition for judicial review of the arguments. Though the Ordinances were ruled as unconstitutional, this was not the end of things. A revised version was brought to the American Congress as the Pornography Victims' Compensation Act of 1992. This doomed proposal was opposed by feminist groupings such as Feminists for Free Expression (FFE). Senators and Representatives were somewhat surprised to find their model 'feminist' legislative bill vehemently opposed by leading feminists such as Betty Friedan, Jamaica Kincaid and Erica Jong.

Daughters of Minneapolis have emerged in Canada and Britain to mixed effect. In the late eighties, a version of the Ordinances was brought over to the UK in a failed attempt to further criminalise an already heavily restricted domestic porn industry. The Minneapolis definition of porn as depicting women 'as objects, things, or commodities' was employed in Labour MP Dawn Primarolo's Location of Pornographic Materials Bill of 1989, which proposed to restrict sales of adult materials to a few tightly regulated sex shops.[8]

In Canada in 1992, the Minneapolis version became accepted into law under the Canadian Supreme Court ruling known as the Butler decision. The Canadian Supreme Court was allegedly persuaded to make its ruling after being shown gay porn videos. It was these films, feminist anti-porners alleged, that truly got the point across to the male judges how the male performers who were penetrated were being abused in being treated like women.[9] Such a repetition of the homophobic cliché – that a man penetrated by another man is effectively made into a woman – was offered triumphantly and without apology. Henceforth Canadian customs were empowered to seize materials 'degrading' or 'dehumanizing' to women. What was often seized was actually gay, lesbian and feminist books and videos. So a law partly birthed in homophobia was then used to censor gay, lesbian and feminist expression.

The publishers of *Libido* magazine, a feminist erotic magazine, speak of how the Butler ruling was used against their magazine by Canadian customs. 'Our own experience at *Libido* is instructive in that we found out from Canadian subscribers that our Spring 1992 issue had been ... seized by postal authorities as "degrading." At issue was a series of photos by an American woman photographer, Della Grace, documenting the London lesbian leather/punk scene. That means we had photos of women by a woman declared degrading to women by people who in all likelihood are not women.'[10]

Meanwhile, life on American college campuses during the nineties finds the Minneapolis version of porn featuring prominently. In the banning of public displays of porn, the Massachusetts Institute of Technology precludes any display in which the 'Subjects are ... presented in a dehumanized way as sexual objects, things, or commodities'.[11]

Where did our love go?
(on how porn came to be a 'feminist' issue)

The Ordinances were hugely significant in making porn almost the leading 'feminist' issue of the eighties, as well as making prohibition the high-profile 'feminist' response to porn. They remain the foundation of the anti-porn feminist's position. In time, however, one aspect of the antis' argument has become more central: that porn not only might cause harm but is in itself, in representing heterosexual sex, an act of violence against women, for the entertainment of men, who are, according to Andrea Dworkin, 'distinguished from women by their commitment to do violence rather than to be victimized by it'.[12] Around this definitional objection spin additional declarations on porn: 'the graphic depiction of the lowest whores';[13] and 'the undiluted essence of anti-female propaganda';[14] on men: 'With lovers like men, who needs torturers?';[15] and on heterosexuality in general: 'The basic elements of rape are involved in all heterosexual relationships.'[16]

Such dismissals of men and heterosexuality arrived less than a decade after a sexual revolution famous for its commitment to free expression and to sex. 'In the sixties, part of what my generation did was the sexual revolution,' Camille Paglia recalls. 'Women of my period were bawdy in our speech. We were trying to break down the old middle-class conventions and part of this was the fabulous sex magazines at the time.' Things have certainly changed. 'But now, in the puritanical revisionism of things, it's like *Deep Throat* is the ultimate symbol of a woman being raped . . . It's loathsome. There has been a horrible retreat into puritanism since the sixties.'[17] From fucking for freedom to sleeping with the enemy within less than a generation – this was a case of either fast-track advancement for the cause or its serious derailment. The question is, how did this happen? How did things get so reduced, with sex seen as the site of female oppression?

At some point during the seventies, feminism and sex became joined together in the forward logic of female emancipation. In part this was due to the over-valuation of sex in modern culture – as a way to explain ourselves and our relations with others. Also, sex was a very sixties kind of revolutionary thing, entwined with broader liberatory aspirations. Way back then – when guru thinkers such as Reich and Marcuse spoke of sex as an essential force, something good hemmed in by civilisation, which was bad – sex was going to set you free. This orgasmic potential became a kind of will to power. Of course, the second wave of feminism was more than just about orgasms; a range of issues like contraception, health care, abortion, equal pay, equality in the eyes of the law, parenting and domestic violence were also key concerns. Yet the emergence of the contraceptive pill, decoupling sex from procreation, did concentrate the revolutionary mind upon the potential within the sexual for political change.

The view of sex as liberatory created unreal expectations. The positive recognition that women had a right to sex without stigma, and good sex as well, got turned into a notion that orgasms were themselves the key to emancipation. 'The sad truth,' writes Lynne Segal, '[is] that having orgasms – however plentiful . . . does not confer upon one power in the world.'[18] When orgasms failed to deliver, it didn't take much for things to get switched around. This view of sex as the site of liberation got reversed, and sex became the site of female oppression, the engine room of patriarchy. At this point, porn started to become a key issue for some as the alleged visual demonstration of male power.

The focus on porn was historical as well as circumstantial. There was perhaps a growing impatience concerning the speed of change in society, a frustration with the apparent intractability of patriarchy. Following the legal triumph for American feminism concerning abortion rights with *Roe* v. *Wade* in 1973, a lull occurred. A loss of drive and a growing mood of fragmentation within the women's movement (over matters of racial, economic, social and sexual difference) created the desire for a new single issue to revive the ebbing sense of unity. In the eighties, these features started to commingle with a steady decline in confidence in men and a rise in disillusion with heterosexuality, particularly following the emergence of the New Right and a backlash against the previous gains of feminism.

There was also the growing awareness of sexual harassment, of domestic violence and rape. For many in the feminist movement the vision of women gaining from sexual liberation clouded over, as the stress that had once been placed on the need for women to affirm their sexual desires slowly became engulfed by the disquiet concerning male violence. In some quarters, the junction of male sexuality with male violence became established almost as a kind of inner truth of heterosexuality, with male violence perceived as the motor of male dominance in society at large, and porn a representation of this reality.

This stress on a relationship between the actual and the representational has been a key feature of the porn wars. The concentration on porn occurred during an era of growing political engagement with the world of media and media theory. With the medium now defined as being the message itself, the nature and the meaning of its signals were viewed as a vital ideological battleground. The content of media became carefully analysed and highly valued, causing dubious assertions to be made. 'Pornography,' writes Catherine MacKinnon, 'makes it impossible for men to tell when sex is forced, that women are human, and that rape is rape.'[19] But porn is the representation of a simulated sex act between consenting performers, whereas rape is a real act of violence, tied in with such complex issues of gender power, the family, child rearing and education, and the law. The fundamental differences between the real and the representational cannot simply be overridden through rhetoric.

It would be wrong to claim it was nearly so simple, sudden or uniform as that, or to assert that all straight women stopped enjoying sex, and started hating men for fucking them into social submission. Clearly most heterosexual people carried on having sexual relationships, with all the messiness, trial, trauma and good things they tend to bring forth. However, for quite some time the loudest or most listened to voices in feminism tended to figure heterosexuality as a problem, according to Andrea Dworkin: 'Getting fucked and being owned are inseparably the same.'[20] Rather predictably, this swerve away from (het) sex occurred just as the wider culture was getting into it: as feminism appeared to be switching off, everybody else was turning on. And ever since, hardly a month has gone by without *Cosmopolitan* luring readers with the secret to the ultimate (multiple) peak experience between the sheets. Such dissonance is a depressing feature of recent times in feminism: 'a dramatic lack of fit,' writes Lynne Segal, 'between what one very visible group of feminists were saying about women's experience of sexual victimization, and what the overwhelming majority of women were reporting as their experiences of sex, and its importance in their lives'.[21]

For a long while, popular images of feminism have mostly been negative. This is not simply a patriarchal conspiracy. In the autumn of 1996, the British writer Natasha Walter questioned the use to most women of a kind of feminism that reviles them for wanting to dress up. 'When young women now hear of the women's liberation conference which published a paper saying "fashion equals control equals violence against women" ... or when they read contemporary feminists saying that women who buy chic clothes are "poisoning their freedom" with "a dark vein of self-hatred . . .", they naturally find the idea of feminism a turn-off.'[22] A year or so earlier a BBC news programme had conducted a brief 'whither feminism' report. A pair of young women working in a clothes shop in Covent Garden in London were asked what they thought of feminism. They said it was bad. And did they consider themselves feminists? Definitely not. The reasons given were that feminism was anti-sex and anti-men. One of the women said, 'I actually get on quite well with my boyfriend, I enjoy being around men.'[23]

Speaking in tongues
(on the wars over porn within feminism)

The irony is that the anti-porn position is only one grouping within feminism, and does not represent 'the' feminist take on porn, or heterosexuality in general. Betty Friedan, Nancy Friday, Kate Millet, Nadine Strossen, Erica Jong, Jamaica Kincaid, Nora Ephron, Anne Rice, Lynne Segal, Thelma McCormack, Pat Califia and Lisa Palac are all noted feminists who oppose the anti-porn position, who do not blame women's multifaceted experiences of inequality on a series of sexual images, and doubt the virtue of focusing on porn, considering the consequent neglect of more pressing and complex problems faced by women.

Unfortunately, the feminist anti-porners mostly deal with the challenge from within the women's movement by acting as though it doesn't exist, or by declining to debate with the women who do not share their point of view. Feminist anti-porners have sometimes declared women who don't agree with them as no longer feminists,[24] as 'house niggers,' according to Catherine MacKinnon, 'who sided with the master'[25], or as 'fellow travellers of the pornographers', as described by Andrea Dworkin.[26] 'It's pretty sexist for them to assume we can't possibly disagree with them out of our own experience,' says Avedon Carol, co-founder of Feminists Against Censorship (FAC), 'so we must be either brainwashed or "in the pay of the pornographers." It's as if they do not think women have a self-motivating sexuality.'

The anti-anti-porners – as they are sometimes inelegantly described – are often derided as innocents who haven't a clue. Avedon Carol remembers being accused of 'living in a dream world', of failing to understand the realities of sexual violence: 'But I've been raped and porn didn't have anything to do with it,' she replies. 'Sexual violence was not a bogeyman for me, out there somewhere, some kind of abstract, menacing "thing", but an actuality, something I've experienced, a part of the make-up of my past and my life.'

The porn wars have been going on for nearly two decades and at times have become very intense. In 1982, a women's conference at Barnard College, New York, promoting 'a complex and nuanced discussion of sexuality',[27] was put together by a diverse range of feminist academics, activists and artists, including Kate Millett, Dorothy Allison, Barbara Kruger and Gayle Rubin. Anti-porn feminists not only boycotted and picketed the conference but they also tried to scare the authorities of the conservative women's college by suggesting the conference featured 'sexual perverts' who were also 'anti-feminist'. Women Against Pornography also handed out leaflets at the conference door, including accusations of 'antisocial' sexual activities against named women taking part in the conference.

Ten years later, in 1992, the University of Michigan Law School held a symposium on prostitution to which they invited the artist Carol Jacobsen to curate an exhibition on the subject. The final selection of art-work, predominantly made by women, included Jacobsen's own video piece *Street Sex*, featuring interviews with prostitutes in Detroit; *The Salt Mines*, a documentary about transvestite sex workers in New York; the activist Carol Leigh's video on global efforts on the part of prostitutes to improve their work situation, *Outlaw Poverty, Not Prostitution*; and Veronica Vera's *Portrait of a Sexual Evol-*

utionary, her film about her times as a porn actress and porn director. Vera's tape was removed from the exhibition when a speaker at the conference complained. Jacobsen reinstated it, stating that either the whole show was to be allowed, or all of it should be censored. A meeting of student organisers of the conference with Catherine MacKinnon and Andrea Dworkin (MacKinnon teaches at the law school) resulted in the total exhibition being closed, rendering a two-day conference on sex work entirely bereft of any input from sex workers.[28]

In Britain, FAC first gathered in the late eighties to resist censorship in society in general and in the feminist movement in particular. Likewise there were American groupings such as FFE and the Feminist Against Censorship Taskforce. Traditionally, censorship has been a tool used by the state against dissent. The history of women's rights in North America and Britain has partly been one of a struggle to gain information. Earlier this century, Marie Stopes and Margaret Sanger faced censorship and court action when they attempted to disseminate information on birth control in Britain and America. During the seventies the British feminist magazine *Spare Rib* was banned in Ireland for carrying similar information, while the landmark feminist book on women's health, *Our Bodies, Ourselves,* was repeatedly harassed in parts of the USA throughout the seventies and eighties. And yet assorted feminist anti-porn groups were now approaching the patriarchal legal systems in North America and Britain and demanding censorship. This marked an abandonment of a previous attachment within feminism to a countercultural politics that questioned the potential for change through patriarchal institutions such as Parliament and the law. Apparently the feminist anti-porners found explicit materials a special case, where it was acceptable to argue against patriarchy while simultaneously pressing for it to step in and take action against porn.

Campaigners in Britain have argued for anti-porn laws similar to the race-relations legislation of the seventies, a legal measure that can be seen as dealing with racism only insofar as it poses a threat to public order.[29] In terms of addressing the deeper, more complex structural problems of racism, the race relations laws are mainly found wanting.[30] Rather than recognise such difficulties, Catherine Itzen of the Campaign Against Pornography and Censorship (CPC) has spoken of the fact that nowadays you can't buy racist magazines in the shops,[31] failing to mention the more coded forms of racism that continue to be endemic in mainstream media. If porn were banned, sexism in the media, and in the world at large, is unlikely to be foiled, or even especially diminished. Part of the allure of censorship is the illusion that it offers a 'quick fix' to difficult situations.

The feminist anti-porners' move to prohibit explicit materials crucially depends upon a definition of porn as sexist. Although anti-censorship groups like FAC and FFE were first started to raise awareness of the perils of censorship, subsequently many have gone on to consider porn itself, often to find it less objectionable than they'd been led to expect. Women such as Lisa Palac, Wendy McElroy, Avedon Carol, Gayle Rubin, Sallie Tisdale and several others have written about the surprise they experienced on taking a good look at porn (see Chapter 9, 'Pornocopia'), especially hard-core porn, a term that sounds so scary from the outside, like the dark heart of something terrible, but is simply pictures and films of people having sex together.

Over time the position of the feminist anti-porners has cultivated the appearance of offering 'the truth' about porn, taking advantage of a popular lack of information concerning the genre. Everybody has heard about porn, has seen its saucy pouting smile on the top shelf, in the red neon light, the video rental stores of the world, and then they have mostly looked away. The mainstream left it at a glance. A fast-moving, fast-growing, multifaceted phenomenon was not properly considered within the broader culture. A gap was left for interpretations, and the feminist anti-porners filled this space.

The existence of other feminist viewpoints undermines the anti-porners' sovereign claim to 'the truth' of porn. To characterise the content of porn as wholly sexist and misogynous is to give an interpretation that many do not share. Some find the depiction of women in mainstream media far more questionable. Though aspects of the iconography of porn, especially soft-core porn, can be read or argued as being sexist, there also exists within porn the depiction of women as strong, autonomous and in control. In hard core, women are often seen seeking out sex and enjoying sex. These scenarios are not coercive, dangerous, nor bearing the heavy moral duty or unpleasant repercussions that so often accompany the depiction of desiring women in mainstream movies like *Fatal Attraction*, *Betty Blue*, *Body of Evidence* or *Basic Instinct*. In hard core, desiring women have multiple orgasms not mental breakdowns, and they're not psychotic or destined to die. These depictions hardly reveal porn as the unequivocal assault on women it is alleged to be.

A question of harm
(on the allegation that porn hurts women)

The linkage of porn and harm is central to the position of feminist anti-porners, whose legislative proposals seek to make porn-makers and porn-sellers legally culpable for the damage that is caused, the anti-porners allege, by porn. If such a link could be established, and it could be said that by removing porn you'd also remove sexual violence, then many who oppose censorship might nevertheless be prepared to accept the need for rooting out the offending porn.

Using arguments adapted from the Civil Rights movement, the Minneapolis Ordinances categorised porn as 'fighting speech', proposing it as a form of expression that presented an actual, demonstrable danger to women. Fighting speech is the kind that might directly cause a fight to take place, an assault to occur. The Ordinances allow a person to take action in the civil courts for damages due to being 'harmed' by pornography. This particular tack meant its advocates could claim that they were not proposing pre-restraint, or censorship. However, the threat of a future damages suit can be just as inhibiting as pre-publication seizure, or the threat of being raided by the police.[32] If a woman who has been physically assaulted claims that the assault was due to a porn image, and that claim is accepted, then it follows that everybody involved in the production and distribution of that image is legally culpable. In theory, therefore, the woman who posed in the image could be required to pay damages to another woman for the actions of an assailant who, because he has come into contact with these materials, is no longer held to be entirely responsible for what he's done. (In *Only Words*, Catherine MacKinnon suggests that porn rendered the criminal defendant Thomas Schiro unable to recognise the wrong he was doing, diminishing his responsibility for the sex crimes he'd committed.)

In American law, 'fighting speech' will be exempted from the normal constitutional protection of free expression if it can be demonstrated that such utterances and the immediate causing of harm are unequivocally related, and that only through curtailing the speech will immediate harm be averted. In the twenties, US Justice Oliver Wendell Holmes famously described such harmful speech as offering a 'clear and present danger', citing the example of someone shouting 'fire!' in a crowded theatre when it wasn't true and causing pandemonium. Another more recent example could be the false alarm caused in Britain in the autumn of 1995 concerning reports of the alleged side effects of certain brands of women's contraceptive pills. This resulted in an immediate, steep rise in the number of unwanted pregnancies. However, such direct causal linkage can't be demonstrated where porn is concerned.[33]

Until about thirty years ago no real studies of porn and the possible effects it might have on a person had ever been conducted. By the late sixties, however, this lack was quickly being rectified. Early efforts focused on fears for the moral fabric of society. However, psychologists like Berl Kutchinsky reported no antisocial changes in sexual behaviour through short-term or long-term exposure to porn. There was some ambiguity about whether seeing new sexual positions caused viewers to experiment in their own sex lives. Findings were more conclusive, however, in suggesting that people did not develop new sexualities from porn, that we are not what we watch. A person of conventional sexual tendencies – so-called 'vanilla' appetites – wasn't going to turn into Queen Whiplash after watching an s/m video. Likewise, a batch of scenes featuring 'regular' sex was unlikely to cause Queen Whiplash to hang up her switch.

With the growth of the feminist debates on porn, the focus of research shifted from seeking signs of a coarsening of the subject's moral world view. Studies started to consider porn viewing and possible connections with aggressive behaviour. In the late seventies, Dolf Zillmann sought to prove that watching porn causes men to commit rape. He was unable to do so, but he did suggest that he had found that male porn users show an increased 'callousness towards women'. Zillman's use of the word 'callous' was very personalised and unorthodox. As his work continues to be cited as proof of porn's dangerous message, it is important to be clear what Zillman meant by 'callousness': which is that the subjects in his study started to consider women as more sexually autonomous through watching porn than they had previously, seeing women as having an interest in sex, as well as life options other than childbearing and keeping house. Porn, in other words, might lead men to become less conventional in their outlook, and such 'callousness' was not felt to be desirable for traditional family values.

After Zillman came Donnerstein and Malamuth, both of whom looked to find empirical links between porn and violence. At first both reported that they had found such links. During a quarter of a century of similar testing nobody has been able to replicate their findings. Subsequently Donnerstein has distanced himself from his earlier work, retracting suggestions that he'd made a connection between watching porn and an increased likelihood of violent behaviour. Donnerstein has also declared that his work was misrepresented. Other research in this area has showed how convicted rapists have had *less* exposure to porn in their formative years, as well as during the period when they were offending. In Denmark in the late sixties, Kutchinsky conducted a study of possible correlations between the removal of all of the country's restrictions on porn and levels of sex crimes, and found a reduction in the incidence of such offences. In the USA, Baron found that it was in states where porn was restricted that women experienced the highest levels of inequality, whereas states with the least censorship, and a preponderance of pornography, were more likely to be tolerant communities, to have greater levels of gender equality in terms of politics, economics, social and legal rights. Similar correlative evidence has been found in Scandinavia and the Low Countries.[34]

The problem with research studies is they are inevitably unrealistic and artificial. 'There can be few things more contested,' writes Segal, 'even from within its own theoretical framework, than the relevance of the controlled and contrived social-psychological laboratory experiment to human action in the world at large.'[35] The studies take place outside the world in which people actually live as well as providing subjects with options that bear very little connection to normal conduct and behaviour. For example, would the viewer be more disposed to administering an electric shock to a person after having seen porn? Possibly, at least according to some lab tests. However, behaviour in such situations largely seems to depend on how the person to whom the shock is (apparently) administered behaves towards the viewer prior to the experiment. If they're friendly then they're unlikely to be buzzed; if they're unfriendly then the viewer might administer a shock. These conditioned responses seem to have little to do with porn. Other researchers, meanwhile, have found empirical evidence to suggest that men are more likely to behave pleasantly after watching porn.

Implicit in such behavioural studies is the conviction that we can know a person. The researcher believes in people having fixed identities with fixed responses, and that since we can know this person we can probably know how they will respond, not just now, but always and for ever. And yet a significant characteristic of modern times is the profound doubts that swarm around concepts of identity. The more the self has become privileged socially and culturally, the more any confidence in the unity and certainty of the self has been undermined. If we are the authors of our own selves, constantly working on the script of who we might be – in the light of experiences, sensations, changing perceptions, memories and many other things – then we are also aware of how things change. Do I feel like I felt five years ago? And, when I walk down the street in public, go out for lunch with someone, try to mingle at a party, have a telephone conversation, read, play sport, watch television, have sex, wait in the queue at the supermarket checkout – am I always the same in every situation? It's true that your tightly monitored, self-conscious performance in the social sphere doesn't necessarily equate with how you are, slumped out on your own, watching porn. However, by this stage, knowing how you act, having recognised the potential within yourself for identity performance, how can you be sure any longer there was ever a rock-solid you to begin with? The idea of an image as a behavioural trigger seems dubious when we acknowledge that identity is intricate and changeable.

The authority of lab tests is further impaired because of assumptions about how viewers watch materials. For example, will men watching a heterosexual sex scene automatically associate with the man? Many porn users often report otherwise (see Chapter 9, 'Pornocopia'). Additionally, the viewer's relationship with fantasy is more complex than behavioural models often allow. A viewer may watch a fantasy scenario, be sexually aroused, and that will be the end of the experience. The pleasure often resides within the fantasy alone. Lab tests, however, view the pleasure as deferred, as a craving created that's still to be satisfied, while also, quite paradoxically, neglecting to pay full attention to the most likely behavioural response to porn: sexual arousal and sexual gratification. Porn is mostly used as part of an erotic repertoire. People either masturbate or have sex together after or during porn. In lab studies, however, what happens to subjects after viewing porn is that they are tested for aggression. The fact that even a hand job is out of the question has to devalue any results.

The conflicting interpretations put upon the data of behavioural tests also point to their limitations. In 1990, Cumberbatch and Howitt reported to the British government on the available research and found a world of confusion. 'Inconsistencies emerge between very similar studies,' they wrote. 'Many interpretations of these have reached almost opposite conclusions.'[36] Even the Meese Commission of 1986, which was decidedly anti-porn, cautiously limited itself to saying, 'The link between porn and rape seemed plausible, but might also be totally non-existent.'[37] This part-admission of failure came after Meese commissioned and heard from C. Everett Koop, then Surgeon General for the United States, who had conducted a review of what the research literature actually said on causal links. Koop reported that no link could be demonstrated. In its Final Report the Meese Commission erased any mention of Koop's review.

A pattern emerges. In Canada in the early eighties, the Metropolitan Toronto Task Force on Violence Against Women asked the leading feminist Thelma McCormack to analyse the available research into the effects of porn. McCormack was unable to find any connections between porn and violent behaviour. Her report was suppressed. In New Zealand, speaking before the Indecent Publications Tribunal in 1990, John Court, one-time spokesperson for the Festival of Light, the British Christian moral rearmament movement from the seventies, was asked to confirm the existence of research that proved there was a link between porn and violence. He replied, 'We do not have evidence that there is such a causal link. I cannot sustain it from my data and I don't know anybody who can.'[38]

It follows, therefore, that we might not know a rapist or sex murderer by the kinds of magazines he reads, the videos he rents. Discussions of media effects on behaviour often revolve around the person with a so-called 'predisposition' to do harm being sent over the edge by media stimuli. Not only is it hard to predict what these things might be – it could be *Penthouse*, or the movie *Ben Hur*, the Bible or *Catcher in the Rye* – but also, at some level, people do have to be held accountable for their own actions. This is not simply a reiteration of the commonplace regarding personal responsibility, but a rejection of a trend that finds modern societies knee-deep in films, pop music, video games, graphic novels, porn, looking for clues as to why acts are committed, rather than looking at individuals and their particular situations. This desire for simple ready-made answers partly explains the popularity of the feminist anti-porn position in the mainstream. Blaming porn, however, may hinder research into the causes of sexual violence, while diverting attention away from the real concern, which is rape and sexual violence.

The lack of proof that porn causes harm has not always deflected feminist anti-porners. 'Women don't need scientific proof to know what is killing them,' proclaims Bonnie Klein, director of the anti-porn movie, *Not a Love Story*.[39] Of course, if porn and rape are deemed as good as equivalent in the anti-porner's litany, when it isn't just a case of porn is the theory, rape the practice, but one is the actuality, the other the actuality taped for people's entertainment, when such a muddling of image and reality takes place, then the idea of evidence does probably start to seem superfluous. But some kind of proof does need to be established beyond speculation, gut feeling, or dread. Previously communities have been sure, feeling in their bones that they knew what was wrong, and what they needed to do. As US Justice Brandeis observed, 'Men feared witches and burned women.'[40]

Vanilla porn
(on the allegations of porn being violent)

A significant flaw in talk of the harm of porn is the virtual absence of violent imagery in the genre. Those who campaign against porn allege that it is intensely violent and getting worse all the time. This isn't true. Porn has become less violent during the eighties and nineties. It wasn't very violent to start with. During the seventies there was a scattering of movies proffering rape myths and dramatic performances of non-consenting sexual fantasies. By the turn of the eighties such scenarios were fast vanishing as porn, like the rest of society, became wise to the fact that it wasn't every woman's secret fantasy to be raped – in contrast to what Woody Allen's character suggests in the movie *Play it Again Sam*.

The 1986 Meese Commission on porn heard from an inquiry into the content of men's magazines. This inquiry found that only 0.5 per cent of magazine porn imagery could be argued to depict violence of the broadest description. All mention of these findings was absent from the Final Report. 'In more than twenty years of reviewing pornography,' says Avedon Carol, 'I have never found an image of a woman bleeding in any porn vendor's in the United States, nor in any private British or American collection, nothing which corresponds with the descriptions used by the antis.' Concerning this elusive violence, in conversation with porn star and activist Nina Hartley, the writer Wendy McElroy admits to searching through movies and magazines, but is unable to locate anything bad or even offensive. 'Yet I keep reading radical feminists who claim that 75% of porn is violence, containing scenes of rape or torture.' To which Hartley replies, 'They are out to lunch on that . . . especially on rape scenes: they were passé by 80, 81.'[41]

One reason you don't find violence in porn is because it's illegal; any efforts to feature violence would risk dire legal repercussions. What is meant by 'violence' isn't simply the record of real crimes. In the USA the 'performance' of make-believe violence within the pornographic genre is effectively illegal. American censors won't allow the connection of fantasy violence with fantasy sex. Dramatic depictions of violence like the ones you see all the time in mainstream Hollywood films are not advisable in hard core.

In general, people don't realise that porn isn't violent. The repeated talk of coercion and violence and of so-called 'snuff' movies has fixed the notion in the mainstream culture of the worst imaginable things as being the essence of porn, and this, like a modern urban myth, has proved difficult to shake.[42] No police authority anywhere has actually found a snuff movie. It is possible to write to authorities like the FBI and have them confirm that they have never come across such materials.[43] It is conceivable that someone might commit crimes, including sex crimes, and record them for their pleasure. It is even conceivable that such materials could be distributed. But this would be very risky, and the British vice police, for example, have no records of having ever seen or heard of such underground materials.[44] Nevertheless such recordings of criminal acts would have nothing to do with the adult industry, nor anything much to do with porn users.

Meanwhile the restriction of access to adult materials in America and Britain continues partly because of the snuff fiction. Fearing the very worst makes it possible to build a case for censorship covering all explicit materials. The association also creates a sense of guilt, suggesting that anyone who likes porn is somehow complicit with non-consenting violent acts of abuse against women. As with the false linkage of child porn with adult materials, the effect is to make any anti-censorship or pro-pornography argument sound callous and complacent. (see Chapter 6, 'Child Story'.)

Despite an absence of violence, many feminist anti-porners continue to speak of porn as an ongoing atrocity exhibition. There are many reasons why they might do this. One is that what is meant by violence is consenting s/m, a minority sexual practice so easily misrepresented, which only accounts for a tiny fraction of porn. 'Feminist anti-pornography ideology has always contained an implied, and sometimes overt, indictment of sadomasochism', writes Gayle Rubin. 'The pictures of sucking and fucking that comprise the bulk of pornography may be unnerving to those who are not familiar with them. But it is hard to make a convincing case that such images are violent.'[45]

S/m sex, and s/m porn can be difficult to read if you're not familiar with the codes and forms. One thing it is not is the depiction of indiscriminate acts of violence inflicted on non-consenting participants. Plausibility and authenticity are so valued in s/m that the depiction will often feature performers who are in some way part of the 'scene'. It is because s/m sex is a complex, ritualised sexual performance between adults, a carefully negotiated manipulation of power relations, that issues of consent are so vital. In this way, s/m practitioners are perhaps more aware of issues of sexual consent than most other people.

The shock value of s/m and its potential for causing unease

have been further exploited by the conflation of a wide range of activities or events under the single banner of 'violence'. Vital distinctions are blurred and lost. Representations of 'torture' could mean the notorious pictures of state atrocities taken by George Dumas in China in 1923, or a 'punishment' scene from the film *Mutiny on the Bounty*, or something between a dominatrix and her consenting male submissive. Context does matter. The American sex rights activist Pat Califia recalls watching feminist anti-porn slide shows concerning the 'violence' of porn which disregarded the varying realities of different images: 'No distinction was made among a photo of a woman's genitals, the act of gang rape, an advertisement for spike heels, the act of child abuse, a photo of a woman who was tied up, and the act of wife beating.'[46]

These shows urged people to view female nudity and serious sexual and physical assault as being inextricably connected. Gayle Rubin observes, 'A great deal of anti-porn propaganda implies that sadomasochism is the underlying and essential "truth" towards which all pornography tends. Porn is thought to lead to S/M porn which in turn is alleged to lead to rape.' This is part of a broader cultural narrative, featured in hit movies like *Silence of the Lambs*, *Basic Instinct* and *Pulp Fiction*, which suggests that 'perverts' commit all the sex crimes. 'Anti-porn literature scapegoats an unpopular sexual minority . . . for social problems they did not create.'[47]

Fantastic tales of porn 'violence' has rendered the production of specialist s/m materials more difficult, while also perhaps encouraging moraltarians to develop a new line of attack on favourite abominations such as gays, lesbians, fetishists, s/mers, transvestites, and transsexuals. 'We are suffering an onslaught upon gay culture,' says Mark Rose, a gay bondage film-maker from New York. 'It is all part of a general backlash against gay culture and gay rights, and liberal rights all over, and perverts, and porn, especially my kind of porn, is a very good place for the conservative right to fight this battle.'[48]

All pimped women
(on women who work in the porn business)

The negative depictions of minority sexualities represents a kind of sexual orthodoxy on the part of the feminist anti-porners, concerned with a right and a wrong way of being erotically. Plainly to work in porn would be a wrong way. Thousands of women appear in porn of their own volition. However the voices of porn women go mostly unheard. As a consequence of this relative silence, others often speak on their behalf. They don't make it sound very nice. According to Catherine MacKinnon, 'Empirically, all pornography is made under conditions of inequality based on sex, overwhelmingly by poor, desperate, homeless, pimped women who were sexually abused as children.'[49]

Porn women are frequently depicted as victims, forced, drugged, bribed, tricked into taking their clothes off; victims of the rough end of capitalism, or of no-good men: all kinds of victim. 'Some people think that because you're an actress in this business, you had a bad childhood or you're fucked up somehow,' says the porn star 'Jenteal', 'that there's something going wrong in your head otherwise you wouldn't be doing it. Which is not the case. People aren't willing to accept the fact that people are doing this because they enjoy doing it . . . If I felt I was being exploited, then I wouldn't be doing it.' Porn actress Brittany O'Connell similarly disputes the depiction of porn women as social casualties: 'They always say they have a low self-esteem. That they only like it because of the money, or because they feel it's the only thing they can do. They can't be in this industry because they enjoy making the movies . . . I graduated from high school at the age of 17. I've been through two years of college already. My major was astrophysics. And I enjoy what I do.'[50]

There is an élitism in the anti-porners' attitude to porn women. Comparisons made with the social purity movements of the last century are apt, when upper-middle-class women intervened in the lives of women from the working classes who turned to prostitution on a casual basis when things were tight.[51] These 'poor' women needed saving, protecting, controlling. The legal scholar Drucilla Cornell warns of a feminist fantasy inherited from the last century which depicts women sex workers as the ultimate victims. 'Feminists in the porn debate have bought into this fantasy to the degree that they see all sex workers as one woman – a woman degraded simply by the reality that she *chooses* to be a sex worker.'[52]

Zak Jane Keir works for Northern & Shell, one of the largest soft-core magazine publishers in the UK. 'People working in any industry may be exploited at some time,' she says. Keir has been deputy editor of *Penthouse* and *For Women*, and contributing editor to *Forum* and *Eros Digest*. 'The subject of exploitation is dear to my heart. As a woman working in the porn industry I sometimes wish I was paid more for what I do. Who doesn't?'

The word 'exploitation' is easily sent forth into the conversation – especially on sex work. Often, what is meant is not so clear. 'Before this work,' says Keir, 'I did low-level secretarial, clerical work and got paid maybe £100 a week for ten hours a day, five days a week, and, I had to be a nice girl, and I used to have to dress in a particular way, wear make-up and look pretty and make the tea and get pushed around.' We live in a 'lookist' culture. All across London, in hundreds of restaurants and bars, attractive women are waitressing. These women get paid a very low basic wage, are employed partly on the basis of their looks, and need to smile and be extra pleasant to earn those increasingly vital tips (see also the good-looking boys and girls in Habitat, Jigsaw, Heals, Emporio Armani). 'Think of the levels of exploitation in fast-food joints. A woman who's been born with good looks, the kind that people want to take pictures of, and is happy to do this – given the choice between the two, I think I'd rather get my kit off and get paid £150 a day; it's better than £2.50 an hour.'

And, if a woman switches jobs, turns from waitressing to stripping – therefore going from £3.00 to £50 an hour – and yet is still described as 'exploited', then it can't merely be an economic thing being spoken about, but something sexual too. The nudity is the 'exploitation', as though being naked goes to

the core of something. Here the cause of sexual equality con-
fuses sexism with sex. The objections may also come down to
sexual modesty. When watching porn or, to a lesser degree,
striptease, there are times when one thinks of something Pat
Califia wrote about group-sex parties, and how it gave her
pleasure looking around and seeing other people's faces when
aroused and in the heat of the passion, with their eyes rolling,
cheeks flushing, mouths gaping. In porn you will see some of
the things Califia describes, and, you may enjoy watching this
or you may find it embarrassing or distasteful. 'In this culture,
where sexual curiosity too often mutates into sexual shame,'
writes Carol Queen, 'we often find our first exposure to porn
uncomfortable or shocking. After all, we know it's supposed to
be dirty. We've never had the opportunity to get used to the
sight of people fucking!'[53] People who feel ill at ease in front of
nudity, exhibitionism and explicit sex may hide their discomfort by speaking of exploitation, rather than simply looking
away.

After more than a decade spent working in porn, the
American actress Nina Hartley sees both good and bad things.
'I'm not saying that the sex industry, under patriarchy and
capitalism, doesn't have a lot wrong with it,' she writes. 'As
with 98% of all business in the U.S., it is still dominated by
men (good ones and bad ones).'[54] In San Francisco a performer
voices her grievances about job security and an improved
working environment. 'Sex work can be fun . . . and people
better realise that we're here to stay . . . but we need labour
rights.' During the early nineties the actress Ona Zee spent a
period trying to unionise workers in the porn industry. She
became known as hard core's 'Norma Rae', but was not successful. Porn tends to be capitalism in the raw where any talk
of collective action is disdained. The porn milieu is also not
conducive to unionisation due to the fast turnover of workers,
as well as the legally outcast nature of the business. However,
Zee continues to stress a need for unionisation and for porn
women to speak for themselves.[55] Nina Hartley agrees: 'We
women have only begun to make our voices heard . . . Now is
not the time for feminists to add to efforts to stifle our voices

. . . Bring porn and sex work into the light of day. Promote worker control . . . Legitimize its existence.'[56]

Like mainstream Hollywood, movie porn remains dominated by male directors and producers. However there is a long line of women directors dating back to Ann Perry-Rhine and Joanna Williams, and including Veronica Vera, Svetlana, Gloria Leonard, Toni English, Tera Heart, Brandy Alexandre and Tianna Collins. During the nineties, women are increasingly producing in porn. People like Candida Royalle, Kym Wilde, Ona Zee and Rebecca Bardoux are also running their own video lines.[57] At Vivid, the largest American hard-core film company, the head of production is a woman, the chief financial officer is a woman, and foreign sales are managed by a woman. 'There's no glass ceiling at this company,' I was informed. Ex-wrestler Tiffany Million has launched her own string of porn videos, Immaculate Video Conceptions, while during 1996 and 1997 Shane, the smart-talking former sidekick of porn producer Seymore Butts, brought out her own brand of so-called 'gonzo' porn – handheld video hard core. *Shane's World*, the ongoing series, features Shane out and about with friends, making porn on the road, in trailer vans, elevators and the back seats of fast cars on the highway. Like excerpts from an MTV infomercial for a young person's lifestyle, plus enthusiastic hard-core sex, the series has been a big financial success, and further encouragement for aspiring female producers in California's porn valley.

If the Minneapolis Ordinances were to become law across America, then women like Shane, Tiffany Million, Ona Zee and Nina Hartley would either be out of a job or be working illegally, and therefore denied their already restricted legal rights. A key issue for feminism has been that a woman has control of her own body, and has equal rights before the law to make her own choices. Feminist anti-porners would deny porn women these rights. They seek to justify this by suggesting that porn women are not politically aware and are unable therefore to make autonomous, adult decisions. 'Women are conditioned by sexism to conform to stereotyped images of femininity and womanhood,' explains a statement of CPC from the late eighties. 'Unaware of the ways that they are misrepresented and mistreated, [women] often willingly agree to participate in the misrepresentation and mistreatment and can even feel that they "enjoy it", or, "don't mind it".'[58]

In other words, women who work in porn and who claim they are at ease with this don't know what they're saying. 'In talking to reactionary feminists,' writes Nina Hartley, 'it becomes clear that they view me, and others of my ilk, as brainwashed, deluded, woefully misled or out-and-out lying about our experiences.' Hartley doesn't appreciate the way her reality is so easily dismissed. 'How DARE these women tell me, to my FACE no less, that my experience was not my experience and, furthermore, could not ever BE my experience? These so-called pillars of the feminist establishment are no better than any patriarch who callously dismisses women's testimony about their own lives.'[59]

The dismissal experienced by Hartley recalls the élite vanguardism of Marxist analysis, where the advance party sees what everyone else, still mired in a state of 'false consciousness', cannot see. In considering the porn wars, the critic Andrew Ross urges a 'historically proven need to question the privileged voice of the . . . intellectual in hot pursuit of his or her own model reforms'.[60] Such vanguardism risks devaluing the vital feminist issue of consent. When a woman says 'yes' to being in porn, yet feminist anti-porners won't accept she really means 'yes', it revives memories of rape trials where it was suggested that a woman saying 'no' to sex didn't really mean it.[61]

Sex objects

(on arguments on what porn might do for a woman)

The view from the advance party likens porn to a submissive version of prostitution. Susan Griffin characterises women in porn as 'whores . . . literally for sale', guilty of making the life of every woman wretched: 'and now, as her likeness shines out onto the public sidewalk, she has become all women . . . Each sale of a pornographic image is a sadistic act which accomplishes the humiliation of all women.'[62]

When describing the porn image 'shining out' into the broader culture, Griffin submits a common primary complaint against porn: that it objectifies women. But what is meant by 'objectifying', a term that is easily offered, but lacks any concrete meaning? Every representation necessarily involves removing the person from the context of their real life, repositioning them within another context, be it the family snapshot, art-work or sexual fantasies. Certain meanings are necessarily partly diminished by such repositioning, particularly a sense of authenticity and wholeness, while other meanings of memory, nostalgia, loss, aesthetics, desire and fantasy are enhanced. In all such contexts the person has become objectified. If sexual 'objectification' occurs within fantasy literature, photo stills or video porn, geared as it is towards sexual arousal, then this seems more apt than if the 'objectification' seeks to cause sexual arousal when its representational purpose is to advertise a car or a wristwatch or a type of food.

The focus on sexual 'objectification' suggests a serious overvaluation of media, downplaying the particularities of real life. Sexism is far more insidious: it tends to occur at home, in public spaces, at work, concerning harassment, violence, pay, health, law, childcare, education, etc. The anti-porner's position reduces women to a singular, essential, universal state. '[There is] no such thing as Everywoman, degraded by the simulated sex act of any one sex worker,' writes Andrew Ross; '"woman" is in fact always specific "women", differentiated by age, class, ethnicity, sexual orientation, and sexual diversity.'[63]

In asserting that all women are 'damaged through the pornographic image', feminist anti-porners pass over diversity and difference, advancing instead certain fixed notions of how women are, that all women don't like porn, or shouldn't like porn. But not all women feel this way. Concerning Catherine MacKinnon, Kerri Sharp writes in an email to the author, 'Her smug, quasi-holy expressions and wagging fingers of disapproval set my teeth on edge . . . Her opinions negate the fact that women have their own autonomous sexuality; we're not being 'forced' to read, write and consume porn.' It has been suggested that 40 per cent of American porn video rentals are made by women.[64] This is probably an exaggeration. At hearings on new zoning proposals for porn retailers in New York in early 1997, Rachel Hickerson of FFE testified that something like 20 per cent of the customers of adult videotapes in the USA are women. This statistic is supported by the annual retailers' surveys in *Adult Video News*, which estimates that perhaps as many as 25 per cent of adult sales and rentals in America are made by women alone, or by women in the company of men, and that 62 per cent of trade involves men alone. How many of these men are taking porn home to share with a lover, and how many women are getting materials through the post, down a cable, or online, remains unknown. 'In a long-term relationship,' suggests Tuppy Owens, 'the woman brings home an adult video with her, and she gets fucked a million times better than she did last week.' Avedon Carol refers to the *New Woman* magazine readers' poll in the UK of 1994, in which one-third said they enjoyed looking at porn with their partners. 'Feminists Against Censorship receives many queries from women who want to know if there is anything beside gay male material that is "hot". The interest is definitely there.' When women are using porn by choice, and other women voluntarily appear in porn, then the idea of an 'everywoman' objectified by porn becomes unsustainable. The turn of the nineties saw the rise of porn subgenres such as 'readers' wives' and amateur videos. These revolutions of commonality find non-professionals making porn for little or absolutely no financial reward, and without having to look like a model to be a model. At some point, all these consenting, autonomous women making their own choices must cease being objects to become subjects instead.

Feminism in the nineties amounts to a broad range of voices, reflecting the diversity of women's lives. In the midst of such heterogeneity, the anti-porners try to speak for all in defining what is degrading to women. This fixing of the limits becomes a culture of prescription. Anti-porners characterise images of

women having penetrative sex as 'bad objects'. A representation of a woman fellating a man may also be defined as
dehumanising. A lesbian sex movie where two consenting adult
lesbian women have sex together, filmed by women, to be
watched by other women, is defined as demeaning.[65] Because
of the existence of what Catherine MacKinnon calls the 'pornographic mind', all graphic representations of sexual activity
are vulnerable to 'distortion': 'What in the Liberal view looks
like love and romance looks a lot like hatred and torture to the
feminist.'[66] In 1994 the American writer Ntozake Shange was
criticised for appearing in a shoulderless, lacy top on the cover
of the magazine *Poets and Writers*. Commenting on this, Andrea
Dworkin observed, 'It's very hard to look at a picture of a
woman's body and not see it with the perception that her body
is being exploited.'[67]

The porn wars of the eighties and nineties have seen a
faction within feminism surrender to a kind of puritanism of
sexual correctness.[68] 'In the end,' writes the social historian
Jeffrey Weeks, 'it is difficult to avoid the conclusion that the real
objection to porn is moral, however that is coded.'[69] It is also
difficult to avoid the conclusion that only women fully clothed,
not pouting, nor returning the voyeuristic gaze, will be acceptable.[70] And when women were demurely covered up last
century, did they feel liberated?

It is highly unlikely that the world would turn out any less
sexist if porn were banned tomorrow. It probably wouldn't
even be any less pornographic, for that matter, as the industry
would simply go underground. Meanwhile, it could be argued
that sexual violence would not only continue in society at large,
but it may worsen. This touches on the so called 'pressure
valve' argument. If porn is helpful to distressed people, then
banning it removes a safe outlet.[71] The cultures in which we
live are heavily sexualised, with sex used to sell pretty much
everything, including the idea of being sexy. Paradoxically, this
is also a culture that makes sexual appetite seem unsafe, as it
also exploits a sense of sexual shame. In a world of such confused signals, porn offers a less complicated message about
sexual desire, as well as a place where a person's mixed-up

feelings over sex might be partly resolved. Though sex offenders tend not to use more porn or find porn any more arousing than others, it has been suggested that the sexually repressive culture that bans porn, and a lot of sex talk with it, raises sex offenders as well. A sexually repressive culture is also traditionally one where women are less likely to be able to speak about sexual abuse.

To argue against restriction, however, is not to argue for porn being forced on people who don't like it. There are women who do not like the fact that porn exists. In the broadest sense, these women are forced to live in a society that tolerates the existence of porn. There is no ready-made solution for dealing with differences of opinion in the public domain, for settling the 'boundary disputes' that clog and enrich a society of pluralities. In response to such feelings of distaste or disapproval, arguments are made for being discreet about where pornography is seen or goes on sale. There should be zoning laws, it is suggested, where adult materials are sectioned off from the rest of the community. With porn locked away like this, however, it can easily take on the identity of the bogeyman. Making public spaces porn-exclusion zones, driving adult back to the edge of town, will also help to reaffirm porn's traditional status as a male-only preserve, restricting access to adult material for a lot of women. Quarantining pornography also means reducing the possibility that women may challenge and remake the porn genre. It is hard, therefore, to support the pressure for driving it into the night. 'Rather than denude our public square of the diverse, provocative messages that will inevitably offend some who pass through,' writes Strossen, 'we have two other remedies . . . First we can simply walk on by, averting our eyes, ears and attention. Second, we can engage in counterspeech.'[72] The writer Wendy McElroy concurs, 'My decision to consume porn in no way infringes on another woman's ability to walk right past it. She can speak out against it. What she must not do is introduce the force of law.'[73]

The porn wars have helped perpetuate certain cultural stereotypes of women as victim, made vulnerable through sex, thereby sustaining anxieties many women have over desire and fantasy. After all, how bad should a 'good girl' let herself be, how far should she stray before she slips over into the realm of the politically incorrect fantasy, or the pornographic desire? 'For many women, the real trouble with pornography is that they don't know how to use it,' argues Lisa Palac. 'We're told not to look because it's dirty, or worse that it can only be interpreted as degrading . . . The very concept of looking at an image and feeling so turned on by it that you have to come is unfamiliar to many women.'[74] Tuppy Owens suggests that many women might look at porn and masturbate later on, but won't see the two events as causally related, or they don't admit to themselves that this is partly what is going on.

The disapproval some women feel for porn may actually stem from the experience of becoming aroused on seeing it. Often these very unexpected feelings will be reorganised and expelled in a reassuring blast of invective. A woman friend tells of when she was in puberty, still shaking off the residual effects of a long embrace with Christianity. The bookish thirteen-year-old was the voracious reader of all kinds of fiction: Agatha Christie, Jean Plaidy, Mills & Boon, or, going a bit more upmarket, John Steinbeck, John Wyndham, George Orwell – whatever she could lay her hands on. One day in the second-hand bookshop in town she came across *The Group* by Mary McCarthy. She started to read this protofeminist novel with pleasure, but couldn't believe the sex scenes it contained. These she read in disgust, but also with great care. And then she read them again, still in disgust. And then, deeply piqued, she threw the book away. She had been aroused by what she had read but was not ready at this stage to admit this to herself: reading smut, and liking it, being a 'bad' girl, in other words, was not the kind of self-image she'd been brought up to have. The writer Sallie Tisdale feels her porn interests were partly determined by the fact that she still felt shame in her sexual life and felt a hypocrite because she advocated no shame: 'I could hear that little voice from long ago: *Bad girl. Mustn't touch*', she confesses in *Talk Dirty to Me*. 'I was propelled toward the overt – toward pornography . . . I needed permission. I needed blessing.'[75]

Women might actually gain from sexually explicit materials. With fewer road blocks in their way, more women might want to start making and using porn. 'We have to understand the potential there is in porn for women to speak about ourselves,' writes Bobby Lilly, an American feminist free-speech advocate. It is possible to find in pornography other stories about sex and sexualities contrary to those provided by the dominant sexual ideology – and its continued stress on romance, monogamy and reproductive heterosexuality. It can also be of use to women in offering information. Tuppy Owens refers to parts of the Middle East where Arab women have hen parties featuring porn videos: 'It's very educational, and livens up their sex lives. They see a blow job and think, yes I'd like to give that a try. Whereas in the UK we might already know about blow jobs from other sources.' Betty Dodson, the advocate for women's masturbation, previously used to masturbate regularly, but always worried that maybe she'd done it so much she'd put her vulva out of shape. The way she found out she was 'normal', that women's genitals come in all shapes and sizes, was by looking at 'split beaver' shots in men's magazines. In 1973 she decided to put together a 'cunt positive' show to spread the word.[76] Lisa Palac, guru of the cybersexual, observes how many women don't masturbate, and feels that it was only when she began looking at 'dirty pictures', and masturbating in response to them, that she 'became sexually autonomous . . . in complete control of my own erotic destiny'.[77]

Porn enables a woman to fantasise about sex without the complications of dating, a relationship, contraception, romance. 'Sometimes, you just don't want the hassle of getting ready to meet a partner, dressing up, going out, etc.,' writes a female porn lover. 'Masturbation is just as valid as two-way sex, I think. Porn does make me feel happy. It reminds me I'm alive.' Porn offers imaginative sexual fantasy, delivered within the safety of the home, perhaps helping to remove some of the shame that many feel about both sex and desire. For some people, confronting their sexuality also means confronting their fears. The feminist film critic Gertrud Koch suggests that, for some, watching is the only way they can contemplate such things. 'Only through the image can the observer confront that which would otherwise frighten him or her . . . in the case of pornographic cinema, the camera becomes a device for creating distance and the medium of harmless voyeurism.'[78]

Not everybody will feel inclined to use porn. Many women remain sure that it's not for them. It is true that, to date, pornmakers have not addressed women as directly, or as often, as they might have. This generic weakness is compounded by the fact that there are still not enough women gaining power in porn to consider doing things differently. A lot of women have also been excluded from hard-core porn because of the coverage it receives in the mainstream. 'More men than I care to count have insisted that women are not excited by erotic images,' writes Anne McClintock. 'Arguing that a quirk of anatomical design has left women numb to erotic images is both implausible and reactionary.'[79] However it isn't just men who say such things. In December 1995, the listings magazine *Time Out* did a series of reports on sex. The journalist Susannah Frankel was sent to buy a hard-core video and find out how she got on with it. This was Frankel's first time and, unfortunately, she did not have a good experience – 'Endless close-ups of penetrative sex' were not enjoyed. Feeling frozen out by her first hard-core video experience, she proceeded to tell the readers that porn can't provide for women, *all women*. Women might be sure that they're not for porn because of their social background, their cultural and sexual values, but also because the only women's voices they hear in the broader culture tell them porn isn't something women like. As much as it is easier for journalists to write the same article that's been written so many times before, it is perhaps also easier to read that you wouldn't like it, and that it's not for you – easier than it is to wonder about it. It's time we heard more from women who are porn lovers – women like Tammy Cole, Rachel James, Lisa Falour, Carol Queen, Carol Leigh, Sallie Tisdale, Lisa Palac, Tuppy Owens, Susie Bright, Nettie Pollard, Cherie Matrix, Erica Jong, Anne Rice, Camille Paglia . . .[80] And it is also time the porn wars ended, and the arguments within feminism moved on to another level of tolerance and exploration.

3
Some history

The humble and obscure life of stag

In Pimlico, London, in the mid-1870s the police raided a house and carted off a massive heap of dirty photos. The seized cache of pornographic stills rose stacks high in the air, a haul as big as many seizures of today. Porn has never been slow to embrace new technologies. The folk history of nude photography suggests that the day after the guy invented the camera he had his girlfriend come round and persuaded her to get naked for the sake of record. It's a bit like this with the history of cinema. In 1896 cinema projection began, the same year the actress Louise Willy shed her clothes in the French short, *Le Bain*.

Pre-cinematic devices like the praxiscope had already delivered up images of nudity before the Lumière brothers had filmed the train arriving at a provincial French railway station. Most often the nudes were female. If it were a male nude, then certainly some additional activity such as throwing a javelin would be required. Thus an early cinematic installation of a gendered distinction is made, which finds that men must *do* while women can simply *be*.[1] At amusement arcades and travelling shows, Thomas Edison's kinetoscope – better known as the peepshow – promised the world to punters. Advertisements for the 'peepers' suggested glimpses of carnal wonder. In reality alluring titles such as *What the Butler Saw* and *Love in a Hammock* delivered little. Here the practice of conning the viewing public, the porn fleece, was extended.

Despite such tame content, the new technology received some degree of heat from the establishment. The peepshow and the cinematograph were new and unregulated. They were also the fancied pleasure of the masses, perhaps the biggest sin of all. Fear of the mob required that the cinema be brought under control. The process of regulation was slow and would begin under the guise of ensuring that the places for screening were sanitary and safe. In the meantime, people demonstrated their love of the crude and dubious, as an array of cinematic goriness and exotica (proto-mondo) was paraded before their eyes: executions from China, dead elephants, belly dancers, the usual full-blooded stuff.

The fully fledged moving image became the hot new media of the emergent twentieth century. Beyond the public free-for-all of distribution and exhibition, short porn movies, 'stag' films, were turning up in the shadow realm of men's clubs, private societies, brothels and 'smoking rooms'. The wrangles over licit cinema – who was showing it, and where, and who was controlling the new mass medium – didn't really concern the stag or porn 'smoker'. It was not the whole world and his uncle ogling such new delights, but mainly the Edwardian gentlemen. Stag was not a mass medium, and therefore not a public affair. Beyond legality from the start, it also found itself to be mainly exempt from juridical attention.[2] Because of this fugitive status, as a film genre porn stag was 'fated to lead a humble and obscure life'.[3] Later, and as stag actually started to receive more attention from police and judges, its fugitive and shadowy character only intensified. Therefore the story prior to the 1970s, when porn emerged from the underground in a feature-length, theatre-distributed form, is scanty and elusive, rife with rumour, hearsay and patchy recall.

Gertrud Koch talks of stag in 'full bloom' in Germany by 1904. Porn was soon to make a global impact, with sightings in Moscow, Paris, Vienna, Cairo and Buenos Aires. South America was particularly quick into the porn fray. Tom Dewe Mathews tells of a band of enterprising Brazilians buying one of Thomas Edison's first batch of cameras, hot off the American inventor's production line. They took it back to Brazil and started making dirty movies.[4] In Buenos Aires, Norbert Jacques reports watching a nudie short in a large hall that was supervised by the local police, and where the stag was shown as a kind of 'pace-setter' for boosting business at the adjoining brothel.[5]

As far as plot is concerned, if early stag had a story to tell then it was likely to be either something fantastical or sprung from the semi-real. The former featured naughty prelates and passionate sheiks in titles such as *Secrets of the Cloister* and *Scenes in a Harem*. Movie shorts like *A Free Ride* (a.k.a. *Grass Sandwich*) from 1915 and *The Casting Couch* from the twenties tended to position the action in a rather less removed fictional space. *The Captain's Wife* is a story of infidelity, jealousy and rage, resulting in a scene where a cuckolded husband comes to blows with the interloper in his wife's boudoir. Such levels of angry realism are rare to porn. Contemporary hard core is one film genre where jilted parties don't punch their rivals on the nose; they are far more likely to be straight off with their kit and joining in.

The cinema of stag offers a keyhole view into a distant, somewhat uncanny, lost world. A secret history of the marginal and the furtive, the semi-criminal as well as the semi-clad. Far more, perhaps, than with contemporary porn, modern viewers will find themselves wondering about the lives and stories of the people on screen. However, the effort of tracking down what survives of vintage stag will not be rewarded by glimpses of lost cinematic highs. The stag genre, all the way from the dawn of the new medium through to the sixties, was mainly a muddle of jerky camerawork and slipshod editing, most often featuring so-so-looking performers – clearly not brought into this world to act naturally in front of a camera – screwing busily in shabby motel rooms on rickety beds. The stag product mainly depicted nudity and rutting, with fixed master shots. Close-ups on genital detail and penetrative acts were less common than in modern porn. Likewise, the external ejaculation. Lost in its criminalised underground of clandestine production and exhibition, porn as a genre quickly became rigidified into a restricted visual experience. It's hard to think of a comparable art form that could so swiftly burgeon and so swiftly become effectively stuck in a long-term generic rut. There may have been heat in the porn stag for the viewer, but the absence of critical and public light allowed forty to fifty years of porn sex to remain uni-flavoured and monotone.

Nonetheless the fascination remained strong. The product, as far as we can know, was cranked out with gusto during the twenties, thirties and forties. Just so long as you weren't arrested. Making stag was a criminal offence. Exhibition in gentlemen's clubs might have been semi-tolerated, but any kind of fledgling industry, in terms of a regular production line and distribution to greater numbers, was policed. Inevitably this made for connections with organised crime and the adjoining mob-controlled activities of gambling and prostitution, as well as alcoholic speakeasies during the Prohibition era in America. Any tales of porn racketeering on a grand scale conflict, however, with the reality of porn-film production down the years, which, as Di Lauro observes, 'has been a haphazard, high-risk, low-profit, regional activity.'[6] The association of porn and the mob, though made out of the illicit circumstances, continues in many peoples' minds today. There is, however, nothing intrinsic to making sex films that automatically has it locked in with gangsterism, just as there isn't with cigarette distribution, olive oil or cement, for that matter.[7]

By the start of the postwar period, access to movies was getting a little easier – at least for some. Eight millimetre, black and white, five or ten minute shorts on single reels, or 'loops', became more readily available if you lived in certain urban spaces, and you knew where to look. In big American cities like Los Angeles, San Francisco, New York and Chicago, men could buy porn loops from newsstands in red-light districts as far back as the early fifties. These were gay as well as straight loops, featuring naked men swimming in sun-kissed lakes, making mock-Grecian poses for life art studies, or simply well-built guys being beefcake nudes together.

For gay and straight porn fanciers, access was never so easy, so safe and so universal, however, that you took it for granted. You couldn't just buy your loop at the video shop on the corner. You had to be able to go to Soho, or equivalent red-light district, and take your chances. You could borrow the precious loop from a friend instead, or send away for something advertised in a shop window or the back pages of photography magazines, often waiting months for it to arrive, if it arrived at all. You also had to have things like a cine projector and a white sheet or the right-sized patch of white wall at home. These projector tools were the video cassette players of their time, but never as widespread. During the fifties and sixties, film projectors would be found in perhaps a fifth of American homes, mostly the middle to upper-middle classes.[8] The cine movie was never truly a conduit for mass entertainment. Neither was it much of a banker. Flimsy film stock would very often break, or the projector bulb would cause rutting torsos to melt and the scene of carnal excess to go up in flames before the distressed eyes of the stag party. Porn stag remained a relatively select and risky pleasure, restricted by factors of class and location, as well as by the time of life – college-going years – or times of the year – works and bachelor parties, and other such ritualised gatherings for men to bond, and watch.

In the early fifties, in the middle of family-centred, clean-living America, in a motel in Tennessee, a certain Juanita Slushes made a stag movie called *Smart Aleck*. Juanita changed her name to Candy Barr and became stag porn's first screen idol. Barr is perhaps the only star of stag during its fifty or sixty years. Because of stag's underground location in the culture, this means that she was simultaneously famous and unheard of: a popular secret, known and lusted over by countless viewers in confidence, truly the cult celebrity. A decade or so later, the last illegal loops were being turned out. Titles like *Dogorama*, directed by Lawrence T. Cole, and featuring little-known performers Eric Edwards, Linda Marchiano and a dog. Within a few years Edwards and Marchiano – by then known as Linda Lovelace – would find themselves living through the heady, happening era of the new legal porn, of porn chic, and experiencing the first ever porn celebrity that dared speak their names. (The dog, however, would remain a nobody.)

During the postwar era of French stag, titles included *The*

Woman in the Portrait and *Family Spirit*. As a nation, France was so revered for its stag movies that 'French film' became synonymous for some with sex film. British-made stag titles from the postwar period included *Pussy Galore*, *100% Lust* and *End of Term*.[9] British porn film-maker Stanley Long started out taking nude photographic stills. Harrison Marks, Britain's most famous home-grown sex film-maker, also started in this way. Women would stand naked, knees together and no lewd poses, and it would be passed off as art-work. Nature shots, art studies, physique culture, all the usual alibis. Later on, Long started to make short films of women undressing. Strip movies were a kind of British stag, several featuring the versatile and voluptuous Pamela Green, icon of postwar Britain's demi-monde. Gay pornographer John Barrington also made similar materials for the gay customer. They would be advertised around Soho in newsagents' windows.[10] The nudie loops made good money for a few, and were the precursors for the legal, certificated naturist movies of the early sixties.

From nudies and mondo to action beaver
(on the road from secret stag to cinema hard core)

In the realm of licit cinema, acceptable levels of nudity were tightly policed for what was a very long time indeed. British sex-film historian David McGillivray describes a fifties of people rushing all the way across London just for a momentary flash of nipple in a racy 'Continental' movie. And then there was change. During the fifties and sixties, Hollywood responded to the growing impingement from television by creating new technologies for that special big-screen experience. To run newfangled 3–D, wider screens, improved colour and sound effects, the movie houses needed to install costly machinery. The independents who couldn't afford to modernise didn't get the A-list movies any longer and they had to seek out a new audience. Art house and Continental films made up some of the shortfall. Theatre managers were quick to notice that movies with a more adult story line, especially those featuring the briefest glimpses of flesh, tended to do pretty good box office. European films like *And God Created Woman*, *Summer with Monika* and *Touchez Pas au Grisbi*, and earthy European glamour-pusses such as Anna Magnani, Sophia Loren, Harriet Anderson and Brigitte Bardot kept many second-tier American cinemas in the pink.

There were only so many Brigitte Bardot movies you could show, however. Likewise, there was a limit to the number of sleazy urban-jungle B-movies, featuring raunchy young misfits in tight sweaters – cautionary moral tales concerning the dangers of sex, drugs and dark nightclubs that revelled in the vices they denounced. A hole in the market was emerging for cheapo, opportunistic, so-called 'exploitation' movies, and there were plenty of people out there ready to plug the gap. (In this context the 'exploitation' involves any 'hot' subjects worth filming to attract a paying audience through a love of money rather than such lofty goals as 'art' or 'the truth'.) From the late fifties and into the early sixties there came a rash of nudist pictures. Nudies were 'educational' films, don't you know. Films like *Take Off Your Clothes and Live* and *Naked as Nature Intended*, from Britain, and *The Garden of Eden*, from the United States, wished to offer the audience deeper insights into the naturist lifestyle.

There was also the rise of the cinematic genre known as 'mondo', where intrepid camera crews would travel the globe – and the world was much bigger then – seeking out anthropological curiosities and exotica, as well as dark tales of prostitution, venereal disease and teenage pregnancy from the naked city. Titles such as *Mondo Cane* continued the dubious tradition of the so-called 'jungle' movies of the forties, featuring at least one segment with native tribal African women dancing topless. It was just like *National Geographic*, only the breasts moved. Such fleshy exposures, however, would be dispersed among other less titillating scenes of global difference and weirdness: decapitations in Borneo, or dodgy surgical practices in the upper reaches of the Amazon.

Mondo and nudies were short-stop transitional staging posts on the journey from privately exhibited stag shorts to full-length cinematic hard core. Junoesque blondes with goose bumps patting beach balls on windswept beaches could only do so much for the libido. Nudity is one thing, action and sex quite another. One trick was to get away with depicting alternative fictions within a dramatic context, featuring looser morals and a general mood of greater sexiness. 'Exploitation' pictures such as *The Dirty Girls* and *Dark Odyssey* arrived on the independent and drive-in circuit in America, as well as *The Immoral Mr Teas*, the first of the many varied works of Russ Meyer, which would use the bare outline of a story to justify showing bikini-clad lovelies doing vigorous things, making their voluptuous breasts bounce up and down. People like Meyer, David Friedman and Radley Metzger took things sideways as much as forwards. At first, Meyer's movies might have shown less flesh than the previous nudies; they were successful, however, in being able to show whatever they showed for longer portions of a feature-length movie. His movies were also far livelier, less likely to pall with an audience – which is what happened in time with the nudies and mondo – and were therefore more lucrative. A kind of level of acceptance as well as a viewing trend was thus established by Meyer and friends.

In the world of art house, cinema's new kitchen-sink social realism began to mean the inclusion of not everything but certainly more. In *Room at the Top*, the subject of sexual wantonness was openly depicted. In *A Kind of Loving*, so too was actual flesh. A version of sexual frankness was increasingly 'in' with the censors as the sixties started to swing. Just so long as they weren't getting too far ahead of public taste, or, indeed, slipping too far behind. Film-makers from Ken Russell to Roman Polanski were in communication with the British film censor John Trevelyan. Clothes were increasingly shed, though always in the interests of art, science or politics, of course, rarely just sex. In 1967, Sweden's Victor Sjorstrom gave the world *I am Curious – Yellow*, his sub-Godardian treatise on film-making, radical politics and sex without love. *Yellow* featured sound bites from figures like Martin Luther King and Olaf Palme, as well as a greater, franker exposure of the male and female anatomy than had even been shown before. It was for this reason alone that the film gained some kind of notoriety. Once riskier films were out on the market, *Yellow* would be left behind, a creaking historical relic.

Both art house and (s)exploitation in the UK and the USA continued to be carefully monitored during this time to ensure that they didn't slip into the realm of straight porn. No matter the extravagant promises, 'exploitation' actually delivered only so much, and no more. While nudity and sexual frankness were permitted, pornography was not. Porn was still the dark, unacceptable background that allowed other kinds of expression to come into the legally defended foreground. Ironically, such efforts to outlaw depictions of sex for the mere sake of it actually helped to make sex into a suitable case for treatment, scrutiny and debate. Nevertheless, in order for the licit and illicit to merge, the latter would need to dilute its product during a transitional stage. A series of what were called 'beaver' loops were made, featuring women stripping to show their pubic region. In 1967 a second-tier cinema in San Francisco started to run beaver loops in amongst its usual titles, and got away with it. Soon after came a selection of 'split beaver' loops, where the legs were spread, and possibly even the labia. (By the late sixties, San Francisco was one of the three key production sites for underground porn loops in America – including the *200* and the *OZ* series of colour loops – as well as New York and LA, with the *M* Series, and the *Playmate* series respectively.)

The next tentative shuffle forwards came in the shape of the 'action beaver', where naked women were active with each other on screen. There was no penetration, not even by finger or tongue, just stripping, rubbing, touching, kissing. So-called 'girl–girl' action became inscribed as a generic staple in hard core's prehistory partly due to its ability to show some kind of love action without showing the erect male member. Moreover, girl–girl was able to function partly as a substitute for showing heterosexual couplings which, if shown without erections or penetration, might be felt to be lacking erotic punch and therefore something of a disappointment to the viewer.

The first films containing hard-core porn shown in public cinemas in America were two documentaries about porn in

Scandinavia: John Lamb's *Sexual Freedom in Denmark* (1970) and *Censorship in Denmark: A New Approach* (1969) by Alex deRenzy. This short-lived mini-genre was the last disguise prior to porn finally coming out in full, cinematic hard-core relief. The two films started showing in San Francisco in 1969. By early 1970 they were also showing in Los Angeles and New York, and soon to be joined by Gerard Damiano's *Sex USA* (1970) and deRenzy's *History of the Blue Movie* (1970). As 'documentaries' the films carefully removed themselves from being just about sex by having 'doctors' offering instruction as to what fucking was all about. They were also careful to claim that their business was partly making a sociological inquiry into how the relaxation of the porn laws in far-off Scandinavia was working out. The films tended to be very grainy. The hard-core action was often inset within the overall frame, playing on a screen within the film, or in the background. All of this was done so as to be able to argue for the movie having some socially redeeming value, so that the producers could hope to escape a prosecution for obscenity.

Porn chic

(on when porn was suddenly all the rage)

Following sex 'documentaries', the final step in the game of brinkmanship was proper movies, with stories as well as explicit sex. Bill Osco's *Mona, the Virgin Nymph* (1970) was the original; Richard Lerner's *Hot Circuit* (1971) came next. Lerner's movie would be the first of many porn films to employ the roundelay device, a carousel of seductions, borrowed from Schnitzler's *La Ronde*, going from A through to Z and back to A again. *Schoolgirl* (1971, David Gerber) and Anthony Spinelli's *Act of Confession* (1972) were other pioneer titles. The latter still rates as perhaps American porn's most controversial movie. This tale of a lubricious nun includes a closing scene that features a bearded character in white vestments walking on water while being fellated. It was never commercially distributed and has been seen by very few people. Shortly after came *Deep Throat* and the era of porn chic was just about to start.

Deep Throat is estimated as one of the all-time top ten moneymakers in film history. It charts alongside *Star Wars* and *ET.* That's a lot of people, a lot of bums on seats, and video rentals too. The film opened at the New World Theatre in Manhattan, New York, in 1972, and was an immediate success. Like the other hard-core features at the time, Gerard Damiano's *Deep Throat* would get busted early on in its run, but unlike the others it kept bouncing back, picking up a lot of news coverage and a growing media fascination. Notoriety led to fame. Porn was the talk of the town, soon after becoming part of the done thing for the smart set. 'When *Deep Throat* opened up . . . in New York, it became chic to go by there at eleven o'clock and try to get into the theater,' remembers porn director Anthony Spinelli. 'All you saw were limousines – tons of limousines parked all the way for fifteen blocks with the chauffeurs waiting.' Hepcats like Sammy Davis Junior went to see what the fuss was all about. Johnny Carson made jokes about *Deep Throat* on national television. The film became a must-see and a mood caught. 'People in their evening clothes would come out of a Broadway show and say "let's go see *Deep Throat*." You could not, you could not get into that theatre.'[11] Every evening this happened, porn inched a little bit further away from being part of the obscene, part of the utterly without merit. It became tougher to convince a jury that such a 'plain view' movie entertainment was in violation of local community standards when part of the community was so obviously 'digging' *Throat* – as they used to say back then. The underground stag had become the hard-core movie on the big screen and seemingly, at least for a while, was rushing towards becoming almost part of the mainstream.

Deep Throat is actually a pretty awful porn movie. What it had was a catchy title and a very catchy premise. The lead woman, played by Linda Lovelace, is unable to achieve orgasm, until it is realised that, through a trick of nature, her clitoris is located in the wrong place. This being porn, the wrong place also turns out to be the right place. Her clitoris is in the back of her throat. Only by repeated bouts of 'deep-throat' fellatio can she reach sexual nirvana. The film, its premise, and its main visual event, were all one and the same thing: the blow job. *Deep Throat* was right on time. A newly sexually enlightened and sexually vigorous America was gagging for the blow job, for the knowledge, the thought, the learning of the technique of the blow job, for the witnessing of such exotic oral entertainments. 'You had middle-class women,' recalls Camille Paglia, 'going with their boyfriends and husbands to porn theatres to see *Deep Throat*. That was a breakthrough. We'd never even heard of oral sex, much less seen it demonstrated.'[12]

Here was a film that not only showed oral sex on screen but actually featured a real story like 'normal' movies have. Not a completely fake 'narrative-alibi' kind of storyline, this was a proper sexual narrative, starting with a problem, finishing with a solution, and featuring scenes of hard-core sex as integral to the story's flow. This was radical for porn: a dramatic set-up, no matter how slight, featuring a quest, which eventually results in a happy discovery and an emotionally satisfying closure. And the quest, the problem being solved, again and again, was that of the giving and experiencing of oral sex as part of lovemaking. By this stage, in hindsight, Damiano starts to look like a porn genius. 'Damiano made our industry, we owe him so much.'[13]

In fact, in terms of form and content, *Deep Throat* doesn't really stand alone. *Deep Throat* reflects a broader concern of cinematic, story-based hard core to recognise the problematics of sex. *Deep Throat* dramatises and seeks solutions to the problems inherent in the pursuit of sexual pleasure. Previously, in stag movies, the question of sexual satisfaction, both male and female, was hardly ever posed. As feminist film critic Linda Williams says, 'To insert a penis into any orifice was automatically presumed to be satisfying to both man and woman.' With hard core the proof of male orgasm, the visible ejaculation, became the staple goal and visual climax of the hard-core encounter featuring a man and a woman. Previously it had only started to feature with any great frequency towards the end of stag's era. In the absence of a commensurate, 'unfakeable' female equivalent, the male ejaculation, it could be argued, came to figure as the overall sign of pleasurable climax and satisfaction, as well as closure within a porn number. Without the come shot, a hard-core, problem-solving scene could conceivably last for ever.[14]

In *Hard Core*, Linda Williams sees the money shot in sex films as taking 'unseen pleasure made visible . . . to the next stage'. Brandy Alexandre, former porn actress and film-maker, sort of agrees: 'You've got to have the come shot, you've got to have the heat. And this, at present, is where the heat is. Once it was a glimpse of ankle, maybe then some cleavage, some thigh. They then got naked in time, and they fucked, and they showed them penetrating. But they also want to show pleasure, and internal come shots aren't so pleasant or pleasurable, but come shots are deemed to be so. I don't have a problem with them,' she admits, 'but I expect that in time they will become old news.' Writers like Williams and Wendy McElroy have also defended the external ejaculation as educative, giving women who might rarely see the physical process of an ejaculation an idea of what it looks like – as well as noting that if men often ejaculate on themselves when masturbating, then why is it so deplorable that a man is seen ejaculating upon a woman. Steffani Martin, an executive at Bizzare Video, agrees. 'What's so negative about a come shot? It's a life-giving, rather than a negative, force.'[15]

The reason hard core came to be legally tolerated in many parts of the West in the early seventies was not merely because a loosening of morals occurred in society. Nor was it just a case of a few hardened, hardy pioneers of graphic, profit-making sexual expression, pushing boundaries to the maximum. Hard core arrived as it did partly as a consequence of the politicisation of sex within society at large. Part of this politicisation concerned the pursuit of more sex, and the pursuit of new kinds of sex, less fettered by traditional moral and social exhortation. As with the endgame of stag, however, it was also realised that sex in and of itself wasn't necessarily going to deliver up the erotic paradise that the sexual revolution had promised. At this point, the pleasure of sex became the issue. When the pursuit of quality sex, of proper orgasms, began to loom as a large part of the carnal story, so hard core arrived, speaking not just of sex and fucking, but of better sex. Hard core engaged with the problem of sexual gratification in a familiar cinematic narrative form while also offering solutions. Some of these were practical, informational solutions, and others were clearly highly metaphoric. In terms of *Deep Throat*, the narrative is heavily oriented towards the phallus. However, such phallocentrism apart, a movie like *Deep Throat* is also very much concerned with female enjoyment. Although the gratification of Lovelace's character arrives in a way that is arguably more about enhancing male sexual gratification than anything female, in less literal terms the whole organisation of the narrative is concerned with female pleasure: the getting of it, the enjoying of it.

The 'problem' of female sexual pleasure is central to *Deep Throat* and many other porn movies of its era. A problem in terms of the dramatic structure that is in need of fixing, but also a problem in terms of the search for some kind of visible sign of a solution. The female orgasm cannot be certifiably visibly proved to have happened – at least not in any equivalent fashion to the male pop shot. Some male porn fans will talk at length about pink flushes, flared nostrils, dilated eyes, banshee wails, 'her pulsating, spasming clitoris'. 'Believe me,' says one, 'I know when a woman's fully pleasured . . . I promise, OK?' The truth, however, is that they don't know; even the most cocksure must recognise deep down that they really can't be certain.[16]

In Freudian terms, this 'lack' might be said to be partly compensated through the fetishised stand-in of the male pop shot, figuring as proof of pleasure for both male and female participants. Less theoretically, this interest in early hard core in the problem of female pleasure, and the lurking anxiety regarding the absence of any visible proof of such pleasure, should go at least some way to dispelling the argument that film porn represents the scene of masculine affirmation. Did you come? Was it good for you, darling? These questions that haunt the heterosexual male's sexual psyche are perpetuated as well as intensified in the arena of early hard core.

The golden age
(on when porn was almost a mainstream film genre)

If *Deep Throat* was felt to be creating male panic across the land and over the seas, then it didn't show at the box office. This was a movie that made a fortune and started a trend. A string of other big-name hard-core feature films were soon to follow, like *Touch of Sex*, *Sleepy Head*, *3am* and *China Girl*. Although porn chic didn't last for ever – once people got used to the existence of hard core at the cinema, the fashion wagon rolled on – porn producers rather enjoyed being fêted as 'out there', the new sex radicals. It certainly made a change from being chased by the police. Moreover, where profits were concerned, the new phenomenon of not only men but also some women coming to check the product out – so contrary to the male-only regimes of the stag – had alerted porners to a new and potentially lucrative market opening up before their eyes.

The American porn industry went in hot pursuit of the couples market. Sophisticated adult movies started to roll off the hard-core production line, movies a lot better than *Deep Throat*, featuring plenty of narrative – ladies, it was believed, are suckers for a good story. It started with titles like *Devil in Miss Jones* and *Behind the Green Door*, and continued during the following decade with numerous other releases, including *Private Afternoons of Pamela Mann*, *Eruption*, *Amanda by Night*, *Talk Dirty to Me* and *The Voyeur*.

The second half of the seventies and the early eighties were what came to be known as porn's 'golden age'.[17] The golden age was pre-VCR – a fact of great importance. This was a time when sex films were actually films – shot on film, that is, and watched in cinemas. It was because the product was cinema-bound and often harboured a producer's up-scale pretensions that quite a lot of porn movies were actually made like 'real' movies too. Lots of loving care and, more vitally, time and money were given over to many productions. Golden-agers tended to be feature-length movies with proper scripts, sets, costumes, good filming (mostly), a sense of a director's presence, and a pool of acting talent. Not only could the actors act but they were also sometimes rehearsed, even coached by acting instructors, and had seen the script and worked on their lines prior to the shoot. Such luxuries were pretty much to vanish from porn after the onset of the video revolution in the mid-eighties, and were only seen to be starting to return again in the mid-nineties.

Not all the movies of the seventies were like this. Many were just well-made porn movies renouncing any theatrical pretensions, which simply set about delivering filmed sex. These were known as wall-to-wallers, effectively a string of loops inside a single movie, maybe held together by a vague thematic link. Performers like the legendary Seka didn't much care to act, couldn't act, but Seka was quite the powerhouse as a sexual performer – queen of the wall-to-wallers.

The golden age was porn dreaming. Dreaming of becoming a regular movie genre just like any other, free from legal hassle, social opprobrium. Dreaming, also, of picking up a broader, more affluent, cross-gender audience as a big-time boost to the revenue inflow from the regulars – presumed to be 'loners' and 'raincoaters'. It seems bizarre now, because it probably couldn't happen these days, but movie porn's early years were imbued with a feeling that a convergence with the mainstream was coming. It was not just a desert mirage, but was almost achieved when films such as Chuck Vincent's *Roommates* (1982), with its high production values, quality acting and absorbing story line, pretty much crossed over and played to art house and independent cinema audiences.

In a similar vein, *Dixie Ray, Hollywood Star* from 1983 is a high-quality porn noir, with John Leslie in the role of a hard-boiled detective. Originally planned as a mainstream movie, titled *It's Called Murder, Baby*, the director Anthony Spinelli hedged his bets by doing some explicit sex scenes to accompany the movie's catchy plot and glossy look, and a sex film is how it finally came out. *Dixie* is good enough to watch for the story alone. You could fast forward through the sex if you felt so inclined. *Eruption* (1977) was another porn noir, a reworking of *Double Indemnity*, which took three weeks to make on location in Hawaii. That's a long time for a porn film. Previously, Anthony Spinelli also made *Sex World* in 1978, the duly extolled porn version of Michael Crichton's *Westworld*, set within a futuristic theme-parked holiday resort which caters to the guests' every erotic fantasy.

Many porn creatives of the time, like Spinelli, Radley Metzger, Georgina Spelvin and Paul Thomas, had already made mainstream films and were now making full-size porn movies instead. Many other porners of the time believed they were embarking on a journey leading towards a career in Hollywood. In fact, being in porn, with all the stigma it brings, was actually taking them further from this goal. From the middle of the 1980s onwards – because of the impact of video, the rise of the antis, the revival of censorship, and a general shift in the culture – porn found itself beyond the pale again, and dreams of a porn–mainstream merger became an impossibility. Though it continues to feed off Hollywood, borrowing and playing with titles, partially mimicking it with its own star directors, contracted performers, studios and awards, American movie porn remains separate and cut off, almost a parallel cinema.

Devil in Miss Jones
(on when hard core became an art form)

In the seventies, porn wasn't the only kind of cinema preoccupied with sex. A lot of mainstream, particularly art-house, cinema seemed equally determined to render the full erotic range on the big screen. Movies such as *Maitresse*, *Ai No Corrida*, *Last Tango in Paris*, *Les Valseuses*, *Bad Timing*, *Salo* and *Immoral Tales* suggested the dawning of an era of sexual frankness on screen that would inevitably lead to the convergence of the previously belligerently divided selves of art and porn. From time to time, there was even talk of a mainstream film director doing a porn film. The names of Scorsese and Roeg came up, while the contentious Brian de Palma actively courted notoriety by suggesting that *Body Double* would be the first mainstream X-rated thriller and would also feature porn superstar Annette Haven. As it was, porn didn't really need de

Palma, Roeg, or Scorsese to make art, or explore the dark, confused side to sexual desire, the tortures of Catholic guilt. If sex, sin and eternal damnation were the kind of hard-core package you were looking for, then porn had the director, and the movie. With *Deep Throat*, Gerard Damiano created an epoch-making dud; with *Devil in Miss Jones* (1972) he made a porn masterpiece.

In order to think differently about porn, to take it seriously as its own cinematic genre perhaps, it's worth departing from the narrow path of relating some history to stop and spend a while assessing a few key films. In 1997, the American reissue of *Devil in Miss Jones* featured a box-cover photograph of a semi-nude blonde woman playing with a devil's fork. Porn box-covers are a vital part of the selling process, and they are mainly misleading. This is no exception. The cover suggests a devilishly playful romp. In fact, *Devil in Miss Jones* is one of porn's darkest movies. Like the mainstream film *Carnal Knowledge*, it could be said to make the sexual revolution look like a very bad idea. One to scare the hell out of every carefree sex advocate.

Devil in Miss Jones opens like a horror film, using spine-tingling piano music straight out of a Cronenberg or John Carpenter movie. The dark photography, grainy textures and patchy colours make you think of *Carrie* or *The Exorcist*. The vivid sound effects of wind and echo add to the chill factor. If erotically pleasuring the audience is what Damiano has in mind, then what's with all the gothic stuff? This is one sex film where hell, as well as heaven, is just round the corner. Having led an unhappy life of boredom, Justine Jones takes her own life. In a dank, dark, spooky bathroom, after sloshing about in a grimy, tide-marked tub half-filled with water the colour of cold onion soup, she slits her wrists. Justine is greeted in purgatory with the news that since she has committed the terrible sin of suicide there's no hope of her making it to heaven. The only way is down. However, since her life was one of complete carnal abstinence, her sin credit rating is very poor. She needs to sin a lot, and quickly, if she's to make it to hell and avoid an eternity of utter dullness in purgatory. In a porn spin on Nietzsche's notion of eternal recurrence, Justine Jones is invited to live her life again, but to live it differently knowing what she now knows. She is invited to live a life, in other words, 'engulfed, and consumed by lust'.

Returned to earth, Miss Jones immediately embarks on her lusty mission. She is greeted by a character called the Teacher, played by the moody Harry Reems, who offers high-quality instruction in the erotic arts. Justine goes about the carnal business of losing her inhibitions under his guidance. In early hard core, women were often depicted as being in need of erotic tutelage. The sexual revolution was still new. Apparently, the notion of a woman being able to instigate sinfulness single-handedly just didn't ring true with the porn auteur. The assertion, however, that this is one more gullible bimbo ready to be thoroughly de-frigidified by an all-controlling male is too glib by far. It just doesn't ring true. Justine Jones features as the desiring subject, and not a malleable object. The feminist critic Anne McClintock has suggested that Justine's life-taking act represents an act of sovereignty of a dissatisfied woman finally taking control of things.[18] This impression is underscored by the magnificent Georgina Spelvin's performance in the role of Miss Jones. A one-time stand-in for Shirley Maclaine, Spelvin was a powerful actor in her own right. Part Joan Crawford, part Barbara Stanwyck, in a hard-core setting, with *Devil in Miss Jones* Spelvin delivers one of porn's great performances.

As a sexual novice, Miss Jones may need some technical pointers, but soon she's pretty much setting the pace herself. Indeed, over time Justine Jones cuts loose from the Teacher to pursue new carnal conquests of her own making and predilection. Once she's got the hang of basic shagging and rudimentary fellatio, there's no stopping Justine. In due course she becomes greedy for the phallus. You better watch out for your shower attachment, your fruit supply, even your pet snake (oh, the joy of religious symbolism). One could, of course, read this as a typical male fantasy of the virgin woman transformed into a cock-hungry sex banshee. That reading does have some validity. But it would be only partly true. For a woman wanting, seeking out and demanding her own sexual pleasure remains one of porn's truly positive messages.

In spite of being saturated in a sense of doom concerning the conflict between repression and desire, or maybe because of it, the sex scenes in *Devil in Miss Jones* are highly erotic and passionate. There's a tremendous sense of vigour and frankness. The hard-core phenomenon was pretty fresh, and generic convention is absent. The visuals and the performances teem with a new-world energy. Spelvin, Reems and co. come across like sexual pioneers, revelling in their new-found explicitness, the newly won expectations for female lust and erotic participation. In spite of Damiano's grim Catholic pessimism for the soul, there's a momentum within the sex scenes, an eager, hungry goal-seeking, that is partly driven forward through a sense that the end is not necessarily predetermined or known in advance. This exploratory charge is not something you often see in porn these days. It isn't something you could really expect after a quarter of a century of so many sex films. The establishment of genre conventions and expectations is unavoidable, where certain goals are inevitable and counted upon.

In the broadest terms, the early porn master works of the seventies are more sexist than the high-end product of the late nineties. The overall culture was more sexist back then. Porn may be a thing apart, but it doesn't get made in a social vacuum. Though women were sexually liberated, the sexual liberation was still predominantly described in male terms. Today in porn there is a far greater equality and mutuality between men and women. Porn has responded to shifts in the sexual politics of the wider culture. However, although less sexist, today's sex movies are, rather paradoxically, more fantastic, where the sex seems less real. For example, in *Devil in Miss Jones* the performers' pubes aren't shaved down to nothing, and the man doesn't immediately start with a full-scale erection: you see a man's penis grow, a rare sight in porn, rising from a slack nub to a studly 'love tower', and in approximately real time. Nowadays, male and female depilation is preferred in search of maximum porn visibility (shaving also makes a penis look larger), while instant erections have come to be expected as a key visual indicator of total virility and unstoppable lust.

It is interesting, looking back, to see bodies that aren't siliconed, or hypertrophied through working out. The body on view in *Devil in Miss Jones* comes from a time prior to the sports ethic – not only pre-collagen, but pre-jogging. Also, the hair is less teased and glammed up. The film's sensibility is different, very Greenwich Village, very New York City, drenched in old European dread and anxiety. Nowadays, if you're looking at the American porn product from a company like Vivid, the *mise-en-scène* of its chief image-maker, Paul Thomas, is a kind of California noir with muscles, souped-up hair and lip gloss, the visuals of mainstream movie-makers like David Lynch, Tony Scott and Katherine Bigelow, and Michael Mann's postmodern, surface-led, LA aesthetic.

Sexual numbers and preferred positions have changed. When Justine Jones was first experiencing the hard-core life, positions such as reverse cowgirl (RC), and reverse anal cowgirl (RAC) simply hadn't been invented. Reverse cowgirl features penetration with the women on top, straddling the man but facing away from him – riding him like a cowgirl rides a horse, only backwards. (RAC is the anal variation.) Because, back then, porn was trying to communicate the feeling of having sex, RC would not have been an obvious choice. Nowadays, because porn wishes to put on a top show for the happy voyeur, RC is a much preferred position because it provides both a favourable view of the women's body and clear and erotic spectacle of the genital action and actual penetration. This reflects what has over time been a more general shift from porn being about 'real' people having hot sex to body-sculpted, silicone-enhanced superhumans 'performing' hot sex. It's partly about the continued rise in voyeurism, partly to do with the growth in vicarious sex during a time of AIDS. Watching beautiful superhumans 'perform' sex on our behalf is a lot less risky, and considerably less tiring.

Speaking of indolence, there are fewer sightings of men selflessly pleasuring women in early porn. Slothful heterosexual males had things pretty well sorted. With liberation and greater sexual frankness, with the ascension of the blow job through *Deep Throat*, if not its apotheosis, Mr Lazybones of the mid-seventies could expect his sexually reborn lady-friend to provide a full and thorough sexual servicing. All he need do was get comfortable, lie back and enjoy the time of his life. Apart from the obligatory humping and rutting, and the male performer needing to keep a hard-on through till the end of the scene, it's tough to see how seventies porn men were working so hard. These days the man really works for his money. Alex Sanders, Peter North, Jon Dough, Steven St Croix and TT Boy are required as contemporary studmeisters not only to recognise what their tongues are really for, but also to be weightlifter, actor, matador, gigolo and second string. Always second string, because the women bring the star rating and the men provide the come shot.

However, one hesitates to receive messages from seventies hard core as a low point for male sexual sloth long since passed. An issue of the *Village Voice* from 1996 suggests that in certain quarters some things never change: 'I have a serious problem,' confesses a reader to the paper's sex counsellor. 'My husband doesn't give me any foreplay or oral sex. I put it to him very nicely, but it just doesn't get done: his knees always hurt, or he has a backache . . . I haven't had an orgasm in three years.' The sex counsellor responds: 'Here's a snappy, smartass line that might do the trick: "Eat my pussy or I'll break your legs" . . . or, "does my babylamb want a blowjob? Well, fuck off you selfish unresponsive bastard. Suck your own goddamned dick, you mutherfucker!" '[19]

Justine Jones isn't shy about asking. She continues to be demanding, even pleading for her pleasuring at times. It is around this point that you twig that all this fucking and sucking isn't going to make for a happy ending. As the movie progresses, the players are revealed as the truly damned. The lustiness of Miss Jones will not deliver satisfaction; it will merely make her want more. All this sex, you start to realise, is driving her crazy. Hot for perversity of every type, her sexual appetite, once stimulated, proves insatiable. It's the kind of appetite that porn films were made for. The catch is that appetite can go on, but movies must end. Rather than plump for the narrative closure of sated lust, Damiano denies Justine true orgasmic release, consigning her for the rest of eternity with an itch, which she alone apparently cannot scratch: 'Damn you, help me. I can't do it by myself.' Stalled on the outer rings of hell, with a nutcase for a partner – a man so deliriously lost within his own ranting existential gloom that he's of no use whatsoever – Justine has no option but to call out for somebody to fuck her. It's a dark ending to a dark, sober film.

Devil in Miss Jones can be read in many ways. It has been described both as a deeply gloomy, sex-negative movie, depicting untrammelled erotic conduct as sheer hell, or, alternatively, has been hailed as a powerful attack on repression. It might be suggested that Damiano blames puritanism for creating this torrid mess of unfulfilled desires: if you suppress sexual desire, you are sowing the bitterest sexual harvest for all. Any movie that shows a desiring woman being driven mad is open to accusations of misogyny. As a plot line it is a staple of modern mainstream cinema, from *Betty Blue* to *Fatal Attraction* to European art-house favourite *Breaking the Waves*. *Devil in Miss Jones* at least recognises women's right to want sex and demand it for themselves, though clearly it remains pessimistic of a woman's chances of ever getting properly laid. Arguably the insanity comes from the tension caused by the Christian moral requirements that 'good' girls don't hunger after sex, and that if they do they shall be cast out and doomed to an unhappy life. Maybe. You just wonder why it had to be so dark in spells, and why no one saw fit to scrub the bath the day of filming. *Devil in Miss Jones* is a troubling film. Sex films were supposedly built for pleasure, but Damiano requires that pleasure costs. Susie Bright calls it, 'A must for every recovering Catholic'.[20]

Though Damiano seems undecided as to whether desire or repression is the problem, the bleakness of Justine's future prospects suggests a last-minute side bet, erring on the side of caution, a 'just-in-case' from the moral pornographer. This partly reflected a perceived need for your hard-core movie to have a moral angle, for it to culminate with the restitution of proper social values in order for the porners to be able to argue in court that their product was socially redeeming, morally intact. In the early days, porn was often to be seen atoning for its sins. Losing its nerve. After all that sin, better chuck in a dose of damnation, just to be on the safe side. Or maybe just a wedding, some kind of resumption of conventional morality. Although it might be argued that this is how films are made, following an order-disorder-order trajectory – and hard core dearly wanted to be like the movies – there's also an underlying tone suggesting that guilt catches up with everyone in the end. All that fucking, the multi-partnered action, the orgies, the every-which-way promiscuity, was rounded off with the same old monogamy. Mainstream cinema is the same. *Fatal Attraction* is a movie of fine upstanding values which, like its lead character, indulges itself with a hot fling – plunging headlong into infidelity and pot-boiling, kitchen-sink fucking – only to wake up feeling wretched with itself (himself) the next morning, and be set to spend the rest of the movie feeling shameful, eager to restore a sense of decorum, to reinstate the proper moral attitudes, if only the furious, spurned Glenn Close would go away. Desire is fun, but it may also be damning.

What's plot got to do with it?
(on why porn deserves to be treated like a proper film genre)

Affording sex films normal critical analysis might seem a rather peculiar thing to do, a case of straying from the point. After all, porn is supposed to be a sex thing. Certainly it's a mistake many critics of porn make, treating porn like normal films. 'Don't analyse it like fine cinema; [it isn't],' says the writer, Carol Queen. In many respects, she's right: porn is not that kind of art. 'It is really just a spectacle,' suggests Paul Thomas, a leading American hard-core film director. 'Most porn films are really stupid. Even the good ones are really stupid. The ones I make they're not really good films. I tell a detective story, it's not a *really* good detective story.' Your best-ever porn drama is never going to be as engrossing as *The Godfather* or *Wild Strawberries*, and your favourite porn film isn't likely to make it onto your list of best-ever films (just as *The Godfather* won't ever make it into your top five sex films). Watching porn like you're watching mainstream cinema won't much help you tune in to what porno is truly about, and will probably leave you thinking that porn is cheap, lowbrow, not very good art, and all the other put-downs that have launched a thousand mainstream magazine articles on the subject.

Indeed, in a genre where sex must come first, the virtue or use of cinema's classic narrative system is questioned by some. Steve Perry, a British porn director, has his doubts: 'The problem you have with porno is that a straight drama requires a lot of time to tell the story but porn takes a lot of time to show the sex. If you want the drama in porno, you'd need hours for both.'[21] Some might also suggest that if people are watching porn, and enjoying it, the likely outcome is arousal, and so they stop watching the film to have sex, and where does that leave the story? John Stagliano, America's top heterosexual pornmaker during the nineties, won't work with story lines, doubting that they have any place in the genre: 'For years people were saying you got to have a plot. They'd criticise a movie for having no plot. I mean, who gives a fuck if it doesn't have a plot. That's the most ridiculous criticism I've ever heard!'

Such declarations are not so convincing, however. The reason feature-length cinema and porn came together in the first place was primarily for the sake of an alibi. Many porners get a kick out of copying Hollywood, it is true, but, pretensions apart, things like narrative, art and themes make a hard-core movie less likely to be branded obscene. Furthermore, many porn users need adult movies to closely resemble regular movies if they're going to watch them, preferring adult films to be just like Hollywood, except for when the actors have sex and, instead of something coy and euphemistic, you get a full-scale hard-core sex scene. Additionally, many porn viewers do actually watch narrative-based porn like a regular movie right through to the end before contemplating sexual activity. In such instances, plot and story matter to the viewer.

If handled well, story will add something to the hard-core mix, providing interesting dramatic set-ups and psychological details that contribute to the anticipation and erotic build-up. The best of the golden age movies would typically provide a combination of a good story and well-filmed sex. Ideally the sex would be properly integrated and more naturally flowing from the film's narrative. The balance between plot and porn is a fine one, involving a careful selection of material. The story needs to be short and sweet and ideally one that is pertinent to a romantic or sexual fantasy. This way the sex makes more sense, and is made more erotic, because it makes sense. Accordingly the plot for *Devil in Miss Jones* is an ideal set-up, not least because of the number of sex scenes it can realistically deliver without being accused of carnal overkill. If Justine is a dead virgin reborn to lust, and this her only reason for being reincarnated, then what else is she going to do but have sex? She's hardly going to be wasting time getting a job, buying groceries, or struggling to pay the rent at the end of the month. Life's daily anxieties, the commonplace binds that both porn and straight-movie fantasy mostly abstain from delving into, don't arise.

Devil in Miss Jones justifies its singular focus with a plot line about sex and nothing but. In *Desires within Young Girls* (1977), Georgina Spelvin again features in the lead role, this time playing a recently widowed mother who seeks to guarantee her long-term financial future by marrying off her two daughters. She invests her last pennies on trying to fix them up with a couple of rich men. All does not go as planned. The film's scenario plausibly allows for a string of sex scenes. The same is true of *Little Girls Blue* (1978), a version of the familiar erotic scenario of college girls exploring each other's inner sexualities, as well as those of some of their teachers. (The film was directed by Joanna Williams, one of the first women porn directors.)

In Henri Pachard's *Between Lovers* (1983), Jessie St James discovers that her husband John Leslie is having an affair. Deciding to even the score, Jessie has a fling with Joey Silvera when away on a business trip. The trouble starts when she falls in love with Silvera and marries him. This leaves her with two west-coast husbands, one in San Francisco, the other in Los

Angeles. The situation only worsens when Silvera and Leslie happen to meet by chance and become the best of friends. *Between Lovers* has a narrative that naturally allows the sex to figure as less forced.[22] This is not the case with two more recent porn movies from the mid-nineties. Both *Hawaii* and *Blondage* are set in the milieu of erotic dancing, the idea being presumably that because striptease is sexy the private lives of strippers will be equally sexy. This isn't necessarily so. It all depends upon the scenario. Directed by Toni English, *Blondage* features some lamely constructed backstage shenanigans concerning 'Blondage', the best erotic dance duo in the land, and a rival would-be club-owner, a 'really sleazy guy', who gets his girl-friend to try and bust up their strip act to put his competitors out of business. The film features Julia Ann and Janine (Lindemuller); it would do, since 'Blondage' is the name of the duo's real-life dance outfit, making this more like a piece of merchandise than a porn film. In due course, the club-owner's scheme backfires, and the women finish with one last dance routine. Not a moment of drama, suspense, or erotic tension occurred between the opening titles and the closing credits of the movie.

Hawaii is also directed by Toni English. This time the director gets better performances from the cast. Moreover the vibrant location photography in a lush, tropical paradise adds to the viewing experience. (Alfresco hard core can be fun to watch. People get bored with being inside all the time, yearning for the great outdoors.) *Hawaii*'s story is almost as poor as *Blondage*, once again concerning some backstage monkey business. However, some erotic potential is generated through a subplot in which Chasey Lain's character has a passionate fling with Dyanna Lauren's husband, played by Colt Steele, Lauren's real-life lover of the time.[23] The adulterous coupling in the sand dunes is erotic, not because Lain and Steele are a dynamite combination, but because we know she's cheating on her best friend in the movie, whilst also having sex with another performer's real-life partner. Previously in the narrative, Steele's visible interest in Lain, and her preparedness to indulge him, to flirt back, has made Lauren annoyed with the both of them, making the betrayal more meaningful. The double infidelity, real and fictional, makes a difference, and is an example of simple storytelling adding something to the hard-core action. Otherwise, the rest of *Hawaii*'s story line is silly, not only bereft of erotic potential, but also mainly taking the film away from the sex, rather than towards it. This deviation is exacerbated when the film suddenly drops a hard-core scene into the proceedings more or less out of nowhere, simply because it's time for one. This is jolting and unerotic, the kind of hamfistedness that makes viewers feel stupid for watching the film in the first place. And there's nothing quite as unsexy as stupidity.

Often, contemporary porners working in what is now a very low-cost, rapid-output, video-based industry will choose the path of least resistance, dispensing with narrative subtleties, and merely providing viewers with a series of scenes featuring naked bodies fucking. Not that there's anything wrong with this; it's just that without a sense of erotic tease, of any kind of seduction between characters, or between the film and the viewer, even the best-filmed, best-acted sexual performances can get to feel a bit lacking. Anthony Spinelli's *Talk Dirty to Me* from back in 1980 is porn's ultimate seduction movie. The porn version of Steinbeck's *Of Mice and Men*, it tells of the progress through the world of smooth-talking Jack and his slow-witted partner Lenny. Jack gets the girls and Lenny gets the leftovers, if he's lucky. Viewers warm to Lenny's limitations, and his moments of envy. We can perhaps empathise more with his limitations as a man and as a romancer than with the godlike genius of Jack (brilliantly played by John Leslie). Nevertheless, though we warm to Lenny, we are in awe of Jack, seduced, like Jessie St James, by his charms.

St James plays the beautiful, happily married woman whom Jack bets he can lure away from monogamy within three days. He does this by talking dirty to her. It is a curious flirting technique, and not necessarily recommended to all would-be lotharios. The point is that Jack is so charming he can make gutter speech part of a successful seduction. Whether or not the viewer believes this is of little matter. The thrill of the chase, the tease of the courting, creates an atmosphere of erotic seduction that lasts the length of the movie. The story is not complex or muddled, but slimline, and the pornographic achievement considerable.

Play Misty for me
(an extended look at the best porn movie ever)

In an altogether different style from *Talk Dirty to Me*, *The Opening of Misty Beethoven* achieves an equivalent formal harmony while similarly trading off a very familiar literary source. Made in 1976, *Misty Beethoven* is widely considered the best porn film ever made. Director Radley Metzger had spent the sixties and early seventies making rather elegant 'sexploitation' movies like *The Lickerish Quartet, Erotic Quartet* and *Don't Cry for Me Little Mother* – his pre-*Evita* spin on the Eva Peron story. Metzger was very smitten with Euro-sophistication and fashionable things. Hence, in 1974, at the tail end of porn chic, he changed his name to Henry Paris and made a quintet of hard-core movies: *Private Afternoons of Pamela Mann, Barbara Broadcast, Maraschino Cherry, Punishment of Anne* and *The Opening of Misty Beethoven*. Later he would resume as Radley Metzger back in straight cinema, directing a rather dull version of *The Cat and the Canary* starring Honor Blackman. (The thought of a hard-core porner and the original 'Pussy Galore' making a dud is rather dispiriting.)

The Opening of Misty Beethoven uses Shaw's *Pygmalion* as its classic literary launch pad. Jamie Gillis plays a character called Doctor Love, an expert in erotic brilliance. Doctor Love is in need of a new challenge, as well as a subject for his next hit book on sex. He goes looking for a likely caper in a porn cinema in Paris. There he finds Misty, an uncomplicated hooker, dispensing her standard, plain-ordinary hand job to a punter who is dressed, for some reason, as Napoleon. Misty as the-matter-of-fact sex artisan, with her perceived lack of sexual sophistication, is the antithesis of Doctor Love and his world of exquisite refinement. Love and his fellow debauched creatures are part of the super sex élite of high culture. Misty is just a force of nature, raw and without a trace of cultivation. He shall remake her, his art shall remodel her. Misty will be his greatest challenge, his greatest triumph. Galatea to his Pygmalion.

Plot theft has always been an intelligent move with porn films. People who tend not to watch porn see the habit as indicative of the genre's asinine nature. They hear the titles – *Interview with a Vibrator*, *Edward Penishands*, *Splendor in the Ass*, *When Harry Ate Sally* – and they think that they indicate that porn is both definitively silly and parasitical in character. And clearly it is, in a way. But the mistake is confusing silliness with stupidity. In terms of narrative economy, ripping off a mainstream plot makes perfect sense. It won't always work. However, *The Opening of Misty Beethoven*, *The Tower*, and *8–4*, are three fine examples of mainstream turned into porn gold, *Pygmalion*, *Sliver* and *9–5*, respectively, being the original source materials. Using well-known plot premises and dramatic set-ups means the viewer is already with you, and the director can avoid the labour of having to get through too much back-story. For an excess of plot clogs the works, getting in the way of the hard core.

Without further ado, Misty is removed from her humdrum life in the back stalls, whisked away by Doctor Love to a variety of swanky apartments and opulent chateaux. Love and his crew are part of the international glitterati, moneyed and mobile: 'Let's go to Rome.' 'We can stay at my place.' Meanwhile, amidst all the swanning around, there's work to be done. The plan is to make Misty the greatest lover ever known to man, for at least this season. Misty is to be reconstructed, to unlearn all her bad habits and begin anew: 'Misty, in order to be something sexually, it is absolutely necessary to begin by being nothing sexually.' The culmination of Misty's overhaul shall involve her seducing the magazine publisher Lawrence Lehman, a young, good-looking, jet-set groover, whose *Goldenrod* magazine annually selects their 'Golden Rod Girl' – every man's dream lover. Misty, our fair lady, shall be the next Ms Golden Rod.

The Opening of Misty Beethoven is a very seventies affair. A Martini-commercial lifestyle of Perspex furnishings, Sacha

Distel haircuts, velvet sports jackets, sheepskin rugs and cheese fondue. A load of swingers' kitsch. However its key movie antecedents come from the sixties: playful, anti-realist, cartoon-strip movies like *Casino Royale*, *Kaleidoscope*, *Modesty Blaise* and *The Thomas Crown Affair*. The movie is a style fest, an abstract mood piece, very aphoristic and full of bad jokes: 'What's the biggest difference between New York and Rome?' / 'There aren't as many Italians in Rome.'

Apart from the historical curiosity of its incidentals, *The Opening of Misty Beethoven* also provides a simple story, a plot, a goal and a moral purpose, as well as some slick direction. The acting is also good, both the dramatic acting as well as the sex. Constance Money plays Misty with the right blending of the carefree ingénue and streetwise softie. Jamie Gillis, meanwhile, manages to shift Dr Love from suave city slicker to bored dandy to brooding malcontent. The scenes bringing the two protagonists together are very sharp and heartfelt. What is especially noticeable, however, is the movie's wealth, its sheer opulence for porn. The production values are extravagant, there's a large cast of extras, allowing for party scenes and movie theatre scenes, the costly trimmings that rarely show in tightly budgeted affairs. The sets are also extravagant, richly detailed and decorated, while the outdoor locations include not just country estates but narrative footage in cities like Rome and Paris, actually shot in Rome and Paris.

The Opening of Misty Beethoven shows you a world of sexual sophistication. Sex is the new thing, the new knowledge – it's what the in-crowd's doing this year. Such sexual urbanity can so swiftly run to tedium and banality, however. So cool it's dull, and no longer so cool. This tension between sophistication and jadedness animates the narrative. Buying his ticket for a trans-atlantic flight, Dr Love is required to confirm his in-flight preferences: 'So, that's first class, non-smoking, adult movie, non-vegetarian. And will that be sex or no sex, fucking or just a little head, sir?' Once airborne, air-stewardesses give optional bjs as well as serving the Scotch and sodas. A female passenger asks if the captain will be free to give her head later on. Settling the bill, the air stewardess says: 'Sir ordered two blow jobs and a brandy.' The passenger complains, 'I've actually only had one blow job, and they haven't brought me my brandy yet.'

Early in Misty's erotic education, she is seen fellating a socialite in the back of a chauffeured limousine. His wife is indifferent to this, as though it were the most natural thing in the world. All she's concerned with is their being late. They stop to pick up another socialite. He says hello to everyone. Misty has an erection in her mouth, so her greeting is garbled. For the first time the wife acknowledges Misty's presence, chiding her for speaking with her mouth full. Is such breezy decadence an all-time high or deadly low? Henry Paris seems fatally charmed, but distinctly critical of the aristocratic high style, querying if Love and Goldenrod are possessed of an inner wisdom on life, or are just a bunch of smug, soulless deadbeats. There's a moral forming in the works. Are perhaps Love and co., with their surfeit of pleasure, immune to real feelings, another generation of lost Americans adrift in decadent, old Europe. After all, *The Opening of Misty Beethoven* is written by someone called 'Jake Barnes', Hemingway's hero from *The Sun Also Rises*, the original lost-generation novel.

Misty is constantly in training, improving her erotic technique, her sexual staying power. They've got the clock on her to see how long she can suck and give hand relief before her mouth gets sore, her wrist numb. At a sex élite training camp, straight out of the training camps in Bond movies like *Goldfinger* or *From Russia with Love*, you see Misty going through her paces and getting better by the day. We see her sucking one butler with his pants down, while she does manual on two adjoining flunkies. We see this a few times, and the men look a bit bored. And then we see them again, but this time they're aroused, because finally Misty is getting the hang of really pleasuring men ('By George, I think she's got it!').

The legend of a girl called Misty starts to grow. Rumours of Misty circulate. She's seen out and about in high society, blowing a count at the ballet in Rome. Everyone is talking about the new, mysterious Beethoven chick. Is she from Belgium? I hear her mother is Hungarian. They say she was once a dancer. That Gatsby myth-making machine in action.

The movie is at its most beguiling and entertaining with such moments and employing a variety of formal tricks: voice-overs, lines slipping over from the previous scene to the next; dialogue that runs across unconnected visuals, or visuals that are telling us what the dialogue is simultaneously recounting. It's a very smart way with storytelling, redolent of early Woody Allen movies, like *Play It Again Sam* and *Annie Hall*. Passers-by speaking to each other in the street about Misty's increasingly infamous sexploits are used to comment upon the action, partly to move it forward but mainly to consolidate it. *The Opening of Misty Beethoven* is a fine example of the movie art of making standing still seem like movement, the self-referentiality, the switchbacks, the repeated commentaries upon itself, all of this serves to intensify the action, to justify the action, but also is the trick of doing something while nothing much is actually happening. This is a very impressive piece of filmmaking. In spells, it can be a bit too clever and gimmicky perhaps, too cute and in love with itself, and has undoubtedly dated, much like any voguish object will date, despite its flare and vivacity.

Moreover, Henry Paris never forgets the sex – the reason we're here, after all. Sex is going on all around, girls are giving blow jobs and playing with dildos left, right and centre. Although full-blown sex numbers are limited to a few major scenes, the blow-job count must be astronomical. As Richard Freeman suggests, 'Henry Paris loves bjs, because he loves them, no doubt, but because this kind of sex doesn't take up as much screen time . . . leaving him more time to deal out a few more droll one-liners and surreal snippets.'[24]

With Paris and other auteurs of the golden age, such as Spinelli and Chuck Vincent, one gets the impression that sex wasn't the big thing for them. These were not smut aficionados. Not like their contemporaries deRenzy and Pachard, or, later on, Stagliano and Gregory Dark. It was the directing of performers, the handling of narratives, dialogue, spots of drama interlaced with sex – the whole porn chic package, that interested Paris. Another reason for all the bjs was that they were all the rage. (When I suggested to a porn director that, twenty or so years later, American films remained perhaps a little too fixated on fellatio, and that perhaps this was because in real life American men felt they weren't getting enough of it, the director was quite peeved at the suggestion: 'That's not true. Here we are more advanced than Europe. For Christ's sake, America invented the blow job, look at *Deep Throat*!')

The abstract mood of *Misty Beethoven* is underscored by the full-scale sex couplings, which are quite druggy and dreamy. Though sex is talked about all the time, constantly fore-grounded with the bjs and Misty's training, Paris tends to clear out some recognisable space for the actual sex numbers. He puts the quipping on hold, pumps up the psychedelics, and segues into the hard core and then out the other side. The sex is often intentionally filmed in semi-darkness, in contrast to the brightness of the rest of the piece, apparently to make it a hotter, redder, deeper thing itself. Like Damiano and Spinelli, Paris isn't so fixed on getting the positions all in a row in his hard-core scenes (as is the case with most porn of the nineties, where directors tend to abide by a hard-core formula which has a bit of sucking inevitably leading to some missionary, a bit more sucking, some so-called 'doggy', and finishing with the pop shot). Sometimes a sex number from people like Paris or Spinelli will pass on a few of the porn staples in pursuit of the right mood. During the orgy scene in *The Opening of Misty Beethoven*, Paris wilfully coordinates it to play like a muddle of bodies, a tangle of organs and limbs. This blurring is accentu-ated by the shift in filming, to jerky camerawork and fast edits. Again, it's people *having* sex, rather than performing sex.

There's a very good three-way scene between Misty, Gold-enrod and Goldenrod's wife on a mattress behind a partition wall during a Warhol-style factory party in Manhattan. The sex scene is erotic, and yet strangely hamfisted. In contrast to his visual precision in the rest of the movie, in the sex scenes Paris goes purposefully sloppy. Some of the pop shots in *The Opening of Misty Beethoven* are interrupted, half lost; a couple actually go missing. Moreover, there is the strap-on dildo scene, a little later on in the film, when Misty anally penetrates Dr Love. A scene that is thoroughly built up for its narrative and thematic suggestiveness is then, at the point of execution, rather botched, not followed through to the close. It's not that the sex isn't erotic, not at all. It's just curiously wayward at times. This waywardness is either a case of inattentive filming, or suggests that maximum visibility, the concern for the camera to bear full, graphic witness to the body's pleasure, had not, as yet, become so rigidly fixed upon as an essential practice of hard-core porn.

As *The Opening of Misty Beethoven* skips and wisecracks its way through Misty's ascent to the mantle of Golden Rod Girl, the exact nature of her transformation, the quality of her achievement, becomes problematic, as does her relationship with Dr Love. We become increasingly aware that Misty is in love. But also that she's not happy. Misty has fallen for Doctor Love. But she realises that Doctor Love doesn't love her back, and so she is blue. To Love, it seems, Misty is just a curious specimen of the moment for him to mould, of no long-lasting interest to him. Here's where the twist comes in. Although she is now a state-of-the-art fellatrix, effectively Misty remains the same. Once she was a bored and couldn't-care-less sex machine working the sex cinemas, and now she's a highly moti-vated, very proficient sex machine. But the mechanical nature of her sex performances hasn't altered. What's missing is the fundamental ingredient. A heart is what's missing. To feel, you've got to love somebody.

Loving is not a problem for Misty. It's a problem for Doctor Love and his chums. Her training had been all about creating the passion that was lacking in the hand jobs she hawked to Napoleon and co. back in Paris. It's all about the decommodi-fication of sex. In Misty's life as a hooker, sex is purely about supply and demand, and the sex is pure routine and barely happening. Doctor Love and his super aesthete cronies, who apparently don't need to work for a living, or need ever worry that the champagne will run out, wish to restore sex to some halcyon higher mantle of delirious excellence, and exorbitant, decommodified luxury. 'She was a sexual civil servant,' it is said of Misty at one point. 'The nadir of human passion.'

But, of course, it is they who are the passionless ones. Dried-up art lovers who have lost that loving feeling, therefore worshipping technique in the absence of sensuality. The inaptly named Doctor Love may be capable of talking a good game, but he knows nothing about passion, not truly, and so can teach Misty nothing. It is from her that he must learn, if he can. He is cold and she is warm, and she has emotions and he is almost too slow to realise that these emotions may well melt his cramping *froideur* to relight his fire – that, finally, Dr Love may actually start to feel love again, and fall in love with Misty Beethoven.

Love's jaded palate shall be rejuvenated just so long as he doesn't let the unhappy Misty slip away from him. As *The Opening of Misty Beethoven* moves towards its final third there is this rising feeling that, once again with a hard-core feature film, as soon as the sex is over there will be a resumption of conventional morality and monogamy. Misty Beethoven is thus required to have a happy ending. After she succeeds in becoming Miss Golden Rod, Misty quietly drifts away. She vanishes from Doctor Love's world, feeling unloved, just at the moment he starts to fall for her. She's gone. But, of course she's coming back. It couldn't end any other way. Without Misty, Love finds life to be an empty affair, a hopeless bore. He continues to go through the motions, the champagne, the fellatio from beauty queens, but his heart's not in it. Where's the love, the feeling? Until one afternoon, bored at home in his luxury penthouse, being so-so blown for the millionth time, and watching a cine film record of Misty's training from before, Doctor Love starts to feel again. Misty has arrived back to the apartment unannounced. She surreptitiously takes over at the helm, and slowly Love's ennui turns to excitement and glee as he twigs. 'She was a sexual civil servant,' he teases. 'The nadir of human passion.' This time it's love for sure, and for ever.

The Opening of Misty Beethoven finishes with further scenes of people out on the street, speculating as to who will be the new Golden Rod girl. Puzzling, also, over the name of the last Golden Rod Girl: 'What was her name?' someone asks.

'Misty Mozart, I think,' says another.

'Whatever happened to her?'
'She just seemed to vanish.'

In fact, Misty's actually ensconced at the love pad, training the new would-be Golden Rod girl in the fine art of fellatio. The former student has become the professor, even quoting her former mentor turned partner: 'Just because they do it wrong doesn't mean that you can't do it right.' Doing it right, serving up the perfect blow job. As before, with Misty's training, the thought of her own pleasure appears to have been missed out along the way. Or is her true pleasure giving men true pleasure? Paris and his contemporaries would certainly seem to think so. Men! They were so bone idle back in the seventies.

Carry on cutting
(on the state of things in seventies Britain)

While American porn was having its golden age, with Damiano delving into the inner recesses of sex, sin, guilt and the afterlife, and Henry Paris making moral commentaries on the international jet set, Britain was awash with images of Robin Askwith's bottom. The nation was embarking upon a brief era of soft-core sex comedies, and Askwith was its chief male lead. This was not a golden age by any description. The sex film historian David McGillivray has written wittily on this small chapter in British film history, and summarises the subgenre's output as 'possibly some of the worst films ever made'.[25]

For a while during the seventies, American hard core and soft British fare almost played hand in hand. While private film clubs got away with showing uncertificated films like *Deep Throat*, *Insatiable* and *Behind the Green Door*, the commercial sector exhibited the home-grown sex movies. The movies were mainly badly made, badly acted, poorly scripted, and very low-sexed. Nonetheless, this was a highly profitable period for British cinema. ABC and Odeon cinemas across the country ran the *Confessions* series of movies: from *Confessions of a Window Cleaner* to *Confessions of a Driving Instructor*, and featuring the inimitably terrible Robin Askwith, whose buttocks at one point in the seventies were voted one of the least-liked sights in Britain (according to a Sunday tabloid paper at the time). In sex comedies such as *Cool It Carol* (Askwith, yet again), *The Sex Thief* and *Can You Keep It Up for a Week*, what you'd get in terms of flesh were tits and bums and pubes and floppy dicks, and more innuendo than you could handle.

Can You Keep It Up for a Week featured Mary Millington, trained veterinary nurse, and one-time girlfriend of sex publisher Dave Sullivan. Millington was as close as Britain ever got to a hard-core star during the seventies. A regular of the domestic soft-core magazine centrefold – as well as the illegal hard-core loops of porn film-maker John Lindsay – for a while Millington ran her own dirty bookstore in South London, while dating the owner of a private members' hard-core cinema club in Tooting. The club was deemed a model enterprise. On one occasion a parliamentary lobby group called the National Campaign for the Reform of the Obscene Publications Act (NCROPA) accompanied a Labour home office minister from the Wilson government on a porn fact-finding mission south of the river. Down in the ministerial car to Tooting, Her Majesty's Government journeyed to sit in on a sex-club screening, to discover that men would sit there, eyes glued to the screen, and some of them would masturbate, while coffee was on sale in the small foyer. The idea of a government minister doing a similar thing during the nineties is unthinkable.

Under pressure from the tax man, facing difficulties with lovers, depression and the police, Millington committed suicide in 1979. She was thirty-four years old. Her suicide note confessed, 'The police have made my life a misery.'[26] Apart from Millington, other 'names' from the brief era of the British sex comedy include singer Elaine Page, Joanna Lumley, Ingmar Bergman's daughter Anna Bergman, and film-maker Jonathan Demme. Demme got sacked from his one and only sex comedy, but would subsequently go on to direct *Something Wild*, *Philadelphia* and *Silence of the Lambs*.

In Britain during the seventies, soft-core porn became established and to some extent tolerated within the culture, the combined sales of magazines such as *Men Only*, *Mayfair* and

Penthouse booming at an estimated million or two a month. A complex set of unspoken rules and practices started to evolve regarding what constituted the acceptable within this licit, widely distributed top-shelf culture, and what strayed into the realm of the obscene. But this was as far as it went. Britain has never had a home-based hard-core porn industry. Not magazines nor movies. There have been a few brief periods of reckless enterprise, short-lived acts of solo derring-do, but never an industry, nothing like it.[27] Hard-core porn is effectively considered to be obscene in the eyes of the law. Obscenity offences will usually lead to a custodial sentence at some point or other. The sex therapist and writer Tuppy Owens, who appeared in a couple of sex movies in the seventies, is sure that one of the reasons she never made a career out of porn is because 'I've always been pretty anti-prison.'

Others have been less circumspect. Mike Freeman, for example, a stalwart on the British scene, made 8mm loops and stags in and around Soho during the early sixties. He then went to prison for obscenity offences. On being released, he came out, and switched from loops to sound and colour 16mm erotic shorts. And then at the end of the decade Freeman did a life sentence for killing a hit man sent to murder him by some people he'd fallen out with – 'It was either him or me.'[28] And so it was back inside again. In the eighties, Freeman was on the scene and making movies again, for a while at least. This time it was a series of full-length hard-core videos: basic, ineptly made outings like *Truth or Dare* and *Happy Birthday*, where Freeman would simply set up the video camera and wait for things to happen.[29] And then he was prosecuted again for making obscenity and sent back to jail. By the nineties, following a series of articles on the British porn scene in the *Guardian*, Freeman wrote in to seriously question their facts. His address was Wormwood Scrubs. Others have similarly tried and failed, and have also mainly gone to jail.

During the sixties and seventies the liberal, democratic, capitalist countries of Continental Europe unanimously decriminalised or legalised hard-core pornography. Rodox from Copenhagen, with its 'Climax' range of magazines, and

Private from Sweden were two of many companies to claim a share of the new market. Following more than thirty years of magazines, Super-8 films, video, novelties, sex toys, CD-ROM, DVD, and cyberporn, the two Scandinavian porn companies remain industry powerhouses into their fourth decade, with Private's line of enthusiastic, luxury porn videos finally making massive inroads into the previously reluctant American market.

Other European porn companies include Seventeen and Helen Duval from Holland, Video Marc Dorcel and Colmax in France, and assorted German lines including Silwa, Dino, Verlag Teresa Orlovsky and Maximum Perversion. Porn deregulation arrived in Germany in 1975. Beate Uhse, a woman who'd been involved with making sex-education guides as far back as the war, quickly became a leading figure in the new hard-core industry. The Uhse empire grew to encompass cinema chains, magazine and film distribution, mail-order novelties, peeper booths, and sex boutiques. By the late eighties, and with the enormous growth in video retail, the Uhse sex hypermarkets were familiar sights in Germany, including a flagship store at Frankfurt airport. Likewise, the swish K7 video hard-core sex shops the size of warehouses are now dotted around France, with Paris-based chains such as Concorde and Hot Video.

As Spain, Portugal and Greece emerged from their respective epochs of right-wing, military oppression during the seventies, they also removed all previous legal impediments to the vending of pornography, both soft and hard. In the late eighties, when people's revolutions in Eastern Europe brought four decades of communist oppression to a close, all previous restrictions upon freedom of expression were removed and annulled – which meant pornography too. Forty years of silence had made it abundantly clear to people living in the former communist bloc that freedom of expression is effectively an all-or-nothing thing, you cannot pick and choose.

In the late nineties, Europe's largest hard-core market is Germany, followed by France, Italy, Spain and the fast booming Eastern European territories. Over thirty years the best of Europorn has been a thing of quality but relatively no-frills simplicity. Porn theatrics, the plots, the pomp, the up-scale productions have mainly been an American hard-core phenomenon. In the mid-seventies Alberto Ferro (a.k.a. Lasse Braun, 'the Pope of porn') made a film called *Sensations*, Europe's all-time biggest porn movie. Two of Braun's films were shown at the Cannes film festival to great acclaim and coverage, as porn chic briefly hit Europe. However, Ferro's porn de luxe turned out to be big lossmakers. Accordingly, Continental porners resumed their regular churning out of a direct, no-fuss, porn-efficient product. Not until the mid-nineties, with the success of people like Joe D'Amato, Pierre Woodman and Luca Damiano, would European film pornography start to be associated with luxury and gloss.

During these times of Continental flux and liberalisation, Britain and Ireland stayed relatively steadfast, and this meant that hard-core pornography was not coming in. There were moments when things might have turned out differently. In the late sixties the Arts Council of Great Britain reported to the British government on the matter of porn and recommended suspending the Obscene Publications Act for five years, to see if Britain wanted to be like Scandinavia. The report was summarily dismissed, however, by James Callaghan, Labour Home Secretary at the time. Callaghan declared that society in his view had already loosened up quite enough during the swinging sixties, and now it was time to call 'a halt to the advancing tide of so-called permissiveness'.[30]

This was the great lost moment for porn in the UK. Up ahead, there were to be future windows of semi-freedom and hard-core exposure in Soho bookshops and cine clubs during the early seventies, or the short-lived loophole of hard-core video of the early eighties, before the new technology got properly wrapped up in legal controls. But these were always pockets of resistance, small-time ventures on the windy side of the law. The recommendation by representatives of the cultural and political élites at the Arts Council that porn be let off the leash was something altogether different and quite unique. Thirty years later, as the century draws to a close, Britain continues to hold out against fully hard-core porn, with little sign of legal change in sight.

The gold rush
(briefly on making a financial killing in porn)

It has been estimated that the first two decades of photographic porn in Europe saw as many magazines sold as the population of the United States, which is about 250 million centrefolds.[31] The gathering and publication of porn statistics tend to be complicated and politically charged activities. Those who wish to rub out porn prefer to raise awareness of its enormous 'addictive' dangers partly through exaggerating its size. Porn itself is also prone to telling lies about size, on and off camera. Sales and circulation figures might be overstated in order to boost company profile, or to convince the world that this is really hot stuff, popular, here to stay and do you have any idea what it is you're missing out on? Hyping the figures gets in the way of telling the true picture regarding the size of porn.[32] The many magazine titles on the top shelf, the fact that they don't gather too much dust, indicates that sales are occurring. But does anyone ever catch a glimpse of an actual sale of a magazine, of an arm reaching up to the top shelf, and do we know where and with whom all these magazines as well as videos finally end up?

'Who the fuck's buying all this stuff?' says David Kastens at Vivid Video in America. 'We used to ask ourselves this question at my last company. Used to joke about it being two farmers in Nebraska. They were buying all the videos and filling their two barns with hard core. We reckoned they'd already filled the first barn, were working on filling the second, and the day they finished, we'd all be out of a job.' There must have been some equivalent couple of farmers and ample barns in Finland for all those hard-core magazines during the first two decades of legal pornography. They'd be filled a long time ago now. On a global scale, the pornography industry continues to grow, in the knowledge that there are territories, markets, tastes and formats that are yet to be properly reached or tapped into.

Although in certain countries, certain delivery systems and genres, porn does plateau, or sees a shrinkage occur, the overall way is up, not down.

In 1971, Lasse Braun and the American porn distributor Reuben Sturman developed the self-contained peepshow machines. Individual and closed-off private-viewing booths, each with its own coin-operated Super-8 projectors and screen, allowed punters to lock themselves away, watch some hard core and masturbate – to 'pay and spray'. Sturman distributed the peeper booths across the whole of the USA from his base in Cleveland, and Braun's Beat films of Stockholm churned out the no-frills ten-minute colour loops to run in them. All those quarters inserted in Sturman's booths were to add up over time. Revenues from the peep show circuit were said to be far larger than box-office takings from the public cinemas exhibiting the hard-core movies.[33]

The number of hard-core cinemas across America had reached nearly a thousand by 1981, with chains like the famous Pussycat cinemas in most of the major cities and towns. Adult movies allegedly accounted at this time for something in the region of 20 per cent of the entire motion-picture industry, and 2.5 million tickets were bought each week. Within six years, however, the adult cinema network had collapsed. Because of video, by mid-decade the number of theatres was down to less than 200 and falling. In the meantime the level of hard-core video rentals had climbed to 15 million.[34] Ten years later, the annual number of adult video rentals from general video stores in America was topping 600 million. That's a lot of pop shots, some kind of porn of plenty. Over time this tale of expansion in hard-core home entertainment would prove to be an ambiguous affair of losses and gains.

The silver age
(on the rise of video hard core)

When the full history of porn is finally committed to paper, video will be seen as a truly major event. Video changed everything, for better and for worse. Video spread the word and video was perhaps the industry's saviour during the times of political harassment. But later on, the new technology and hard economics would also cause a precipitous quality drop in the hard-core product.

The video story actually started out as a glorious revolution of greater access, portability, a broadening out of the hard-core culture to places cinemas couldn't reach. Hard core became available to many more people – those men, and especially women, who didn't wish to go to the sex cinema, to sex shops, or possibly to the red-light districts of the city, but might every now and then pick up a porn title from their local video rental store as part of their leisure-time activities. For some, such video recreation would turn out to be more than just renting and watching; they would set up their own cameras on tripods and make their own porn loops to watch – or later to swap, as would be evinced in the late eighties boom in amateur porn. If porn is democratic, then video porn is very democratic.

Video happened early and profitably for the adult industry. The porn business was quick to recognise the potential of the new technology, and was transferring its product onto cassettes in advance of mainstream Hollywood. In this way, porn was performing its regular duty as a key driver for the economic emergence of a new technology. The rise of video saw the decline of big-budget cinema hard-core productions. The last of the theatre, the costumes, the sets, the glamour. Peaking with movies like *Roommates*, *The Voyeur*, and the surreal, bravura weirdness of Rinse Dream's *Café Flesh*, the golden age passed away, as a compensatory silver age of good-time video hard core got started. In front of the camera there was a changing of the porn élite. The careers of a generation of stars like Annette Haven, Abigail Clayton, Georgina Spelvin, John Leslie, Kay Parker and Seka were running out of steam, as the times of Hyapatia Lee, Brigitte Monet, Nina Hartley and Ginger Lynn were just beginning.

The best of silver age means a pretty good porn film: well made, plenty of good sex scenes, often couples-oriented, and most likely something a little lighter too – fun and throwaway in the best possible sense. For at this stage, light and disposable didn't necessarily mean rip-off or trash, rather it suggested a Ginger Lynn comedy or something by Henry Pachard – like *Sexcapades*, and its sequel *Great Sexpectations*, both concerning the return to pornoland of director Harry Crocker following his years of trying to make it in art-house cinema. *She's So Fine* is another Pachard comedy about a wedding day from hell. 'I tried to experiment a little with the form,' remembers Pachard, almost twenty years later, 'escaping predictability, you know, maybe with using some witty dialogue to accompany the sex.' Instead of the regular moans and groans, and lines like 'Oh your cock's so big', Pachard put some fun and tease into the dialogue, 'It would be "So, are you going to fuck me?", says one; "I don't know, maybe", says the other. Or you have a scene where a couple are having sex and the wife says, "Honey, I want a divorce", and at the point of ejaculation, the husband say, "I'm really uncomfortable about this divorce business, ah, oooh, aaah."'

Pachard directed *Devil in Miss Jones II*, disposing of Damiano's Catholic dread in favour of doing a satire of sex films, and featuring Lucifer, or 'Lucy', going through a mid-life crisis. It wasn't just comedies for Pachard, however. *Jailhouse Girls* is his 'women in prison' movie, featuring the ever eager Ginger Lynn taking a break from screwball comedy and playing an innocent woman in jail, adroitly negotiating the sexual hierarchy behind bars. It's the lighter turns, however, for which Ginger Lynn is remembered. The beautiful hard-core actress had a deft touch and an ebullient screen presence. Her mood, style and erotic enthusiasm through 1984 to 1986 reflect badly upon the dreariness and lifelessness of porn five years later and into the early nineties. Not until the emergence of Ashlyn Gere did American hard core have another really big name star of any lasting presence.

Lynn movies were sure to make a play on her name, whatever the producers could think of in an afternoon. There were titles like *Blame it on Ginger*, *Ginger on the Rocks*, *Project: Ginger*, *Gentlemen Prefer Ginger*, *I Dream of Ginger* and, more accurately in terms of her actual preferred hair colour, *On Golden Blonde*. *The Pleasure Hunt* finds Lynn searching for her rich dead husband's money. Before she can get her hands on it, however, she is required to go through various erotic adventures following a pleasure-hunt map leading her to the buried loot. The movie is the quintessential Lynn vehicle: sexy, lively, bringing the bounce of snappy, harebrained story lines to combine with hot hard-core sex, and featuring good locations too. Lynn's Hawaiian triple, *Pink Lagoon*, *Panty Raid* and *A Little Bit of Hanky Panky*, are also three good-looking affairs, filmed on the islands themselves, and all three of them directed by the talented Svetlana.

As the porn antipathy from quarters of the feminist movement started to build in the mid-eighties, ironically, a porn woman's lot was on the up. Svetlana was one of the best porn directors of her day and, along with Candida Royalle and Joanna Williams, was turning out an appealing, couples-oriented hard core, far from the degradation alleged at the time to be the life force of porn. Further proof of the upswing for porn women was the high earning potential for star performers like Lynn, who was making a small fortune from hard core. Lynn proved a shrewd operator with her business affairs, not only getting paid well but negotiating royalties on all her movies. She also became the first performer to sign exclusively to a single studio, allowing her to pick and choose her roles and work less often and for more money. Lynn continues to earn royalties today. There is also a large commercial web site dedicated to her career. The increased nostalgia for porn of days gone past finds actresses like Lynn continuing to make some kind of return, possibly even a living, from a career that actually lasted only a couple of years. Not what you'd call the hard-luck story of a porn victim.

The big squeeze
(on when they tried to run porn out of town)

Throughout the years of Reagan and Bush, a backlash occurred in America against all things liberal and permissive. In this mood of moral rearmament, pornography's lewd exhibition was an intolerable affront to Christian decency in plain view. In due course the adult industry found itself in big trouble for the first time in more than a decade. A revival in tough anti-porn rhetoric and stigmatisation fostered a coordinated campaign against the industry.

The big squeeze came in different shapes and guises. The early eighties saw Catherine MacKinnon and Andrea Dworkin propose their model anti-porn laws to the city of Minneapolis, contributing to the rise of a more powerful anti-porn lobby from religious groups and parts of the local and federal government (see Chapter 2, 'Porn Wars'). Whether it was coordinated, circumstantial or merely coincidental, the modern 'feminist' language of Minneapolis would in due course feature in the demonology of the Christian right as part of the mood of illiberalism. In 1986 Edwin Meese, President Reagan's Attorney General, empanelled a federal government commission to 'inquire' into pornography. The Meese Commission was a loaded and shrill event, featuring lurid denunciations, staged conversions, impassioned confessions, and the hectoring of the few porn-positive voices allowed to testify.[35] The hype and excess of Meese turned out to be its secret weapon. Nobody took the hysteria seriously. In fact Meese was very serious. Meese made porn look very bad – porners were mobsters, child molesters, rapists, perverts, heathens, pimps, whores, sexist (they got the last one from the Minneapolis Ordinances) – softening up porn, making it a more vulnerable target for rooting out. After all, overground porn was still only a wee thing, no more than a decade and a half old. As far as the conservatives were concerned it wasn't too late to go backwards.

The next six or seven years, from 1986 through to the early nineties, the American Justice Department set about putting the pornocrats out of work and in jail.[36] It was a concerted effort targeting large-scale distributors like Adam & Eve, hoping to cut off the supply route of porn to the masses, while also going after producers through various tactics of entrapment, as well as harassing and penalising sex shops and even general video stores with an adult section. Treating porners as mobsters was often the preferred way of forcing the pace. In

1987, the Adult Film Association instituted a suit to stop the US government using the RICO law against the industry. RICO – the Racketeering Influenced and Corrupt Organisations law – not only perpetuated the porn–Mafia association but also allowed greater juridical intervention, like seizing assets and closing down operations in advance of any case actually going to court. Used in this way, pre-seizures can see a business financially killed off through loss of revenue and liquid assets, and having to meet costly legal payments, before any court action has even occurred. 'A chain owner in Minneapolis was alleged to have seven items which were obscene,' an executive at Vivid remembers. 'His whole twenty-five bookstore chain was shut down. They came in, closed the shops, impounded all the materials, padlocked the shops.' In time such actions were overturned, but by then it was usually too late. 'Once it happens, it happens. They ain't going to give you that shit back. You're not getting that stuff back. And you can't sue the government in those instances.'

Another favoured weapon was regular nuisance prosecutions of stores on misdemeanours. During the Bush administration there was also the more serious, simultaneous, multiple prosecution of several national mail-order companies, where a distributor not only would be prosecuted in a dozen different states in one go, but was also often required to fight each case separately. In a federal political system like that of the USA, individual states, and not the government in Washington, will often have first say in making the community's sex laws. In this way, sex law in the USA has become a highly complex patchwork system, where shifting between states may also mean shifting between very different moral climates. It became a device of federal agents to go to a conservative part of the country, order up a video from California, and then seek to prosecute the company for sending obscenity across state lines – 'Interstate transfer of obscene material'. The test for the obscenity would be made according to the conservative community standards of the address where the video was sent. A porn executive tells of a gay video with a scene where a white guy gave a black guy a blow job, and the black guy ejaculated in the white guy's face. The company sent the tape to an all-white town in rural Alabama and they were prosecuted, and the all-white jury found the image to be against their community standards and therefore obscene (see Chapter 5, 'Not the Wild West').

The porn film-maker Merlin spoke to the writers Robert Stoller and Ira Levine concerning the FBI's 'Miporn' entrapment sting of the mid-eighties. A pair of undercover FBI agents set themselves up as porn distributors in a part of Florida that was relatively anti-porn. They ordered material from an unnamed maker of specialist s/m movies. They said they loved his stuff, but why didn't he put some basic fucking into his films. In the US, to blend hard core with ritualised sex play is to risk courting an obscenity charge.[37] The FBI agents knew this, which is why they suggested the director change his style. Effectively they were soliciting him to commit a felony. The porner, in turn, said he didn't make those kinds of films. They took him for meals, they took him to the racetrack, paid for him to bet, they continued to pressure him over the lack of hard core in his tapes. He wouldn't budge, he said no. 'But . . . these FBI agents really were out there actively trying to convince people who didn't want to do this to go into business so that they [the FBI] could make better collars.'[38]

During the big squeeze, porners, distributors and store owners were drained of funds, not only via numerous fines but through a punishingly expensive legal system, where cases would be drawn out and legal fees would stack up so high that defendants would be forced to plea-bargain, and agree to leave the business. Meanwhile, a lot of people went to jail. At the Free Speech Coalition's Night of the Stars junket in Los Angeles in July 1996, Eddie Wedlestedt, president of *Goalie Entertainment*, a video store chain, reported that during the previous ten years the staff in his eight Dallas area stores alone had gone to jail a total of 1,250 times. The chairman of VCA, one of the largest adult companies, spent time in jail in 1994, and Vivid paid a $2 million corporate fine at around the same period. Following Meese, in a climate of fear and court action, adult material became less available in parts of America. Meanwhile a panicky porn industry revised its self-regulating parameters, making the product less explicit. In a sense porn in America has yet to recover from the experience of these times.

An explanation of this onslaught on porn would require a book in itself, which might consider the intolerance of the eighties as part of a sixties backlash, as well as being part of an American tradition where fear of subversion creates a need to hunt down the 'enemy within' – whether it is communists, gays, immigrants, single mothers, UFOs or porn. At this time a renewed religious fundamentalism was visible in certain quarters of American society, with talk of great Satans, Armageddon round the corner, and the need to stop lesbians kissing on *LA Law*. More specifically, many porners point to a grouping of agents at the Federal Government Justice Department who were closely associated with various Christian right lobbying groups, often appearing at public rallies together. Only when a couple of high-profile members of the Christian right were duly caught out, found to be hypocrites with porn stashes of their own, did this directional drive against porn start to ease.[39] Certain police activities were also ruled as unconstitutional, and Bill Clinton was also elected president, and an especially nasty period of concerted governmental harassment ended. Many in the porn industry believed that with Clinton they'd be far better off, and they were mainly right. Although he didn't actually turn out to be porn's best friend, Clinton was not its main adversary like Reagan and Bush. A fear persists of a day when the Republicans might get back in power, and start assailing porn again. Not this century though: 'The guys at the justice department have all left,' says the porn director Paul Thomas, 'There's no chance of them rebooting up and coming after us again. They were waiting to see if Clinton looked like he was going to do two terms, and when he did, then they chose to move on.'

Hassle and trouble still continues, especially at a local level. Any time a politician needs to raise their profile, or a police officer gets it into their head that porn is a bad thing, he or she will instigate a raid on an adult bookstore or stripper bar. For, if an official doesn't like porn, and would also like to promote his or her work – be seen out and about, doing things – then porn's something worth chasing after. As one anonymous porn-maker says, 'Why haven't we legalised certain kinds of drugs? One of the biggest reasons is because we would put thousands and thousands of agents out of work. Likewise porno.'

This is a low
(on when porn was almost unanimously reviled in Britain, and after)

After the setback with their legal efforts against porn in America, the MacDworkinites came to England to try again. In 1989, Dawn Primarolo, a Labour Member of Parliament, launched her doomed legislative bill concerning the location of the sale of pornographic materials. Her definition of porn, referring to the depiction of women 'as objects, things or commodities', was an almost word-perfect retread of the Minneapolis Ordinances. At this time the Labour party was enduring its long and daunting period of being in opposition, where political parties gradually switch from having beliefs to making reactions. In 1986, the Conservative backbencher Winston Churchill introduced his private member's bill seeking to bring television within the obscenity laws. Rather than attempt to defend freedom of expression, the Labour left responded by suggesting an additional restrictive clause. This was the occasion when Clare Short proposed amending the bill to include outlawing topless models in the news media, notably the *Sun*'s 'Page 3' girls. Short's move was seen as being at least partly connected to the bitter ongoing labour dispute at Wapping, involving the *Sun*'s proprietor Rupert Murdoch, and caused support for the bill to fizzle out.

Meanwhile the Off the Shelf campaign on newsagent porn began. This involved anti-porners charging into branches of Menzies and WH Smith, making some noise, chaining themselves to shop fixtures and ripping up any kind of magazines with women featured on the cover. This assault on cover art not only targeted *Playboy*, *Penthouse* and *Mayfair*, but also often included titles like *New Woman*, *Marie Claire*, *Esquire*, *Cosmo-*

politan, *Company*, *Arena* and *Vogue*. (Such actions continue, in dribs and drabs, a decade later.) At this time, arguments concerning violence and porn were at their most vociferous. The accusations had no basis in reality. The domestic soft-core industry was already heavily regulated, with violence the last thing soft-core titles were likely to feature. Nonetheless the Conservative government of the time commissioned a review into research evidence concerning porn and any links with violent behaviour. The Cumberbatch and Howitt Home Office report of 1990 found no evidence supporting the argument for a causation of harm, stating there were no proven links between porn and violence. Kenneth Baker, Home Secretary at the time, called the report's findings to be another small contribution to the ongoing debate. A report that had been commissioned to make a definitive statement on the complex matter, was now no more than another small contribution. Furthermore it was a contribution that the government apparently sat on, almost failing to publish, with the report slipping out around Christmas time, and on the quiet.[40]

Despite Howitt and Cumberbatch, allegations over violence, harm and porn persisted. These were undoubtedly dark days for pornographers, who were blamed for all kinds of crimes and sins, attacked in law, harassed by the police, embattled in the marketplace, and chased through the streets by highly vexed Christians and feminist anti-porners. Even the civil libertarians briefly deserted the cause, when in the spring of 1989 the Annual General Meeting of Liberty (National Council of Civil Liberties) adopted a policy change agreeing to back any parliamentary activity against porn. This shift towards a policy of censorship and restraint by a group dedicated to freedom caused the formation of Feminists Against Censorship. A loose gathering of media and academic feminists, FAC objected to the way feminism had become associated with censorship and sexual purity, and with depicting women as victims. Along with other interested parties they put their arguments to Liberty at the following year's AGM, and Liberty promptly ditched its previous policy change.

The high-water mark of the antis' pressure had perhaps been

reached and passed. Certainly their dominance of the arguments would never be so complete again. At the end of the eighties there was hardly anybody with a good word to say about porn, apart from the porners, and mostly they preferred to be silent. At this stage, the assertion that porn was altogether sexist, violent and representing the most serious threat to female emancipation had achieved the status of incontrovertible truth. A dread of erotic representation extended beyond porn, and it became the dominant view in the broader culture that exploring sexuality through images was not only offensive but also irresponsible.

During the next few years such certainties would start to unravel. The nineties saw a revival of interest in women and sexuality in cultural spheres. Desire was back. Examples of women being sexually expressive and tuned in to the erotic arts grew apace: there were lovers' guides, erotic novels, Madonna's *Sex*, nude fashion models, Annie Sprinkle and Marissa Carr going naked at the ICA and Smutfest, dominatrices and femtops, pierced leather-clad amazons with whips and guys in chains, lesbians doing bondage – all kinds of sightings of rude women, as well as tanned muscle men dancing naked for crowds of desiring women.

Tuppy Owens remembers the moment she realised the mood was changing in Britain. She had some new erotic materials she'd been working on, and she took them to be photocopied. The photocopier was different from her usual one, so she advised him about the raunchy content. And the guy said that was nothing, she should see some of the 'porn' that the students from the nearby art college were turning out for course work. The anti-porners' assertion that sexual representation is intrinsically harmful to women seemed untenable and increasingly out of touch. Though the porn bogeyman continued to stalk debates, often held up as the unacceptable, the unspeakable and the tacky – the one place where women's visual imaginations didn't want to finish up – increasingly porn ceased to work as a disciplining spectre.[41]

Meanwhile, though much has changed in art colleges, post-feminist circles and assorted 'scenes', hard-core porn remains a thing apart. In Britain, things never flow in one direction where sex and regulation are concerned. Though the nineties has seen a rise in the alternative sex scenes, with swinging, s/m and especially fetishism becoming almost hip and leaking into the mainstream through fashion and advertising, at the same time fetish clubs continue to be bothered by police interventions and legal prosecution. The push–pull nature of the conflict between censorship and rights of privacy and choice continues. In recent times we have seen the launch of porn-friendly magazines like *Desire*, *Headpress* and *Velvet*, and of film companies like Redemption, Jezebel and Purgatory, as well as the controversial publishing activities of Savoy, Delectus and Gay Men's Press. Soft-core porn videos are now on sale in record shops like HMV and Virgin. 1997 saw the inaugural 18 awards celebrating 'art and entertainment for adults', as well as Britain's first ever 'Erotica' trade fair at Kensington Olympia, visited by thousands. But despite the centrefolds in *Loaded* magazine, and billboard hoardings round London during 1997 featuring a giant-sized Kathy Lloyd advertising the Playboy TV channel, the police war on hard-core porn in Britain remains as focused and diligent as at any time since the fifties. In an era of deep anxiety concerning social and economic change, as well as the perpetual dread of the power of the image, rebel media and fugitive cultural representations continue to be vulnerable to censure as well as to being scapegoated. This ongoing story of censorship in the UK will be the subject of the next chapter, while Chapter 5, 'Not the Wild West', will concern itself with bringing the American hard-core scene up to date.

4

An Englishman's relish

'We hear so little, and understand even less.'
   (a disoriented English couple at the start of the film *Casablanca*,
   clueless as to what is going on all around them)

A rainy, grey morning in September in the mid-nineties. In the close, sticky atmosphere of Court No. 4, Highbury Magistrates, everyone smells faintly damp. We are gathered here today in North London, to move sluggishly down the long road to justice. Committal proceedings concerning the case of *Crown* v. *Blank* are about to recommence after a six-month hiatus. Blank, and Blank junior, a father and son porn mail-order operation, and their two partners in crime, face charges of conspiracy and possession for gain under the Obscene Publications Act. Back in early spring, when it was realised this was going to be a long committal, eating up a whole week of court time, the decision was made to adjourn until a block of days could be fixed. At the time, Blank junior, leaving the court, had announced to no one in particular that late September was all very well, but he'd booked a holiday and he wasn't going to be able to attend, 'no chance'. However Blank junior is here in attendance today. He is tanless, it's true, but if he minds not being on holiday it doesn't show, for he keeps swapping amused looks and smiles with his co-defendant pal.

The court action involving the family Blank & Co. marks the culmination of Operation Well, a police stakeout over several months, which led to the busting of a large-scale East End porn-distribution company. In terms of porn, Britain is the most censored nation in the Western world. This is no rhetorical flight of fancy, just the state we're in. Ireland is also a heavily censored nation, but really it's no comparison; Ireland is a kind of theocratic state, slowly thawing out, whereas Britain supposedly embraced pluralism towards the end of the fifties. In 1996 the Area Clubs and Vice Unit of the Metropolitan Police, which covers Soho, seized around 70,000 videos and magazines, worth in the region of £2 million. In the mid 90s, rates of seizures have soared, from 3,000 videos in 1990 to 52,000 six years on. All these materials, by the squad's own admission, are commercially available across Europe and much of North America, and made in Germany, France, Holland and the USA. Available for purchase in swish legal porn megastores in the heart of Paris, seized and destroyed in the heart of London.

In certain circles the world over, Britain is known for the quality of its soft-core spanking porn. Spanking has become known as the English vice. However, in reality it seems fair enough to reposition the term within a broader narrative, where it is in fact censorship that's an Englishman's vice, as well as the relish of certain Englishmen and women. Several months prior to the visit to Highbury Court, I went to a debate hosted by MENSA at Simpsons-in-the-Strand. The subject was the desirability of making porn illegal in the UK, as if there weren't already half a dozen laws controlling it. There are times in this perpetually frowning nation when it seems that some people simply can't get enough restriction.

Accordingly the pornographic materials legally available in Britain at present remain principally soft core. There are the home-grown soft-core top-shelf magazines, as well as video soft core available on cassette or via cable and satellite. The video porn is a mix of foreign hard core crudely and severely chopped down to legally acceptable levels of exposure, as well as foreign and domestic purpose-made soft core. On the home front, outfits such as Electric Blue and Liquid Gold run a restricted gamut from 'reader's wives' frolicking upon floral bedspreads, male and female strip compilations, and lifestyle soft core filmed in exotic locations, where beautiful women fondle their breasts in the shower, or writhe about orgasmically on a beach in the Maldives or Hawaii.[1]

Britain also boasts some very civilised gay and lesbian soft porn, and the occasional spanking and mud-wrestling tapes. But where actual hard-core porn is concerned, Britain has never really allowed the stuff to come into or be sold or exhibited in this country. The only major sightings of a kind of legal hard core have been the series of Lover's Guides to good sex. These were passed and certificated as non-obscene because they were deemed to have educational and scientific value. In 1970 Alex deRenzy's *Sex in Denmark* used the wheeze of employing a man in a white coat to sneak in hard core under a 'scientific' guise. Twenty-five years later, it's still the most secure alibi in Britain. The Lover's Guides were first released onto the market in the late eighties. At the time, Michael Hames, head of the Obscene Publications Squad at Scotland Yard, vehemently criticised such tapes, which include erections and genital action, suggesting they'd make hard-core porn look acceptable, and then how could he and his officers justify seizing such materials?[2]

In the name of the law
(on the legal control of porn in the UK)

As far as the law goes at present, mere possession of hard-core porn is not an offence in the UK. If you import it, publish it, sell or distribute it, you face trouble, and may well find yourself in court as well.

The Obscene Publications Act of 1959 is the foundational law for the present system of censorship. The OPA was launched during an era that sought to deregulate people's private space, to remove Church and State from the bedroom, while also reconfiguring legal restrictions in the public domain. In this sense the OPA was an anomaly in that it remained very much concerned with the person's private space. Though possession and purchasing were never made criminal offences, the criminalisation of selling porn – of possession for gain –

made purchasing it mainly awkward, and often impossible. The OPA effectively drew a line in the ground, on the dark side of which were obscene materials which you would know by their supposed ability to corrupt those who came into contact with them. On the other side of the line was the public sphere, a protected area where, in the interests of civic hygiene, these obscenities should not be legally visible. Keeping the filth out of view, and therefore commercial circulation, consequently makes the exercise of private choice hardly viable.

This legal ruse has been consolidated down the years through the continuing arguments about the effect of the image upon behaviour. Porn, it is alleged, weakens marriages, coarsens minds, causes passive viewers to turn into sex pests. (Porn may well in fact sustain marriages, while causal links between images and behaviour remain unproved.) These allegations sustain the view that porn is more than just an argument about individual rights. In this way do the anti-porners, be they moral or political, preserve the feeling that porn is a social issue, a matter for public scrutiny and legal intervention, and not simply a private matter for the adult to decide about for him or herself.

In the never-ending war on porn the OPA is supplemented by a rack of other laws. The Post Office Act of 1953 makes it an offence to send obscenity through the post. The Customs Act of 1876 makes it an offence to bring such materials into the country. During the 1980s, other new restrictive laws were passed in the UK addressing a whole range of porn matters, tightening up particularly on sex shops, private cinema clubs, and new technologies such as videos and computers.

At the turn of the eighties the spread of the emergent video technology briefly posed a serious threat to the state regulation of porn in Britain. The early days of the video revolution saw the product-hungry new technology experience a shortage of mainstream movies for people to rent. With the major film companies and distributors slow to make their titles available on cassette, porn and other 'lower cultural' forms – like action movies and slasher horror movies – were quick to fill the gap. These were the key genres in the video revolution, the kinds well suited to a more flexible, diversified and certainly less capital-intensive market such as video, especially a market that in Britain started without any form of state regulation or censorship.

However, the straight-to-video racket is the kind of vulgar, low-rent form of expression that generally dips beneath mainstream film criticism's radar. This critical neglect, the consequent lack of legitimation in the culture, can be a liability when matters of law arise. Without critical favour, certain genre pleasures are easily dismissed and thrown to the law. That few people were prepared to speak up for the undervalued genres of the early days of video made the technology vulnerable to scapegoating. In due course a media-led panic ensued in Britain concerning the threat of so-called 'video nasties'. This flexible term referred to a whole range of sex and horror movies which certain powerful and vocal groupings didn't like the look of. Matters worsened when the police announced that they were being overwhelmed by a dangerous, out of control, videographic jumble of sex, brutality, cannibalism and bad actors in Nazi uniforms, and without the proper laws in place for them to do anything about it. There was much myth-making over the actual content of 'video nasties'. These were mainly gory slasher films, the kind of stuff that had been in and out of cinemas over the previous decade. Some of the video titles specifically singled out for complaint had in fact already been released at the cinema with proper film board classification.[3] These myths went mostly unchallenged, as new legislation was drafted and passed into law.

The 'video nasties' furore exploited fears over the imperilled child in order to bring the new video technology under legal supervision. Television, like radio, is a pervasive media. This means it is not possible to ensure that children can be protected from materials that might be deemed as too adult for their immature sensibilities. In the USA the broadcasting media must not transmit indecency. In the UK there is a time watershed before which adult business cannot be shown. Such 'source' restrictions could not be imposed with videos. Instead an extension of the film ratings system into video cassettes was made law. The Video Recordings Act of 1984 made it an offence to sell or rent out videos that haven't been certificated by the British Board of Film and Video Classification (BBFVC), while also making it an offence to sell or rent titles to those under a certificated age.[4]

What sounds quite reasonable also actually amounted to a serious extension of censorship. The new law's immediate impact was to close a legal loophole that had allowed the importation of uncertificated American and European porn on video. Rodox from Copenhagen claimed they sold 50,000 tapes into UK during this period, whilst the Beate Uhse Organisation in Germany is alleged to have shifted 10,000 copies of a single title.[5] In the long term, the Video Recordings Act installed pre-censorship with porn. Statutory film classification smartly circumvented the system of legal test cases, the matter of shifting tastes and evolving cultural values in society. Previously you could have been making or selling hard core in a climate not entirely opposed to images of explicit sex, and, if prosecuted, found a sympathetic jury on your day in court. Now the offence was not having a certificate, with the content of the movie mainly irrelevant. In this way people were denied access to public juries to argue their case for freedom of expression.

The BBFVC does not give a certificate to a film deemed to be 'inappropriate'. This term is no less subjective than 'indecent', or 'obscene', and is therefore determined by an examiners' personal taste, or through the board capitulating under political pressure.[6] A law that had been introduced proclaiming its intention to restrict children's access to adult materials inevitably also became the law that seriously limited access for grown-ups.[7] And not just porn, as in due course most of the 'video nasties' would fail to gain video certification, not even an 18 certificate, once presented to the BBFVC.

In the UK, the story of video and porn has been one of losses and gains. It's likely that because of video's portability more people have access to hard-core porn than ever before. (Also, because video is a technology that doesn't require laboratory processing, it is much harder for the authorities to monitor and supervise production and distribution than it is with celluloid.) However, opportunities for contesting legal definitions of obscenity were seriously curtailed because of video. This is ironic since video was originally vaunted as posing a threat to regulation, only in fact to get turned around and made into a big stick for the censor.

Operation Well
(on when a police surveillance operation nabbed a porn ring)

All the laws and legal action mean that most British porn lovers wishing to lay their hands on hard core will either have to break the law themselves or get their porn from somebody else who does. Even then, availability in the UK is restricted. At present, the best, most reliable source of hard-core videos is mail order. Although to solicit and receive hard core through the post is an offence, it is difficult to track if posted domestically. In response to advertisements in soft-core magazines, customers usually send money to an address overseas, and videos are dispatched in plain-wrapper envelopes from within the UK. What happens is that couriers smuggle hard-core video master tapes into the country, ready to be mass-duplicated and mailed out to customers.

A tactical shift concerning the policing of obscene materials in recent times has seen a far greater focus on mail order. Undercover post office, customs and trading officers in coordination with the police are regularly closing in on the porn duplicators, on Mr Big. In recent times there have been significant raids in Maidstone, Selsdon, South London, Birmingham and Manchester. Raids yield anything from small-time operations running two video machines in someone's front room to major operations featuring a hundred machines duplicating videos round the clock. A Manchester bust in 1995 produced a further seventeen duplicating addresses in London, too many for police to get around to attending to. People found guilty of duplicating will usually be fined in the region of £5,000 per video master. They either pay their fine or face between six and eighteen months in jail.

Back at Highbury Magistrates, the story of Operation Well is unfolding. It all started when one of the offending Mr Blanks fell behind on payments on his company's account with the Royal Mail. The company was registered in Amsterdam, but Mr Blank was actually working out of East London. Each week he would drive up to the sorting office loading bay and remove several sacks of small packages from the back of his red Astra van for mailing within the UK. Sometime during November 1994, Blank didn't pay his bill on 6,000 parcels, one of which had 'come open' while languishing at the sorting office. Its contents were analysed with some interest: it was a brochure for a company called HpF (Hand-picked Films of Amsterdam), featuring graphic colour photos advertising hard-core videos for sale.

The police were called in, and a surveillance team swung into action. Mr Blank was advised about the arrears, which he settled in full. Over the months he would be observed arriving on a weekly basis at the sorting office in the same red van, with further sacks of mail. In time he was traced to an office building in a back street in Shoreditch. This is what the police were after, the heart of the action. In July 1995, the Shoreditch offices were raided. Inside, police discovered banks of duplicating machines, 4,000 video cassettes, as well as business letters, mailing lists, and more glossy brochures for 'top-class erotica'.[8] A father and son, it transpired, were running the video duplication and mailing out, assisted by the son's best mate – the one with the van. During the raid on premises, in the heat of the moment, the son is reported to have declared, 'I never done them brochures!' And he wasn't lying. That was the handiwork of the fourth defendant in court today, a printer from South London. Following arrest and further investigation, all four 'gave a largely no-comment interview', according to the prosecution, and then they were charged, at which point lawyers and courtrooms started to feature.

The barrister defending Blank and Blank junior is the epitome of patrician cool, with a polished accent, smart clothes, fine shoes, good hair and a suave, detached ease with the world. When he liaises with his clients, a social and economic gulf is perfectly visible. Law courts are a key location in modern times where the good, the rich and the well educated are to be seen putting in some time supervising the unruly, the uncouth and the unlucky, where smart lawyers do their arcane stuff and their clients pay through the nose. Certain class fluidities in recent years mask the stubborn continuation of social divisions. The politician Tony Benn once observed similar hierarchies emerging from out of the post-industrial mist, back into full relief, in the way the annual war memorial services are choreographed, with the officer classes laying the wreaths, and the serving classes marching past in drill formation. As barrister and defendants consort, two worlds meet, of different beginnings, housing conditions, diets and text books – the British class system is alive and kicking.

There is little sign, however, as we await the arrival of the presiding magistrate, that the class system rearing up in this way is troubling anyone else in Court No. 4. The defendants seem relaxed and nonchalant – they keep whispering to each other, smiling. The briefs and clerks are bored – they yawn a lot. One is reading a novel, another stares into space, or occasionally, with a puzzled look on his face, into the public gallery at the lone spectator – that's me. He's puzzled because he can't think what could possibly bring someone to this court who had the choice to be elsewhere. The magistrate arrives, and the torpor lifts awhile, only to intensify soon after. The sluggishness in court is breathtaking: nothing runs on time, or runs smoothly. Proceedings are recorded in longhand, with the court clerk asking witnesses to go slowly with their testimony, repeatedly having them go back over what they just said so as to be sure he's got it down straight. The police officers are required by the defence counsel to recount each detailed entry of their stakeout logbook for evidentiary purposes. Further hold-ups occur when witnesses are called who are nowhere to be found, or when a witness is caught chewing gum by the magistrate and made to take it out, and the whole court hunts around for a wastepaper bin. Things almost grind to a halt as one police officer's painstaking recitation of her notes becomes too much to bear. The magistrate finally becomes exasperated, she announces that this must stop! 'Five days for committal proceedings are quite long enough.' This is, she fears, a serious waste of public money.

She's right. The whole performance, the surveillance, the drawn-out court action, the excessive costs, all a waste. To confirm, in a way, the sense of futility, it is mentioned in passing that the defence will not be contesting the obscenity of the videos. There are four master tapes, featuring fun and games with, among other things, an aubergine. All the defence lawyers will allow that according to British legal precedent the videos are 'obscene'. Therefore the court will not need to view them. The irony that the objects that have caused this whole drawn-out and costly affair will be entirely absent from proceedings appears to go unnoticed.

The peeping policeman
(at the offices of the vice police)

It is not unusual for obscenity to pass unseen in the legal context. Most 'obscene' materials seized in the UK are simply destroyed. Nobody views the offending items, not even the police, really; they just go to the burning plants and up in flames. This is because most seized goods might not actually be found obscene by a jury. The reality is that juries are unreliable, often failing to find 'obscenity' in a porn movie. Watching porn may not be their idea of fun, but over time juries have repeatedly found it difficult to accept that depravity follows from watching a variety of consenting adults having sex with each other. Therefore the authorities tend to go to a magistrates' court seeking only a forfeiture and destruction order against porn, with no legal action being taken against the person caught in possession of the offending items.

All seized material is checked to see where it falls on the rising scale of obscenity. A standard vice police report titled 'Metropolitan Police, Tapes for Forfeiture' categorises the offending materials. The single sheet of paper lists twenty videos, each one described as 'part viewed – obscene acts'. A column of proscribed acts runs down the right-hand side of the page: Masturbation; Fellatio; Cunnilingus; Intercourse; Ejaculation; Group Sex; Buggery; Flagellation; Bondage. Each box is to be ticked if the act is seen on tape. Only one tape out of twenty is ticked as containing bondage. None is ticked as featuring flagellation.[9] The lack of 'violence' apart, on this particular viewing day other porn offences were fairly well featured. Most titles featured masturbation, fellatio, cunnilingus, ejaculation – staples of a typical porn film – and were therefore marked as offensive, fit for a court to order their destruction. Obliging magistrates are mostly inclined to pass materials presented as obscene on the nod, agreeing thereby to their being shipped off to the local incinerator. Most people in the UK who have their materials seized – vendor, distributor or holiday-maker returning through customs – do not contest the action: lawyers cost money, it's too much hassle, and you'll probably lose anyway.

Another police report. This time it's just one offending item, an intercepted video tape sent through the post. The video is *Bottom Dweller*, by Patrick Collins. Collins is a mainstream American porn-movie director. People can buy his tapes all across the Western world. The offences listed by the police are as follows: 'Film Starts . . . 02.19 on the counter, still shot of erect penis being held and semen being ejaculated towards face and mouth of female; 02.34, still shot of male having sexual intercourse with female. Male erect penis in female vagina, clearly visible. 11.18, rubs finger in vagina. 11.19 Viewing ends.'[10] The viewing ends at this point because the peeping policeman has seen enough. The sex so briefly outlined is suggestive of the content of the rest of such a movie. This is standard American hard core, which forgoes 'specialty' sex, and will not contain any 'far-out' images or activities. Once again, therefore, *Bottom Dweller* is obscenity of the lower order, for burning not prosecuting. The awkward concept of obscenity will only be tested in a court of law, and before a jury, if the police feel the seized material can be proved to be 'depraved'. Then the more serious offence under section 2 of the OPA, of possession for gain, will be the charge. The police have a fairly clear notion concerning what they think can be successfully argued as obscenity. It is with certain kinds of Continental materials, particularly German products, that an officer's viewing time will likely stretch beyond ten minutes. These are titles that will be watched for the real hard stuff – watersports (urination); bondage and hard-core sex in the same scene; the use of foreign objects, fruit-and-veg porn, bananas and carrots – watched from start to finish, and all the offences listed. Such a tape shall probably go to trial. Usually with raids on duplication plants, such as with Operation Well, the police hope to land three to four of such 'hot' video masters.

At West End Central police station, up on the fourth floor, the viewing area for the vice police is a room with half a dozen video booths. The set-up is much like any row of booths you find in sex shops across continental Europe and America, the only difference being there's no Kleenex dispenser. Around the viewing area, filling every available piece of floor space, large bundles of bagged evidence containing videos, magazines, explicit video box-covers and sales brochures, are waiting to be listed and then shipped via the magistrates' court to the incinerator. And you find yourself asking the question: is this any way to purposefully employ the police force in a modern democratic society – watching dirty movies all day?

Actually, it's not all day. Officers are only allowed to view videos for a maximum of four hours each shift. For the sake of their eyes, I am told, and because, it is muttered in passing, 'we don't want anything strange to happen to anyone'. Presumably it is meant by this that an officer might be 'depraved'. The curious thing, however, is that the police don't really believe that porn depraves people. Recognising that juries might find most materials they seize and destroy to be non-obscene, the police are all too aware of the problems with defining porn. 'The law is weak,' says an officer of the vice squad, 'because the words are too strong. "Deprave and corrupt" is asking too much of a video. Just by watching a video, am I depraved or corrupted? Probably not. The words should be more like "upset, concern, annoy, discomfit".'

The vice officer continues to explain the predicaments of the job. 'The Obscene Publications Act offers us good powers to seize, but obscenity is too hard to prove these days.' He stops and thinks about this awhile. 'It's no fault of the Act really, more to do with how society has gone, has become more used to watching certain things. A lessening of morals really. You have satellite and cable now, legally showing soft core, but people always want more . . . cable soft core leads to hard core, leads to s/m and leads to snuff.'

I asked if he had ever seen such materials, the really vile stuff, that is, the elusive snuff? – 'No, but I'm sure it's out there.'

Has the squad itself ever come across things like snuff? – 'No.'

Any scenes of actual violence or non-consent, any records of a crime? 'No. Generally it's all commercial stuff we seize.'

He tells me that the head of the vice police is always working on persuading government to get the obscenity laws changed, to reconsider the wording. What would happen if the laws were altered, I wondered, if they were made more wide-ranging, stricter, would porn be rooted out at last, finally done away with? – 'No, to be honest with you, it will always be with us. Once there's a market, there will always be people trying to sell to it. Making the buying of obscene materials an offence would help a lot though.'

The Hackney Road versus Florida
(on selling porn in a cold climate)

Until then, however, the police shall have to make do with seizing and destroying, continuing to stop the hard-core supply both at source and at point of sale in Soho and other sex shops dotted about London and across Britain.

In Highbury, following a lunchtime soaking in the rain, everybody returned to the airless Court No. 4 smelling of damp again, and proceedings dragged on through the afternoon. Meanwhile four thousand miles away in Cape Canaveral, Florida, it was mid-morning, sunny and bright, and the Fairvilla Megastore was opening up for another day's highly lucrative porn retailing. Fairvilla is what some like to call the future of adult retail. A 14,000-square-foot, two-storey, one-stop shopping experience, tapping into the still underexploited single women and couples market for sex in America. Here people come and buy videos, sex toys, magazines, T-shirts, lingerie, greeting cards – the whole range. Owned and managed by husband-and-wife team Bill and Shari Murphy, Fairvilla provides a new kind of up-scale porn-buying experience, more like shopping at Gap or Virgin than the traditional adult bookstore, with hardwood floors, a forty-foot domed ceiling with a galleried mezzanine floor, and an adjoining open-air palm court with waterfalls and a coffee shop. There's another Fairvilla store in Orlando and a chain of outlets is planned for both the Atlantic and Pacific coasts in the near future.[11]

Though the situation is not entirely good for porn retailers in some areas of the United States, in this particular part of Florida, and many other regions of the country, things are looking up. Here, couples come to browse and purchase materials that are regularly destroyed in Britain. This very act of purchasing itself, should the police have its way, would also be a criminal offence. In Paris, Hamburg, Frankfurt, Granada, Amsterdam, Brussels . . . similar shopping experiences are also available. Meanwhile, in Shoreditch, scene of the police stakeout for Operation Well, and just around the corner from the Columbia Road flower market, you can find a very different kind of porn-vending enterprise, something very hole in the wall. It was time to be leaving Highbury and the chronically slow workings of justice, time we were catching a bus and heading east for a spot of shopping.

Think again of Florida, the commodious shop interior, the 50,000 videotape titles, cappuccino in the palm court, seventy degrees in the shade, and then think of Hackney Road, in the drizzle, the non-stop exhaust fumes, and this little derelict shop, the window blacked out and boarded up, its insides gutted, a place that doubles as a one-day-a-week porn vendor. You step inside, over bits of plaster and rubble, adjusting your eyes to the gloomy light. There's a guy sitting at a knackered desk, listening to the cricket on the radio. He smiles. 'Have you been here before, mate?'

Let's assume you haven't, that way you get the full guided tour. 'Right, you have the videos over there.' He points at the wall facing us, at three of four long shelves, buckling under the weight of several heaps of boxless video-pornware, with numbers scrawled in marker pen on their sides. 'They're organised in categories, that's German, American, amateur, specialty, gay, etcetera. And then you have this' – he points to a typed sheet of paper pinned on the wall beside him – 'which lists all the categories, and each tape by number, which tells you the title of the video. And then, next to that, you see those letters?' He points at a string of initials and abbreviations, adjoining each individual title on the list. 'They tell you what kind of action there's featured on the tape. You know, g–g for girl–girl, 3w for three-way scenes, a for anal . . . errr, bt – big tits, s/m – well, that's obvious. Anyway, it's all listed.' He points to another typed sheet listing the extensive glossary of terms. 'What you do is, pick the video you want to buy, and you check they're working on the machines back there, because there's no refunds. It's £15 for singles, £30 for double tapes, £40 for two double tapes. And then, next time, if you bring in the old tapes as part exchange, you get a fiver off the next purchase. So, if you could just leave your bag here while you're looking, then we'll all be happy.' He smiles again. You do as instructed.

'Back there', beyond the desk and tapes at the back of the shop, a pair of television sets and VCRs await for testing tapes. In front of them a neat and orderly queue of men has formed, waiting with their porn selections. Apart from the radio, and the muffled orgasmic groans coming from the television sets, all is quiet. Not sombre, not furtive, just a concentrated quiet. The hole in the wall's clientele couldn't be much better behaved, courteous and patient, and respectful of each other's space. Here again, as in court, the social classes meet, but this time the hierarchies temporarily fade away. Middle-class men and working-class men, *Guardian* readers and *Sun* readers, all politely rubbing shoulders, scary-looking big guys, and specky little nerdy guys, college graduates, rugby boys, all patiently waiting their turn to test and purchase and return to the grotty reality of Hackney Road. (But no women, of course. The shoddy, criminal, low-life circumstances of the hole-in-the-waller render the situation hard to access for women, making this porn-retailing situation very men-only.)

Outside London's West End, from time to time, unlicensed sex shops like this will rear up, hoping to go unnoticed or otherwise taking their chances with the law. And from time to time, the law comes and arrests them. There was a raid in Islington in late 1995, for example, that was reported in the local press. Islington Council's trading standards officers and local police shut down a single operation adult 'bookstore' in the neighbourhood. Arrests were made and court action duly followed. Two men were found guilty and each was fined £2,000 for selling uncertificated porn videos. One trader had about sixty tapes, the other about a hundred and fifty. Local politicians were excited about this long-overdue crackdown on serious crime. 'This is firm and decisive action from the magistrates,' said Councillor Paul Jackson (Labour). 'I'm glad to see our trading standards officers getting the support they deserve.'[12] A fellow Labour councillor, Ted Goodman, who is also chair of the Campaign Against Censorship (CAC), contacted his party colleague the following month: '[You are] praising the enforcement of censorship of video recordings made by consenting adults for consenting adults,' writes Goodman. 'Presumably you are therefore saddened by the abolition of all censorship which has now been achieved in the former communist States of Eastern Europe.' Goodman's letter continued with the observation that Britain is one of the very few countries in all of Europe that practises state censorship. 'Even allowing for the fact that the actual censorship itself is imposed by Parliament, its zealous enforcement by a local authority is thus a cause for shame, not pride.'[13]

Across town, in Soho, there are six licensed shops selling soft-core materials, and about forty other unlicensed joints. The situation is policed by the vice squad, with its twelve officers, two sergeants and one inspector. It is a common and understandable quibble: you tell someone hard core is illegal in Britain, and they say, but what about Soho, what about the neon-lit sex shops of Brewer Street, Archer Street, Whitfield

Street, Lexington Street, Berwick Street? Until 1996, the police had no powers to shut down porn outlets in 'Sin Central'. They would raid a shop, cart away the dirty magazines and videos, and temporarily close the premises. The bloke working behind the counter at the time of the raid would be arrested, be charged, go to court, be fined, and, in due course, resume his job of selling illegal hard core, until the number of arrests and prosecutions started pushing him towards a custodial sentence, at which time he would switch to another part of the operation, maybe tape-smuggling or duplication. In the meantime, the day after the raid, the shop would reopen, fully restocked from the duplicator's hidden stash, with someone else working behind the counter. With limited staff and work-hours, the number of times that police officers can go back for more busting, raiding, viewing and taking through the legal system is restricted. This is why there continued to be hard core in Soho, and why the police started redirecting their efforts towards the suppliers.

Additional laws were sought supposedly to deal finally with the porn outlets in Sin Central. From the start of 1997, with the new City of Westminster Act in place, the police, working in concert with the council's licensing office, promised to close down for good any shop selling obscene materials. Shops would either get licences, which are rationed, or they'd be swiftly raided and have their premises padlocked in perpetuity. In theory there'd be no chance of an unlicensed sex shop lasting for any length of time. However, a year or more later, little had changed. The porn shops utilised a third option, which was to keep the hard core off premises, or keep it down to the bare minimum. Here the shop cuts its obscene materials to less than 10 per cent of the overall stock. This is another version of the old sex-shop alibi of fifty copies of remaindered Iris Murdoch novels gathering dust out on the shelves, with five Rodox colour climax hard-core magazines under the counter; or fifty copies of *Gone with the Wind* on video fronting for five copies of *Debbie Does Dallas*.

The people who work in the shops of Soho are rarely the owners, leaseholders, or part of anything that can be connected up. They are mostly just small-time operators. According to the police, and judging by behaviour, few, if any, are new to a life of crime. People involved in the porn industry at the distribution end tend to be old or young lags, who see police pressure, court action and the like as an occupational hazard, and the maintenance of proper trading standards as the headache of the legal retailer. Buying hard core in Soho is a mostly dispiriting experience. Entering a typical sex shop is like going back in time, like going into a dirty video shop twenty-five years ago. Soho's sex shops have entirely missed out on the stylised makeover of retailing. It's as though the shopping revolution of the eighties never happened. The shops are so low-maintenance, because they're so fly-by-night. Most of the men working the stores in Soho aren't interested: 'Porn, can't stand the stuff, mate', 'What d'you say it's name was again, *Deep Goat?*' They don't care; they're passing through, and, most of them, they rip you off. Pre-sale, they promise you everything, promise you the world, any kind of video you like. 'John Leslie's *Chameleons?* Yeah, we've got that, but not here, give me ten minutes will you.' They then disappear for a while, off to collect the ordered materials from their 'stash', returning with the videotape, the requested film's initials written on the spine (CM, for *Chameleons*). You pay up, you take it home, it's not *Chameleons*, it's complete rubbish. And, when you return and ask for some kind of fair treatment, they get very nasty, almost instantly. It's hard to fathom the attitude. There's seemingly no need for it, but still they do it. And then again, if they're likely to be shut down at any minute, to be arrested, why would they bother about treating the customer well? Here we find the short-term nature of advanced capitalism at its most short-term: here today, gone away tomorrow. It's rare to see the same man fronting the shop twice running. Someone's always standing in for a friend, doing a favour for a mate who's sick today, but he'll be in tomorrow. This is Soho; it's the way Sin Central breeds dishonesty. But beyond the inevitability of the sex-shop con trick there does lie a story of how things came to be.

In the early to mid-seventies, at some indistinct moment, the emergence of soft adult materials onto the outskirts of the mainstream became accepted, or at least tolerated, in Britain. Soft core got its foot in the door, and wasn't for budging. It would be inaccurate to say that things have gone smoothly ever since. However, broadly speaking, British soft-core magazines have become an accepted, if neglected, part of the magazine landscape. What has not always been so readily accepted, over time, is where the stuff goes on sale.

It hasn't always been the case that newsagents were the main place to go to for your soft-core magazines. From this point at the end of the nineties it is hard to imagine, or remember, how once this island was dotted with porn emporia. Not only were there a hundred sex shops in Soho itself during the mid-seventies, but from 1978 to 1981 David Sullivan's Conegate company alone opened a hundred or more stores all across the regions, from Colchester to Salisbury, Whitstable to Lancaster, to rival the dozens already out there being run by other firms. For a decade or so, sex shops were boom entities. Conegate was not only opening everywhere, but making a fuss about it. Public outcry was actually pursued, to make everybody aware there was a new sex shop in town. Outlets would regularly be launched into provincial communities with the starting up of a letter-writing campaign to the local press, railing against the rising tide of filth, and duly the customers came flooding in. It was a high-risk campaign, however, and Sullivan was definitely pushing his luck. With neon-lit porn shops setting up near to schools in the heart of middle England, it was only a matter of time before the law bit back.

Concerted local efforts were started up, petition signing, demos by feminist anti-porners, graffiti blitzes, glue in the locks, Christian vigils laying siege outside the flesh spots. Popping into town for a copy of *Whitehouse* was like heading into a war zone. Pressure was brought to bear upon the Conservative government of the time, which eventually, belatedly, rushed through new laws to tighten things up. The Local Government (Miscellaneous Provisions) Act of 1982 afforded local authorities wide powers of control over local sex operations through the granting of licences – or, more accurately, the refusal to grant them. Though chain owners fought a rearguard action, the boom era of the sex shop was coming to a close, and a lucrative new revenue stream for local newsagents was just beginning.

The bulk of the soft-core magazine business relocated from the sex shops to the little shop on the corner. Newsagents tend to stock a lot of top-shelf titles because they're a good moneymaker, and not, as has been alleged, because the wholesalers, doing the job of Mr Big pornographer, are forcing it upon the poor, defenceless vendor. The value of soft core to the newsagents has increased in recent times with the growth of hypermarkets, which continue to impinge upon traditional local community trading. Most kinds of newspapers and magazines are now sold in Sainsbury's and Tesco, except, of course, for porn. Thus the revenue from soft core becomes even more vital to the corner store and newsagent.[14]

There is a further irony attached to the death of the sex shop. Its demise was discontinuous with newly hatched plans within the world of video technology and film classification. The Williams Committee's report on porn of 1979 recommended both the extensive licensing of sex shops and a continuation of film censorship. The latter included the inauguration of a new certificate for sex movies. Following this, the BBFVC responded with the 18R certificate, as a legally supervised conduit enabling soft-core porn to reach the adult masses. The regulated sex shop was fundamental to such a conduit; 18R videos were only to be sold by licensed sex shops. The sustained attack and consequent collapse of these shops, however, meant there was nowhere to sell the videos.

In time, companies tired of the difficulties involved in running sex shops. The struggle to gain a costly licence from reluctant and capricious local government authorities was a draining and unpredictable process. Licensing committees tend to be easily swayed by minority campaign groups prepared to lobby vociferously to block applications. Fifteen years later, getting a license continues to be a hard slog. In the Shropshire town of Naisley, an application for a sex shop licence was summarily rejected by Wrekin district council. A discussion followed on a local radio station, in which the danger of children gaining access to sex shops was raised. When it was suggested that despite legal restrictions children were still accessing tobacconists, a local councillor stated that sex was more harmful than tobacco. Afterwards the radio station admitted they'd experienced no difficulty in finding people to talk against sex shops, but nobody living in the area would speak up for them, not publicly, not by name.[15]

The story of the sex shops is a key, if unglamorous, strand within the larger narrative of porn in the UK. The 18R video classification was mainly a non-event.[16] The opportunity squandered was the continuation and development of a sex shop and sex video culture, with outlets that might, in due course, and following the fuss and bother of outcry and protest, have settled down into the trading community landscape. Such outlets might have become an accepted sight, and a place to visit for not just men but also interested couples and single women, which is how it has worked in parts of the USA and Europe. The potential for acceptance, for an increasingly maturing mainstream sex culture was to be killed off before it ever really got started. People tend not to miss the things they don't already have.

A proper carve-up
(on what's wrong with British porn magazines)

Whether many would miss British soft-core porn magazines should they ever go away is open to question.

At the start of the porn movie *An American Buttman in London*, the leading American porner John Stagliano is to be seen rooting through heaps of British soft-core magazines – *Razzle, Club, Escort* – declaring his affection for Britporn. This partly serves as an establishing shot to justify a trip to London, but is also a genuine love letter to the genre from a long-distance admirer. Stagliano's glowing appraisal is not typical, however. Many porn fans would be happy to see the back of the bulk of Britporn. 'What I don't like about most of the Top Shelf,' says sex campaigner Tuppy Owens, 'is that it is disrespectful to its readers.' Furthermore, 'What it needs is more intimate details, things that might make you feel a lot less guilty about wanking. Girls that pose should have more of an identity, be allowed to express themselves to the readers, so that there is almost some kind of a relationship, so that she's not just a cunt, but a person with a cunt.' These are the kinds of attributes Linzi Drew feels she brought to porn in her times as a glamour model. 'My appeal was that I was the first girl to be a real person who was talking back: 'Yes, I like to be fucked, this is my favourite sexual position.' Talking back instead of just being there with my legs spread, and saying I like windsurfing . . . I think the punters ought to get some realism and I think that realism was what appealed to them about me.'[17]

A lack of realism isn't what bothers Spencer Woodcock, former editor of *Fetish Times*, but a lack of intelligence. '*Mayfair*, it has quite good pictures, is good porn, in that way,' he says, 'But between the porn there is a lot of crap, which tends to treat the reader like an imbecile.' Nicholas White, erstwhile heavy porn user, with a habit so big at one time he confesses he single-handedly kept the British soft-core industry afloat, feels that soft core doesn't treat its customers very well. 'I get the impression that most porn publishers couldn't care less as long as the mugs keep paying up, like the football chairmen who take the loyalty of the fans for granted.' In a letter to the author he writes, 'British soft core doesn't want to grow up. It has always existed in a curious twilight zone between the accepted and the stigmatised . . . It's neither celebrated nor vilified, but merely tolerated, which is artistic death to any genre.'

Over the years there have been four main players in the heterosexual, soft-core magazine industry in Britain. Galaxy, which produces magazines such as *Knave* and *Fiesta*; the Paul Raymond Group, with, among others, *Escort*, *Men Only* and *Mayfair*; Northern & Shell, with a list that includes *New Talent*, *Readers' Wives*, *Forum* and *For Women*; and finally, David Sullivan's stable of titles: that is, pretty much everything else that's featured on the top shelf, *Rustler*, *Parade*, *Love Birds*, as well as, more recently, the *Sport* 'newspapers'. There are also a few independents, such as *Desire*, a magazine for couples, and

Hustler, as well as the 'specialty' field of spanking, fetishism and the like.

There was also a new-look *Penthouse* (UK) on the market from autumn 1997. Though retaining the licensed brand name for market recognition, *Penthouse* (UK) relaunched as a very different kind of porn magazine, devotedly sophisticated, tasteful – appealing to girlfriend as well as boyfriend – and fit for leaving out on one's coffee table. Looking more like a style magazine than something off the top shelf, the new *Penthouse* arrived featuring very soft and very 'arty' photo sets of skinny, semi-naked fashion waifs shot by leading fashion photographers like Corinne Day. During a period when men's 'style' magazines, from *Arena* to *Maxim* to *Loaded*, continued to court readers by running 'soft-core' glamourpuss photos of supermodels and film actresses, the new *Penthouse* (UK) further blurred the point at which 'style' ends and 'porn' takes over.

Whether such a genre-busting magazine would find a readership to sell sufficient copies remained unclear. The leading title in the top-shelf market is hard to ascertain. Only *Knave* is at present audited by ABC, its circulation figure is currently below the 100,000 mark. It is widely thought that the titles competing for top spot are *Fiesta*, *Escort* and *New Talent*. The journalist and campaigner Lyn Proctor used to work for *Fiesta*: 'I enjoyed working for the magazine. Their attitude was that sex is not just the prerogative of the busty nineteen year old, that sex and sexuality is the prerogative of everybody ... *Fiesta* shows women not just as observed objects but as people who enjoy sex themselves.'[18]

Porn is a diffuse sector of the magazine world. Circulations may well be smaller than they were ten years ago but, as any trip to the newsagent will bear out, there's a large range of titles on sale. As *Snappy*, an American 'entertainment' magazine of the thirties, announced on the cover of its August 1933 edition, 'Men like variety.' And magazine publishers like a market where diffusion produced on a low budget can be sold on with a high cover price. Although it is rare to see anyone actually pick up and buy a porn magazine in the newsagent's, somebody is buying them – possibly 6 per cent of men with any kind of regularity – as the soft-core publishing industry keeps hold of its 10 per cent share of the overall magazine industry.[19]

Zak Keir works for Northern & Shell. Does she accept accusations that Britporn is stuck in a rut? 'Some mags do the same things year in year out; it varies from publisher to publisher, from title to title. Some are pretty conservative, have looked the same for years. Whereas with others, it's let's do something different, let's do this, let's do that.' Keir points out that it isn't as simple or singular as some critics or casual observers suggest. 'A lot of it depends on your market, what you are concerned with; there's a lot of variety in the industry. In aims, your fetish fancier is very different than your average *Sun*-reading male.' However, others well acquainted with the form clearly do not share Keir's jaunty assessment. 'I don't think porn is inherently any more passive than most other forms of entertainment,' argues Nicholas White. 'Our whole society is founded on vicarious enjoyment. But it is the mass-production of it, and porn is a major offender in this respect. Pure lust is as enigmatic as love, but expressing its subtle variations has dubious economic value in an industry dedicated to the lowest common denominator. It would be exciting if a subculture of independent sex-zines sprang up.'

It would seem, therefore, that the first thing wrong with British porn magazines is they're not very good. A long look at them, and the suspicion grows that the publishers aren't trying hard enough. They don't have to. Consumers don't have much choice; they can't easily take their porn spending money elsewhere. When other options do arise, with, for instance, the admission in recent times of raunchier American soft core onto the market, then the domestic product starts to leak readers. In the main, however, access to full-on hard-core magazines remains heavily restricted in Britain.

The vision of low-budgeted, domestically produced British pornware being turned into big profits for wealthy porners like Paul Raymond, David Sullivan and the Gold Brothers can sometimes confuse discussions of porn in the UK. Criticism of porn becomes tangled up with an anti-profit tradition on the left.[20] In these times of reconstructed socialism, although some people continue to query the virtue of powerhouse corporatism symbolised by outfits like British Telecom, rarely do they query the morality of making a phone call. With porn such a mix-up nearly always transpires. It seems that porn is in itself bad, and made much worse by the fact that it turns a profit. However, take away the profit issue, as with amateur porn served up free on the internet, and the wrongfulness of porn would still be apparent to those who think it a terrible thing. The issues can be disentangled. It is possible to talk about the morality of porn apart from the morality of corporatism, just as discussions on Sainsbury's and Tesco and the social impact of the hypermarket can proceed without the need to question the acceptability of buying food.

This is not to suggest that all is fine with the British porn-trading landscape, which presently lacks a competitive edge. A small group of large publishers have things pretty much all their own way. New publishing ventures from outside the group tend to flop. A range of factors and vested interests see that they do. It all sort of goes back to the law. Britporn magazines must be certain not to contravene the OPA and Indecent Displays Act (1981). What this means is not exactly clear. There's no point in ringing up the police or the government to find out, as there aren't any guidelines they can just pop in the post. In the early eighties, Kent Boulton, a former strippers' agent, started making porn videos with fellow British porner, Mike Freeman – films like *Knacker of the Yard* and *Flat Sharing Shaggers*. Boulton wanted to know what the situation was with regard to the law. He went to the police, but he couldn't get a clear answer on his legal position. He went to the film censor, but they said they didn't like to impinge upon the film-maker's artistic integrity. They would much rather you did your best, or your worst, and then they'll see what they think about it. 'We'll either censor it or take it to court.'[21] Making porn is partly an art of working in the greyness of the received wisdom and hearsay. And, if you've strayed the wrong side of the line, 'First time you'll find out there's a problem is when they're breaking down your door.'[22]

Due care and self-regulation is required. Any magazine published by the major porn publishers will be meticulously checked over by lawyers for any infringements of accepted levels of nudity, levels of spreadness in the 'crotch shots', angles of male tumescence. No kind of genital activity or genital contact may be shown – according to precedent and common practice, as much as any interpretation of the law. And then the magazines have wholesalers and distributors to satisfy. WH Smith and John Menzies distribute a significant proportion of British top-shelf porn. If they don't approve of magazines and their content, a magazine won't get the wide distribution that makes for the large profits.

The arrangement the big domestic porn companies have with their distributors and the law has over time encouraged a regime of self-censorship to emerge. You don't go to the trouble of commissioning a photo set, or printing up a magazine, only then to check to see what your lawyers, or your distributors' lawyers, think. You do the censoring first. Occasionally lawyers bridle, just a little, but mostly the magazine people have become adept at making sure they don't go too far. Distributors hold an especially stern line on penises, more restrictive, for instance, than anything applied by Her Majesty's Customs. In recent times Customs have readily admitted a regular feed of nearly hard-core magazines imported from overseas, mainstream American titles such as *High Society*, *Velvet* and *Cherry*, showing erections, couples, group-sex scenarios: the very kinds of images that are supposed to be illegal in this country.

For a long period, *Hustler* (UK) was also running virtually hard-core imagery on a monthly basis in Britain, using photospreads taken directly from the photo library of *Hustler* (US), also featuring couples in very nearly fucking, very nearly sucking scenarios, or actual penetration shots with strategically placed hands masking the precise point of docking. The magazine is produced under license from its American counterpart by JT Publishing, which also publishes *Hustler* in South Africa and Australia. The editorial content for all three titles is generated in South Africa. The magazine is then printed in Spain and will be checked by customs as it is brought over for sale in the UK. Not once did customs consider it necessary to block or doctor an issue of the magazine. Distributed by Goldstar, rather than Menzies and WH Smith, *Hustler* wasn't getting into High Street retailers like Forbuoys or Martins. Though the publishers claimed a circulation of around 25,000 a month, in early 1997 they cut back on the nearly hard core in order to reach out to a larger audience.[23]

The liberalisation by customs over levels of explicitness does seriously clash with the present views of the distributors in the UK soft-core market. It goes to show how with porn laws things are rarely straightforward. At *Desire* magazine, an independent magazine for couples, Lesley Sharrock believes that the reason why people don't get to see erect penises in the UK is not that the authorities won't allow it but that most magazines and their distributors won't. *Desire* magazine launched in Britain in late 1994, hoping to become a mainstream magazine reaching out to readers beyond just the sex shops and the top shelf, and running photospreads of men and women as mutually consenting and desiring subjects. However, the magazine ran into difficulties over distribution. 'As for our picture content,' said Lesley Sharrock, deputy editor for *Desire*, 'there are dicks in the mag but they tend to be only in the [solo] guy sets. This is due to the fact that the two major wholesalers, WH Smith and John Menzies, won't handle any magazine which publishes pictures of couples (male and female) where both people are naked. Two naked women are okay but not a man and a woman. Mad but true!' Sharrock despairs. 'And the crazy thing is, that a newspaper can run pix like that but a top-shelf magazine can't. *News of the World* ran a front-cover picture of a naked couple (from the waist up at least) and the guy had his hands over the woman's breasts. While this is allowed in a so-called "family" newspaper we would not be allowed to run that same picture on our cover. This is purely commercial censorship and nothing whatsoever to do with the law.' Such restrictions finally led the publishers of *Desire* to leave the High Street and find its market through subscription and direct mailing.

Publishers and distributors seem to have little regard for the growing call for some kind of 'mutuality' in porn imagery, where consenting adults are featured in the kinds of visual scenarios that bear some similarity to people's experience of sex. The reluctance could be moral, or the fear that such widespread distribution may gain them too much bad publicity, which might then require the police to intervene. However, you also suspect an element of double standards as much as caution or prudery. In August 1994, *Everywoman* magazine had difficulties with WH Smith over a cover featuring a plaster cast of an erect penis, the next issue featured a cast of a female torso and went through without a murmur. In this way is the British porn scene highly sexist.

What is commercial censorship has been masquerading for many years now as moral and legal censorship. The 'angle of the dangle' – the notion that a free-standing penis in a photograph may not rise above a certain angle – is not written in law; it is agreed by four parties – the police, the distributors, the magazine publishers and various lawyers – all of whom seem happy for the arrangement to continue. When an editor at *For Women* says that she'd love to show erections but the law won't let her, this is not telling the whole story. It's ironic that mainstream soft-core porners in Britain have in effect taken to hiding behind the law. For so long, porn searched for alibis to excuse and justify itself before the courts. Nowadays, soft core finds that its alibi for not evolving, for not delivering, actually resides within the law.

The present restrictions in Britporn benefit the status quo. The situation suits publishers such as Paul Raymond and Northern & Shell, neither of whom are vocal in lobbying for the porn laws to be changed. If they were changed, the home-based porn companies might well be outfaced by the larger European porn companies of Denmark, Germany, Holland and Southern Spain – Rodox, Private, Seventeen, New Look, Magma, Silwa, Clarke Entertainment. Most of these continental porners are already multinational, as well as multilingual, carrying an English text box to go with the German, French, Spanish and Italian text boxes. These are experienced, long-term hard-core porn manufacturers who would relish the opportunity to compete in the British market.

Plainly the present laws in Britain are beneficial to what is practically a cartel. The British porn situation is a perfectly tight and cosy set-up for those inside the loop, suiting the police, distributors and publishers. This is not to suggest that once upon a time the different parties gathered in a room together and conducted a carve-up. Merely that over time a snug chain of mutually satisfactory relations came to pass. This is an industry where there are very few independents. Any new company that ventures along and wishes to start up in competition will not only struggle to get a good distribution deal but may also suffer more than its share of legal harassment. (Rumours circulate of bad behaviour – for example, exactly who is responsible for the tip-offs to the police concerning smaller publishers or distributors? – but actual proof is limited.[24]) Closed clubs do not welcome new members, and closed clubs with vested interests to protect can be especially unwelcoming. These are some of the things wrong with British porn magazines.

The love train
(on Her Majesty's Customs and porn)

Tracking the workings of an Englishman's relish for the vice of censorship inevitably leads to the world of Her Majesty's Customs. With the legal support of the Customs Consolidation Act (CCA) of 1876, the granddaddy of British laws of regulation, customs officers stand firm at the stations, ports and airfields of this island nation, holding the line against the threat of foreign contamination. The CCA describes the situation thus: 'The goods enumerated and described . . . are hereby prohibited to be imported or brought into the United Kingdom . . . Indecent or obscene prints, paintings, photographs, books, cards, lithographs and other engravings, or any other indecent or obscene articles.' As time has gone by and new technologies have come on stream, the Act has simply been deemed to be inclusive of all forms and formats of expression.

As back-up for such an ancient law, HM Customs & Excise provide a supposedly confidential set of guidelines for officers to refer to. A recent version advises, 'Seize as forfeit imported material which in your opinion . . . falls within the test for obscenity . . . providing the material cannot be manufactured or sold domestically.' But, as usual, how do we know obscenity when we see it? 'The CCA refers to goods which are . . . obscene but it does not define what these words mean. Therefore they are accorded their normal dictionary definition.' As an attempt at clarification this does not rate highly. At which point the guidelines become rather more precise: 'Prohibited obscene material will include that which portrays explicit sexual activity viz.: analingus [sic.] (oral contact with the anus) . . . buggery (penile penetration of the anus whether male or female) . . . cunnilingus (oral contact with female genitals) . . . ejaculation (emission of semen) . . . fellatio (oral contact with male genitalia) . . . intercourse (penile penetration of the vagina) . . . masturbation (manual stimulation of the genitals) troilism . . . (three persons indulging in simultaneous sexual activity – usually two males and a female) . . . the use of any object to attain sexual gratification.'

This is a pretty thoroughgoing list of restrictions, and yet, as discussed, customs do allow at least some leeway with sexual depictions: 'The display of erection in males and "open crotch" shots of females will not generally be considered to be within the prohibition.' There is also the Personal Use Tolerance: 'Do not seize or detain small quantities of obscene material which passengers . . . import as part of their . . . baggage or effects, e.g.: magazines, books . . . but not videos, never videos, these can be easily copied, and are therefore never tolerated.'[25] They mean it about the videos. For example, should you have sex on holiday and film it as a keepsake, give your partner a blow job in the surf in a secluded cove with the Hi-8 video camera recording, and are searched, going through customs on the way home, and have your holiday memento seized, then you are considered to be in possession of an offensive item: your love-making has become an obscenity. This has actually happened to people. 'Obscene video tapes . . . are the primary target', the guidelines declare without qualification.

Once customs have rooted out the obscenity it's time for questioning. Here the guidelines are keen to ensure that officers don't jeopardise the case by saying the wrong things, urging that any kind of prejudice be avoided. 'When discussing the contents of material, avoid using terms like . . . "group sex", "lesbian" and "homosexual". It is the act which creates the obscenity, not the sex or sexual orientation of those performing it.'

The photographer Rosie Gunn was once stopped and searched returning from Amsterdam. They found she had a few porn videos in her bags. Gunn is a feminist photographer who also leads classes for women on the subject of porn. She was held in custody while they took away her videos for close inspection. After a long wait, a customs official came along and notified her that her videos would be confiscated. He asked Gunn, 'Are you familiar with the terms "fellatio" and "cunnilingus"?', before telling her that this time she was free to go.

When your materials are confiscated you have twenty-eight days to contest the seizure. If you do, you are summoned to a magistrates' court to argue your case. A magistrate may take your side and let you keep your porn. More often than not, however, magistrates will back the law. The cost of lawyers, the bad percentages, means that most prefer to just give in quietly. Meanwhile, those caught in possession of several videos, those who look like the wrong sort, or as though they might figure as a good high-profile offender, will find that matters rarely stop at confiscation. For these people an arrest will probably follow. As will the indignity of having their homes searched and the public exposure that often comes with legal action. 'Prosecution is desirable,' the guidelines advise, 'to publicise the prohibition and the serious view taken of offences.'

In the autumn of 1995 a vicar from Wimbledon in south London was arrested by Customs at Dover for carrying hardcore porn videos. Shortly afterwards, his story was splashed across the front of his local newspaper. He was returning from a trip to France where he'd conducted a wedding service for a friend. He was questioned for twenty-one hours, and his house was searched, where the discovery of additional materials was made. Thirty-five years old, and recently separated from his wife, the vicar's behaviour was described in the news report as 'sordid'. Some of his parishioners were 'shocked': "I've always found him very normal and a sociable sort . . . It just doesn't seem like him.'" Meanwhile, other parishioners, 'could not believe their mild-mannered preacher could sink so low.'[26]

David Webb is the founder member of the National Campaign for the Reform of the Obscene Publications Act (NCROPA), who, for over seven years, has pursued a test case through the British courts on importation of obscene videos from Europe. In 1997 he was still waiting to go before the European Court of Human Rights in Luxembourg. It started in 1990 when it became apparent that, after a period of relative tolerance on the bringing in of small numbers of videos, suddenly more and more people were being detained by customs. A lot of people returning from trips to the Low Countries, especially gay men, were being intercepted and their materials confiscated. Webb decided to see if he could get himself arrested. Returning from a trip to Brussels, with six gay videos in his suitcase, the former actor made himself appear furtive and edgy and was duly stopped by customs. He was not only arrested but immediately whisked away in a car, up to London, on suspicion of being a Mr Big in the video importation business. Three members of the vice squad were picked up *en route* to his house for a thorough search. He was later charged, and a long series of courtroom battles, with Webb conducting his own defence, had begun.

The idea of NCROPA first came to Webb in the sixties during a rainy hold-up making a film on location. Nine years later, after the Old Bailey trial of the book *Inside Linda Lovelace*, he finally set about it. The idea was to form a campaigning law reform organisation to pressure MPs on the laws of obscenity. 'The law has no right in people's bedrooms,' declares Webb from his flat in Chelsea. 'The OPA is based on the concept of obscenity, a thing which is only capable of being interpreted or defined on an entirely subjective level. Depravity and corruption as two concepts are not quantifiable, you can't measure them. To have as subjective a term as obscenity enshrined in any law is wrong; it just shouldn't be.'

From time to time the fuzziness of definitions will be raised in Parliament when they're making new laws. 'And then parliamentarians will try to introduce "laundry lists",' observes Webb, 'saying these things are prohibited – buggery, cunnilingus, etc. – but someone says, "Well, wouldn't that mean *Coriolanus*, Act II?", or whatever, and the proposed law starts to look like an ass.' Webb has often watched debates from the public galleries at the House of Commons. 'So what they normally end up saying is, sod the laundry list, we've got to have a vague law and the courts and the judges and juries can interpret it exactly how they want to.'

Over time Webb has come to believe fuzzy legislation founded on open-ended definitions are actually preferred, to make it a catch-all kind of prohibition. Thus considerable extensions in the activities of the police, trading officers and customs are apportioned. This is the sort of law, in other words, that NCROPA and its sister company, the Campaign Against Censorship, want removed from the statute books. 'We are not opposed to the most minimal law, protecting minors and possibly animals. But that is all. You cannot have a free society whereby anything that offends someone is out, because we are all offended by certain things, but we all differ about what offends and what doesn't, and we have to go along with it. I don't like boxing, but I wouldn't ban it. Just as long as they are not forced to do it.'

When Webb first got his lobby group started, he assumed it would take a matter of five years or so to effect changes. Instead more than twenty years have now passed, during which time a considerable intensification of the regulatory legal framework in the UK has occurred. So entrenched does the UK appear to be regarding law and censorship, it has arguably gone too far for things ever to be turned around, and so it is to Europe that many look for hope of future change. Such optimism can obscure the view a little. The often repeated hope is that Britain's new trading partners, with their greater liberalism concerning pornography, will require that the British stop being so prudish and come to terms with the legally produced porn of Paris, Marbella, Dusseldorf and so forth. Otherwise, what kind of free-trade zone is the so-called Single European Market? Unfortunately it is the kind of single market founded upon laws that allow member states the right to veto the sale of materials within its borders that its domestic laws forbid. Pornography, in other words.

The European Convention on Human Rights, however, may prove more amenable. The argument is that a person living in the UK can have in his or her possession hard-core materials featuring adults; this is not an offence. It is the same in the rest of the European trading block. And yet this person cannot cross borders without being targeted, intercepted, prosecuted and having his or her home searched, because of porn, and this amounts to an infringement of a person's liberty. So far, by 1997, a customs importation case had never been heard on the basis of an abuse of human rights. If Webb should finally make it to Luxembourg, and win, then the Obscene Publications Act will quite possibly find itself out of date, and all the efforts of Webb and his co-campaigners will have been worth something.

Island life
(on why Britain is so censored)

In the meantime, it is incredible to think how a few videos licitly purchased in Brussels, featuring consenting adults having sex, can arouse so much interest, and all that police and court action.

Having offered a partial review of censorship in the UK, outlining the *how* of control, it is interesting to dwell awhile in speculating as to the *why* of such things. In America, when discussing porn, people will often speak of their nation's sexual hang-ups, of a sexually repressive culture that has yet to mature, referring enviously to the sophistication of Europeans back in the 'old world'. And then they pause awhile, as a sliver of doubt enters their head: this is when they think of England.

There may well be experiential differences that partially

explain the English vice. 'I think the UK is heavily censored because of being an island,' suggests David Webb. 'Without that bit of sea, I can't believe that our isolation could have gone on for so long.' Being an island nation, not recently invaded, leaves some British people thinking that maybe we're superior to foreigners. Firstly our army is better – the foreigners may start the wars, but we finish them. Our education system is more ethical, our humour's better, our theatre, too; clothes, television, pop music – all better. Likewise our moral values are firmer: here civil servants cannot be so easily bought, and honest, toiling footballers don't take a dive every time they enter the opposition's penalty box. 'That island mentality,' says Webb, 'they are all wrong, and we are all right. It goes back to empire, king of the castle, holier than thou.' Webb remembers the time he challenged an MP on Britain's anomalous position on porn compared to the rest of Europe, when the backbencher replied, 'Well, just because all those foreigners do it, doesn't mean to say that we should.'

A picture starts to form, a familiar composite of paternalism, chauvinism and puritanism. It is a puritanism that deeply distrusts pleasure, which, according to Pat Califia, is what 'perverts' enjoy: 'for all pleasure is to some extent judged to be perverse'.[27] A chauvinism that not only distrusts all things foreign but maybe considers sex itself as something rather foreign, something suspiciously decadent, too cosmopolitan for a proper Englishman's appetite. A paternalism that doubts the wisdom of certain social classes being left to make up their own mind on things.

In contemporary Britain, the controlling inclinations of the political and class élites persist. In France during the eighties, Jack Lang, long-time minister of culture for the Mitterrand administration, declared it was not the business of the state to prevent adult citizens from seeing, hearing and reading what they like.[28] In contrast, a dim view of the voting masses continues to hold sway for many British parliamentarians. In 1993, Liz Lynne, the Liberal Democrat MP, persuaded over a hundred fellow MPs to sign a motion banning a new edition of Sade's *Justine*. This was a book she said she hadn't read, but

she had culled 'nasty' passages from it for a 'blue file' to distribute and use to convince other members of the wicked
nature of the text. The banning failed. The Campaign Against
Censorship subsequently wrote to the signatories asking them
if they felt they had been corrupted by offending passages. All
those who replied said they hadn't, but that they did not want
the book to become 'generally available'.

A box of scissors
(on a wider culture of expurgation in Britain)

It is necessary to see the story of porn and restraint as part of a
much broader narrative of censorship in British culture. The
notion of a private, personal liberty concerning adult materials
simply isn't tenable within a system of paternalist élites. In a
television interview in the spring of 1993, James Ferman,
Director of the BBFVC, said, 'We can't have freedom for adults
in this country, because we can't trust adults to protect
children.'[29] The desirability of a morality constructed around
the protection of children is debatable. This aside, Ferman's
admission contains the coded message that we fear we cannot
trust adults not to behave like children, therefore we must also
treat them as children.

In the daily realm of television broadcasting, a lack of confidence in grown-ups manifests itself not just within the repeated
warnings that preface assorted shows and films, but also within
the more hidden acts of cutting and dropping. A small selection
from numerous examples gives a picture of disdain for viewers.

The American thriller, *Three Days of the Condor*, is aired
about once a year on British television. This seventies film
about political paranoia builds its mood from suspense and
disorientation rather than through blood and gore. When the
hundred most violent movies list is compiled, *Three Days of The
Condor* won't chart. There is one scene where a regular postal
delivery turns into a botched effort to kill Robert Redford.
There's a hand-pistol with a silencer, a brief struggle and a
couple of muffled rounds go off. Sometimes this movie is
shown with a large part of this scene missing. After ten at night,

a film no more violent than a noir thriller from the forties is cut. And cut so badly. You see the postal officer at the front door, then the film visibly lurches and jumps, and literally the next thing you see is the postal officer lying dead on the floor. No explanation is given for his lying there shot. All sense of continuity has been abandoned.

On the internet, a critic of censorship describes the confused experience of watching a James Bond movie on British television during the nineties: 'TV censorship in this country is getting steadily more severe. Seen a Bond movie on the box recently? Every time you see one of the classic films there are more cuts, making it more and more incomprehensible.' The attentive critic explains how the movies are cut. 'No violence using ordinary objects as weapons is allowed. It's OK for people to be stabbed or shot but clobbering with the poker or strangling with the telephone cord is a no-no . . . Frequently, people who hadn't seen the original version would be hard pushed to figure what is supposed to be happening.'[30]

Programmers are often quite casual in their behaviour. In the television soap *Brookside*, when the character Beth Jordache famously kissed her girlfriend on the lips, and this 'lesbian' scene was removed from an early evening transmission, people got to hear about an overzealous Channel Four. In early 1996, however, when the Australian soap *Home and Away* had scenes cut that involved a brief flirtation between the character Shannon and an older woman, the cuts were made without comment. When chased on the matter by vigilant viewers, ITV announced that Shannon was due to resume being heterosexual soon. A whole episode of *Neighbours* was dropped when the story line was considered too raunchy. These acts of secret censorship represent an indifference towards the viewer that wouldn't be acceptable in other cultural spheres, with a Peter Greenaway film on Channel Four, for instance, or a BBC television production of *Titus Andronicus*.

What is also curious about television censorship is that sometimes the 'bad' scene is cut and other times it's left in. One year, for example, the film *Raging Bull* is transmitted without the bit where Jake La Motta is being teased about his next opponent being handsome, and La Motta says that the guy's so good-looking he doesn't know whether 'to fuck him or fight him'. But the next time the scene is played intact. The third time round, the lines have been dubbed over, sounding something like 'to flug him . . .' With the comedy *Broadcast News*, one time it is shown with the full scene of the return of the mercenary soldier saying 'fuck, fuck, fuck, fuck, fuck' to an unwelcome television reporter; another time it is maladroitly masked, sounding like 'flug, flug, flug, flug, flug'. Who knows which way it'll go next time, stick or twist?

The situation is so bad that when films like *Body Heat*, *American Gigolo* and *Fatal Attraction* are scheduled for BBC1 or ITV they'll have been so butchered that there's little point in tuning in. A kind of mass turn-off might have some impact with broadcasters who, like many of the movies they programme, work on the basis of the tease that goes partially unfulfilled – 'selling the sizzle, not the steak'. With a movie like *Basic Instinct*, the deception is at its most flagrant. Culturally, *Basic Instinct* mainly functions as a licit sex movie, the steamiest adult thriller, featuring dirty sex, weird sex, the crotch shot, and Michael Douglas shaping up at the disco in a V-neck sweater. This is certainly the way that it is promoted for broadcasting.[31] And yet it is cut. Sold on the basis of the tease, the television company then fails to deliver the goods. When questioned about this the channel claims that it's being judicious and even-handed: 'LWT must adhere to ITC regulations regarding sex, violence and language on TV programmes.'[32] This is disingenuous. It would be more honest to acknowledge prior to transmission that the movie has been interfered with.

There should be a switch around; every transmission that's been cut ought to come with a 'censored' warning. The bulk of censorship goes unseen in Britain. (Between 15 and 20 per cent of films released in Britain each year have been tampered with by the BBFVC.[33]) Media splashes over movies such as *Natural Born Killers*, *Kids* and *Crash*, or traditionally a television play from Dennis Potter, give the impression that suppression is the exception, the last resort contemplated with a liberal society's deep reluctance. In fact it is structural and insidious.

They could place a symbol in the top right-hand corner of the television screen (perhaps even the cinema screen) for the duration of the transmission, something like a box with a pair of black scissors.

In 1996, the BBC reported the findings of a survey of viewer attitudes and values that found that in these culturally fragmented times a common standard is hard to find – 'We no longer have a single audience who broadly hold the same jokes funny and the same insults offensive.' The survey did suggest, however, that viewers were becoming less agitated about sex on screen, with only 3 per cent of those surveyed voluntarily querying sex on television. But over in Westminster, in the Houses of Parliament, politicians continue to worry about levels of decency, of what Labour MP Jack Cunningham referred to as 'scenes of gratuitous sex'.[34]

The many rumours and reports of sleazy, dirty politicians who apparently find it so hard to keep their trousers on leave you wondering about their fitness for lecturing on matters of decency. In 1994, the Tory MP Stephen Milligan tragically died in pursuit of the risky erotic highs of solo auto-asphyxiation. It was reported that he was found with an orange in his mouth. The purpose of the fruit was lost on Nikki Wolf, publisher of *Fetish Times*. It was the *Daily Telegraph* who felt sure they knew what the orange was for. 'The establishment are all a bunch of perverts, just like me,' said Spencer Woodcock. In order to catch some 'perverts' in action at Club Whiplash, a private, members-only fetish club, police officers were 'required', during the autumn months of 1994, to go deep undercover wearing full fetish regalia on repeated visits.

So, maybe sex – all kinds of sex – isn't some dubious foreign delicacy after all. Rather an exotic pleasure for the few, that needs supervising when it involves the many. There was the MP who sat on the parliamentary committee on the Video Recordings Act of 1984 who was very critical of porn, specifically alluding to the 'dangers' of gay pornography that required it be kept from the wider public. During this period the very same member was a regular at a nearby house for gay porn nights with the VCR and a select group of friends.

As well as occasionally leaning towards hypocrisy, parliamentarians can often lack backbone. A campaigner tells a story concerning the parliamentary election campaign of the spring of 1992, when his local MP spoke at a pre-election constituency rally of how the Conservative Party was the party of freedom, choice, 'leaving people to get on with their own lives and do whatever they want to do'.[35] During the after-speech questions, our campaigner stood up and asked why, if the candidate's party supported freedom, did its election manifesto make a vigorous commitment to the anti-porn laws. Expecting to be lynched by a gathering of loyal party members, he was actually applauded. Though put on the spot like this, the candidate managed to produce a non-answer before moving on. Then, come the election day, the campaigner met his MP at the polling station, and pursued him on the matter. At this juncture, the MP literally looked over his shoulder, like a guilty schoolboy, checking to see that no one was listening, before admitting that of course the campaigner was right, that he also believed there should be much less censorship. But what could he do? 'My hands are tied,' he said.

His hands are tied to some extent by vocal lobby groups and sections of the media who seek to set the parliamentary agenda on matters of 'decency'. A steady pressure for censorship is maintained by certain vociferous newspapers. The motivation of the papers varies. Some are doing it for righteousness – battling for moral rearmament – while others exploit the frisson that sex stories supply. This titillation requires sponging off the deviancy that is simultaneously being scorned. It often begins in the courtroom. Anne McClintock has written of the trial of brothel owner Cynthia Payne in the early eighties, where the court was treated to long and titillating descriptions of sexual misadventure. The Old Bailey courtroom was filled with whips, belts and chains; turning blue with tales of spankings, lesbian shows, cross dressing; publicly relishing, in other words, the thought, as well the public display, of the very things it was there to condemn and forbid.[36] Such paradox and hypocrisy in the media leads to salacious, eye-grabbing headlines, with journalists detailing every last perversion. The *Daily Sport* covered proceedings at the trial of Club Whiplash. On the same page as a telephone sex ad offering '35 seconds of smutty mouth', the report mixed dismay with loving descriptions of activities witnessed at this 'depraved world of fetish sex': 'breasts were exposed, vaginas were exposed, penises were exposed . . . The music was loud – but the sound of whipping was louder . . . At the bar a woman and a black man and another man of Mediterranean appearance were sitting together [who could fail to note the additional sauce of racist myths]. She hitched up her dress, and had no knickers on.'[37]

High levels of media outrage make politicians nervous. A report in the *Daily Mail* of 23 November 1995 arrived with the banner headline: 'Turn the TV tide of sex and violence, demand MPs.' John Beyer, general secretary of the National Viewers' and Listeners' Association, the lobby group first started up by Mary Whitehouse, argues that a scene in Mike Leigh's *Naked* where you see an actor's limp penis is a suitable case for legal action: 'If that is not obscene by any definition then what is?' Beyer appears to believe that seeing a man's penis might deprave viewers. MPs hear this and rather than laugh they think they had better do something, or at least say something right-sounding. And so former minister John Patten suggests, 'The definition of obscene does need strengthening.' And MPs across the spectrum, including then Labour shadow minister David Blunkett, rush to back the need for toughening up the laws of obscenity.

A small demographic group of elected parliamentary representatives, noted for rarely watching television, are nevertheless convinced that some programmes are capable of depraving their audiences. Evidence indicates that the vast majority of the viewing public don't agree. The police often argue that there are many images on television of an 'obscene' nature but that the jury who would see it this way is almost impossible to find. Therefore what is needed, suggests the Tory MP David Liddington, are 'not only changes in the law, but also changes in public attitude'.[38] When people do not realise they are being corrupted it is time for re-education.

Satellite of love
(on blocking satellite porn)

In some ways these controlling performances may not matter. Parliamentarians may legislate, but people will still gravitate to their pleasure zone of choice, no matter what the *Daily Mail* says. The error is to see things as only top-down, hard domination. Cultural diversity, free markets and consumer power are dynamos that weaken the restrictive traditional moralities. It would be a mistake, however, to assume that people just doing their thing, regardless of law and social sanction, are going to fix everything.

British television porn is an example of a cultural change in the weather colliding with state control. The story of satellite and cable in the UK has been one of both advances and setbacks concerning censorship. (Likewise the internet, another new frontier technology – see Chapter 7, 'The Perils of Cyberspace'.) In contrast to cinema, television or radio, these new media delivery systems generally prove harder to filter totally. Alongside increased availability and access to materials, however, has been the British government's high-handed efforts to stop as much as they can. A service known as Red Hot Dutch was the first to get the treatment. Mark Garner and David Waller's Continental TV service, based in Manchester, organised for a Dutch-based adult film channel to be beamed via a Danish satellite to the UK. People with satellite dishes and encryption decoder cards to make sense of the beamed signal could receive a hard-core porn service. It is impossible for the government to block a signal physically. What they do is make it an offence to sell the decoder cards or to advertise or market the satellite service. To run a company premises in the UK connected to hard-core satellite porn is also against the law. As it is for the British media to accept advertising for the channel. To date, sales on the black market in the UK of porn decoder cards have not been extraordinary. The Metropolitan Police say they've never actually arrested anyone for selling decoders, or even heard of such operations. For the time being it is a crime without profile.

With television porn, two abominations of the British psyche conjoin: the dread of hard core and the fear of a foreign invasion. Accordingly, the British government continues to prohibit any satellite stations that arrive on the scene, like XXX, TV Erotica and Rendezvous. It is difficult to reasonably defend the blocking of satellite broadcasts, or to contend that a restricted feed after midnight is an issue concerning the public domain. Arguing for the protection of minors is hard to accept when the channels go out in the middle of the night and are encrypted. The selling of gateway decoder cards could easily be restricted to grown-ups. Nonetheless the British government banned TV Erotica as 'damaging to children's health and well-being'. An explanatory letter from the Department of National Heritage to the CAC continues, 'One of the perennial challenges in a free society is to ensure that the concerns and sensitivities of reasonable citizens are respected, but without unduly interfering in the rights of free speech and expression . . . it would be unacceptable to allow a complete free-for-all in broadcast material.'[39]

In the meantime, Red Hot Dutch pursues its legal challenge to prohibition through the slow-working mechanisms of the European legal system. Whatever the eventual outcome of this particular case, during a prolonged mood of Euro-scepticism it seems unlikely that the British government will be forced to change its ways.

All to play for
(on the future of porn in the UK)

So much of the story of porn in the UK is about explicit materials being censored into the relative oblivion of criminality, the furtiveness of unspoken pleasures, secreted stashes, plain-wrapper mailing. The positivity of new television delivery systems and extended television services is the moving of sex entertainment further into full view. The ever-spreading cable and satellite television network across the UK will be accompanied by a growth in subscriptions to the legal, British-based soft-core porn channels, reducing the porn fear factor within mainstream culture. The internet has already succeeded in altering the perception of many who thought they'd die if they ever saw a hard-core image. Soft-core television may well achieve similar shifts in opinions. All those gauzy, seductive soft-core movies from Vivid, VCA, Penthouse and Playboy could well see couples and individuals grow to be less afraid of porn, treating it as just another part of their leisure entertainments.

In this respect it doesn't much matter that services like the Fantasy Channel or the Playboy Channel programme a non-stop service of watered-down soft core. Television porn goes beyond issues of hard or soft options. Because of its restrictive porn laws, Britain missed out on its porn share of the video revolution. Though video pornware has been available during the last decade and a half, the positioning of pornography as illicit and separate has contributed to the notion of porn as a secret, bad thing. Twenty years of corner stores in the USA selling porn videos helped hard core to become more firmly established in American culture. The absence of porn at the local video and corner shop has meant that an equivalent cultural shift failed to develop in Britain.

In due course, some viewers of television porn may wonder why they only get the tease and limited nudity, with none of the real love action. At which point some porn pioneers may just start to push the boundaries a little. In America the previously immovably soft-core Playboy has in fact started letting the occasional erect penis show on its subscription cable channel. Although it won't necessarily be to the advantage of the present British sex industry, the viewing public's familiarity with soft core may breed a new market for hard core, as well as an increased advocacy for liberalising the laws.

For the present, companies like Northern & Shell and Playboy (UK) will stay soft. A porn television cartel equivalent to the magazine scene is fast approaching – assuming, of course, that soft-core television porn won't be outlawed in the future. The Church of England sold its shares in BSkyB, objecting to the transmission of soft core. The *Daily Mail* suggested that commercial companies who depend for their profits upon devout and god-fearing families ought to withdraw advertising from a satellite company prepared to 'peddle porn'.[40] These campaigns seem unlikely, however, to prevent companies extending their strictly soft-core markets. The future scenario for British television features digital, cable and satellite significantly adding to the established terrestrial services, promising to take the number of television channels into the hundreds. In such a deregulated landscape, and with the inevitable increase of niche, minority programming, of the *narrow*-casting of subscription, pay-per-view television, Reithian concepts of television being a medium that *broad*-casts to a singular viewing audience of a very tight singular morality will be recognised as no longer viable.

In law, in Parliament and large parts of the mainstream media, the mood remains anti-porn. From time to time, no doubt, newspaper thought-pieces and magazine features will tune in to television porn, and most likely the talk will be of snooze buttons, sad and lonely subscribers, and of viewing figures less than for the Cup Final, suggesting that television porn amounts to a great British turn-off. But they will have missed the point, which is that another line of information will have opened up, communicating to people the notion that sex and desire aren't bad for your health, variety and experimentation needn't ruin your life, and being a little bit voyeuristic doesn't make you bad.[41]

Establishing levels of porn consumption is difficult. It would seem that at present the demand for porn in the UK, especially hard core, is restricted. Nevertheless a buying market is out there. It is estimated that every day somewhere between forty and a hundred videos are sold per shop from the forty to fifty unlicensed outlets in Soho alone. Meanwhile, the extent of mail-outs in the mail-order sectors and the number of magazine titles on the top shelf indicate that there's a demand, that people are reaching out for porn. Poor box-office returns on films like *Striptease* or *Showgirls*, or the short-lived existence of the 'hot' London stage show *Voyeurz*, don't suggest, as many argue, that sex sells badly, more that bad films and bad theatre sell atrociously.

At the same time, state regulation does need rolling back in order for the culture to thrive. Twenty years ago, people could see *Deep Throat* in a cinema club in Soho, or occasionally even at late-night screenings at mainstream cinemas around Britain, without losing their soul. In late nineties Britain, a part of people's lives is being stifled. There's a need for an earth-turning moment when laws are changed. However there's little sign of positive legislation forthcoming from any of the parliamentary parties. Amidst anxieties over social upheaval, and an alleged moral collapse, sex is an easy target for blame, to cover for deeper social problems. Therefore the desirability of sexual censorship remains unaddressed. On the right, a precarious, pragmatic construct seeks to accommodate a version of libertarian economics with acceptable levels of authoritarianism in the social sector. Meanwhile the left, partly fearful of being associated with the blight of 'permissiveness', seems happy to concur. The new Labour administration of spring 1997 was greeted with little enthusiasm concerning the situation on sexual censorship. 'The Labour party in power is likely to be the last bastion in this country of anti-sex feminism,' declares Spencer Woodcock, at *Fetish Times*. 'Whereas say lesbians have pretty much moved on, as have a lot of people, anti-sex feminist arguments are still pretty current in the Labour party.'

The reluctance of the Labour Party to think differently in these areas has its own recent historical roots (see Chapter 3, 'Some History'). However, an anti-porn agenda does also fit into a longer-running puritan strand on the British left, a non-conformist repudiation of frippery, or the red-brick provincialist's distrust of metropolitan values, of the perceived sexual decadence of the bourgeoisie. Such tendencies suit residual doubts over the centrality of matters of sexuality or 'rights' within a political belief system that continues, at least at some level, to perceive economic relations as the heart of things, the hub from which all other matters radiate. Sex will often be noted only when it is perceived as being symptomatic of the pains of capitalism. For instance, the unemployed young man is viewed as more enfeebled through his spending an afternoon watching strippers, or masturbating to some dirty pictures.

The lack of an open-minded analysis of porn issues on the left has stunted the growth of a radical sex culture in Britain.[42] Porn went on selling during the seventies, eighties, and into the nineties, no matter how reviled. Market forces and desire saw to that. Meanwhile the left saw to it that heterosexual sex was rarely discussed other than in the context of exploitation. All that potential for pleasure and bliss was turned off as radical politics switched to greyness, grudge and lots of guilt. 'Anti-sex feminists were such a disaster,' suggests a porn fan, 'because they managed to police the left with regard to sexuality and desire, while not really stopping much porn from being sold. So people were probably still buying their magazine, and having a quiet wank, rather than going down to the Labour club and having an argument.'

The reticence over porn has contributed to its continued restriction in Britain. Any positive shift requires for this to change, for the commonplace perception of porn as a bad thing, far better dismissed and censored than thought about, to be challenged. There are areas of life where people who'd normally think themselves open-minded and tolerant of difference find their understanding runs out. This is often when they're discussing porn. As Tuppy Owens suggests, 'They can't think straight because they've been really indoctrinated about how terribly bad all that stuff is. That's the problem, that people stop being logical, and tend to get all emotional about things.'

The future for porn in Britain remains unclear, partly because of a lack of thought, and a lack of attention. This is the insidious nature of censorship. Prohibition may well increase as it also becomes less noticeable, to feature like the new computer technology increasingly features in our lives – being all around us, while becoming so transparent that, according to William Gibson, we hardly recognise that it's there any longer.[43] In terms of media technologies, a future of ratings and filter systems, of pre-installed internet 'nannies' and television 'V-chips', is slowly coming on stream. In theory the V-chip, the invention of Tim Collings from Simon Fraser University in Canada, will enable viewers to pre-programme their television set so that it will automatically veto any transmission-carrying materials that exceed their personalised levels of tolerance. As with many ratings or filter systems, it sounds reasonable, hardly like censorship, but a thing of personal choice. Of course, some people won't want chips as part of their television diet, as they have already learned to use the 'off' switch when something they don't like the look of comes on. Yet at the buying end, there'll be little choice, as the V-chip will be standard in all new television sets by the end of the decade.[44]

On the launch of assorted tools for controlling internet content during 1995 and 1996, it was suggested that access and browser software would still need to be switched on by individual users, and customised to suit their personal tastes and tolerance (see Chapter 7, 'The Perils of Cyberspace'). But, for how long will it stay like this? And can we assume that people will be bothered anyway? Indolence and technofear are all around. Most people are lazy where technology's concerned. We learn as little as is humanly possible about how to work alarm radios, microwave ovens, VCRs and computers. In order for the V-chip to function (likewise internet screening tools), the filtration will need to be 'switched on' by the manufacturers, arriving to the customer on a default setting of 'family values' consumption. And then those who prefer a bit more liberty will be required to do the disengaging themselves. To do so might require purchasing a de-installer, or to spend time poring over the instructions manual that explains how to switch off the blocker. It won't be impossible to do this, it will just be the harder option.

This kind of industry-wide and government-approved single morality is the alternative scenario for a future of media deregulation. In order for the proliferation of television outlets to go forward – of digital, cable, satellite television, of 200 channels, and niche programming – it could be that it is accepted that one television tradition will be retained in the new landscape, and that is the continuation of a controlled, standardised, and very *broad*-casting morality. A widening of choice might paradoxically result in a narrowing in the range of materials. More may mean less. The mass recliner culture, as described by techno-theorist Manuel de Landa, could beckon, featuring colourless, wall-to-wall mainstream entertainments, while amidst the new-tech backwaters and satellite hinterlands, for the small minority of people with the wit to make their way to such far-flung media holes, there'll be spots of raunchier stuff going on, and swearing too![45]

At York Minster, in the summer of 1996, the video artist Bill Viola was commissioned to provide an art installation. Part of the finished artwork included the video image of a naked man under water. Though the piece was curated with the knowledge and support of the Minster's church elders, it was threatened with removal on police advice for fear of causing offence. A solution was found which saw the display screened off from the rest of the church. All that it needs sometimes is for someone to complain about nudity – or the possibility that someone might possibly complain at a future point – for there to be action taken restricting access or the display of materials. Under such circumstances a multi-channelled pornocopian future seems in doubt.

In Britain there are occasions when we seem in danger of becoming governed by a moral view that deems all forms of nudity as questionable. A pluralist society that allows for discrepancies, whereby soft-core magazines are available in newsagents and images of nudity are removed from a church against the better judgement of the resident clergy, suggests a struggle that is ongoing. It is not desirable that a minority determines the levels of explicitness for all. If a few people don't like it, they can always look away. To re-embrace a universalism in society that upholds a singular moral standard will inevitably involve the exclusion, demonisation and possible criminalisation of deviant sexualities and acts, while simultaneously enabling a restrictive moral code, approved by the few, to be foisted upon the many.

5

Not the Wild West
porn in the USA

Porn USA is based in Van Nuys in the San Fernando Valley in
Southern California. The bulk of the mainstream porn film
industry moved here in the mid-eighties, lock, stock and lube.
It would be entertaining to think that the reason porn people
gathered together in this uninspiring district of Los Angeles
County has something to do with the feeling of safety in
numbers. Spurned and reviled by mainstream society, chased
to the end of the American continent, like in the Westerns, the
porners rounded up their wagons in a tight circle to protect
themselves from the onslaught, maybe to fight their last stand,
or perhaps to survive.

It is a romantic notion. Though it may have some distant
psychological resonance, derived not least from the tendency
some porners have of billing themselves as carnal pioneers,
sexual frontierspeople, outlaws of the flesh – 'We're the last
gang in town,' says director John Stagliano – the truth is more
prosaic. The reason porn in the USA gets made in Van Nuys is
the rent's cheap, the equipment-hire rates are cheap, the
beautiful people who didn't quite make it into nearby Hollywood or television come relatively cheap, and the sunshine's for
free. So no wagon-ring mentality, just opportunity and
common sense. And anyway, as the nineties move towards a
close, and film porn moves through its third decade overground, talk of a frontier spirit seems misplaced; any thoughts of
last stands and rebel yells that there might have been once upon

a time are fast receding, certainly within the larger companies, with their media-friendly porno de luxe.

In these times of an alleged increase in sexual deferment, when, according to the 'Sex in America' survey of 1994, '36 percent of men age eighteen to twenty-four had no sex with a partner in the past year, or had sex just a few times', and during an era when, unsurprisingly, many Americans are reckoned to be reacquainting themselves with the joys of solo sex, the business of proxy carnal gratification is big.[1] A lot of this proxy action for the generation xxx is taking place on screen. Be it hard core, soft core, rented, piped in, or sent away for, *Wet-TV* is a boom phenomenon. An estimated 20 million American households have access to porn subscription channels, via satellite and cable. Out on the road, plenty of hotel chains offer programmed, pay-per-view cable featuring soft-core adult movies.[2]

During the middle to late nineties, the sales volume for the adult video industry in America is around 4 billion dollars. Despite the fact that there are several 'taboo' states and 'non-X' districts across the country, the adult share of the overall video market in the USA is around 15 per cent. Which makes porn a bigger draw than Disney.[3] In more liberal regions such as the West Coast and Northeast, adult's share of the video rentals market is 40 per cent. General video stores in these two regions stock on average 600 to 700 adult titles. Meanwhile the boom in sell-through continues. Though some people are still happy just to rent *Buttslammers 3* along with Scorsese's *Casino* for the weekend, others are buying them outright at ten dollars a throw, theirs to keep for the rest of eternity. Porn-makers are also diversifying their markets. New formats and new technologies, such as laser discs, CD-ROM, DVD, and subscription sites on the world wide web, provide new revenue streams. As porn in the USA grows, it is also evolving into a regular, mature industry. The tone at production companies like Vivid, VCA and Wicked may not be so starchy just yet, not quite conservative, but it is focused and corporate, and certainly not the wild west.

All about Teri Wiegel

(on America's new porn acceptability)

On my first night in pornland I was invited to go see a movie by its director. *All About Teri Wiegel* – 'So good, it would make Pat Buchanan sick' (*Hustler*) – was directed by Gino Colbert. Gino used to be an actor in gay porno who switched to director-producer in the early nineties. He now makes gay and straight movies, both as a freelancer for large production companies and as an independent. *Teri* is a pet project: not only did Gino direct and produce, he also financed, edited, organised the publicity, and did just about everything else. He even came to pick me up, driving me to the film and back again afterwards. For the Friday and Saturday late shows, Laemmle's Cinema, a regular multiscreen on Sunset and Crescent, was running Gino's movie. Last week it did the same with a gay title he made. Laemmel's is not a low-rent dive but a trendy cinema. Apart from *Teri*, the line-up that night included *Chungking Express*, *City of Lost Children* and John Schlesinger's *Cold Comfort Farm*. Outside a crowd of young hipsters were queueing for *Welcome to the Doll House* on the first weekend of its release. But it turned out that some of them were actually there for *Teri*. Ms Wiegel is a big name in porn, a former *Playboy* centrefold who crossed over to hard core, a still relatively rare career move for a star of soft core. (The reason she did, she tells us in the movie, is she 'loves to suck dick'.) On this particular night *Teri* actually did better box office than John Schlesinger.

The cinema was three-quarters full, including a lot of single men, but also several couples. There was a couple in the row in front of me, and the girlfriend kept looking round at the audience before the lights went down. She seemed a bit anxious about what she'd been persuaded to see. A quarter of an hour in, with one hard-core scene down and another already under way, she was nudging him in the side, whispering in his ear loudly, before finally they both got up and left. Everybody else stayed put however, joined by some girls from another screen who crept in without paying. The audience seemed entertained, but perhaps not always in a quintessentially pornographic way. A gang of teenagers at the front, three girls and three boys, were highly enthralled, lurching from loudly amused to loudly grossed out by the graphic sex – the explicitness made more arresting because the video, blown up for a large screen, had turned the performers' genitals a shade of purple.

There was certainly a lot of laughing during the film. A lot of which was likely down to embarrassment. If the laughter bothered Gino, he didn't let it show. He just seemed happy to be having his film screened alongside regular movies, a small dose of the spirit of 'crossover' redolent of hard core's golden age of the seventies. But not a serious bid for mainstream status. Though it was interesting to see a hip young audience taking in an adult film at the multiplex, this was not the way the new porno credibility of the nineties was shaping up.

As I was to learn, mainstream Porn USA is currently having a good run of things. Profits need to be worked for, and legal harassment remains a worry, but, for the first time in two decades, movie hard core is almost cool again. An industry that has always been on the margins has partially come in out of the cold and is finding itself more socially acceptable than it has been in a long while. Acceptance has come through video, in the main. More recently things have speeded up because of the impact of cable and of such phenomena as Howard Stern, and the radio host's fondness for having hard-core stars on his show.[4] And then in late 1996, the porn stars Janine (Lindemuller) and Nikki Tyler were on *The Tonight Show* with Jay Leno and, according to *Adult Video News*, 'the adult industry reached a new level'.[5] There's also the internet. Millions of porn users are not only swapping dirty pictures but also having conversations about their favourite hobby for the first time ever, discussing best movies and favourite stars without feeling furtive or guilty. People are curious about porn again and the sleaze factor is somewhat in abeyance. 'Once it was a question of taboo,' writes a porn fan, 'but slowly, perhaps because of the internet, it is returning to its status of quotidian that it had in the seventies.'[6]

During 1996 and into 1997, even Hollywood seemed to be falling for its poor little orphan cousin, with a boomlet of hard-core-related projects in the pipeline. There was *The People v Larry Flynt*, produced by Oliver Stone and directed by Milos Foreman, and *Boogie Nights* with Marky Mark playing a porn stud. Gossip had Christopher Walken and Abel Ferrara making something about porn. There were even rumours circulating of Ron Howard, director of *Splash* and *Apollo 13*, doing the Linda Lovelace story. After all, porn's a pretty good story to tell about. And yet were these movies going to tell it like it is?[7] Rarely does the outside world visit pornland without a hatchet in its haversack, with the word 'sleaze' carved in its handle, ready to bury it deep. I wanted to do something else, to demonstrate how this newly confident, newly socially acceptable porn industry of the second half of the nineties is also a proper industry. 'People don't realise that this is a very professional business,' says the porn actress Julie Rage. 'I think it is important that people try to learn that,' adds Jenteal, 'It's not a fucked-up industry.' The hard-core industry is not only a lot safer and more proper than readers might imagine, but the bulk of its product is getting tamer by the year. Another reason why we talk of not the wild west.

At the Waag
(on the set of a porn film)

The day after my night at the pictures with Gino in West Hollywood, I got a cab to the Waag Building, an aeroplane parts warehouse in the middle of nowheresville, Van Nuys. It's Sunday, on a holiday weekend, and it's a rather desolate part of the San Fernando valley, next to the railway tracks, on the other side of which squats a large Budweiser factory. The production is a post-apocalypse, retro-futurist science-fiction film in the style of *Blade Runner* or *Strange Days*, with hard-core sex as the main event. The movie is called *AD 6969*. It stars Christy Canyon, and features Julie Rage, Melodie, Stephanie Swift, TT Boy, Jon Dough, and Sindee Cox.

This is a five-day shoot, featuring a decent-sized crew, and costing over $150,000 – a lot for contemporary porn. The movie will be shot on film, not video, and have a proper plot and story line, an extensive, detailed script, including expository scenes and non-sexual action sequences, and even a spot of kung fu. This is 'high end' porno. Not all the porn made in the Valley is like this. But late-decade, high end is where the big porn story is occurring. This is day four of filming. Sindee's day. Her big sex scene with TT Boy is coming up later. David, production manager for the shoot, takes me through to make-up to be formally introduced. First he checks that she's decent. Sindee is indeed decent and currently in conference with the make-up man over the state of her hair. We shake hands, and she resumes her root panic.

The story concept for *AD 6969* is that men are an endangered species. Every time men copulate, they die. So they don't copulate. Imagine all that enforced celibacy, that pent-up testosterone, building up and bursting to be a pop shot. The opening scene of *AD 6969* occurs in a post-apocalypse warehouse (in other words, this late twentieth-century warehouse, plus green and red lighting and blasts of dry ice). The men in frame are wearing distressed jerkins, shredded loincloths and plastic girdles painted with crude phallic symbols. *Thus Spake Zarathustra* is playing, as they gather around an ice box, relic from the twentieth century. One of them opens it up and they all go crazy, 'yipping and yahooing', it says in the script. In the commotion the ice box is accidentally knocked over, disgorging its fearful contents across the floor. Without comment the camera closes in on a fanned selection of vintage *Playboy* magazines. I think we get the picture. Hugh Hefner would be delighted to learn that the only things from the twentieth century to survive are ice boxes, the need to have sex, and *Playboy*.

In between the sex, *AD 6969* will involve assorted action sequences, chase scenes and shoot-outs. 'It's a basic good guys bad guys syndrome', explains Julie Rage. There are also to be various futuristic trappings and gadgets. That is to say, toy store camouflage combat hats, shiny bin liners, squirt guns painted silver with toy aeroplane wings glued on the sides, gold sprayed shin pads, to go with the silver *Barbarella* dresses. For it doesn't matter how high end you call it, $150,000 doesn't buy a lot of props. 'I play a good guy,' Rage continues. 'I play a scientist who has discovered the cure to keep men from dying after they ejaculate, and I am banished from civilisation by Christy Canyon for trying to administer it to my lover, who is also her lover. And so we escape into the "wild country", and Christy programmes a female cyborg to go after me and kill me. But in fact the cyborg falls in love with me instead.'

And the ending? 'And the ending is I'm pregnant. Which makes me the first female to be pregnant in about a million years.'

Ordinary People

(on 'couples porn')

AD 6969 is a Vivid picture. Vivid is a producer, manufacturer and distributor of adult erotica. The company brings its product to the masses in the form of video, direct broadcast cable, interactive CD-ROM, DVD, laser discs, novelty merchandise, and its own web site which receives 1 million hits a day. Cyberspace aside, Vivid, I'm told, 'is in every country in the world that will handle it'. Even the UK takes Vivid in its soft-core incarnation on video and the Playboy cable channel.

Vivid has been trading for over a dozen years. In terms of volume of product and turnover it is the largest hard-core entertainment company in America. Worldwide only Sweden's Private is in the same league.[8] There are at present around a hundred people working for the company. Vivid is on a big growth curve, with profits climbing in the region of 20 per cent a year. The long recession in California didn't really hurt a lot. Porn is an industry that tends not to suffer in times of cutback.

Paul Thomas is the producer of *AD 6969*. PT, as he is generally known, is a figure of some significance within the industry. He was a regular film and theatre actor in the early seventies, performing on stage in *Hair*, and playing Peter in Norman Jewison's film version of *Jesus Christ Superstar*. In 1975, PT made his life-changing switch to porn. 'I got in because I loved it. Because it was a lot of fun. I found it unbelievably wonderful to be paid for doing this.' Later he started making his own porn films. Now the director-producer works exclusively for Vivid and is the company's chief image-maker. Thomas is the master craftsman of the high-end 'couples' movie – good-quality porn with a story and a cut-price luxury sheen to go with the sex. Hard core that bears some passing cinematic resemblance to movies they show at the local multiscreen, and not at all like the hard-core loops they used to run at a 42nd Street peepshow.[9]

A 'Paul Thomas' film – one with PT as producer or director – will be in the range of seventy minutes long, will feature a dramatic set-up and look a real picture: shot on film, with good photography, featuring nice locations, as well as the best-looking talent working in the business. Considering the product-hungry assembly-line conditions under which he works, Thomas turns out a fetching, seductive erotic package. You watch a PT movie and marvel at how opulent it looks on the low budget he's working with. Such glossiness will come as quite a surprise – and who knows, maybe a turn-on – to those who thought they knew what porn was, thought that it was some kind of greasy, non-stop fuckfest filmed on a rancid mattress in someone's garage. Five or six sex scenes should be expected in this kind of movie (though it can go lower), but double penetrations and gangbangs should not. Like his directorial rivals in high end such as Andrew Blake, Michael Ninn, Cameron Grant and Candida Royalle, Thomas offers porn for people who don't want simple, in your face – or in somebody else's face – hard core. A porn for newcomers perhaps, for high end tends to be gentle with first-timers and couples.

The notion of the 'couples market' is mostly a thing of hunch work in the absence of market research. The hunch is that there's a genre of porn video that has an audience of couples out there, ready and eager for it – be they watching at home on video in glorious hard core, or the soft-core version available on cable subscription, or piped into their hotel rooms, while on a trip out of town. During a prolonged stay in dreary Van Nuys, where there's nothing to do, every night in the motel I saw waiters going back and forth from the restaurant building delivering room service. Next day, trays with stacks of empty plates were waiting to be collected outside the rooms. Everyone was staying in and watching television. The hotel provided eight pay-per-view cable channels to compliment the regular service. Four of the eight channels were showing a non-stop feed of soft-core porn – Vivid movies, starring Christy Canyon, Chasey Lain, Jenteal, Racquel Darrian. All those couples staying in and nesting, night after night. All that porn on tap.

Couples are porn's dream viewership, bringing mutuality, respectability and a steady inflow of revenue. The kind of demographic unit that when renting from the video store might pick up a Disney movie for the kids, a family movie, something like *Forrest Gump* or *Independence Day*, and an adult title for after the kids have gone to bed. A Paul Thomas film maybe. Ideally this video rental transaction would be taking place at the local chain – Blockbusters, in other words. But Blockbusters for the time being has a strictly no-adult policy with its stock. Therefore, companies like Vivid need the local, independent, so called 'mom and pop' stores. Likewise mom and pop need Vivid. It's a very symbiotic relationship. Adult is a good investment for small shops. It doesn't cost a lot wholesale and it rents well, and for a number of years. Most of all, it's one thing Blockbuster doesn't stock. Sometimes this can give the small-timers the edge. A porn retailer told me a story about a little corner shop outfit in New York. In the early nineties a Blockbuster opened up across the street. You'd have thought this was curtains. Not so. The independent continued to thrive while Blockbuster eventually closed down. And the suggested reason for this famous victory of David over Goliath? The little corner shop had adult videos and Blockbuster didn't.

'Adult has always been a fringe part of the economy. But we've become increasingly more mainstream with video cassettes,' says a Vivid executive. 'We now have a complete generation that has grown up with the video store on every corner, where baby-boomers brought home an adult video from the corner store, so they're used to it. It's a slow process, but the video story started in 1980 and it is now 1996. And these days, what we are seeing is people now aspire to be in our industry . . . Things are changing.'

The novelist Anne Rice has talked of the way eighties America sent out mixed signals on sexual freedom. 'I think it was in 1980 that I saw *Kramer vs Kramer* . . . and I felt at that point that we were for a backslide into puritanism . . . But the strange thing was that this neopuritanism or whatever it was . . . as soon as it started to gain momentum, you had movies like *Dirty Dancing* cropping up.' Rice remembers the 'real' fifties, and it wasn't like *Dirty Dancing*, 'We didn't dance like that in the fifties! Nobody did! The dancing in that movie is shockingly erotic. Yet obviously the American people wanted that movie.' The American public wanted other things too: 'They wanted X-rated videos, and they wanted them in the corner store. They wanted to take them home and play them on their VCR. They simply didn't settle for the new puritanism, whether it was being packaged for them by the Republican administration or by the feminist movement.'[10]

Wake up sleepy head
(on some of the things you see on a porn set)

It's not until late in the afternoon that PT shows up on the set of *AD 6969*. And then shortly afterwards he's gone again for the day. He tells me he likes producing because you don't have to work long hours. The director working the long hours is Jeremy Sullivan. Jeremy is in his early thirties, skinny, pale, bearded – cine nerdish and manically busy keeping things rolling. He's the son of porn director Ron Sullivan, also known as Henri Pachard. Pachard has been in the business from the start. He has made over a hundred hard-core films and countless videos, including *Devil in Miss Jones II*, *Sexcapades* and *Great Sexpectations*. Henri is noted for being good with comedy and for always featuring a sex scene in the toilet. Late last night he 'wrapped' his latest project. It was a 'she-male' video, although he says the performers told him not to call it that. Today he's making a brief cameo performance for his son's big film. He plays a eunuch in sunglasses and a monk's habit, wearing his severed testicles in a chain-mail pouch around his neck. Henri is now into his fifties, with his glory years well behind him, and his son is using him as a eunuch monk. But Henri doesn't seem bothered about the casting; he's just happy to be around, emotionally confessing to me how proud he is that Jeremy's gone into the same business.

It takes a couple of hours to get started in the warehouse. There are two sets erected at the same time. The director and crew flit between them, preparing the set-ups and fixing any technical problems. Anyone who thinks porn productions are a big party, with orgies going on all over the place, can forget it. 'A porno movie is just a film with sex in it,' says the director Steve Perry (a.k.a. Ben Dover). 'A Hollywood movie is a film without the [hard-core] sex, with a bigger budget so there's four people to move the light instead of one. But we make films in the traditional way.'[11] The mood on set is relaxed, and not too intense, but at the same time people are busy getting on with things. Some of the crew are young film-school graduates who see porn as a fast-track route to getting close to the filmmaking action. They talk a lot about technical stuff, really interested in the demands of filming, with Hollywood and MTV hovering over their shoulders.

I look at the shooting script. Usually a porn script is minimal in length, three to four pages, but this one is twenty plus. It's written by someone called Guillermo Brown. Which sounds like another *nom de porn*. There's a lot of them about. Starting with flagrant they pass through funny, to silly and beyond. There's Julie Rage, Christy Canyon, Chasey Lain, Jenteal, Nico Treasures, Nikki Sin, Misty Rain, Champagne, Chardonnay, Cortknee, Monique DeMoan, Tina Temptress, Lisa Lipps, Scarlett Fever . . . The list is endless. Few porners stick with their real names (Janine Lindemuller and Paul Thomas are rare exceptions). Everyone has his or her reasons. In porn the primary motivation is protecting privacy, avoiding the stigma, and making firm the split between who you are and what you do for a living.

Most porners get into the swing of having a different working persona, this idealised, sexy version of themselves. 'I couldn't possibly be as outgoing, or eccentric, or sexual, in my jeans and sweaters,' says the actress Jeanna Fine. 'When I put on the false eyelashes and the dominatrix boots and my costume, over-drawn lips and full drag queen make-up . . . I instantly find the character.'[12] In the video *Behind the Scenes*, about life on a hard-core movie set, a young actress, 'Mona Lisa', is in make-up at the start of the day, freshly scrubbed, wearing her regular clothes, and a member of the crew says, 'You look like a college girl,' and she replies, 'I *am* a college girl.' Later on she shows up on screen totally made up as a hot and horny sex diva.

Likewise on set today. Sindee Cox has now also gone into her porn megababe persona. From regular-looking in jeans and T-shirt she's become the love goddess from planet sex in exotic make-up, big platinum hair, combat trousers and a cut-off top that barely covers her stupendous siliconised assets. She looks gorgeous, if unreal. Sindee laughs a lot, apparently unfazed by, if even particularly aware of, being the porn woman sur-rounded by a mostly male film crew. The men are very natural with her. There's a lot of joking around. Sindee says she likes being on a long shoot such as this, because you get to know the people a bit. She and Henri rehearse their forthcoming scenes together. They improvise from the script, 'bending' their lines till they feel right for them, even try 'slipping on each other's lines' a little. They agree they like to do this, improvising quite well together. But the shame is, once they've got the lines, they almost immediately start to lose them again. Meanwhile, Sindee's romantic lead for today, the actor TT Boy, arrives late on set and then proceeds to talk to nobody other than himself. TT Boy is porn's would-be rebel and reportedly the least favourite male lead with the porn women. Described by an industry chum as 'a life-support system for a penis', he flexes his muscles a lot and occasionally lands a semi-punch at pieces of furniture, glowering amidst the camaraderie.[13]

Three short link-scenes are shot over the next couple of hours. Scene one has Sindee typing, with Pachard tied up in the chair beside her. Sindee's playing a villain and she's just seized the computer from Henri. In the next scene she has Pachard, who is still wearing his sunglasses despite the dark, pornocopia

take over at the screen. She hands him a sex chip to be inserted in order to bring her cyborg lover to life. TT Boy's the cyborg, rather appropriately. 'Modelled on a twentieth-century porno star,' says Pachard, improvising. As the chip kicks in the cyborg stops being statuesque and becomes a man. 'Good evening,' says TT Boy.

On to scene three, in which TT Boy and Sindee play house together. This third set-up is from another segment earlier on in the movie. 'An abandoned medical facility,' according to the shooting script, 'with plastic crates and junk stacked around the various pieces of medical equipment. ARIANA sleeps naked on an x-ray machine table. She is a blonde beauty. At the head of the x-ray table is a TV and video playback unit, its wiring exposed. Suddenly the blank screen lights up with the picture of a 20th century WOMAN sleeping in a 20th century bedroom.'[14] This is the scene being filmed. The twentieth-century bedroom is minimal, a black curtain for a backdrop and a mattress. It is early day, the morning of their fifth anniversary, and Sindee is sleeping. Meanwhile TT Boy is fooling around with the video camera that's her anniversary present to him. I don't think TT Boy is a cyborg in this particular scene. He is prowling with his video camera, especially around the sleeping Sindee. In porn, you're never far away from some kind of reference to voyeurism. He lifts up the cover and slowly scans her curled-up body. Sindee's twentieth-century bedwear is a pair of high-riding, black latex shorts, a black latex crop-top, and a pair of patent stilettos. Well, you didn't really expect striped pyjamas and fluffy slippers did you?

Gently TT Boy rouses Sindee from her slumber: 'Wake up sleepy head.' Sindee stretches and yawns. Blinking at the camera, she lightly scolds TT Boy for opening his present early. And then it is her turn. He hands Sindee a package. She opens it up, and inside is the skimpiest net vest, a barely fabricked thing. It's just what she wanted, she says. He suggests she try it on, she does, and for the first time today the scripted dialogue stops – silence ensures the viewer is not distracted from the body show. We are now in the moment, we have nudity.

Sindee has a great body, for sure, but her breasts are simply amazing – like two large, plastic globes. The nineties has seen a burgeoning of silicone and saline implants, both in porn and the mainstream. A woman new to Los Angeles told English *Vogue* about when she and some friends were sunbathing in the park, and she looked around and realised that something wasn't quite right, 'My colleagues' breasts were all rigidly saluting the sun – they were like pith helmets – while mine slouched miserably towards my sides.'[15] Whether porn fans like fake chests is a moot point. In recent times there's been a small-sized backlash against silicone. A company called Realistic Pictures insist on using real-breasted women in their productions, as, in the main, do directors like John Leslie, John Stagliano and Patrick Collins, while the actress Jenteal tells me the chest doctor's definitely not getting hold of hers. 'Because of the frequency of implants in the industry, a lot of people are really interested in seeing natural-breasted women. Their chests just look so big and fake and it's getting really old hat.'

Back on set, Sindee has put her chest away, just about covered by the net suit. TT Boy is filming her up close. Sindee mugs for the camera while he choreographs her movements, having her pose this way and that. 'Put your legs in the air and spread 'em.'

With Vividtude
(on the producers and the state of the industry)

Tucked away off the main strip and down some sleepy residential streets in suburban Van Nuys, you'll find Vivid HQ. This ordinary-looking, single-storey breeze-block affair – basically a series of small warehouses strung together and uniformly painted yellow – is where the bulk of the operation is housed. David Kastens, an executive at Vivid, used to work in the music business before moving into porn in the late seventies. He gives me the brief tour of the shop. From the modestly plush front section for the executive staff, we move back through international, where they sell the fantasy product globally. There's a woman on the phone, speaking French. Kastens tells me that she sold a hundred Vivid movies to German cable television the other day. We move on past post-production – where the guys edit down the raw footage into pornware, and curse about the camera operator's failure to keep in focus – and through Interactive, the testing suite for their new-technology applications, which are researched and developed at another site. Then onwards through sales, publicity, offices, stockrooms and so on.

Vivid releases four new titles a month, around fifty in an average year. I checked out the colour-coded tape stock filed away: Vivid Straight is blue, Vivid Gay – yellow, Vivid Cable – black, and so on. Vivid Gay is a line of gay materials put together by Jim Steele, whose Heart of Steele Productions produces exclusively for Vivid. Though not as important to Vivid as straight, because the hetero market is bigger, gay nonetheless remains a valued sector, commanding a higher price, as buyers tend to be more loyal and more affluent, and mostly more easily reached. Then there's also the Vivid compilations, gay and straight, which account for an extra dollop of releases onto the 'adult erotica' market. And let's be clear about the product, what we're talking about: this is not porn, this is adult erotica. The words are important?

'The words are important,' says Kastens, 'I've never been comfortable with the word pornography. I truly wish the Greeks had never invented it. But we're stuck with it. You see the problem is porn in the US tends to be lumped in with other materials which are considered to be obscene. Vivid do not trade in obscenity.'

It's the middle to late nineties, twenty-five years since hard-core porn became part of the entertainment landscape, since porn stopped being underground and under the counter, stopped being stags and loops and started being proper movies. Twenty-five years since *Deep Throat*, and the birth of the adult entertainment industry. By the mid-seventies, following a year or so of *Deep Throat* and porn chic, hard-core porn had established itself above ground as an ongoing industrial concern, apparently beyond snuffing out. However, no one ever actually said porn was legal in America, constitutionally protected free speech: they never said it about *Deep Throat*, and they haven't ever said it since. In the seventies the US Supreme Court decided to leave it up to community standards, which means there's no common legal standard or certainty for the adult industry (see Chapter 1, 'Definitions'). Though filming porn is licit in the state of California, there are parts of the state where you won't find adult videos on sale, even parts where just a few years ago there was talk of banning string bikinis. 'We're like a schizophrenic country,' says Kastens. 'Anytime you have a country with 260 million people, you're going to have a lot of different views.'

Although the adult industry had a rough time in the late eighties, during the Reagan and Bush administrations, by the mid-nineties it finds itself to be a fairly stable and settled business. Apparently porn is here to stay. And yet, strictly speaking, porn isn't legal. It is hard to think of an equivalent business that occupies a twilight world of legally trading but is not quite legitimate. That's the strange thing, porn is a business always in danger of being prosecuted. People who make porn go to jail sometimes. This creates some peculiar situations. Video piracy remains a problem in the porn industry. To combat this companies are supposed to use the FBI on copyright infringement. But this is the same FBI that's often trying to put the porners in jail. 'They really don't want to go out on these cases,' says Kastens. 'There have been instances when companies have had to go to court to force them to do something about the situation.'

It was video that saved porn in the USA during the eighties and the dog days of the backlash against the industry. Porn continued to grow because of video. Without it, restricted only to sex shops and sex cinemas, hard core might not even have survived. You can shut down adult cinemas because of lewd behaviour, can make mail order sales too risky for producers, and chase adult stores out of 'good' communities, saying they lower the tone, and hence neighbourhood property values. Over time, however, zoning video porn out of existence proved not to be possible, as adult sections in local video rental stores dug in. In this sense, video porn became part of too many people's lives to bust and harry into oblivion.

What survived the big squeeze, however, often turned out to be not that great. The so-called 'silver age' of porn was quite a short-lived affair. Within a few years of video coming to dominate the market, hard core experienced a serious drop in quality. As the adult video market grew, the industry itself expanded and opened up. Hard core had once been like a cottage film industry distributing to a more controlled movie house market. With video instead of a few cinema chains, there was a larger, more flexible distribution and retail scenario, and therefore a more competitive marketplace. More producers entered the industry, exploiting the cheaper video technology to turn out more and cheaper product. Suddenly $20,000 budgets were too high. Competitors were doing movies for $18,000, $15,000, $12,000. A lot of porn made in the valley came to be shot in a day. A movie would go into production in the morning and, six scenes and six pop shots later, following twelve to sixteen hours of hard labour, another 'one-day wonder' would be finished. One-day wonders were made with as little fuss as possible, a video-camera operator, a bed, a slice of pizza for lunch. In the main, cinematic art was no longer a big concern.[16] Getting the requisite number of pop shots and an okay distribution deal was what mattered. The only real care invested was in producing a sexy box-cover to lure the punter.

From about 1986 to 1990 the output from the adult industry was mainly low-grade material. The sex became mechanical sex a lot of the time, formula porn: 'blow, dog, mish, pop!' – 'blow-job, then doggy style, then missionary position, followed by pop shot', as Jeremy Sullivan explains. And then amateur came along. Once the mass-produced video cameras emerged onto the market, a lot of ordinary people started committing their lovemaking to videotape posterity. Avedon Carol suggests that amateur was a women-led development. Women who as teenagers took their new partners into a photo booth for a strip of pictures of them together, maybe kissing, spotted the potential with video and took a lead. 'Women like to take pictures, to have records of events. How many people have private collections, one can only guess. And the next step is, why don't we sell this?'

In the mid-eighties, early murmurings started off an amateur network, a future trend, with outfits like Susan's Video Exchange offering a swap-and-buy service in home-made hard core. Though technically a lot of amateur wasn't that brilliant, by this point neither was a lot of the commercial porn. 'It really was just couples in Nebraska,' remembers Jeremy Sullivan. 'And it was hot sex a lot of the time and the feeling was refreshing for the viewer.' Amateur hurt the industry, draining off sales. For a while people panicked. 'I was at a trade show,' remembers David Kastens, 'and a shop owner in Detroit said, "You can walk into my store and you won't see one Vivid or VCA tape. All I have is amateur, that's all I get asked for."'

But the excitement didn't last. The novelty palled. 'People realised that they didn't always want to watch ordinary people fuck,' says Gino Colbert. 'The girl or boy next door getting nailed has limited erotic appeal.' After panicking, the porn industry's more measured response to amateur was to swallow it up. The majors started distributing it, or running their own ranges, as well as mimicking its style. 'Amateur' became a bunch of long-serving members of the industry cooking up a show at 'home', yet marketing like it was part of the original pioneering amateur spirit. Though there continues to be an avowedly amateur scene, the threat of amateurs has been reduced to no threat at all, and to just another subgenre.[17]

Porno de luxe
(on how porn went upmarket again)

At the turn of the nineties, following the impact of video, amateur and the rise of the one-day-wonders, a few of the large hard-core production companies such as Vivid and VCA took stock of the situation and decided they needed to do something, to invest a little in their pornware and bring the quality of the product back up a little to stand out from the rest of the pack. Around this time a director called Andrew Blake started making exquisitely polished, relatively high-cost hard-core movies that made their producers a large profit. This was a key moment in the story of nineties hard core. This success marked the end of the undisputed reign of the one-day wonder.

Blake's *Night Trips* and *Hidden Obsessions* are stylish, glossy, impressionistic mood pieces, and quite a lot like hard-core pop videos. *Hidden Obsessions* is a portmanteau movie made up of vignettes that link together as the fantasies of a woman novelist. Between the fantasy scenes the novelist, played by Janine, is to be seen masturbating. There are twelve short scenes. In 'Diamonds and Pearls', Randy West and Francesca Le play sex games together, with blindfolds and shaving and pulling jewellery out of intimate orifices. It's all very *9 ½ Weeks*. In 'Diamond Rain', huge diamond raindrops fall as Celeste and Woody Long make love. Then there's 'Thirties Fantasy' with Melanie Moore and Randy West screwing in period gangster clothes. 'Espionage' is shot in black and white, with Dominique playing a spy in a hard-core situation. Most famous of all is 'Ice Dildo'. Shot at night in a luxurious penthouse overlooking the glittering downtown LA nightscene, it features Janine and Julia Ann playing with a transparent dildo. As they proceed to insert the dildo inside each other, it begins to melt, as the dildo is made of ice. Intercut with this are shots of Janine the novelist masturbating alone by her swimming pool. The scene ends with droplets of water from the fast-disappearing dildo falling onto her tongue. It is the best-known image in modern porn.

Blake is the most technically accomplished director in porn. His 'look' is greatly admired. He lights scenes beautifully, and makes everybody look gorgeous as they play out fantasy scenarios straight out of Nancy Friday. His kind of porn is what you might call 'artistic', or what others refer to as 'coffee-table erotica'. This is not everyone's all-time favourite brand of 'artistic'. Nevertheless, Blake offers a kind of hard core that can and does arouse many viewers; a lot of women speak highly of his work. 'Blake has something,' says Kastens. 'He had a very big impact on this industry.' Not least in terms of inspiring a string of imitators. In Blake's undertow there followed Cameron Grant, and movies like *Elements of Desire* and *The Dinner Party*. Hard core's journey into designer sex continued with Michael Ninn and *Sex*, *Sex 2*, *Latex* and *Shock*. Ninn's hard core was hailed as the pinnacle – or the nadir – of the genre. A Ninn suite offers a visually arresting concoction of impressive photography and boasts all the trick shots that Ninn picked up during his time in advertising: the slow-mo, the fast camera switches, the barrelling, twisting lens-work, the dry ice, the *homages* to movie classics like *Citizen Kane*. Ninn also uses good sound, elaborate make-up, costumes and props and, for porn, super-sophisticated special effects meshed with the live-action footage, including morphing and other computer-generated illusions. The computer effects for *Latex* were made by the same people who did *Batman*. In terms of the adult industry Ninn's films cost a fortune to make and an age to turn out. A film like *Latex* marks quite a transformation of the hard-core scene from the bargain-basement porn of half a decade earlier, and it was a massive hit.[18]

The elaborate visuals of *Latex* were the part realisation of long-term speculations made by the producers VCA in the new computer technologies. Putting money into hardware was another side to the porn investments of the nineties. Reflecting the growing confidence, other aspiring American firms like Wicked, Sin and Ultimate were doing the same, likewise Marc Dorcel in France, Berthe Milton's Private, and people like Helen Duval, Hans Moser and Sarah Young in Europe. Vivid has also invested heavily in this direction. 'In terms of Interactive, Vivid are the top producer in US, if not the world,' says Kastens. The seriousness of the company's future intent saw the two owners of Vivid split their responsibilities, as one went off to look after Interactive exclusively, and the other took charge of the company's many other concerns. The fruit of such speculation and toil are games like *Club 21*, a virtual Las Vegas where success comes in the shape of live-action video footage of strips and explicit sex. Likewise *Alleycats*, an interactive bowling game where a full strike gets the player an eyeful of hard-core action.

With the new technology a lot of capital investment is needed upfront. This is dependent upon a stable political environment, and is far from compatible with a return to the costly witch-hunts of the late eighties. 'There is a sense of a major upswing in the industry, it's true,' says Kastens. 'But there are a lot of things tied in: you need money and expertise to make these kinds of movies and stuff, but you also need the right kind of political atmosphere. Twelve years of Republican administrations was very stifling, the amount of money lost fighting legal battles in the courts, the amount of people who went to jail, served time. But there's been none of that during Clinton.' This is why in every porner's dream of the future there's a place that is far from digital and very much constitutional. Ultimately, First Amendment protection is the goal. 'We always look to the time when we don't have to deal with all this hassle.'

The Vivid Queens
(on porn's 'contract players' studio system)

The third and most crucial strand of Vivid's capital investment has been in people, speculating heavily in real-life flesh and blood. It doesn't matter how good the script or the digitalia are, whether it's film or videotape in the camera, this kind of adult entertainment depends upon bodies and beauty. Vivid is famous for its beautiful contract players, also known as the Vivid Queens. It was the first company to offer exclusive contracts to performers, with Ginger Lynn the original Vivid Queen in the mid-eighties. Though other companies have followed suit, Vivid still leads the field. Wicked, VCA, Ultimate and Sin are all doing it, but with still only a maximum of three contracted performers at any given time. During 1997 Vivid was expanding its roster from six to nine women, and rising, as well as signing up a couple of men. 'I'm not sure a lot of other companies can afford to do it as much as we can,' says Kastens. 'Vivid players make a lot of money working on fewer films than any other actresses in the business.'

The performers sign exclusively to the company for all their film work, with an agreement as to how many films they'll appear in. The length of a Vivid contract can vary. One year renewable is the average. Given the chance, almost everybody renews. 'Usually if they're with Vivid, they don't like to leave.'

The contract gives the performers a large say in whom they work with, as far as additional actors and actresses are concerned, as well as directors. Though they don't get script approval, they get input. If they are interested, and show some directing talent, contract players are then encouraged to take it up.

Talk of a proper industry, of not the wild west, stems firstly from broad-based observations of how porners go about their work in the nineties. 'It is a business where the women make the choices,' says contract player Jenteal. 'The girls who are making the movies are the ones who are making the choices.' Accordingly, working conditions on a lot of porn sets are improving, with proper meals, showers and some level of privacy. These basic comforts are not uniform, and things are far from perfect – for one thing, small budgets won't buy a lot of luxury – but it's getting better. They even close the set for sex scenes on a lot of productions. In the shooting of *AD 6969*, the production manager had been concerned for Sindee's rights of privacy, and then, with the full scene between Cox and TT Boy finally upon us, the director closed the set. A lot of actresses told me they preferred it like this. The crew and invited guests are one thing, but no hangers-on or lurkers. As people gather up to leave, I am told that as the visiting writer I can be an exception, and if I want to stick around then that's okay. I'd thought about this; it's something you're not sure about, whether you'll watch the actual sex scene, or whether you'd really rather not. The few writers I'd read who had visited a porn set had stayed and goggled. But with the disapproving words of performers ringing in my ears I shuffled outside with the other discards. 'If they want to watch me have sex,' says Chasey Lain, 'they should buy the video.' And that was it. I ducked out. Despite further invitations to watch from directors and performers (including Julie Rage inviting me to sit in on an anal scene she was shooting the following day, 'I'm going to be fucked in the ass by Melodie with a strap-on. It should be fun!'), I never did go all the way.

A Vivid contract may also specify what kind of sex the performers are prepared to do on film. Some will choose to only have sex with their real-life partner, while Janine Lindemuller, one of the biggest porn actresses of the decade, doesn't have onscreen sex with men at all. Not this far, in a career lasting half a decade. What started out as a relationship-saver became both her signature and career asset, and would feature in her agreement with Vivid.[19] (In 1996 Lindemuller was accurately boasting that she could 'write her own cheque' if she were to agree to do a boy–girl number on camera.[20]) However, choice is a relative term sometimes. For instance, not every porn woman can decide who she'll work with. Although a contract payer may decline to work with a particular performer, and freelance stars like Felecia or Stephanie Swift may set limits on what sex they'll do and still do very well, other freelancers who are less in demand have the choice to refuse and then possibly lose the work.

High risk
(on hard core and safe sex)

Safe sex is another option offered to Vivid performers in their contracts, and most of them take up that option. Inevitably this is an issue that haunts the hard-core industry. During my stay in porn valley I met with John Stagliano. Stagliano is a director, producer and manufacturer of porn movies. His Buttman movie series, about a shy, horny guy with a Hi-8 video camera and a sizeable fetish for backsides, have made him one of the most successful and admired figures in American movie hard core. In the porn 'zine *Batteries Not Included*, an adoring Tammy Cole places Stagliano in the lust pantheon. 'If Russ Meyer is the tit man of the century, John Stagliano is the ass man of the millenium.'[21] On the usenet, at alt.sex.movies, a reviewer, 'Imperator', puts it like this: 'When in doubt, rent Stagliano ... Stagliano continues to rule contemporary porn.'[22]

During a long day of interviewing Stagliano, this handsome, accommodating, trendy fortysomething – the finest rebuttal of the fictional stereotype of the porner as sleazy bloke – we spoke of many things, of genetics, religion, Camille Paglia, anatomy as destiny, but also the situation with regard to safe sex and porn. This conversation would prove tragically ironic. 'The hard-core industry is disease free,' he told me when I asked how risk of infection was dealt with. 'The self-imposed norm is an HIV test every six months, and a DNA test every two months. I also require an antibody test every thirty days for performers. These things are more important than rubbers, which are very non-sexual, and some girls are allergic to them.'

For a man who makes a point of taking a lead with practising good ethics in the industry, Stagliano was disappointingly inflexible on this issue. 'I have shot with rubbers four to five times, with people I really wanted to use. But if people say they want to use rubbers, then usually I won't hire them.' Gino Colbert told me that on safe sex the straight industry was stupid, or ignorant, or both. 'They just don't understand. They still seem to think that it is some kind of gay-only complaint.' Colbert told me he always offers performers the choice of using condoms. With *All About Teri Wiegel*, four out of the five couplings declined the offer, saying condoms affected their performance, making them feel less sexy. Colbert believes straight porn needs to eroticise condom use, to stop saying they aren't erotic. Typically, Stagliano argued that with gay movies safe sex is vital, and that with a transsexual movie he was about to produce the decision had been to go with condoms. 'Transsexuals tend to be very sexually active,' he tells me.

Later, I thought of *Face Dance*, Stagliano's best film. Exorbitant and mesmeric, this highly wrought, multilayered piece of pornwork weighs in at a massive four hours forty minutes long. In *XXX*, Wendy McElroy admits to watching the opening scene from *Face Dance* and being left open-mouthed.[23] On the subject of risky sex, there's a particular scene that comes to mind. Rocco Siffredi plays an Italian porn actor who goes to America to make a regular, non-porn movie, only to find himself tangled up in a mess of neuroses and double-dealing. He is kidnapped at airport arrivals by a seductive intermediary sent by Buttman, blindfolded and driven to Buttman's abode, where he features in a stag party game, called the Face Dance – organised to celebrate Rocco's coming to America. The game involves four blindfolded men with four women dancing close to their faces. The women rotate, changing partners. In due course the blindfolds come off and the situation evolves into a choreographed orgy, while Stagliano films the action. It's basically the fantasy version of the bachelor party game taken to the limit. The Face Dance involves a considerable amount of swapping and switching of partners. Every performer, it would seem, gets to be intimate with everyone else. This, by any definition, has to be sexually active. If anyone on the shoot had been infected, all eight of them would have been exposed before the day was done.

The scene was filmed at Stagliano's Malibu home. If you've watched a few of Buttman's tapes, it probably means you've also seen his love palace. The long, blue sofa I sat on is recognisable from various Stagliano movies. If furniture could talk, it could tell of assorted three ways, four ways, and 'reverse cowgirls'. Not just the furnishings, however, but the extensive sun-deck, the luxury sculpted pool, the great view of the ocean, the art, all of what in *Face Dance* he calls, 'my reward for being a pervert'. When American *Penthouse* profiled Stagliano, he was photographed in dinner jacket, bow tie and Hawaiian trunks, draped over the side of the pool and sipping champagne. Buttman in real-estate heaven. The dream home is part of the arousal. Buttman's abode is the alluring extension of the fantasy scenario of his most excellent life. Stagliano's movies are consumer wank fantasies, offering viewers the arousing hallucination of blissful, luxury living, of the achievement of uncomplicated and carefree states of being. Accordingly a lot of his fans reckon that John Stagliano is 'the luckiest guy in the world'. 'John, honestly, I watch your movies,' writes a fan. 'I see the things you do, the things that happen to you, and I reckon sometimes you must think you've died and gone to heaven.'

It's not always so heavenly, however. One evening in December 1995, Stagliano's girlfriend, the actress Krysti Lynn, was driving back from a bar to his house, when she lost control of her car and plunged down the side of a hill. Both Lynn and her passenger friend were killed. The following summer, at the Video Software Dealer's Association annual awards ceremony in Los Angeles, a rare occasion for main-stream Hollywood and its hard-core shadow to share a platform, Stagliano's *Buttman's European Vacation 3* was voted the best video in the adult category. While the actor Robin Williams made quips about wanting to be Buttman too, Stag-liano dedicated his award to Lynn. Shortly afterwards he left for Europe for another *European Vacation*. Further Buttman titles were to follow over the following months. But the emotions raised by the loss of Lynn apparently continued to trouble Stagliano. In a moment of depression, what he later called a 'temporary death wish', he had unprotected anal sex with a Brazilian transsexual prostitute. And then, in the Spring of 1997, it was reported that John Stagliano had tested HIV positive and that, for the time being at least, the 'ass man of the millenium' had stopped making porn movies.

Stagliano rarely had sex on camera, being a director first and foremost. Nevertheless, the aftermath of the news of his infection saw the porn industry's complacency regarding safe sex deeply undermined – at least temporarily. A lot of people in straight hard core are always eager to stress that though there have been incidents and some scares, so far no straight actor in porno has been infected making porn. The only reported AIDS death in straight porn was John Holmes, whom – people assure you – got infected through being an intravenous drug user.

Assuming this is true, you can't help feel it's some kind of miracle, whatever kinds of precaution are taken. A few years earlier, the actress Busty Belle voiced the doubts she had: 'I don't care if you had an AIDS test two weeks ago, who were you with last night?'[24] Accordingly, when the news broke about Stagliano, an actress who'd recently been with the director was fired off the set of a major porn movie. The nerves were further jangled with the news that an actress had also tested HIV posi-tive and, it was rumoured, had been aware of her status while continuing to work. Either the industry-approved testing procedures weren't so reliable, or they weren't always being scrupulously applied. Memories of the Barbara Doll 'incident' from 1995 were revived. When the visiting French actress tested positive the whole American industry had shut down for a fortnight, and collectively had seemed on the verge of making a far larger commitment to condoms. And then, miraculously, Doll tested again, and this time she came up negative. She left the States and returned to France and set up her own porn video production company. However rumours of a 'cover up' persisted, claiming that maybe Doll was positive after all.[25]

Because of its wagon-round mentality, many in the straight porn industry reckoned that the community was 'protected', that regular testing and the social cordon that mainstream society has placed around hard core meant the industry could shield itself against infection. This collective act of finger-crossing is proving increasingly less viable. At the time of Stagliano's announcement, the outer fringes of the gossip market were talking about an accident-prone industry in danger of being shut down as a public health risk by its various enemies in society. Though the chances of such vengeance seem pretty remote, hard core's best protection against both backlash and infection remains a greater acceptance of condoms. Vivid's safe-sex guarantees for performers were starting to look like a possible front-end of a future industry-wide change of heart.[26]

The women of porn
(on what it's like to be a porn actress)

Back on the set of *AD 6969*, in the darkened interior of the warehouse, Sindee and TT Boy are doing their big sex scene together. The screen lovers are hard at it for three to four hours, the time it takes to film a choreographed porn scene. Outside in the parking lot, in the hot sun, other performers, extras, remnants of the crew and we assorted hangers-on all sit around on the baking asphalt, waiting. There is nothing else to do. Time passes slowly. The mood grows drowsy. It's like siesta time, except of course for Sindee and TT Boy.

Henri Pachard passes by, stops a while and then retires to his car to catch up on his sleep. Other conversations similarly start up and peter out: Stephanie tells Melodie how pretty she looks, and they discuss their shoes as they both disappear into make-up. Christy Canyon arrives. She is the Vivid player on the production, and conducts herself accordingly – 'I work for Vivid', she declaims at one stage, meaning, 'I don't have to take any shit.' She also disappears into her car. As a deep lull descends, I talk with Julie Rage, sprawled out on the floor in her futuristic warrior gear.

Rage used to be in the army. I had been told that she'd left the service because she wasn't getting enough sex. Was this so? 'Not exactly. Although I did get into trouble for pinching a guy's butt.' She was an army combat medic. 'I guess it meant I was pretty familiar with bodily functions, where things are at, anatomically.' While pursuing her new porn career, making use of what is reputed to be the longest tongue in hard core, Rage is also studying part-time to be a coroner. 'Somebody's got to do it.' Her porn earnings are paying for the retraining. 'The nicest thing about working in porno is the cheque.'

Rage tells me that she liked porn movies prior to getting into the industry. 'It had always been my secret little fantasy, but I never thought I would ever do it in reality. I stumbled into it, really.' Out of the army, she responded to a local newspaper ad for nude modelling and was recommended to try out for screen work. Her partner wasn't too keen on this, she tells me, and then she smiles. 'But he's not my boyfriend any more.'

Sitting out in the car lot, talking to the porn actress about her career switch from war to sex, about the fun she was having, the money she was making, her future plans in the dying business, I keep thinking about the myths regarding the adult industry that continue to circulate in the broader culture, which have it that porn is about violence and coercion and women victims. I remember what the British porn-maker Steve Perry once said: 'People still have this in-built idea that porno is made by two men in a back street in Tooting, who hang around dole offices to put guns to young girls' heads and drag them back to have sex in front of a camera.'[27] Or Californian porn is a rickety shoot at an abandoned hovel, where a dodgy hard-core scene turns into a filmed slaying to be commercially distributed at a later stage. 'There's no coercion in porno,' says Rage. 'That's just ignorance. People are banging down the doors, trying to get into this business.'

So, they're banging down the doors, but why? How come so many people want to get into porn? For the money, seems the first and fundamental truth of it. 'For fuck's sake man, that's the reason I'm in this business,' says Taylor Wane, an actress originally from England. 'I get at least $500 a scene and with dancing around the country – which pays the best money – I can earn $15,000 a week, not bad for an ex-shop assistant at Boots. Now I've got a nice sports car and a really nice home.'[28] Porn actress Savannah, a big star of the early nineties, used to make $5,000 per night for dancing engagements. Shortly before she died, in an interview on the *Joan Rivers Show*, Savannah had said that the thing she really liked about the porn business was that she didn't have to look at price tags any more.

Traditionally, another reason for getting into the porn business has been to try to use it as the springboard to other acting jobs and screen work, of parlaying porno celebrity into Hollywood stardom. So far, this has mostly proved a lot of wasted effort. No matter how big the porn star is, he or she is just small fry in the bigger star pool. Not a single hard-core star to date has gone on to make a real splash in mainstream movies or television. The stigma is too great. Rumours concerning Hollywood stars who've done hard core, those big, unprintable names, are simply myths.[29]

The porn past is tough to live down, and hard to conceal. One of the problems is that a performer courts maximum exposure and celebrity for the larger earnings to be made on the dance circuit. Such fame makes it difficult to achieve crossover later on into the straight entertainment world. In the early eighties Annette Haven was originally cast to play the lead in Brian de Palma's thriller, *Body Double*. But then Columbia found out that their new star was fully X-rated, and this was not felt to be desirable, so Haven was removed from the film.[30]

Ginger Lynn has made several B-movies since hanging up her G-string – going from porno diva to straight-to-video schlock. Titles like *Bound and Gagged: A Love Story*, *I Was a Teenage Sex Mutant* and *Vice Academy* suggest a kind of typecasting. She also got a small role in a couple of episodes of television's *NYPD Blue* – she played a hooker. Porn's most famous crossover is probably Marilyn Chambers. The one time *Ivory Snow* girl and star of *Behind the Green Door* took the lead in David Cronenberg's *Rabid*. Lately, Ron Jeremy has done cameos in *The Chase* and *Killing Zoë*, and Ashlyn Gere, porn's top woman of the first half of the nineties, has landed small parts on television shows like *The X-Files*.

Another version of porn motivation figures performers as inadequate types. Britanny O'Connell hotly disputes this: 'They always say that the only reason girls are in this industry is because they have problems.' Old-timer Henri Pachard thinks there's some truth to the rumour. A self-confessed needy person – every time he improvises a line on set, he asks people whether they realise he made that line up himself – he is convinced there must be something wrong with him and his porno compadres: 'We wouldn't be in this business if we weren't somehow socially dysfunctional, fucked up.' Paul Thomas agrees. 'We're all misfits. Everyone here on this set, if you dig deep enough, you'll find some basic personality flaw, something wrong with them which explains why they're here in the first place.' At which point he paused and looked at me, 'Including you.'

The gay movie director Jim Steel feels such talk is mistaken: 'Incest survivors, that sort of thing . . . It's ridiculous to make any generalisations about these people when you look at how much product there is out there . . . It's all business now.'[31] It is difficult to dispel the impression that references to damaged people is much a case of victim culture coming through, where everybody's got a tale to tell of how they're fucked up, and porners are no exception. The thing is, porners are in fact victims of a social stigma that shuts them out of the regular world. 'It's very hard to hang around with anyone who's not in the business,' confesses Jenna Jameson. 'I don't meet very many people not in the business. I'd like to, but it's sort of hard.'[32] Jenteal says she's lost friends through entering into the hard-core life. 'I was at a wedding and this [ex-]friend specially came up to me and said, "Are you still doing that disgusting porno?!" And that was all she said.' Being labelled and semi-outcast in this way may need some explaining, causing some to feel that they've maybe brought it upon themselves.

With the reputation you get for being in porn, Henri Pachard is sure that nobody grows up dreaming of working in the business. 'I certainly did not grow up thinking, well I am going . . . to do sex movies,' says Candida Royalle.[33] Dyanna Lauren, though, who's been in the industry for fifteen years, begs to differ. 'This is something I've wanted to do most of my life,' she says. 'I grew up with a different mentality than most kids, I guess. I grew up wanting to be a Gypsy Rose Lee.'[34] Some may find this hard to believe. Perhaps because they're not exhibitionists. Carol Queen is a self-proclaimed exhibitionist. The former stripper and peepshow dancer feels people need to take such things into account: 'To really relish a peep show or porn career you have to be a dyed-in-the-wool exhibitionist; for some people it would be discomfiting to know that strangers are masturbating to memories or pictures of you.' This discomfiture, she feels, part-explains accusations of porn as objectification: 'Many who assume it would feel degrading to fuck before a camera or dance naked for strangers are not the least bit exhibitionistic . . . How, then, could they understand that such activities could be exciting?'[35]

Many porn women describe the experience of having the camera upon them as being sexual – 'It's definitely flattering,' says Kaylan Nichole. 'I always like being the centre of attention.' – that it gives them the permission to be sexy, to be a 'bad' girl. 'I had fun. I felt great with my first sex scene,' says Rage, 'I felt like I could let go. For that moment in time in front of the camera, I could be whoever I wanted to be.'

Several women speak of porn giving access to alternative sexual experiences. 'I was never the type of person who could approach someone in a club and say, "I'm bi-sexual. Want to come home with me?"' says Dyanna Lauren. 'But making adult films gives me the opportunity to do some of the things I wanted to in a comfortable environment.'[36] Chasey Lain, another Vivid Queen, acknowledges that porn allowed her to 'get in touch with her bisexuality'.

So called 'girl–girl' is a thriving, popular subgenre in the nineties. Lesbian action is easier to cut for soft-core versions as required by the cable market. The preponderance of 'g–g' is also due to aesthetics. People like the all-body flavour of g–g. A common misconception over 'lesbian' action in hetero hard core is that it serves only as an appetiser in advance of the arrival of the male stud, wherein his sexual pleasure becomes the central event. This is one way a scene might head, but it is far from guaranteed, with many videos being exclusively devoted to all-women scenes. Traditionally the female body is considered more beautiful to look at. In this way girl–girl scenes are well suited to the requirements of high end. In the soft-focus image system of porners like Andrew Blake there's nothing more beautiful, elegant or sophisticated than the sight of two gorgeous women languorously amusing each other. The last thing you need is some bloke with a raging hard-on ruining the look.

Many porn women like it this way. In fact the prevalence of girl–girl has much to do with their improved situation in the business. What was damned for so long as being particularly reprehensible, especially exploitative of women, has turned into a key site, or sign of porn women's growing power. Janine Lindemuller's no-men policy is not unique, while many women spend a long while working in the business 'doing' only other women prior to their first onscreen screw with a man. 'It's not so hard emotionally for women working with girls,' says Jenteal. As well as keeping real life relationships intact, there's the issue of safer sex, as well as the greater efficiency in contrast to maybe waiting an hour for the guy to get, and keep, an erection.

The loneliness of the long distance toolpacker
(on porn men)

The increased girl power in hard core finds leading porn women picking their screen paramours. Several decline to work with any men other than their real-life partner (see Chapter 1, 'Definitions'). This means that either they work less often, they do a lot of girl–girl, or hubbie gets to be a porn star too. 'It used to be that the man got the job to win over the girl,' Susan Faludi observes; 'now he must win over the girl to get the job.'[37]

The male presence onscreen in hetero porn is a curious thing. It might be argued that the men are more objectified than the women, with barely an identity beyond that of the guy with the erection, the anonymous toolpacker servicing the porn queens. It is not as straightforward as this. Although they will often go unmentioned, there have been many distinctive men of porn. It could be they're famous for being supermen, like the preternatural pop shots of Peter North; or then again for being regular guys, like Steve Perry and Seymore Butts; or then maybe they're good actors, charming, as with John Leslie, Richard Pacheco, Mike Horner and Randy West.

Ron Jeremy is likely to be the only male porn actor that non-porn buffs will have ever heard of. A well-endowed, amusing character, Jeremy (a.k.a. 'the Hedgehog'), is not so representative of the contemporary male talent, nor even the old-style porn stud. Men like John Leslie, Paul Thomas, Jamie Gillis and Harry Reems were neither hedgehogs nor fatsos, but suave performers who could act as well as screw on screen. Now with cultural trends like the muscle culture, a new kind of male has come into the industry: good-looking, tanned, muscular, but also wooden, sometimes, cloneish and not particularly skilled at acting. With the return of high end, some of these men are required to find the actor within their stud bodies, while also delivering an erection, and often getting paid less than the porn women. Some levels of resentment have been noted. However the day-to-day reality continues to find the men and women of porn sticking together, going out with each other, getting married, having affairs, getting divorced, then getting married again. Most of the women speak with fondness and respect for their male counterparts, people like Steve Drake, Jonathan Morgan, Alex Sanders and Steve St Croix. 'It's hard not to have intimate feelings about some of the actors I work with,' admitted Jenna Jameson. 'How can you do all this stuff with these guys and then feel nothing for them?'[38]

In the spring of 1995 the feminist writer Susan Faludi wrote about the plight of the porn male for the *New Yorker*.[39] Written around the time that male actor Cal Jammer shot himself outside the home of his estranged wife, the actress Jill Kelly, Faludi's piece became a venturesome dissertation upon the deepening state of crisis in American malehood. With an industry seemingly in thrall to the demands of its megababes, apparently porn was no longer the engine room of male dominion, more like the scene of masculine obsolescence.[40] However, the porn power stakes are not best viewed through such a singular, gendered lens. Though certain shifts in power relations have occurred, relatively few performers, male or female, are actually under contract. Talk of all women calling the shots in the porn industry is exaggerated. This is more like some women calling some of the shots.

The bulk of hetero porners are freelancers getting paid by the scene. Working this way can put some amount of strain on the porn man – the difference between a pay cheque and what Linzi Drew describes as BFH (Bus Fare Home).[41] 'The pressure to perform was enormous,' writes porn veteran Richard Pacheco, describing his hard-core debut. 'I really had no idea that a man could experience such a dissociation from his dick.'[42] The porn man has to get an erection on request – the getting or copping of wood – and most likely in front of a film crew.[43] He has got to hold it there – to wield wood – for however long it takes to shoot a full hard-core scene. All the while the man is wary of the problems of losing it – of difficulties with wood. And then, after all this time and effort, when the director says now's the time, the man has to ejaculate in a minute, to bring it all home. These are demands not to be laughed about. But of course they are laughed about, we can't help it. Often this will only make things worse for the sensitive woodsman in the valley.

This situation is perhaps exacerbated by the fact that the rates of pay for men are lower than for the women.[44] But it is also true that the men work more often, good woodsmen particularly, and that their careers last longer. With the women, a turnover in new faces is a feature of the business. Things tend to be a lot less fickle for the men. Their careers can last seemingly for ever, and the opportunities to move into directing are great. John Leslie, Paul Thomas, Jamie Gillis, Randy West, Joey Silvera and Jon Dough are some of the many porn men who have switched to consolidate their careers in this way.[45]

Faludi's version of the porn chain of command placed the 'grunts' (as Paul Thomas called them) pretty much at the bottom. But she did not dwell on the booming career of the black star, Sean Michaels, who not only has successfully moved into producing and directing, but, like gay icon Jeff Stryker, has commenced with 'branding' and 'merchandising' his porn celebrity – anyone for a pair of Sean Michaels's briefs? Likewise Rocco Siffredi, by far the biggest earning performer in the whole porn world. Actor Steve St Croix became a contract player at Vivid in 1996, with his man-tool insured with Lloyd's of London after he bought himself a fast motorbike. People like St Croix are prized assets in porn: good-looking and able to act, keep an erection and pop-shot on cue. That kind of person gets well taken care of.

A few days after the *AD 6969* shoot, Woody Long, a former male lead, drove me out to John Stagliano's house in Malibu. *En route*, we talked of wood and other things. 'Porn guys, they're horny types,' says Woody. 'They're the guys at school who were always feeling horny, non-stop, all day long.' This simple motivational truth is often lost in efforts to 'explain' the porner. Says Woody, 'Men, they do it for the money and the sex, and because they can.' When he talks of porn studs, Woody modestly talks of 'them', the others. Though he's done his fair share of wood-work, he declines to put himself in the same bracket as the legendary men of wood: the Peter Norths, the Rocco Siffredis, the Joey Silveras. These are the stalwarts, the rock steadies, the jism kings. North is notorious for three things: his unchanging hairstyle over more than a decade of porn-work; the fact that he was also once Matt Ramsey, gay porno stud; and, most profusely, being a human freak in the spray department. Font of the endless pop shot, North is a gushing geyser, known as 'his voluminousness' to some.[46] In his autobiography, *Penetrating Insights*, North puts his superman talents down to treating his body like a temple. Steve

Perry suggests an unusually powerful prostate. Perry also recommends that performers keep off spicy foods like Italian and Indian as a mark of respect to the female talent. 'It makes your spunk smell disgusting.'[47]

Despite his rather boastful *nom de porn*, Woody Long is happy to come clean on one of porn's biggest lies: those big dicks aren't as big as they look. Male readers should know that John Holmes and Ron Jeremy are exceptional cases, and most studs are little more than average-sized. Famous porn stars with 'enormous' cocks look so big because the scale is hard to judge, especially if he has clipped his pubic hair or is using a vascular device to pump up the size temporarily. And anyway, when all is said and done, big isn't necessarily best. Kitten Natividad, a Russ Meyer superstar, did some work with the truly sizeable John Holmes, 'It felt like a snake,' she told *Boing Boing* magazine. 'There was no end to it.' But though it made a career for Holmes, it didn't bring him sexual happiness. 'He didn't like to get oral sex or fuck. He had no feeling in his dick, that's what he told me. And he couldn't really get it completely hard.'[48]

Woody is convinced that the secret for good wood-work is temperance. Holding back off the set. 'You just need to save yourself. Go two days without a screw if you have a big performance due. No more than three days, however, because then you prematurely ejaculate and that is no good.' Long acknowledges that this kind of regime places some pressure on a stud's personal romantic existence. His relationship with Vivid Queen Celeste didn't last the course.[49] Now that he doesn't act any more, he too is working on extending his hard-core career into directing.

The post-porn syndrome
(on difficulties after leaving porn)

The career of a porn woman can last a dozen years or it can be a short-stop affair of one or two films. Whichever way, eventually all good things must come to an end. One day you're banging down the doors to get in, another day you're trying to move on. At which point problems may arise with stigma. The choices that porn women make as young women can have an impact upon their lives for years to come. 'Think very hard about it,' Kaylan Nicole advises aspiring porn women, 'because it's not the easiest thing in the world to deal with after.'[50] Following porn, Candida Royalle found her career horizons narrowed: 'My name was dirt . . . I was a spoiled woman.'[51] The 'post-porn syndrome' will often result in career trouble for any woman recognised from her former career in hard core. Brandy Alexandre had to leave a couple of jobs for this reason. Whenever she's looked at too closely by someone in the workplace she worries she's been recognised, and it's time to be moving on again. 'You just never know,' says Brandy. 'This is for ever.'

This tends to limit an ex-porn woman's career options. Some ex-performers do lingerie ranges, others will do counselling. Hyapatia Lee was a major star who, when she quit, relocated to an Indian reservation, where she is involved in natural health cures. Porn women make a fair share of their money from adult offshoots that can continue after they've finished with films: running fan clubs with merchandise to sell, from signed pictures to 'used' panties (there's also the Jenteal replica vibrating vagina and the Christy Canyon blow-up doll), and everyone's getting their own commercial web site.

Some ex-porn women drift into prostitution, a business that tends to hang over most performers during their hard-core career. Porn women often make lucrative personal appearances at adult book stores. Apart from selling signed posters, some stars will do nude Polaroids with the fans. For twenty dollars they'll sit on laps and smile at the camera while letting the punter hold on to a breast. For ten dollars they'll do it topless. Such up close interfacing between porn star and the fans continues with the one-on-one, fantasy 'chat' booths. Here the porn star sits in a booth, and for five minutes and for twenty dollars, she'll strip, play with herself and say rude things to the guy on the other side of the glass screen. (Until recently the Vivid Queens did a 'talk-nasty' telephone sex service.)

In the summer of 1996, the topless bars and dance halls of

Memphis, Tennessee were shut down by the local vice police. Among the usual racketeering, obscenity and prostitution charges, several adult video stars on the dance circuit, including Chasey Lain, were named as 'featured prostitutes'. This was clearly a slur. But, although rare, prostitution is not unheard of during a successful career, especially with gay porn stars. So-called 'Outcall' and 'custom-made' videos are, for obvious reasons, a little talked about side to the industry. Custom-made came out of the video revolution, a subculture of video porn, where wealthy customers commission a video to be shot to their exact requirements. A woman accepts an order, and will get a trusted party to video her as she performs and talks to the camera/client as she goes along. But custom-made can also involve the client performing with the star.

The rules of engagement
(on the legal restrictions put upon porn-making)

In California, making porn used to be against the law. During the seventies and early eighties they used to film a lot of hard core around San Francisco, where the police turned a blind eye. Filming also went on in Los Angeles County but was a lot riskier. In the mid-eighties, in the hills above Malibu, John Stagliano used to scout for houses abandoned after forest fires as safe places to shoot hard core away from the prying eyes of the police. In 1986, the producer Harold Freeman had a porn production shut down by the police on the charge of 'pimping'. The county district attorney argued that the exchange of money for sex on a porn set equalled prostitution. Freeman was charged with five counts of pimping, one count for each woman whom he paid to perform in his film (the male performers were not charged). Freeman was found guilty. He went to jail and paid a $10,000 fine to go with legal fees approaching $100,000. Freeman's attorneys filed a routine appeal to the California Supreme Court, not expecting much to come of it. Instead the court not only read the case, they threw the conviction out. The justices found it self-evident that the LA district attorney's actions had little to do with prostitution, and was all about an anti-porn drive. This set a legal precedent, making porn-production legal in California. Soon after, nearly the whole American porn industry came to settle in the San Fernando Valley.

These days, porners filming on location in Los Angeles County pick up their shooting permit from the same place where the people at Disney or Universal get theirs. And doing things like taking to hills for underground shoots seems like ancient history. The way the porn industry goes to work in the late nineties indicates that this is no wild west business. And when you look closely at the legal situation, any residual notions of wildness and lawlessness fade away. The hard-core industry is a proper industry partly as a consequence of the tight grip of censorship and the law. The censorship of porn comes firstly in the shape of specific laws making specific requirements, and it also looms in the threat of action in the courts – thereby effecting the way producers make films.

In terms of legal restriction, one recent law has had a big impact on the adult film industry in America. This concerns the keeping of performer records. During the Meese Commission hearings of 1986 it was suggested that it was difficult sometimes to tell if a performer in an adult movie was of legal age simply by viewing the tape. This was considered to be a possible loophole in the laws against child porn. In time the US Congress passed the Child Protection and Obscenity Enforcement Act, which became an operative law in 1995. The Act requires that anyone who makes a video should keep extensive and detailed records to prove that none of the performers were under age at the time. This is required, however, of every performer; there are no exceptions. A production company that makes tapes exclusively featuring middle-aged actors has to keep records. If the producers at Fantastic Pictures, who specialise in 'pensioner' porn, slip-up on a fifty-year-old's records then they will be sent to prison. It is against the law in America to make porn that depicts sexual acts involving minors, or simulated sexual acts involving minors. The adult industry does not make child porn. The reality is that all adult porners want to do is earn a living; they do not wish to break the law or go to jail. However, with the Child Protection Act, the offence is not really making child porn, but failure to stick to the record-keeping mandates. This is a bad law, not because it's desirable to have under-age performers making porn, but because it makes it more difficult to produce adult porn.

All the porn companies like Vivid, VCA and Evil Angel now have a lot of additional administration to deal with. On *AD 6969*, there was a man playing a small, non-sexual role who hadn't worked in the industry before. After he was finished, he had to wait around for several hours before they paid him, while a photographer was called out to come and take his photo. 'Basically it's a big pain in the ass,' says Kastens. And far more than a pain for the smaller, independent companies. While the large-scale producers can afford to pay people to take care of things, it's the independents who really struggle to deal with the extra paperwork and costs. For a tiny-circulation, four-page, stapled-together 'zine dedicated to the work of Carol Leigh or John Stagliano, which 'borrows' an image from one of their films, the possibility exists that a government official could come round some day and ask the editor if they have the records for the two performers featured in this photograph. It might not ever happen, but the threat is always present. 'This law,' observes the porn 'zine *BNI*, 'can be easily used to close down a large segment of the underground 'zine scene.'

Despite the complaints, Henri Pachard thinks the records law is a good thing. Henri would like the industry to raise the performer age to twenty-one. 'If a girls slips in under the twenty-one minimum age net, she might come in at eighteen. But slipping under the eighteen minimum age requirement could mean somebody could end up using a fifteen-year-old in hard core, by mistake, and this does not look good.' Traci Lords was an actress who slipped in under the legal age during the eighties. Lords entered the business when she was only fifteen and appeared in hard-core movies. When her true age was revealed, the under-age videos were suppressed in America. Her original movies are illegal in America. Anyone caught in possession of one of her tapes is committing the felony of being in possession of child porn. In Paris, France, you can go into a shop and pick up a Lords video – her tapes still do good business – in the US, you'd go to jail.[52]

The Traci Lords affair cost the adult industry dearly, in terms of money and bad publicity. The story is that nobody in porn knew her real age. 'Traci Lords was doing porno with the body of a woman, from age fifteen,' complained the producer Jim Holliday. 'No one knew she was under age.'[53] Certainly Lords used very good fake identity papers, so good they even tricked the US government into issuing her with a legitimate passport that said she was of age, enabling her to go to Japan to promote her films. How she got her ID, who brought her into porn, who tipped off the police about her – these queries remain unsettled.[54] Neither is it certain that the record-keeping laws would stop someone else with similarly good fake documents fooling the industry again.

Four fingers and a thumb
(on the threat of legal action)

The second types of censorship faced by American porners comes not in the form of an interdictory law but the threat of action in the courts. This is an issue of obscenity, of materials that might be deemed obscene by someone, somewhere, at some point. The way to steer clear of this kind of trouble is to avoid sending adult materials to people or places in America that object to representations of nudity or graphic depictions of sex.

This is the 'community standards' story. You make a porn movie in California. Perhaps part of the operation you run is a mail-order service. You publicise your new video and wait for the orders to come in. An order arrives from Mississippi. You forget that Mississippi is a 'taboo' state and send the tape. This is a big mistake. Because sometimes the person who ordered the video turns out to be a government agent, and the government can now charge you with 'interstate transportation of obscenity'. And they will take you to court. Not in Van Nuys, but in rural Mississippi, where the local values are of a more traditional, less cosmopolitan flavour. And the jury's going to be shown scenes featuring people having sex, and if they find that this video offends their moral standards then it is declared to be obscene.

By this stage you're in very big trouble. 'Here at Vivid it cost us half a million dollars shipping one tape to the wrong place in our mail order business,' says David Kastens. 'Nobody went to jail; it was a corporate fine. At VCA, the owner went to jail for eight months in a federal prison in 1994. And paid a 2.2 million dollar fine.' (The irony, of course, with a corporate fine for obscenity is that the way the company raises the money to pay up is through making and selling more of the same.)

Mention the two words 'community standards' to a cool, laid-back, having-a-good-time porner in California, and watch them shudder. 'In Las Vegas, a few years ago, the FBI took over somebody's local operation, ordered in some product, and then busted some people. It's just one of those things you've got to live with.'[55] John Stagliano also has dozens of war stories to tell. 'Traci Lords. When it was found out she was under age, everybody pulled their tapes, destroyed them. Nobody went to jail. One guy, he was pulling them from his shop and putting them in his attic. A really stupid thing to do. A year later he got a call from someone in Hawaii saying, "Do you have any Traci Lords tapes, my customers keep asking for her?" He said, "Yeah, you know, I've got a whole load in my attic, sure you can come and take them." That guy turned out to be a government agent. And the shop owner, he went to jail.'

So, back to the start again. You're in California, you've just made your video, where can you send it? What places will accept images of copulation and what places won't? As far as Vivid is concerned, 'It is impossible to tell every county. What's a safe county, what's a taboo county. So mostly you go by state. Utah's a non-X state. You don't bother shipping to Virginia.' All the producer can do is be very careful, and know that their distributors are very careful too, and believe that they know what they can sell in their locality. And keep his or her fingers crossed. 'Sticking to your older distributors is a smart move,' says Kastens, 'people who've been around a while, who went through the wars of the sixties and seventies and eighties. I remember years ago a New York distributor pleading with manufacturers not to open up links with any new distributors, and everybody thought he was just looking after his own business and trying to stop others getting started in the industry. And yes, he would've kept it to himself, but he was right; if we'd all listened to him, nobody would have gone to jail, nobody would have been busted.'

Plainly porn in the USA can be a very precarious business. For distribution is always a risk. On the Federal, nation-wide level, only child porn is specifically illegal. Anything else may be deemed to be obscene, which, as there is no such thing in America as a laundry list of offending articles, ultimately depends on subjective readings. And there's no way that a company can indemnify itself against such things, is there? 'No, the only way you can indemnify yourself is through internal censorship,' says Kastens. 'Know what you're doing, be aware of every piece of tape leaving the building, and don't push the line!'

As in Britain, it proves hard in most parts of America to get obscenity convictions from juries for tapes featuring regular heterosexual sex. Anal sex is not as hard to convict in certain parts of the country, especially gay anal sex. Other, more 'controversial' sexual practices, such as bondage and domination, especially when in conjunction with hard-core sex, or the insertion of foreign objects, will often be deemed as obscenity. These controversial depictions are too borderline to be even contemplated by mainstream producers. 'Vivid don't look to cross the line. In terms of numbers of fingers and foreign objects,' says Kastens. In this way does the industry censor itself, and the term 'rule of thumb' takes on a whole new meaning. In straight tapes, the unwritten understanding is that where so-called 'fisting' is concerned the thumb must always be visible. In gay hard core, such fisting is most often filmed and included in the master tape, but cut from the version shipped interstate to sales and rental outlets.

The rules of insertion can prove ridiculous at times. In *Cop A Feel*, Brandy Alexandre directed a scene with a guy playing a traffic cop, during which she takes his truncheon ready to use it on herself as a substitute dildo. But all you see in the American version is her facial expressions and then she puts it down. The insertion scene was cut because a policeman's truncheon is not specifically a sex toy, and because also, since the 'cop' touched the truncheon first, in advance of Alexandre, the whole scenario could conceivably be read as him somehow 'urging' the truncheon on her, and therefore as depicting non-consenting sexual activity.

Not only does the more licentious stuff stop getting made these days in pornland, but old-style raunch now receives a retrospective make-over in the editing suite. Nostalgia for porn's golden age amounts to a lucrative revenue sideline for companies sitting on a quality back catalogue. The problem is, they did things differently then. Golden age films would occasionally feature story lines like incest or dramatisations of non-consenting sexual situations. In the middle to late nineties in America, that kind of scenario isn't allowed in hard core, including any reissued films. A company like VCA continues to release 'classics' onto the market where scenes have gone missing.[56] In *Baby Face*, in the orgy scene, the actress Kristara is playing with a candle, ready to insert it, but every piece of footage where she does has been cut. Hilary Summers used to be one of the stars of the film *Taxi Girls*, but because her only scene involved a 'fisting' with Nancy Hoffman, Hilary Summers is no longer there.[57]

It's rather like after the Russian invasion of Czechoslovakia following the Prague Spring of 1968, when all the official photographs featuring Alexander Dubček were doctored, and the disgraced former premier was simply taken out of the picture. It is easy to go back in time and to find in the arts values that do not fit with those of today. One only has to think of Shakespeare and anti-semitism in *The Merchant of Venice*, or old-style versions of *Othello* where a white actor 'blacked up' to play the lead. The thirties Hollywood tear-jerker, *Jezebel*, is a wonderful film that also features crude and racist characterisations of southern blacks that wouldn't be tolerated today. But that's how it was then. Should the film now be cut? Do we just edit out the bits from our past we'd prefer not to see nowadays?

In the nineties, US hard-core producers and distributors need to watch carefully over the mood and the style of the sexual activities depicted. There will be no watersports, for sure, and no rough-housing – absolutely nothing that could be argued to be pressured sex. (For some producers this can even mean that you don't push the performer's head close to the groin, you 'steer' it.) It doesn't matter if it is clearly acted, because, as far as some people are concerned, the fact that porn is fictional is not entirely clear. In other words, when we see the actor Bruce Willis shoot up a gang of villains in a *Die Hard* movie we don't for a second believe this actually happened. However, because the sex in porn is seen as being for 'real', an equivalent shoot-'em-up in a porn movie could also, by association, be viewed as for 'real', and therefore against the law. You may feel as a porn producer that you have to have a story to go with the sex, to protect your film from charges of obscenity. But your story can't be too convincing and feature the kind of 'true to life' fight sequences you get in films like *Kalifornia* or *Twelve Monkeys*, or carry story lines about assault or abduction, or have an onscreen murder depicted with the sort of cinematic realism you get in films such as *Jagged Edge* or *Fatal Attraction*. 'Porn is uniquely restricted to a set of established narrative conventions,' writes Gary Indiana. 'Its legal status places it between fiction and nonfiction, potentially illegal if it's strictly documentary, and also if it's too imaginative.'[58]

For *AD 6969* to appeal as an action adventure hard-core romp, the film needs to have some action. The finished piece will feature assorted moments of 'real' screen sex, and plenty of fantasy science 'fiction', and occasionally there will be scenes of cartoon commotion as part of the story, featuring Melodie's deftly choreographed kung fu kicks and toy gun shoot-'em-ups between Julie and Christy – scenes that were carefully filmed during the last afternoon of the shoot. However, to avoid any representational confusion, the scuffles and skirmishes were filmed to be as farcical and slapstick, as 'unreal' and playschool as possible, while also being carefully cordoned off from the hard-core sex.

Where's the heat?
(on the problem of low-intensity sex in high-end porn)

Stories were porn's original alibi, and a major contributory factor in the emergence of cinematic hard core at the start of the seventies. A quarter of a century later the director and producer Paul Thomas continues to make films laden with story. 'People who liked the porno they made in the seventies, they like my stuff,' he says. 'I'm single-handedly keeping the golden age of porno alive.' As a director, Thomas is a 'touch' player. *The Masseuse* and *Steamy Windows* are good examples of narrative porn, achieving a balance of tightly compressed story, intrigue, beauty and sex. *Bobby Sox*, *Beauty and the Beast* and *Justine* aren't bad either. Then again there's *The Coven* and *Layover*, messy, cold-fish erotic entertainments to test the viewer's patience.

Companion 2: Aroused is a film from 1996, a kind of steamy porn noir, reminiscent of the novels of James M. Cain. The story concerns the mysterious disappearance of Randy West's wife, the bitchy Christina Angel, and the tense aftermath which finds a lugubrious West the object of the competing affections of Asia Carrera and Ashlyn Gere. During the movie Thomas himself appears in a non-sexual role, playing a detective trying to find out what happened to West's vanished wife. This is a whodunit that only Thomas, as character as well as director, seems interested in. The viewer is not fussed. As far as they're concerned, judging by what we are offered by way of some grainy, over-stylised flashback sequences, the wife was a conniving minx, and who cares what happened to her. There's too much story in *Companion*. If we were looking for tons of plot, we'd have watched *The Usual Suspects*. The 'wifey' strand of the narrative requires a lot of plodding exposition, while taking us further away from the intriguing battle of wits occurring between Gere and Carrera, and the potentially more lusty couplings this might engender.

Thomas has a weakness for overelaborate stories and is not as bothered by the sex as he might be. The couplings in *Companion 2* are rather low temperature and mechanical. Though well filmed, the editing creates an awkward whole, made worse through the occasional spot of looping – using the same footage twice, as if nobody would notice. This trouble with sex and plot as interconnected flaws are PT's signature. 'In a way, I don't know who watches my movies,' he confesses, 'I'm amazed they're so popular. Because I give so much story. I really get you to watch, to get you to understand these people and why they're fucking. And most people I know, they just really want to watch the fucking.'

This problem with low-intensity sex is not confined to Thomas, but is a growing feature of hard core during the nineties, especially high end. Richard Pacheco accuses industry leaders like Vivid and VCA of making tepid love action the 'house' style. 'They must be cutting these together with their eyes closed these days. They couldn't possibly have had any hard-ons in the editing room.' Similar criticisms track the movies of Michael Ninn, Cameron Grant, Candida Royalle and Andrew Blake. 'Blake, his stuff is like pretty pictures in a magazine which you can't jerk off to,' complains John Stagliano. 'When I first saw hard core, and I was yet to actually have sex in real life, I was a little bit turned off. I thought this stuff is gross. It made me a little uncomfortable, too many bodily functions, too many close ups of fucking. Now, of course, I love that stuff. But it was a process of getting into it.' Stagliano thinks it is the same for a lot of people the first time they're exposed to hard core. 'So, if you watch Andrew Blake you think this is better, because this stuff has got all these great production values, and the sex is not in your face. But really, in the end, it's porno for people who don't like having sex.'[60]

It's not so much that the sex in high end has become vanilla, although self-censorship will create a habitually, generically tamer product over time. What seems to have gone missing is the sense of 'real' bodies having 'real' sex. The detached air is often blamed on the performers. A commonplace in the industry pitches the real porn stars who 'love to fuck', like

Julie Ashton, Tiffany Minx and Rocco Siffredi, versus the Vivid Queens and the like who'd rather pose, and claims that where erotic is concerned, some performers haven't a clue.

The way the sex is filmed can also find a coolness setting in. Flowing and properly integrated sex scenes are not the norm in high end. All of Thomas's movies are shot with soft core half in mind. On the set of *AD 6969*, the sex scenes were filmed twice. After TT Boy and Sindee had been going at it for a couple of hours, the torpor out in the parking lot was ripped by the sound of Sindee wailing from inside the warehouse, as she and TT Boy finally reached the peak of human experience together. Shortly afterwards, TT Boy emerged from the dark for a breather and weighed himself. After make-up had refixed one of Sindee's false eyelashes which had come unglued, the screen lovers resumed with filming the scene all over again. Second time round Sindee and TT Boy replayed their carnal adventure in a more discreet shape and form. The soft-core version means there'll be no erection, no penetrative sightings, no ejaculation, just backside to lap, lots of humping, face spasming and strategically placed cutaways. 'Woman's legs in the air, it's soft core,' says PT; 'legs on the floor, it's hard core.' Legs in the air the woman's genital area is obscured, and therefore so is any kind of actual genital contact between performers. Legs on the ground, and viewers see a whole lot more.

In the hard-core version the couplings switch uneasily between coy mid-distance views and close-up shots of genital detail – not quite tunnel vision, but getting there. This juxtaposition of euphemism and explicitness, even with the deftest transitional edit, can be jolting, like switching between different television channels and two distinct porn subgenres. A singularly made-for-hard-core movie doesn't need to finesse in this way, and a singularly made-for-soft-core is all finesse, and both therefore can possess a visual unity and harmony that the high-end, hard–soft shuffle struggles to emulate.

To add to these difficulties with high end's divided self, a lot of the directors have a weakness for fancy camerawork, fast edits, slow motion, messed-up focusing, a lack of ambient sound, and other distancing effects like the computer-generated imagery. All of these things are not necessarily best suited to filming hard-core sex. Such efforts of high-end porners to imitate the visuals of the MTV culture often result in a version of rock video cool, with feelings, spontaneity and other unhip things kept at arms length.

Porn in the 'burbs
(on how the future looks from here)

In the main, what there is of a porn media in Britain and the USA applauds the high-gloss hard core, relishing the return of porn glamour. In *Desire* magazine, Sal Volatile heaps praise on this 'brilliantly stylish pornography': 'With Ninn, the day of the sex-vid as high art is nigh.' High art for some perhaps, but low heat to others. A quick trawl through the online world of alt.sex.movies or rec.arts.movies.erotica finds that not all the porn fans out there think high end means good porn. In the broader cultural context of nineties buzz-word phenomena like 'genderquake', 'white male anger', and 'masculine role anxiety', some figures in the porn industry see the triumph of 'coffee table' erotica as proof of the industry succumbing to 'the feminisation of Hollywood'. As Bill Margold explained to Susan Faludi, 'Even this business is losing its masculine fibre.'[61] This certainly doesn't sound like the wild west any more, more like the plaintive cry of a defeated old-timer, out of step with the new world.

The term 'adult erotica' does suggest a more civilised X-rated product, the kind that abjures a driven carnality in favour of a tasteful erotic sensuality – to 'capture the whole mood of the erotic moment', as Candida Royalle describes it.[62] Nothing too vulgar, in other words, the right kind of desire as opposed to a wrong kind of lust. But beyond any reformist agendas in high end, a far more practical matter most likely explains the reserved feel of the sex, and this is economic. 'A Paul Thomas film' and 'A Vivid production' are the embodiment of self-made changes in porn in the USA which have caused the product to alter. The changes are the greater capital investments during the nineties, and a coextensive opening of newer, more diverse markets. The porn industry echelon, the dominant high-enders, have decided that the way ahead involves creating a flexible, eye-catching product that can fit in various formats and media. Why court the one consumer, when you can wangle the product to work for a range of consumers. Vivid foresees a future involving a variety of delivery systems, delivering different parts or versions of their single, homogenised sex product to a variety of niche markets. It might need some chopping, might mean the product won't perform brilliantly in any single format, but as long as it proves mutable enough to make the sale then apparently they're happy.

High end is all about maximising profits by creating the kind of porn product that will pay three or four times over. What looks like big investment may well be trying to get away with doing things on the cheap. This is not meant as a criticism, merely an observation about how a tightly costed industry tends to work. However, it must be confessed that on the set of *AD 6969*, before filming Sindee and TT Boy's sex scene, the sound engineer was having difficulties getting good sound. The rustling of the plastic wrapper on the mattress was picking up on the soundtrack. 'Take it off!' said one of the crew. But another said that if they removed the plastic they wouldn't be able to take it back to the shop.

The Vivid strategy depends upon the seductive mood of the PT movie to keep pulling in the big chunks of cable revenue and foreign sales, and, most crucially, the hypability of the contract players to drive a subscription web site and to sell those expensive interactive games. A Vivid Queen's sexual glamour will also keep the lucrative spin-off ranges turning over, from comic strips to love eggs to laser disks. Going up-scale has made it feasible to consolidate while also extending. 'Film creates a product which reaches out to a larger audience, a mainstream audience, which Vivid is striving to do,' says David Kastens. He pauses a second, realising how this might sound to the hard-core die-hards. 'Not that we'll ever forget the market that we're biggest in, but we want to stretch out. That's what the billboard is all about.'

The 'billboard' was a publicity stunt from Vivid. The company rented out a giant advertising space on Sunset Boulevard in Los Angeles. The previous tenant had been Universal Pictures trailing 'Jurassic Park: The Ride'. When Kastens approached Ginnett Outdoor Advertising with the idea, they were not smitten. "'Porno!" they said. "You can't do that!" So I said, tell me your parameters, and I sent them in the photo art, and they said it was totally acceptable, no problem.' Vivid were the first hard-core company to do such a thing since the seventies. The billboard featured all the Vivid contract players pouting and posing in their sexy gear – the Lurex hot pants, the nipple-hugging boob tubes – with a strapline saying 'Vivid Adult: Video That Goes All The Way'. The Vivid Queens are the killer application bringing it all together, the unifying, seductive front end of the company, rounding up the diverse, scattered punters, as many waifs and strays as possible, and bringing them all to the varied product line. No matter that it often lacks the real porn heat.[63]

Whether the high-end porners will succeed remains to be seen. Porn-lovers are the kind of people who though they have the best intentions find that sometimes their lust centres get the better of them. The head is saying, Don't buy another soft-focus high-ender that won't deliver, but the libido is screaming, Wow that box-cover looks hot! The lust centre has no memory, and sometimes it forgets about the lack of real raunch, and hankers after the top-of-the-range beauty. 'Won't get fooled again' is the oldest, most repeated and least convincing statement in the history of porn.

A possible view of the future starts to form. The heterosexual hard-core industry seems sure to enter a state of total product-glut before the turn of the century. In the mid-eighties, the writers of *Porn Gold*, the first serious inquiry into the porn business, were analysing an American industry making 400 adult movies a year. A decade or more later, and the number of releases is going through the roof. In 1995, 5,000 porn titles were released on to the US market. In 1996, this had risen to around 7,500 releases, and in 1997 it was topping 8,000. Plainly the porn industry has become fixated with size.

America is a land of plenty, and porn does not condemn sexual appetite, but most people would agree that there's too much porn being made. Overproduction can't go on indefinitely. The industry appears inexorably to be closing in on a state of grid-lock, which will inevitably lead to some companies going out of business. 'At a point in the not-too-distant future, supply will far exceed demand and some people will be forced to vacate.'[64]

Such a shake-out occurred at the start of the nineties with the more advanced gay porno industry, when several studios went under. Meanwhile profit margins for straight porn continue to tumble. Where once they were huge, now they are squeezed for large parts of the industry. In the mid-eighties the finished product from a one-day shoot could expect to turn a $15,000 investment into $150,000 in a few months. Not any more. The wholesale cost of a single cassette is well under five dollars. When video started out it was $90, and for a long time held at around $35 – and this for larger bulk sales. While retailers are in a position to keep a good profit margin, some porn producers are having to cut theirs nearly to the bone. This is hardly the story of quick and prodigious fortunes that porn was once rumoured to be.

When glut becomes no profit, then the wealthier firms with their stand-out product are the mostly likely to be able to ride out the storm. After the shake-out, high end won't be the only hard-core product left, not by any means; big-selling porners like John Stagliano, Ed Powers, Seymore Butts and John Leslie will also thrive, as will outfits such as Private and Video Marc Dorcel on import from Europe. Amateur and even some hardier survivors in the middle end will remain on the market. However, none of these will provide the whole American porn package. The high enders will have bought up most of the beauty and the glamour, and, if that's what the viewer wants, they'll most probably be watching a movie directed by Thomas, Blake, Ninn or Royalle, and produced by Vivid, Wicked or VCA.

The detached high end could turn out to be the leading as well as the defining American porn of the future – a porn more about mood and drama than simply sex. This evolutionary

6

Child story

One morning in June 1989, a businessman in Northern England called Lawrence Chard got into his car to go to work and take his children to school. At the moment when his wife brought the children out of the front door, a car came speeding round the corner, stopping in the Chard's driveway. Three men got out and surrounded Mr Chard. They were police officers, and he was under arrest, charged with taking indecent pictures of his children under the Protection of Children Act 1978 (POCA).

A camera film he'd put in at the local chemist's for developing had been queried concerning its content and the police had been contacted. One recent sunny afternoon spent at the Chards involved their two kids and their friend running about naked. The children had all been swimming. They were playing about in a suntrap in the Chard's back garden. In the presence of Mrs Chard and the other child's mother, Mr Chard had got his camera and captured the moment. As far as the police were concerned such innocent images were sexual poses.

Fourteen months of anguish were to follow for the Chard family, before Lawrence Chard was unanimously cleared by a jury at Preston Crown Court. The photos were innocent, while the juridical intervention by the state was highly intrusive and also, arguably, indecent. It included interrogations over sexual acts that never took place, with the children reduced to tears while also being exposed to the sight of their parents being browbeaten by suspicious police officers. The family subsequently changed their name and relocated to another part of the country.

In 1994 a woman in Ealing, West London, was arrested at Boot's the chemist concerning a picture of her friend's four-year-old son, taken at home, with the boy climbing over a seat with his trousers half down. The arrest occurred the day after the funeral of the woman's father. The woman's partner was a probation officer. Therefore in addition to the emotional strain, this investigation posed a threat to the man's future work prospects. The couple vigorously complained about the police action. Charges were never brought, but the pictures were not returned.

These two stories are representative of ongoing problems in Britain concerning nudity and images of children. During times of deep anxiety over child sexual abuse, the searching after external pointers to this mainly private, hidden crime has made innocent photographs suspect, with images of child nudity viewed as a possible symptom of abuse. Where once analysis of the content of media was a progressive thing, worries over child sexual abuse and child pornography has led to the situation where nearly all images of children are sexualised and seen as open to doubt. This often causes anxieties and energies to be misdirected, most likely to the neglect of the more tangled, demanding actualities of real abuse. The situation is perhaps also symptomatic of difficulties in the broader culture concerning sexuality and children.

To mention to someone that you are writing a book about porn is often to prompt the question: but what about child pornography? Although this book was planned to be about adult porn, the dominant cultural demonology that finds the adult porn industry and the sexual abuse of children as somehow conjoined needs addressing. The unfortunate slippage may be partly about the public nature of porn in contrast to the elusive, secret reality of the sexual abuse of children that mainly occurs in private. As Linda Williams observes, 'Because of this . . . exhibitionist quality, it is often porn, and those who can be vilified through its use or production, rather than real sexual harassers, who end up being blamed and punished.'[1]

Panics over child porn, though mostly caused by a heartfelt and salutary concern for child protection, can also be roused in order to make adult porn look guilty by association, as though watching a video of two adults having sex somehow connects the viewer with the darkest of abuses. The placing of the word 'child' in front of porn, forcing into people's minds an image of a child being made to perform unspeakable acts in front of the camera, thereby forestalls any reasonable discussion of adult porn. The reality is that the adult entertainment industry employs only adults to produce porn entertainment for adults. It is necessary to make clearly separate a regulated, large-scale business exclusively featuring adults, which goes on in full view and brazenly advertises its existence, from the unconnected, highly secret and underground recording of acts of child sex abuse.

Before now

(on when the production of child porn was legal in parts of the world)

There is a history of commercially produced child pornography; it is a grisly story, but one long since ended. In Denmark in the late sixties, the Danish government legalised production of all forms of pornography. During a period lasting between 1969 and 1979, this even included the toleration of a small, commercial output of magazines, as well as some films, of the record of sexual crimes involving children below the age of consent. In the seventies, Rodox produced a series of ten-minute loop films of child pornography. The precise circumstances of such film production remains unclear and rather lost in time now. The *Lolita* series, both stills and, presumably, the actual movies themselves, continue to this day to be a leading contraband exchanged between interested paedophiles. Likewise the magazines *Children Love*, *Incestuous Love* and *Nymph Lovers*. *Bambina Sex* was another child-porn magazine produced in Denmark in the seventies, and put together using materials sent to the publisher by individual paedophiles. This was allegedly the first ever photographic child-porn mag, published in 1971, and with an alleged print run of 20,000.[2] The publisher Willy Strauss came from Copenhagen and was also responsible for the magazine series *Lolita Sex*, also made up of amateur, private material sent in to the magazine. Strauss estimates that he published another forty to fifty one-off titles during the ten years of legal immunity in Denmark. In Holland, in the same period, there was a magazine series also called *Lolita*, and its contents were home-made images sent to the magazine. A lot of seizures of the eighties were of this small booklet series, as they are today. Any hard-core child porn being distributed on the internet will most likely feature scanned-in images taken from the Dutch *Lolita* series.

There is no history of commercial child-porn production in the UK. In Soho in the late sixties and early seventies, child-porn magazines from Denmark were available for purchase in some sex shops. (A similar situation transpired in red-light districts in some North American cities in the early seventies.) At the time a prosecution to test the legality of such materials was not launched in the UK, or in fact anywhere on mainland Europe. Such palpable evidence of sexual crimes against children only led to prosecutions in the USA in the middle of the seventies, at which point the Federal laws were changed, making the sale or possession of such materials a felony.[3]

The trade in child pornography was made illegal in Denmark at the turn of the eighties. Willy Strauss continued an *ad hoc* production. His activities led him to be entrapped by America's NBC in its 1984 news show, *The Silent Shame*. No prosecution followed. Strauss then switched to *Lolita Slavinder* (*Lolita Slave*), which was a series of pornographic stories with line drawings, something that is not illegal in Denmark. Following *The Silent Shame*, and US Senate hearings on the matter describing Amsterdam as a modern Sodom and Gomorrah, the Dutch government moved to make all forms of child porn illegal as of 1985. Around this time the Dutch police went looking for commercially produced porn in Holland of recent provenance, and found none. Some privately made material was uncovered, mostly originating in the USA. It is also alleged that much of the content of European child-porn magazines of the seventies originated in the USA and Canada. North Americans would send their pictures to magazine outlets in Holland and Denmark, who then published the materials, but with the bulk of the print run actually being in the USA.

A similar story occurred with illegally produced and distributed home-based American magazines of the seventies. *Lolitots*, the best-known title, would rehash European materials with domestically sourced private contributions. Otherwise, there has never been a commercial child-porn industry in America. The only noted child-porn producers in the USA in the eighties were probably the US government itself. During that decade, US postal inspectors continued to publish *Wonderland*, the paedophile contact magazine, as part of an ongoing entrapment ploy, even though the publisher had died. The writer Laura Kipnis tells of the case of two men in Virginia who were sentenced to thirty and thirty-three years' imprisonment after being convicted of conspiracy to make child pornography, when what had happened was that FBI undercover agents lured them into discussions of producing such materials.

In September 1995, a so-called FBI 'sting' operation concerning child porn in cyberspace, conducted through the gated online service AOL, led to the arrest of a dozen subscribers. The FBI investigations involved what might be described as 'active entrapment'. This included an adult agent pretending to be a teenage girl and convincing a suspect to cross state lines on the basis of the promise of their having sex together. Apart from suspects responding to such active entreaties from agents, nobody was arrested for seeking to make contact with an actual child.[4] The classified pages of gay magazine *The Advocate* have also been unwittingly used in federal government sting operations. Meanwhile US government agents have run film laboratories offering 'confidential' developing services, as well as also producing and distributing catalogues offering child-porn videos. These are currently the only publications in the USA that solicit, advertise, sell or offer to purchase or exchange child porn. Such extensive operations have resulted in few arrests of actual child pornographers, and fewer convictions.

Once the laws changed in Holland, further crackdowns

occurred in the eighties and nineties. Dutch police reported that much of the materials being seized was often the same goods they had been confiscating twenty years earlier. In 1992, two Dutch academics, Schuijer and Rossen, carried out an investigation of child pornography and found pictures still circulating from the seventies, concluding that virtually no new child porn has been produced on a global, commercial scale in over a decade.[5]

A poor law
(on the problems with POCA)

In London, in 1994, the Metropolitan Police Obscene Publications Squad was split in two, becoming the Vice and Clubs Squad, with adult porn as part of its remit, and the separate Child Porn and Paedophile Unit. This restructuring made sense in recognising child porn as being unconnected to adult materials industrially, generically or in terms of sexualities. It is also sensible to treat records of sex crimes against children as part of the broader issue of child sex abuse. However, it was suggested that the restructuring was made necessary because the child-porn problem had grown so big. This seems to suggest the fairly large-scale distribution of underground materials. But not through sex shops – there's no such availability in places like Soho.[6] To sell such materials would be too risky, assuming of course there was the desire to do so in the first place, or a large enough market to make it pay.

The Metropolitan Police are convinced there is a big market for child pornography, that the recording of child sexual abuse is taking place – on video and Polaroid – and these records are being passed around in small rings. Furthermore the police allege that rings of paedophiles are buying and distributing child porn made elsewhere.[7] (What is partly meant by this, perhaps, is the likelihood that individuals are returning from visits to Asia carrying mementoes of their exploits as child-sex tourists and, if they are part of a 'ring', perhaps swapping them amongst like-minded people.[8]) Examples of child-porn rings have been uncovered; they are, however, few and far between.

This isn't to say there aren't more to be uncovered. During 1996 and 1997 cases emerged of two possible rings in Belgium and France.[9]

Nonetheless, the feeling exists that the police and customs in the UK, and their counterparts in North America and parts of Europe, have become overly preoccupied with the notion of rings. The fear of rings, as pointed out by Linda Williams, 'can be seen as the product of a conspiratorial view of society, it ensures that the extent of pedophilia is unfathomable and that rare examples of ped networking can be construed as merely the tip of the iceberg, hidden by the conspiracy'.[10] With conspiracy we tend to project outwards, giving a kind of shadowy presence to villainy while placing crimes against children in nasty, dark, 'other' situations, rather than in the place where children appear to be most at risk: in families, in children's homes, in foster families, etc. The need to avoid underestimating child porn is equivalent to the need to locate the true dangers, the real offences, and to separate these from any false panics or stand-in anxieties. Conspiracy theories reflect the desire for easy answers and clean solutions, but they risk turning a society's attention away from the wider problem of abuse.

In Canada, for instance, in London, Ontario, in the winter of 1994, police chief Julian Fantino called a news conference to announce the apprehension of a major child-porn ring. At his side were piles of video tapes. It turned out later that these tapes contained only commercially available materials – images of children taken from mainstream media. Though numerous arrests were made, and some charges were brought, most people were released. All charges, so far, have been withdrawn, and to date nobody has gone to trial, let alone jail.[11]

The secret nature of child porn makes it difficult to speak of with any true authority. In the UK, researchers have to pick through information from court cases, police reports and convicts' testimonies, as well as anecdotal evidence, horror stories, rumours and fears, and try to piece together some kind of profile of the phenomenon. Statements about the content and prevalence of material are speculative or provisional at best.

Though the making of records of sex crimes against children does occur, as recovered videos and photographs demonstrate, the amount of evidence in cases brought to trial is not considerable. Legal researcher Stephen King has made a study of the workings of the POCA, the principle anti-child-porn law in Britain, which shows a lower number of prosecutions than one might expect during a period in which child porn has supposedly been on the rise. In the early nineties, the POCA resulted in around forty-two prosecutions per year in the UK. A good third of all police cases are dropped, and will never go to trial.[12] One doesn't doubt that child pornography exists. What one questions is how much there is, and how readily available it is. (It's certainly not in the sex shops. Issues of availability in cyberspace will be discussed in the next chapter.)

In the meantime, the bulk of *visible* police and judicial activity in the UK concerning child porn actually involves images of a non-pornographic nature – family snaps, naturist images and art-work. This is due mainly to the misuse of a bad law, the Protection of Children Act of 1978. The POCA allows any nude photograph of someone under the age of sixteen, such as those involving the Chard family and the family from Ealing, to be deemed as indecent, depending upon what the viewer thinks. This will happen when a law speaks of indecent photographs, rather than the more straightforward concept of the photographing of indecent behaviour with or towards children (as it is defined in German law). When a Rochester city councillor's home was 'raided' in June 1994 by five policemen acting under the POCA, according to the councillor, one officer asked his superior how to spot an 'indecent' photo from among a collection of family snaps. 'Anything with genitals showing,' he was told.[13]

In Britain during the nineties the suspicion has grown that in the absence of sufficient prosecutions for actual child pornography, and the lack of more successful seizures of child-porn materials, other innocent individuals and innocent materials are being required to fill in. It is widely thought that a shortage of results for the police, customs and the Crown Prosecution Service, during an era of anxiety over the existence of child sexual abuse, has led these authorities to become what a representative of Liberty has called 'moral entrepreneurs' – in the business of creating crimes to make arrests and secure convictions. It is certainly possible that at present all nude images involving children are being lumped together by the relevant authorities under the term 'child pornography'. This doesn't mean to say that records of child sex abuse won't make up a part of the paedophile unit's haul. It is difficult to know for sure. The vast majority of what is seized by police and customs in Britain is not seen by anyone else, apart from the Crown Prosecution Service and the occasional jury, and so may be described in whichever way the authorities choose using their own interpretations of a dubious law.[14]

In 1993, a senior officer at the Metropolitan Police's Obscene Publications Squad, who was involved in the arrest of the photographer Ron Oliver, was speaking by phone to Oliver's London solicitor, and had this to say on the matter: 'Any photograph taken of any child in the United Kingdom without clothes is indecent.' The police officer went on to declare that prosecutions wouldn't be directed against parents who took nude photographs of their children.[15] This view was in accord with the Home Office, which suggested in a letter in December 1995, 'The law is not intended to penalise parents who are simply taking family snaps on the beach or in the garden . . . harmless photographs of this nature are unlikely to be considered indecent by the courts.'[16] Clearly this parental exemption did not occur in Rochester or with the Chard story. Nor in the case of Julia Somerville and Jeremy Dixon. On 2 November 1995, television newsreader Julia Somerville and her partner Jeremy Dixon were arrested by Scotland Yard's Paedophile And Child Pornography Unit and taken in for questioning. This was following a complaint received from a branch of Boots, over a roll of film featuring shots of Somerville's naked daughter taking a bath. Two days later the story broke in the national news media, naming all parties, including Ms Somerville's daughter. Somerville and Dixon were put on police bail and their file was passed on to the Crown Prosecution Service, which in due course failed to find evidence of wrongdoing and advised the police not to proceed with their allegations. Somerville spoke of 'a deplorable invasion of my privacy and that of my family'.[17] At the time, the photographer Ron Oliver remarked, 'The real tragedy is that the police investigate everything as if there's something terribly wrong already – guilty until proven innocent . . . the damage to reputations and families is done when the police bash down the door.'[18]

This is exactly what a few forward-looking parliamentarians had predicted when the law was passed in 1978. In 1977 to 1978, the so called 'kiddy porn' scare crossed the Atlantic from America to arrive in the UK. Though unsupported by actual evidence, tales of a million kids in America being abducted annually, some of them press-ganged into a multimillion-dollar child-porn industry, achieved maximum impact, resulting in a private member's bill by backbencher Cyril Townsend being rushed through Parliament and onto the statute books as the POCA.[19]

At the time, adequate laws were already on the statute books in the UK to deal with acts of indecency or sexual assault against children, whether or not they were filmed or photographed, and the Home Office advised against adding to these. The absence of a deluge of child pornography in Britain was in fact admitted by those calling for the new law. It was also noted in Parliament, in passing, that allegations of a massive child-porn industry in America didn't match with efforts by researchers to track down examples during visits there. (For example, sightings of child-porn materials in sex shops, on both sides of the Atlantic, were in fact long since a thing of the past.) All of this was seemingly of no significance.

The new law made the taking of indecent photographs of persons under sixteen years of age to be a criminal offence. Crucially the term 'indecent' was not defined. Some parliamentarians did pause to wonder as to whether it needed definition. Worries were expressed over the possibility of 'innocent' images being queried. Following the Home Office's announcement that there was a 'desperate need' for a better definition which could be uniformly applied across the country, Emlyn Hooson MP suggested that 'What is a perfectly decent photograph to a doting parent, who has photographed a nude child on a mat in front of the fire, may nevertheless be an indecent photograph to a man who has that peculiar twist of mind.' Lord Northfield spoke of 'a real risk' of the new law impinging upon family photographs. Audrey Wise MP assured members that pictures that showed nude children on the beach would not fall foul of the Act, that this was not a bill against nudity 'as such'. With impressive foresight Lord Houghton of Sowerby predicted that such a loosely defined law might lead to innocent people being arrested, and also convicted in the mind of the public by the simple fact that the police had raided them. Two weeks or six months later, when the allegations were proved to be groundless, it would be too late.[20]

These warnings went unheeded. And yet the POCA did make it possible by the early nineties for any posed nude picture of a child to be deemed indecent by the police. The police have also proved reluctant to see dropped cases as reason to reconsider their approach. A nude photo of a child will be cleared of all charges of indecency, only for the next day to see a similar image causing a new investigation to be launched. Meanwhile time and resources and significant sums of public money are used up, rather than being channelled towards detecting real cases of child sex abuse. Though clearly children are abused within the family, there is an awful irony in the situation where a family's innocence is ruptured by a team of vice police ostensibly seeking to defend innocence. And it seems that, while child sexual abuse continues to be uncovered in social care facilities, foster homes, church groups and other respected social institutions, too often the police are to be found rooting through innocent family snaps.

Child naturist magazines
(on British customs)

The issue of definition proves less troublesome for Her Majesty's Customs & Excise. On average, customs were annually making seventy-five seizures of child imagery in the nineties, until 1996, when the figures started to rise steeply, almost trebling. Many such seizures were actually of art photographic books, including the work of well-known photographers such as Sally Mann, David Hamilton and Jock Sturges, as well as what were at the time legally produced naturist magazines. Mostly, with such seizures, prosecutions would not transpire.

In 1992, H. Holt, a teacher, a single man, living with his parents, was raided by customs officers and charged with importing a French naturist magazine, *Jeune et Naturel*, and a similar German naturist title, *Sonnenfreund*. Previous orders of these titles had been opened and inspected by customs and sent on. Holt had actually approached officials asking for guidelines over what was an acceptable importation, and was told that the naturist magazines were not considered a problem.

There are specifically three 'naturist' magazines that have caused the majority of seizures by police and customs of so called 'child porn' in the UK. The magazines exclusively feature pictures of nude kids taken in naturists camps around Europe. As of 1997, *Jeune et Naturel* was legally on sale in France, and likewise *Jung und Frei* and *Sonnenfreund* in Germany. Similar images of naked children in non-sexual situations in naturist camps have also been made available on video for purchase. *Jeune et Naturel* and its sister publication *Jung und Frei* were at this time actually both produced in the UK by the company that produces the leading naturist magazine, *Health and Efficiency*. Neither title went on sale domestically, and from 1996 were no longer available in Britain through subscription (meaning the loss of about thirty to forty subscribers). During 1996 considerable pressure was being brought to bear on the French and German governments to make both titles illegal. The third exclusively child naturist magazine, *Sonnenfreund*, is produced in Germany.[21]

These naturist magazines feature nude pictures of children of all ages up to eighteen. However, prepubescent children do appear to form the largest featured age group. The need for such magazines is certainly rather unclear. Peenhill, publisher of two of the titles (until the end of 1996, when the company ceased to exist[22]), says that they feature as an introduction to naturism for children. In the right kind of context, this might be true. However, considering that *Jeune et Naturel* was not for sale in France to under-eighteens, this argument lacks plausibility. Although photographs of children on holiday in a naturist camp does not constitute child pornography in the sense of records of indecent behaviour with or towards children, the exclusive focus on children and the omission of photographs of children in a family context, as is the case in other naturist titles, might suggest that a paedophile market is being courted. Likewise with the child naturist videos sold through the magazine *Sonnenfreund*.[23]

It took two years for the case of H. Holt to eventually come to court. In the summer of 1994, he was acquitted on all counts concerning these naturist titles. Holt argued that if these images were not indecent – that they were simply portraying naturist children in naturist locations under no coercion and engaged in normal activities – and didn't involve indecent acts, then exactly where was the 'indecency' taking place? It was also suggested that, if it were not an offence to produce the magazine in the UK, then it made no sense for importation to be an offence.[24] After the trial, Holt wrote to customs and subsequently the British government asking for the return of his magazines. Customs would not comply, arguing that although the court did not find the magazines indecent, this did not mean they weren't, and that therefore they saw 'no reason to alter their policy in respect of their seizure'.[25] Holt's communication with the government also concerned the American artist Jock Sturges, whose work has been exonerated in the UK and the USA from accusations of indecency but often still features in seizures made by British customs and police. These authorities will often refuse to return such materials as well as seeing ownership as suggestive of a paedophilic nature. 'The Jock Sturges book you mention is considered indecent by Customs,' writes a government official in a letter to Holt. 'Furthermore I understand that the police do consider taking action over the sale of such books if these sales are brought to their notice.'[26] In the summer of 1996 the same Jock Sturges book, *The Last Day of Summer*, was prominently displayed in the window of

Zwemmer's, the art books store on Charing Cross Road, London.

Images and behaviour
(on controlling thoughts)

Policing child naturist magazines like *Jeune et Naturel* involves policing the indecent thought. Rather than wonder why someone would wish to look at pictures of nude kids playing on the beach, what needs to be ascertained is whether possession of such images features as an accompaniment to committing actual offences. There is no clear evidence at present that such material is causally linked to sexual crimes against children. Also, although the production of actual child pornography constitutes a sex crime, whether people watching such materials also sexually offend against children is not clear. 'The most reasonable assessment based on the available research literature,' writes David Howitt in one of the most extensive, far-reaching analyses of available research data to date, 'is that the relationship between pornography, fantasy and offending is unclear.' Additionally, if there are connections between fantasy and reality, they are 'not straightforward'.[27]

The intensification of interest in the shrouded phenomenon of child sex abuse is still relatively recent. There is a lack of meaningful studies regarding individual offenders and the precise character of their behaviour. Within the field of prevention, detection, and treatment of offences and offenders, disputes over the centrality of imagery to behaviour continue to arise (along with accusations of complacency or counter-accusations of misplaced energies, and bad science). Theories of 'validation', 'escalation' and 'grooming' feature in such disputes.

The argument with validation is that paedophiles will see their criminal activities as less terrible, or less 'un-natural', the more they see other pictures of similar crimes. This sounds plausible. The police have certainly seized child porn from child sex offenders. However, this fails to take into account the large number of child sex offenders who have no experience with or use for such materials. According to group studies conducted in Howitt's inquiry into paedophilia, 'Very little interest in child porn was expressed by most of the paedophiles.' Furthermore, 'Some of the offenders expressed strong distaste for that sort of thing although few had actually seen it.'[28] To see child-porn imagery and child sexual abuse as inextricably linked is a mistake. The sex offender and the camera do not necessarily go hand in hand. In fact, it is likely that in a majority of cases the camera is not present to record such crimes of abuse. One reason many offenders might not use or need visual aids is because they have actually lived out their fantasy through some kind of direct sexual assault. Much paedophilic sex offending involves acts that do not require sexual arousal for their execution, and paedophiles will not necessarily achieve orgasm during the sexual assault. The offence is an experience that provides fantasy material for later masturbation. Thus the offence itself becomes the pornography.

There is a dread of the power of the image in Western culture. This dread underlies a lot of discussions of child porn, especially theories of escalation. The escalatory model suggests that a person may come across images of child nudity and might as a consequence develop paedophilic tendencies. This version of events figures human sexuality as deeply unstable, and pornography, particularly child pornography, as a highly toxic substance that can cause people to develop desires they would never have felt otherwise.[29] However, in the specific context of child porn, not only do many child sex offenders fail to make use of illegal materials, but many resort instead to making exclusive use of materials from the mainstream media. These licit images may be taken from children's clothing catalogues, television commercials, pictures in national newspapers and magazines, Hollywood movies, even Disney animation films.

The argument that suggests that certain materials produce a desire for child sex is speculative. Most likely the desire already exists. 'In none of the case studies in our research can be found instances of individuals who had experience of pornography of any sort prior to their early sexualisation,' says Howitt. 'There is no evidence that early exposure to porn was a cause of later offending.' Furthermore, 'Whilst some therapists see fantasy as part of an escalating offending cycle . . . the direct evidence for this is slight.'[30] There is a counter-argument, in fact, that suggests that naturist materials incorporated into a paedophiliac fantasy may actually provide a safe outlet for satisfying urges, and therefore possibly make sexual offences against children less likely. In the present climate of Britain in the late nineties, such an argument is unlikely to be acceptable in court.

The knowledge that general media images depicting children can be appropriated into a paedophilic fantasy has caused some observers to argue for the removal of a lot of mainstream imagery featuring children. In his book on child pornography, the journalist Tim Tate criticises mainstream media for being slack. Children featured in the advertising campaigns of *Vogue* and *Harpers Bazaar* in America, he suggests, are potentially a direct address to the paedophile. Partially undressed children being used to sell make-up, or perfume, may cause a frisson of excitement with the wrong kind of viewer.[31]

In Milton, Ontario, in 1994, a man was arrested and tried for possessing child pornography. The prosecution argued that confiscated video extracts from the art-house movie *Death in Venice* and American television's *Little House on the Prairie* were child pornography, due to the 'context' in which the material was found. In other words, the way in which the defendant saw and perceived the extracts was deemed criminal. His lawyer suggested in defence that 'thought crime' is not a part of the Criminal Code.[32] In 1996, a long-running series of Safeway supermarket commercials in the UK came under attack. Somewhat an imitation of the film *Look Who's Talking*, the ads featured a 'cute' little boy and his precocious observations upon the world, delivered via an adult actor's voice-over. This 'adultisation' of the child, it was argued, made children more attractive to paedophiles and the ads should be removed.

The critic Gilbert Adair has offered a version of the Kuleshov Experiment in such instances. Kuleshov sought to show how a film image gains meaning from its contextual arrangement with other images coming before and after. So, the neutral, unchanging expression of an actor's face in close-up, intercut with an image of a tiger, a steak and naked woman, can be seen by the viewer as expressing fear, hunger and lust respectively. 'A child's body is a beautiful thing' is Adair's opening statement, which he then contextualises with three different qualifications: '1, in the eyes of a parent; 2, in the eyes of an artist; 3, in the eyes of a paedophile ... All of these statements are, I submit, unarguably true. The problem is that, because the third expresses an unpalatable truth, the first two – in Britain at least – have been irredeemably corrupted.'[33]

To locate and root out every last image that may cause a paedophile excitement would prove a never-ending project. As Howitt observes, 'Paedophile stimulation from mass media is only fully understandable if we assume that what the offender puts into the experience of the media is important, not just the media's objective content.'[34] The hopeless job of supervising the mental impulse is never done. You are never going to be able to stop people having thoughts. The excessive monitoring of nude images of children may only guarantee their sexualisation. In this way is indecency located everywhere, while being required to be absolutely nowhere. The potential for distorting such imagery is not exclusive to jaded, hard-bitten vice cops, but exists at large in British society. One example is the unfortunate story of the young father in Essex who was photographed naked from the waist up, and holding his naked baby in his arms. This picture was taken down from the display window of a Debenhams department store in 1996 following complaints from members of the public. This iconic image of the eighties – the caring new man, clutching a naked baby in his strong but gentle arms – was now an image that was felt to be dirty and suggestive of terrible things.

Uncivilised conduct
(on child sexuality)

The so-called grooming theory also proposes links between imagery and sex crimes. It suggests that child porn is used by offenders, shown to their prey, to make the offence seem normal. Calls for the suppression of images of child sexual abuse on the internet derive partly from theories of 'grooming'.[35] Research evidence, to date, does not provide much support for this theory. Howitt found that few of those child sex offenders who have possessed child pornography spoke of using these materials as part of their 'wooing' techniques.

The grooming theory connects to broader social dilemmas concerning children, knowledge and power. If grooming should play a part in some abuse scenarios, one possible counterbalance would be equipping children with a greater knowledge of sexual matters. Having children better informed may empower them to dispute the acceptability of such conduct, to thus repel unwanted advances. Lifting the veil of secrecy that often makes sex a furtive, dirty, unspoken business may also give children the confidence to speak candidly to someone about unpleasant experiences.

The call for children to be sexually informed in order to help protect themselves can conflict with the dominant cultural imaginings of childhood as a period of innocence: imaginings that often vigorously resist any efforts to inform children. Childhood innocence is arguably an adult projection, some-thing that emanates perhaps from the conflicts and insecurities we experience as adults, which require the sentimental reassurances of a lost childhood Eden. These projections do not agree with the reality of childhood. In Britain in the nineties, according to an article in the *Daily Telegraph*, 'No one who knows small children can have failed to notice that they exhibit signs of sexuality from infancy.'[36] Eighty years ago, in his 'General Theory of the Neuroses', Sigmund Freud wrote, 'And then it turned out that all these [adult] inclinations to perversion had their roots in childhood, that children have a predisposition to all of them and carry them out to an extent corresponding to their immaturity.' Freud went on to observe, 'No doubt you will feel inclined at first to deny the whole business . . . overlook the sexual activities of children (no mean achievement).'[37]

Despite the far-reaching cultural acceptance in British and American society of many of the insights of Freud, as well as most people's actual experience of infants, the existence of child sexuality continues in the main to be denied or suppressed. This is due in part to the uncivilised character of child sexuality, which appears to be without barriers, failing to observe the distinctions between the masculine and the feminine, the oral and the anal. 'As long as the adult members of a society permit them to do so,' observes the American sexologist Leonore Tiefer, 'immature males and females engage in practically every type of sexual behavior found in grown men and women.'[38] Rules and normality come later. 'Normal is a moral category,' writes Judith Levine. 'We really don't know anything about normal children's sexual behavior.'[39]Part of the process of childhood involves disabusing infants of what Freud called their 'nuts and bolts' fascination for their own or other people's bodies. Before 'normality', child sexuality is an exercise in bad behaviour, an affront to good taste. Like the sexualities of other 'foreign' entities – the rustic, the urban poor, the native cultures of distant lands – over time child sexuality both demystifies sex and offers an alternative, polymorphous account. And this we really don't wish to know about.

A society that denies the existence of child sexuality, and that has also become troubled by child nudity, will most likely often seek to discourage sex education. This is to be expected. As Freud observed, 'Strangely enough, the people who deny the existence of sexuality in children do not on that account become milder in their educational efforts but pursue the manifestations of what they deny exists with the utmost severity – describing them as "childish naughtiness".'[40] Keeping children innocent can also mean keeping them ignorant. How ignorance helps young people look after themselves remains unclear. This desire to keep certain realities out of children's lives is linked to issues of power. Children are to be protected from knowing about the outside world and all of its dangers, but also its information and its choices. A child that is no longer ignorant may also know a thing or two, and might therefore challenge an adults' pedagogical authority. Books, films and urban tales about dangerous kid gangsters, of precocious, demonically possessed infants, of communities under siege from a gang of angelic nippers (and the tall story of the six-year-old boy holding up the corner shop with a pistol; films like *The Omen*, *The Exorcist*, *Little Devils*; books such as *Turn of the Screw* and *The Midwich Cuckoos*) all suggest that sometimes society is not always clear about who needs protecting from whom. A possible subtext of these fictions is the adult's urge to resist the emergent autonomous child, to hold off that moment when the child declares its 'demonic' state of independence.

The desire for maintaining child innocence finds some campaigners arguing for the age of consent to be raised and globally standardised as a part solution to child pornography.[41] (These campaigners cannot be pleased that, as of February 1996, Italy cut the age of consent for sex between consenting teenagers to 13, one of the lowest limits in Europe. 'You cannot punish love,' announced MP Alessandra Mussolini.[42]) Sixteen, eighteen, even twenty-one could be a standard age. It is difficult to see how this will help protect an eleven-year-old child in jeopardy. Such measures may in fact have more to do with a disapproval of teenage sexuality than with issues of sex abuse. To raise the age of consent would inevitably lead to the disciplining of consenting teenagers sexually involved with other consenting teenagers. When 'cures' for child porn criminalise teenage sexuality, you suspect that other supervisory 'moral' issues, like the rate of teenage pregnancy, teen violence and teen curfews, lurk in the background.

The urge to suppress child sexuality for as long as possible is also one that wishes to strictly monitor it, to channel and control it, to be sure the eventual adult sexuality that comes forth will be the 'right' kind – that is, heterosexual – and not the 'wrong' kind – unconventional and self-defining. Anxieties over what happens once the child and his or her sexuality grows up are at issue. Television shows like *Happy Days* and films like *American Graffiti* (or, more recently, the less saccharine *Dazed and Confused*) provide nostalgic, misty-eyed narratives of American teenhood. The tightly structured regimes of being a teenager in love, the graduating systems of reward and restriction – of carrying books, first dates, first kisses, going steady, wearing his ring – once seemed, from a distance, like constructed rituals in the melting-pot experience, part of the ongoing process of becoming an 'American'. However, such mawkish conventions were also the means for moulding and disciplining sexual identities. And, when such moulding fails, when the child's sexual behaviour doesn't turn out the way it was meant to, then the adult world's difficulties with child sexuality may run to hostility.

In August 1996, in Idaho, America, a seventy-year-old law, long since fallen into a state of disuse, was revived under pressure from the local tax-raising and spending authorities and the lobbying of the Christian Coalition. The law makes fornication outside of marriage illegal, and a custodial offence. The authorities started using it against teenagers to stop them having sex with each other. The authorities said they didn't like youngsters having unwanted pregnancies, and the state having to pay for it. But the absence of family-planning classes in school suggested the intrinsic dislike of teen sex. Fifteen-year-olds touching each other in parts of Idaho were now under threat of going to jail.[43]

Lost innocence
(on art-work)

A fair portion of police and judicial activity in Britain over 'indecent' images of children – apart from family snaps and naturist magazines – involves photographic art-work. In the late summer of 1989, Arthur Cotterill, a professional photographer and artist, was arrested under the provisions of the POCA for taking indecent photos of children. A few weeks earlier, while on a visit to a naturist club in Kent, Cotterill asked a twelve-year-old girl and her father if he could take some pictures of the girl as a study for a painting he was due to embark upon. She and her father happily obliged. He subsequently visited the family and took more pictures. When these were sent in for processing a lab worker complained, and the police were brought in. Cotterill's house was raided, other photographs of boys and girls taken for his work were seized and placed before a local magistrate, who found that some were indecent and fined him £1,000.

Photographs from the Cotterill case include a picture of a naked twelve-year-old girl lying on a bed in a modest pose. This picture was considered not indecent in court. There were also pictures of a boy, naked and leaping off a small podium, which were also deemed not indecent. Other pictures showing him in the same situation but waving his hands in the air were, however, found indecent by the magistrate. The logic in this is hard to grasp. Differences between all the images in the Cotterill case and pictures of a family on holiday, where the kids are nude on the beach or at play at the campsite, are non-existent.

Cotterill appealed his conviction to the Crown Court. The three presiding judges looked at the 'indecent' photos, and found none of them actually to be so. It was also declared that Cotterill had 'legitimate reason for possession of the photographs'. When making art-work depicting children, artists will frequently use photo guides, as it is rare that children will remain still for any length of time. Judge Rubin declared, 'Artists have very good reasons for having all sorts of photographs of human beings in all sorts of states of dress and undress.'[44]

In November 1992, the pen-and-ink illustrator Brian Partridge was arrested under suspicion of taking indecent photographs of children. Suspicion was aroused at a processing laboratory over photos that Partridge had taken of several clothed young girls. The way the children were posed and the fact that their underwear was visible in some pictures had made a lab worker uneasy. A visit to Partridge's flat in Cheltenham uncovered a stash of photos, including a collection of scrapbooks featuring cut-out pictures of young girls taken from various High Street shopping catalogues. In May 1993, Partridge was charged with five offences of taking indecent photos of children between 1983 and 1992. When the legal researcher Stephen King saw these images in court he admits that the question that ran through his head was: 'What the hell was he thinking about? What was his motivation.' King did not feel happy with the images and their drift. The poses assumed by the child models were of Partridge's construction. Although permission had always been gained, the parents were not always present during the sessions. No child had complained that any kind of actual contact had taken place, but one had said that she had felt uncomfortable, that Partridge's manner made her feel ill at ease, and she wouldn't wish to sit for him again. Partridge faced trial at Gloucester Crown Court in late November 1994 and after one hour's deliberation was found guilty on two counts. He received a year's probation.[45]

Partridge is considered a superb draftsperson. He had previously collaborated on a large art project around the subject of Alice in Wonderland, involving more than two dozen artists including the noted painter and photographic historian Graham Ovenden. During the raid on Partridge's house, police found work by Ovenden, and by the child photo-portrait artist Ron Oliver, given to him in appreciation of his work. There were also letters from Ovenden. Letters and address books mean a lot to the police. If you believe networking to be an intrinsic part of paedophilia, then they provide a possible way of uncovering a ring. Under the circumstances and considering the materials in Partridge's possession, it is understandable how the police might have wished to make further inquiries.

Raids on Ovenden and Oliver were conducted during the early months of 1993. Both artists were taken in for enquiries. The day after the raid on Ovenden, the Daily Mail ran a story announcing that the police had broken a major child-porn ring, stretching back twenty years. The article named both Ovenden and Oliver, clearly suggesting that both artists were deeply implicated, if not guilty. A 'suspect's' entitlement to some level of discretion in the preliminary stages of a sensitive investigation was discarded. The story in the Daily Mail did not mention that Ron Oliver's photographic portraiture was mainly of clothed children, and all the work had been commissioned by their parents. It also didn't mention that photographs by Oliver, typical of the 20,000 photographic images of his that were hauled in by the police and referred to as child porn, are part of the permanent collection at the Bibliotèque National in

France. Instead, guilt was presumed over a body of work that didn't feature a single depiction of indecency.

As a painter and a member of the Ruralist Brotherhood of Artists, Graham Ovenden has spent a lifetime contemplating through his creative efforts the meanings of childhood and notions of child innocence. His approach and style is in keeping with a long-standing tradition in fine art of nude child portraiture. Ovenden's paintings seek to capture the spiritual and physical beauty of mainly the changing female body: charting a transformative passage of time before, as he describes it, 'the apple has yet to be eaten'. Ovenden's aesthetic is rather bucolic and misty-eyed. His depiction of childhood can be sentimental, and his characterisation of young women is arguably rather paternalistic. It has been said that in Ovenden's preliminary photos, as well as his finished paintings, the eyes of the subjects are 'disturbing', 'erotic', that the viewer–subject eye contact can be questioning – the returning of the voyeuristic gaze, perhaps. That Ovenden mainly photographs young girls will trouble some people. (If he photographed mainly boys, this would trouble many others.) However his choice of subject touches upon broader cultural issues: of young girls being seen as prettier than young boys, of young girls being socialised to present themselves as pleasing to the eye, often therefore making girls more eager to pose.[46] All these matters are secondary, however, to the fact that in due course the police were to realise that they had made a mistake, that Ovenden's work was not indecent, and that they hadn't stumbled across a child-porn ring after all. Leading figures in the art world, from David Hockney to the Exhibitions Director of the Royal Academy, were swift to come to Ovenden's defence. No charges were brought against him.

As a portrait photographer, Ron Oliver gains commissions to photograph parents as well as their children from all over the world. The work he produces is considered to achieve a very high level of technical and printed excellence. Oliver's images of children are highly sympathetic, tasteful and decorous. The notion of indecency is totally absent from his work. Even any sense of child sexuality is mainly absent. In the work of photographers such as Sally Mann, Ovenden and Diana Blok, such issues are raised and to some degree explored. With Ron Oliver's family portraiture they are not. This is why it is particularly striking that such work should be the cause of investigation.

A small amount of Oliver's portraiture involves nudity. These images are always taken with the consent, if not at the request, of the parents who commission the work. Oliver's portraits will cost a client a small fortune – between £6,000 to £15,000. His work hangs prominently in the family homes of diplomats, bankers, industrialists, politicians and assorted public figures in Britain and across Europe and North America. As Oliver himself says, making sure to place his clients properly on the social scale, 'These are not the children of "ageing hippies" or "eccentrics" nor are their parents naive.'[47]

Five years after being raided, charges had not been brought against Oliver. But the 20,000 photos that were seized, virtually the sum total of Oliver's working career at that stage, had not been returned. In possession of his passport, and not on bail, or under any restrictions of movement, Oliver left Britain with his family some time after the original police raid. Under the glare of publicity, the threat of future police harassment, and a lack of clarity within the law regarding how he might continue to work in the UK, Oliver felt it time to find a new country in which to live.

It might be argued that parents and photographers should not to be left to decide if a child is photographed nude. For, once the child has grown up, they might regret such images were ever made.[48] It might also be suggested that because children don't understand what nudity means to adults, or what being nude will mean to them when they are grown up, then neither are they in a position to make such choices. This would imply that nudity is shameful, and would preclude the production of most nude imagery of children. (In late 1995, in the light of the Somerville case and his own experiences, Ron Oliver observed, 'The way it seems morals are in the UK, the only solution is for every person never to take nude pictures of their children.'[49]) In such discussions, seldom do the subjects themselves get to speak on the matter. Wishing to make it clear what constituted his photographic relationship with his clients, Oliver requested and received support from children he'd photographed over the years.

Many of these models were now grown up. An ex-model, aged nineteen, describes how when she was nine she was photographed by Oliver: 'I remember being very excited about it. My mother discussed it with me privately and left the final decision to me whether on not I should agree. . . . Ten years later I still have some of the pictures Ron took of me on my bedroom wall. All of them were taken with great taste and sensitivity, including those showing full-frontal nudity . . . I am very proud of the pictures that Ron took and still show them to my friends . . . I have often gone into bookshops to search the shelves and have been thrilled whenever I have found a book or a postcard which contains a picture of me.' She concludes, 'The idea that these pictures may be indecent or obscene has never entered my mind.'

Another one-time sitter for Oliver offers an opinion: 'The few naked pictures he took were normal for me. There was nothing sexual about the sessions or the way in which the pictures were taken.' Another concurs: 'I am still amazed and horrified by the accusations that Ron's work is in any way indecent, obscene or pornographic. My sister and I have nothing but happy memories of Ron Oliver and his work with us.' These excerpts are representative of many letters expressing similar sentiments. Finally, another former sitter, now grown up, elaborates on the matter: 'I am to be married shortly and I sincerely hope that Ron will be able to attend the wedding. When I eventually have children of my own it will be my dearest wish that Ron Oliver will agree to photograph them . . . his photographs are something to be treasured for a lifetime.'[50]

None of Ron Oliver's work even came close to being a record of indecency. Neither the content nor the compositional style offers even the faintest suggestion of such acts, nor does the way subjects are posed.[51] The eagerness of the children to work with Oliver, the fact that they defend their involvement many years after the fact, asserting some agency in the production of the images, these are significant features. The writer Lawrence Stanley has described child sexual abuse as a symptom of entrenched power relations within society.[52] The work of Ron Oliver (also that of Baylis, Sturges, Mapplethorpe and, most notably, Sally Mann) will often visually empower children as photographic subjects. This pictorial autonomy may cause some of the discomfiture felt by some adult viewers. The subjects of Oliver's work often break free of the restrictive sentimental conventions of child portraiture. As the mother of one of Oliver's studies observes in her letter of support, 'If I had wanted just "another pretty picture", I wouldn't have commissioned Ron Oliver. Today there are only a handful of photographers who have the skill and the inclination to photograph children without a smile, looking directly into the camera saying: "Here I am, look at me, look at who I am." '[53]

The traditional faith in the 'truth'-telling of photography is obscured in the context of allegations of 'indecency'. The photographing of a child could amount to sexual abuse. It could be a situation that is non-consenting in the sense that it is urged or pressured, and yet the photo itself offers no evidence of such manipulation. In other words, the photo may not tell the whole truth. Conversely, when an image reveals nothing, when the subject of the image says there was no indecency, still indecency has been alleged, because some believe it must exist. In the family photography of the American artist Sally Mann, the 'truth' gets turned around. These beautiful images of what at first glance appear to be the record of a family event – a boating trip on a lake, for instance – on greater reflection begin to reveal themselves as very studied, skilled constructions of normality. The 'authenticity' of Mann's work is assumed partly due to the fact that this is her family, the subjects are her children, this is their lives together gathered on black and white photographic film. The record of a summer's afternoon drawing to a close, that captures the emotional turbulence of tired children, the petulance, melancholy and affection – these raw, untreated emotions of children in the moment have to be for 'real'. And yet, alongside these notes of authenticity, hovers a distinct feeling that this record of events is a treatment of what happened. Mann's children are willingly playing themselves in their mother's carefully posed 'documentary' piece.[54]

Mann's choreographed performances of the family photo challenges our faith in the camera's reliability. Her work asks that we recognise how the 'truth' within the image is actually made, in part, by the viewer – depending upon what they bring to it, and what they find there. Similarly, in defending his work, Ron Oliver has said that the photographic event is in the eye of the beholder, depending upon who takes the picture, and whoever looks at it – including the police. Talk of viewer's 'constructing' the image, imputing dark meanings to innocent art-work or family snaps, brings us to the established photographic subgenre of the 'trace' photograph. The 'trace' will be literally trace-like sometimes, a photo of a scene from which the subject has just left. Something very Mary Celeste: an after-dinner dining table recently deserted with perhaps a still smouldering cigarette in an ashtray, conveying the strong ghostly after-presence of the recently departed.

The 'trace' directly dramatises and foregrounds one of the key emotions within photography, which is a general sense of absence. So many pictures, especially family and holiday photographs, convey an absence, of people no longer here, no longer with us, of times spent that have gone by and are irretrievable. In seeking out visual indicators of sexual abuse, the police and other authorities have perhaps looked at a nude child and 'seen' in this nudity the trace, or the portent, of sexual abuse. Also, on a more abstract, more hypothetical plane, there's perhaps a 'trace' within images of children of lost childhood and lost selves, and within images of nude children the trace of a lost, or perhaps suppressed, child sexuality. Child historians like Carolyn Steadman have written about the idea of childhood as a Western-made, bourgeois invention of recent centuries, and this childhood coming to symbolise for adults a departed 'lost self'. Talk of childhood is often filled with plaintive sentiments because of the things we relinquish in order to grow up: 'our lost potential selves', as Elizabeth Wilson describes it, and, perhaps more pertinently, 'our lost "polymor-phous-perverse" sexuality'.[55]

The adult gaze that falls upon a photograph of child nudity is partly troubled perhaps by the flickering 'trace' within the image of more personal losses. As a theory this is perhaps too neatly packaged, too Freudian for some, and yet it is also rather more forgiving than other arguments, with their suggestions of an unsavoury, indecent eye on the part of the authorities. If you work in the field of child protection, and by now you're aware that there are some who find the most innocent image of a child arousing, you yourself can no longer see just innocence, or, if you do, it appears tremulous, vulnerable, connected to sce-narios of abuse and loss of innocence. Perhaps when you know that awful kinds of child sex abuse can be perpetrated and recorded with Polaroid and video, you want to do whatever you can to stop this from happening, to be sure also to make society wary of being complacent. Hence the projections, the misread-ings, the negative fantasies that see rings and danger everywhere. You therefore will not allow that images in adver-tising, kids in art-work, toddlers in catalogues, family portraiture, nude families on holiday at a naturist spot, family snaps in the bath or the back yard, can be licit, innocent and none of your concern. As Frank Lubbers observes, concerning the work of Ron Oliver, 'The unprejudiced viewer of these photographs will just see gentle, innocent and modest nudity. The biased mind sees only its own confused contents.'[56]

The danger in seeing bad things everywhere means that real acts of cruelty towards children, including sexual abuse, could be missed. For these reasons it would be better if an image were judged as an offence when it is a record of an illegal act, and not because some people – and clearly it needn't just be sex offenders but police officers too – look at them and see indecency. It would be more sensible perhaps if the authorities were to recognise that the act of sexual abuse is the crime, and not a piece of film.

7

The perils of cyberspace

There are two leading stories told about pornography and the new media technologies. Both, in different ways, offer a narrow, rather troubled vista. One account finds a dispute between cyber-sceptics dreading a further alienation of people from 'real' life and those cyber-boosters who proclaim a new dawn of sexual rapture via telecommunications. These disputing claims will be assessed in the next chapter, 'Future Sex'. Meanwhile, the other new tech and porn story concerns risk and danger, illegality and censorship, and revolves around the 'young person' and fears for their exploitation in a variety of cyber-malpractices.

In *The Secret Museum*, Walter Kendrick speaks of the birth during the last century of an entity known as the Young Person, who was forever in peril of being corrupted by certain hot texts, nasty photos or amoral comic books. The need to protect the vulnerable young person was used as justification for censorship throughout society, to control or forbid items that might, as Dickens's Mr Podsnap put it, 'call a blush into the cheek of a young person'.[1] During the twentieth century the defence of the young person as an argument for censorship lost ground for a while, and even fell into temporary disuse. At the trial of Haga Revelly, in 1913, the presiding judge advised against fixing a public morality on the basis of the very young: 'To put thought on a leash to the average conscience of the times seems tolerable, but to fetter it by the necessities of the lowest and least capable seems a fatal policy.'[2] But in recent times in the

UK and the USA there has been a revival of the Young Person. Anxiety over the safety of children, and of their coming into contact with materials made for adults, can re-emerge as justification for sweeping censorship for all.

With computers, it is not always clear whether the young person is at risk from *seeing* something, or being *involved* in something. During the nineties these two interconnected scares are running parallel, fluctuating in levels of prominence. For a long while exposure was feared most, or at least mentioned most often. In 1994, a British parliamentary select committee reported on the 'new horror' of computer porn, a thing so virulent, according to Labour MP Frank Cook, it was 'tantamount to the injection of heroin into a child's school milk'.[3] In the high-temperature language of porn demonology, if the analogy isn't Dachau, it can be hard drugs, or a viral infection: computer porn is 'technology's HIV, a law-resistant disease that so far has no effective check'.[4]

Evidence from up and down the land of school desks hiding floppy disks full of the hard stuff was scanty to say the least. Nevertheless, talk of school-yard porn rings was all the rage. A police officer in Luton boasted of breaking up a playtime exchange network and seizing 700 or more porn floppy disks. In due course it turned out that every disk was actually clean, but the headlines by then had moved on. A government-funded research unit at the University of Central Lancashire announced that a third of British schoolkids had disks with porn on them. This was a statement apparently based upon what some teachers from a small sample of schools were saying was true, or, as was conceded, more likely guessing to be true.[5]

In time the internet started to gain a notoriety. No longer was it just a case of playground swap meets, but a whole datasphere out there waiting to trade. A place that knew no bounds, hosting sites that catered to every kind of sordid sexual practice for cyber-nippers to stumble upon by mistake. A mistake almost impossible *not* to make, according to a *Time* magazine cover story from late June 1995, which described the porn presence online as 'ubiquitous'. With dramatic artwork, including an image of what looked like a man fornicating with his computer, *Time* announced the new social panic: 'ON A SCREEN NEAR YOU: CYBERPORN. It's popular, pervasive and surprisingly perverse.' The report by Elmer deWitt leaned heavily on the findings of a study from Carnegie-Mellon University of Pittsburgh: 'Marketing Pornography on the Information Superhighway'. The study, it was implied, had quantified 83.5 per cent of all image-based online traffic to be pornographic (or at the very least suggested that 83.5 per cent of online newsgroup image-based traffic was pornographic). The research was the sole scholastic output of Martin Rimm, a thirty-year-old undergraduate who was using 'data' gathered for a spoof on net filth he was hoping to get published.[6] Rimm's grasp of basic statistical measurement techniques was found to be limited. His research, which crucially hadn't been peer reviewed, lacked a clear methodology, offering assertions without evidential back-up and results that were impossible to replicate. Though esteemed researchers had alerted the magazine to serious flaws in the Rimm study, *Time* still published its story – a story that in itself communicated a mixed message. For, deep in the text, in distinct contradiction to the attention-grabbing story lead, it was noted that Rimm's research did not find 83.5 per cent of usenet files to be pornographic in content, but rather that: 'Pornographic image files, despite their evident popularity, represent only about 3 percent of all the messages on the Usenet newsgroups, while the Usenet itself represents only 11.5 percent of the traffic on the Internet.'[7]

So cyberporn was not so 'pervasive' or 'ubiquitous' after all. Another misleading feature of Rimm's report and the story in *Time* was the way the world wide web and usenet, two different areas in cyberspace, were confused with bulletin board services (BBSs). BBSs are a separate dimension of the online world, offering a direct-dial, computer-to-computer relationship. Access to a BBS is less simple, usually requiring a credit card for membership, and can often involve a lot of costly long-distance calls that would soon show up on a parent's telephone bill. Hardly something that children are likely to stumble across in their regular surfing. Even then, much of the content carried on the majority of adult related BBSs will be images scanned from magazines available at newsstands and adult bookstores.

The problem with myths like *Time*'s cyberporn panic is that they take on a life of their own. Once these misleading scare stories are out, there's no easy way of pulling them back. Soon afterwards, Ralph Reed from the conservative Christian Coalition group in America 'quoted' from *Time* on the American television show *Nightline*: 'According to the Carnegie-Mellon University survey, one-quarter of all the images involve the torture of women.' This was simply untrue. Neither the study nor *Time* made any such claims. A report that had grossly misrepresented the reality of the internet was now itself being travestied. Such net demonology leaked across the Atlantic, causing a similar panic. The Labour MP Barbara Roche, as well as some 'concerned academics', called for the government to take action in the fight against the increasingly sordid datasphere. Newspapers wrote gleefully of the dark side of the internet, of its being 'a heavily used red-light district, sending pornography into millions of homes'.[8] This image of porn being sent into people's homes was commonplace, like a very bad dose of something nasty that people were unable to resist.

Online self-advertisements from filtration software manufacturer SurfWatch asked the burning question, the concern of parents, educators and employers: 'How can porn be prevented from coming into computers?'[9] The mainstream image was already fixed, of the viral porn coming to get you, emerging from out of the cyberchaos and pulsing down telephone lines, under the sea, under ground, under your street and up into your home through your modem – suddenly bursting out all across your computer screen. As though you didn't go looking for it, which is how the bulk of people tend to come by their pornography.

Porn is certainly out there in cyberspace. There's quite a lot of it – although not nearly as much as some have suggested, or as might first appear, as the same images and materials have a habit of re-emerging with some regularity. More important than size is the issue of access. Small amounts of net porn can show up where it's not wanted, or be trailed at inappropriate places. However, the vast majority of online porn isn't available for easy consumption, or can be easily avoided. Certainly, porn is no blushing violet. Not when it's selling itself, and not even when it's giving it away for free. Generally, you don't go to the effort of scanning an image of your nude partner, or a paparazzi snap of Farrah Fawcett caught getting out of the car with no knickers on, to then lose the image on the net. You tend to post it where others will find it, so to brag, to offer trades, to contribute to a shared system of lust. Porn brazenly advertises its existence; you then either choose to look at it, look away, or block your child's access to such things. Of course the non-linearity of net spinning can sometimes lead you into foreign places. However, during the explosion of interest in the net, there were increasingly fewer open porno sites on the world wide web that didn't carry a warning plate at the front door – 'WARNING: The following pages contain sexually oriented adult material intended for individuals 21 years of age or older. Access is prohibited to minors! If you are not 21 years old, you must NOT continue and you MUST follow this link.'

In time, a much more effective barrier to inappropriate viewing or unwanted porn experiences in cyberspace would emerge in the familiar shape of commerce. The main porn vendors had slowly but surely moved into the datasphere and were making their sites pay-per-view. A few coy tempter images were offered at the front end of commercial sites, but any further revelations were dependent upon payment in advance. Young persons in cyberspace were starting to find that their modems were no longer good enough to guarantee access to many of the really hot online parties. What had often been the case on BBSs was increasingly common on the web. To access a private view with Gina De Marca you had to have a credit card or you were out of luck. If you really needed to see another shot of Christy Canyon in her morning glory, you required a Mastercard-purchased user name. Once upon a time it was the technical effort of extracting binaries that made prospecting for net dirt a chore, then it was belated parental/societal inter-ference, and now it was commerce.

Blockers and PICS

(on rating and filtering the internet)

On launch week in 1995, Penthouse's subscription web site received 3 million exploratory hits per day, reportedly melting the system for a while. It was just like a decade earlier when new dial-a-porn telephone sex lines had caused telephone networks in several countries to collapse on the first night. Headline stories are made of such events. Once again porn was demonstrating its power to drive new technology forward while also dragging it through the dirt, ably demonstrating its inadvertent knack of softening up a new and unruly media system for regulation. Repeated talk of online smut had finally brought forward the time to block. Blocking measures were in place at university campuses in America. In the UK, Oxford University, having found that during October 1995, 4,000 connections were made to one usenet newsgroup supposedly trading in erotic materials, instructed Ukerna, the company linking the university to the net, to check offending groups.[10]

But that was mainly gown-town titillation. The serious blocking was in the home with a whole new range of filtration systems like Cyber-Watch, Surf Patrol, Net Nanny, promising to keep the cyberporn from sullying any child's net experiences. SurfWatch was the creation of a man from Vancouver called Bill Duvall, who started paying a team of college graduates to be smut hounds, sniffing out as much net filth as possible to add to his 'trick book' of 'nasty' cyber addresses. By 1995, ten addresses per day, per hound, featuring 'sexual frankness', were being transferred to the SurfWatch computer program which would, in theory, automatically block access to such high-risk cyberzones. Then there was Net Nanny, a software programme available any night of the week to babysit cyberbrats, to watch over their on-screen activities and communications. Any age-inappropriate behaviour in the live chat rooms and online meeting places, any leading questions from cyberstrangers like 'What's your name?' and 'What's your phone number?' and, according to *Time* magazine, 'nanny pulls the plug'.[11]

There are, however, problems with such filtration systems. Firstly, they don't always work very well. In the USA, in May 1997, *Consumer Reports* magazine ran a story on filtering applications. Senior editor Jeff Fox reported trying to access two dozen sites featuring sexual material while running the filtering software, Net Nanny, Cyber Patrol, CyberSitter and SurfWatch. 'None of them blocked all the adult sites we tried to get into.'[12] Filtering software has also been criticised for being too heavy-handed, for blocking access to non-porn sites that might feature discussions of gay sexuality or breast cancer, because such sites use key words like 'sex' or 'breast' which the filter system is configured to veto. 'It definitely has problems,' admitted Ann Beeson, staff attorney for the American Civil Liberties Union.[13] Additionally, a filtration company's hit list of unacceptable sites might be too restrictive for people's tastes. *Hotwired* journalist Declan McCullough found that the list of proscribed sites of one cybersitter database included the National Organisation for Women, and the famous Bay Area online cybercommunity WELL. Since these databases may be treated as commercially confidential, people might have to take a company's word that their criteria for blocking sites is realistic rather than oppressive.

In the wake of these *ad hoc* blocking measures, industry leaders in the field of new technology, like Apple, America Online, AT&T, IBM, Microsoft and Netscape, decided to team up as a formidable net posse to do something more concerted about the tarnished image of their bright new revenue stream.[14] Soon afterwards the World Wide Web Consortium came up with an industry-wide plan to clean up cyberspace, launching PICS – the Platform for Internet Content Selection: 'an easy-to-use labeling and selection platform ... that empowers people worldwide to selectively control online content they receive through personal computers'.[15] The PICS system of content labelling could be implemented at site, or by service providers offering access to the internet. Content could be labelled in the style of viewing guidelines for cinema. This might mean a level of '12' for very mild, non-explicit nudity; '15' for discussion of adult issues; '18' for levels of blue language,

explicit sex or violent imagery. Parents could then either con-
figure the software to a level of consumption they felt happy
with or, alternatively, incorporate a ratings system provided by
a reputable organisation such as the American Parent Teachers
Association or Boy Scouts of America.

The development of ratings and labelling systems necessarily
raises questions over whose moral standards will mark the lines.
Historically the story of ratings has seen an imposition of very
exacting moral standards. Comic book guidelines from 1954
required strict morals for superheroes: 'Illicit sex relations are
neither to be hinted at or portrayed . . . sexual abnormalities
are unacceptable. The treatment of love-romance stories shall
emphasize the value of the home and the sanctity of marriage
. . . Divorce shall not be treated humorously nor shall be represented as desirable. Crimes shall never be presented in such a
way as to . . . promote distrust of the forces of law and
justice. . .' By 1971, following the Beatles, Woodstock, the
Vietnam war, and television news images of a naked, napalmed
child running down the street, an 'updated' set of guidelines
proved as eager as ever to stress the need for homeliness in
comics: 'The comic book medium, having come of age on the
American culture scene, must measure up to its responsibilities. To make a positive contribution to contemporary life,
the industry must seek new areas for developing sound, wholesome entertainment.'[16]

A rating system will inevitably encode certain values. These
may not be as buttoned down as the comic codes of the past,
but are bound to offer a value system proposing, if not
requiring, the norms of marital-heterosexual-'vanilla'-mon-
ogamy, at the same time as blocking and disposing of
alternative or conflicting points of view.

A rating or labelling system hurried into place by an
industry in fear of being regulated by government is likely to
end up being its own censorship system (and likely to be one
that is commercially beneficial to those who create it). Values
apart, ratings and certification tend to carry with them
additional powers of restraint. PICS also claimed to offer
worried employers the technology to block members of staff

from accessing recreational sites on company time, as well as enabling governments to block materials they don't approve of from coming into their territory. In other words, this sugar-coated solution was pretty serious.

The future in cyberspace as promoted by PICS could be similar to that of cinema and video distribution – where near-compulsory ratings and certification is required and all materials are carefully monitored and patrolled. How exacting supervision might be under such a regime is still not clear. For instance, what does the future hold for any non-certificated web site, or non-certificated newsgroup, should, in time, PICS and co. become the industry standard in America? With video in the UK, if you don't have a certificate, it doesn't matter what the content is: you are breaking the law. According to those pushing for PICS, the labelling system would remain 'volun-tary'. Nobody, it was suggested, will be 'made' to label their web pages by law. However, internet service providers may require it as part of their service contract with users, if not least to avoid allegations of being responsible for 'publishing' or 'disseminating' 'obscenity'. Any user infringements, like mis-labelling, and it's time for the subscriber to find a new service provider. How many internet service providers in the US are going to risk offering internet access to rebellious users? And even if some do, with most of the other servers not running any 'unlabelled' pages, those users who would rather not adhere to a non-negotiable system of norms imposed from above may face a future where if their contribution to cyberspace fails to achieve widespread distribution they'll be banished to its outer fringes instead.

Another bad law
(on the Communications Decency Act)

For a period in America, a future involving the outer fringes even seemed in doubt once lawmakers started taking an interest in bringing the new media into line. In the summer of 1994, James Exon, a Democrat senator from Nebraska, launched a campaign to regulate online communications. Exon proposed an amendment to a pending telecommunications bill, which would become known as the Communications Decency Act (CDA). The CDA made distribution of 'indecent' materials via telecommunications media punishable by up to two years in prison and a $250,000 fine. Though Exon's legislative initiative was much criticised and protested, its constitutionality seriously doubted, in February 1996, with the presidential and congressional election season looming, it was hurriedly passed into federal law as part of the Telecommunications Reform Bill.

Almost immediately a joint action was launched against the new law in a federal court in Philadelphia. Plaintiffs included, among many others, the Electric Frontier Foundation (EFF), CompuServe, AOL, Microsoft, Apple, the American Libraries Association (ALA) and the American Civil Liberties Union (ACLU). Four months later, in June 1996, the court struck down the CDA as a law that 'went way too far in criminalising protected speech'. The Philadelphia court ruling observed that 'The strength of the Internet is chaos, so the strength of our liberty depends upon the chaos and cacophony of the unfettered speech the First Amendment protects.'[17] As this bad law moved on from Philadelphia *en route* for its inevitable burial in the Supreme Court, hackers entered the US Justice Department's web site in a small gesture of rebellion, rechristening the site 'Department of Injustice', and flooding it with swastikas as well as pseudo-images of a 'topless' Jennifer Aniston.

The underlying intention of the CDA had been to characterise the internet as a form of 'pervasive' or '*broad*-casting' medium, equivalent to American network television and radio. In the USA, such media are denied the normal First Amendment constitutional protections for free speech. Instead they need to adhere to the far stricter requirement of not transmitting indecency. In this context, 'indecency' effectively means working on the basis that if a kid might see it then it must always be suitable for their consumption. (This explains why the briefest sighting of the actress Sherry Stringfield's bottom in an early episode of television's *NYPD Blue* caused such a furore.)

In late twentieth-century societies of diversity and plurality, the acceptability, or desirability, of organising freedom of expression around the protection of the young person's sensibilities seems difficult to defend. Once such sensibilities become entwined with a censor's decision-making process, then restriction will most often win out over liberty (especially with censors in the habit of making political expediency their guiding light). To some extent it has to be dependent upon parents to keep porn out of reach of their children. 'As a parent of a soon-to-be teenager,' writes a woman fan of porn on the net, 'I am concerned about the accessibility of unsuitable materials . . . but I accept responsibility for keeping them out of her hands . . . and educating her when the need arises.'[18]

American anti-porn campaigners hoped that the CDA would extend the 'pervasive media' restrictions on network radio and television to cyberspace, while those opposing the new law argued that online communications should enjoy the same freedoms available to the printed media in America. Expanding 'indecency' to cyberspace was part of an ongoing endeavour of right-wing Christian groupings like Morality in the Media and the Christian Coalition to make 'indecency', and not the far raunchier 'obscenity', as the constitutional norm rather than its exception.

In late June 1997, as expected, the US Supreme Court ruled the CDA as unconstitutional. Its ruling found that the internet is not an 'invasive' medium in the way of television or radio and so shouldn't be subject to the same extensive controls. Justice John Paul Stevens compared pornography on the internet to the legally accepted dial-a-porn operations in the USA. 'The dial-it medium requires the listener to take affirmative steps to receive the communication.'

Before the short, unhappy life of the CDA had been brought to an end, the anti-porn lobby groups had already started regrouping and redeploying upon the complex, daunting field of state law. The bad law-making of the CDA was to be followed by a whole series of worse bills at state level all across America. In Florida, a draft amendment to the state's porn statutes would make online transmitters of adult material liable to pay victims of sex crimes. The Virginian state legislature redefined constitutionally protected artwork as net-distributed 'child pornography', even when there was no child involved in their production. In Connecticut, a state censorship bill was signed into law which could put netizens in prison for the wrong kind of 'flaming'. In another case in Florida the ACLU were also contemplating a First Amendment lawsuit against the Orange County Library System which had been filtering all user access to the internet. 'You can't subject adults to library content that is only suitable for children.'[19] During this intense bout of restitching America's highly complex patchwork of state sex laws, how tenable or durable such new bills would be was, for the time being, anybody's guess.

The American cyberdream
(on the fight for a free datasphere)

At a federal level the push to regulate the new media was by no means over – it was just coming from a more acceptable source. On the day that the CDA was rejected by the Supreme Court, as the cyberactivist Bruce Ennis declared, 'the Internet is now basically safe from government regulation in the future,' the stock value of the Net Nanny company rose almost 60 per cent on the Vancouver Exchange. Ira Magaziner, a senior policy adviser to the Clinton administration, announced that he would not support another law like the CDA. In his view, the key to making cyberspace a clean and safe place for America lay not with laws but with self-regulation within the industry. 'The administration therefore supports . . . (the) adoption of competing ratings systems . . . to assist in screening information online.' At the same time the Software Publishers Association repeated their call for parents to safeguard their children by using the filtration software made by some of its members.[20]

During the legal struggle against the CDA, the American Civil Liberties Union had been quietly ambivalent over the desirability of blocking software, while co-plaintiffs the America Library Association were in fact partly backed by filtration companies such as SurfWatch.[21] Whether the ill-conceived CDA was ever likely to amount to more than an act of playing to the electoral gallery is doubtful. However, industry-led initiatives such as filtration and rating systems were proving more durable, the apparently acceptable face of regulation. Just so long as it kept the big bad government out of the cyberian's back yard.

The battle scenario with the CDA had explicitly pitched 'big brother' against the rugged American individualist. In a society where every step taken by the federal government is greeted with profound distrust by at least some grouping or other, the CDA was always going to be vigorously resisted. (The USA in the late nineties is after all a country where federal government buildings are bombed by militias.[22]) The new technological environment tends not only to accommodate but often to amplify libertarian tendencies. The American cyberdream was partially founded upon a belief in the manifest destiny of the radical cyber-individualist, of their 'small is beautiful, chaos is excellent' mores. 'I do not think the Net will be regulated/ censored by the government,' a woman porn-lover writes in an email to the author. 'The deciding factor, I think, is the large number of 'baby boomers' online. Our attitudes were shaped in the permissive sixties, and we tend to be anti-government, in general . . . and dedicated to personal freedom, and freedom of expression. We won't let it happen.'[23]

For censorship to stick, therefore, it needed to emerge from within the digital sphere itself. Which, of course, had already started happening with PICS and the like. These were censoring tools, restrictive filtration systems, but they came to the net community not via Bill Clinton, but through 'libertarian' technocrats who said they only wished to keep government off their back, to 'enable' netizens, while making the datasphere a safe place for people to roam. Nevertheless, the US government couldn't really have hoped for more from an industry ready and willing to meet the 'need' for restriction. In another era, the sight of various mega-corporations ganging together to create such coordinated control systems would be treated with the gravest suspicion. Because deregulation is part of the founding myth of the information led economy, it was possible for many to overlook the obvious reality that some of the people credited with helping to forge this new world frontier were now producing the software to affect its enclosure. In the eye of the storm over the CDA, such cartelism was greeted not only as the net's saviour but almost as though it were the continuation of its historical process.

Casting the net
(on the realities of net seduction)

Accompanying so much talk of porn flying into the computer were tales of what became known as 'net seduction'. Stories of children being spirited away by their computer, vulnerable to online predators, of being drawn into dangerous real-life situations. Some stories were true. One sixteen-year-old boy spent three weeks with a man he met in cyberspace and then returned home. A thirteen-year-old girl left home to be with man in San Francisco who'd promised 'that we can run around our room naked all day and all night'. In the USA, Ernie Allen, Executive Director of the National Center for Missing and Exploited Children (NCMEC), acknowledged that in 1995 there'd been ten to twelve 'fairly high-profile cases' of children being lured online into dubious situations. Whether all of these situations had featured an off-line, real-life dimension was not always clear. However, NCMEC was very keen to point out that in a country where 800,000 children are reported missing every year, these levels of net seduction were currently not their main concern. Oliver Clarke, chairman of CommUnity, a UK-based online campaigning organisation, as well as a police sergeant in Manchester, was also eager to place any such hazards in perspective: 'Children are far more at risk of falling prey to a paedophile whilst standing at the school gates than they are surfing the Net.'[24] Even *Time* magazine's cyberporn 'exposé' downplayed the threat: 'There is no evidence that it is any greater than the thousand other threats children face every day.'[25]

For the troubled, worried parent, online reassurances were flooding in. 'The Net is a far safer place for your children than

Disney World,' writes one concerned parent surfer,[26] while
another volunteers assorted handy hints: 'Suggestion: stay in
the room where the computer is when your kid is on IRC
[internet relay chat, live discussions] or anything else, and keep
checking to see what they are saying or having said to them.[27]
Experienced online people were keen to point out that children
could spend their whole childhood in cyberspace and never
once encounter a child predator or even have any inappropriate
material passed their way. These strenuous efforts to quell any
incipient panic conflicted however with the news media's love
of a good story. Broadsheet newspapers ably rose to the challenge. Scary cartoon illustrations were mocked up, featuring
kids in front of their PCs and a hand reaching out from the
screen grabbing them by the neck, about to drag them off into
the cybermatrix. It was an adult fairy tale of the nineties to
rival Hansel and Gretel but with the added twist of something
straight out of the eighties horror movie *Poltergeist*.

Around this time, reports emerged of the number of homeless children in UK exceeding 300,000 during 1995, of the rise
in the number of families living in poverty in the UK to nearly
20 per cent, and of increased incidence in the UK of violence
in the home: 'Researchers estimate one in 100 marriages is
characterised by severe and repeated violence affecting at least
750,000 children each year.'[28] These more commonplace tales
of woe for children in the nineties were often offered up in
snippet-sized reports that tended to be buried at the foot of
page five of any given newspaper. Such stories never fronted
the 'Weekend' section, and they never came with a handy
cartoon illustration of a young child being kicked around the
living room. This would have been in poor taste.

Arresting images
(on child porn online)

During 1996 the focus of fear in the UK visibly shifted from
stories of net seduction, and child exposure to lurid online
materials, to the highly emotive anxiety over the distribution of
child porn on the internet. As far back as 1985, and *PBB* from

Woking, Surrey (one of the first adult bulletin board services in the UK), the world of telecommunications has been troubled by the shadow of child pornography. After rumours that paedophilic porn solicitation had taken place in one of its special interest groups, *PBB* was pressured into closing down in 1987. In the same year, across the channel in France, *Ballet Rousse*, a bulletin board based in Lille which ran on the French Minitel computer-telephone information service, had ceased to function following rumours that an exchange of paedophilic information and images had occurred on the service.[29] In Australia in 1993, one of the first successful prosecutions was made against an internet user for posting child porn on a usenet newsgroup, while in March 1993, in the US, 'Operation Longarm' resulted in forty arrests, and two indictments, for trading in child porn on the net. In the case of 'Operation Longarm' the illegal images being posted and traded were scanned photographs from *Lolita* magazine from Holland and originally published over twenty years previously.[30]

The most noted court action in Britain up to 1998 was Operation Starburst. According to the National Criminal Intelligence Service's annual report for 1995, NCIS 'assisted Birmingham police in the first ever internationally coordinated effort to target suspects distributing child porn on the internet . . . (which) has led to prosecutions in a number of countries, including America, Holland, Estonia'.[31] The targeted activities actually involved a direct dial-up Bulletin Board Service. Alban Fellowes, a research assistant at Birmingham University, was charged and convicted under the Criminal Justice Act of 1994 for computer pornography crimes. Fellowes and a friend ran a BBS known as 'the Archive', which held a store of paedophilic materials, including scanned images of sexual activity between children and adults taken from the *Lolita* magazine of the seventies. The Archive was run on the basis of access to the service being dependent on a new caller having something to trade. The full content of the Archive was apparently not discussed in court. Fellows himself was sentenced for three years' imprisonment in May 1996 on the basis of being in possession of three indecent images originating from *Lolita*. Stephen Arnold, his co-defendant, received a six-month sentence for distributing indecent photos.

Clearly the new telecommunications technology makes the wider availability of child porn a possibility. (Though turning this possibility into a fear of the technology itself often occurs in pursuit of an altogether broader, regulatory agenda.) What is not so clear, however, is whether such technologies are responsible, as is often implied, for stimulating a larger market for such materials, causing new materials to be made, and therefore, in turn, leading to more instances of child sex abuse. When in cases like Operation Starbust the hullabaloo over transnational, internet child-porn rings ultimately amounts (in the UK at least) to the possession of three images dating back a quarter of a century, people are bound to wonder about the true nature or extent of the dangers of child porn in cyberspace.[32] The suspicion continues that a lot of the materials being branded as child porn are in fact non-pornographic, in the sense that they do not have an explicit sexual content, and, furthermore, are not records of criminal acts of sexual abuse of children. As far as can be established in such a fast-moving, elusive realm, judging from court action to date, and from monitoring of the few offending paedophile newsgroups that have actually featured image files, a lot of the materials described as 'child porn' are in fact nude pictures of children taken from art-work, family albums and naturist materials.[33]

The strange phenomenon of 'pseudo-photographs' also features in anxieties over illegal materials online. These digitally manipulated photographs of indecency 'featuring' children were made illegal in Britain under the Criminal Justice Act of 1994.[34] Pseudo-photographs are representations of things that never took place. The product of sophisticated image-editing software, they have no substance or ontology beyond their computer-digitalised construction. (The high winds in the blockbuster movie *Twister* also did not exist; they were just sculpted light and magic.) The CJA defined an indecent pseudo-photograph to be the construction of 'what "appears" to be an indecent nature involving a child under the age of 16'.

As is common with such law-making the concrete definition of 'indecency' has been avoided.

On a beach by the sea, two teenage girls in bathing costumes stand alone on the right hand side of the frame. On the left-hand side of the frame, quite bizzarely, stands a man in full frogman gear. This is not a fetish-style frogman, this is one who has apparently just climbed out of the sea. The frogman's semi-erect penis is sticking out of his wetsuit. One of the girls has her hand reached out in the direction of the penis, but not touching it. This is a child pornographic pseudo-photograph. This is not the visual record of a crime. The meeting between the frogman and the teenage girls never took place, its only 'reality' is within the digital domain. Once a man stood on a beach in full frogman gear with his penis sticking out, and two teenage girls once stood on another beach, one with her hand slightly reaching out. Someone has taken these two distinct moments in time and place captured on film, and sewn them together using digital technology. The two spheres of the pseudo-photo are not actually distinguished by a discernible stitch line down the middle, but distinction between the varying cloudscapes, light and types of sand and beach, and the distinct grains of the two joined images – the fabricated nature of the pseudo-photograph, in other words – is quite clear to the eye.

The fact that a pseudo-photograph is not real, nor an actual record of abuse, is not to say that it isn't offensive or deeply troubling for most people, therefore making it 'indecent' (if not 'obscene'). Nevertheless, putting the prevailing disapproval of such imagery to one side, it should be recognised that a vital feature of pseudo-photographs is the viewer's thoughts. It is the knowledge that some people have 'indecent' and 'illegal' thoughts that finds a share of the anxiety over actual child sex abuse displaced into the realm of imagery, into the arguments about how seriously pictures and thoughts should be taken. The relationship between paedophilic imagery and the com-mitting of actual offences (as discussed in the previous chapter, 'Child Story') is not at all clear, or even demonstrated. It could be argued that pseudo-photographs might serve as a fantasy substitute to an actual act of abuse, a 'harmless', pressure-releasing way of skirting the temptation to offend. That such theories remain speculative is secondary, however, to the fact that in society at present such ideas are non-starters as they're simply too offensive to the vast majority of people.

In the meantime, if child sex offenders are producing new materials – actual records of their abusive behaviour – and are also distributing these images in cyberspace, then they're taking enormous risks. In announcing themselves so publicly, offenders face possible detection. Self-declaring paedophile exchange systems online provide opportunities for discovering offenders, and for monitoring sex abuse. In the autumn of 1996, a Catholic priest in Scotland was convicted for possessing child porn pictures on his personal computer. He was caught after speaking on the internet of some of his 'conquests' of younger parishioners. In this case, the priest was apprehended not because of his posting child porn in cyberspace but for bragging online. It was the internet, in other words, that led to his being caught. In seeking, therefore, to eliminate offending newsgroups, the authorities may actually be jeopardising a source of good leads as well as making sex crimes harder to track.

The internet may be used to police sexual abuse. This does assume, however, that the prevention of the sexual abuse of children is the main concern. Although the heated nature of discussions does partly stem from the fact that people are truly offended by paedophile activity, and desperate to do something about it, nevertheless the way the issue is often handled suggests that other agendas are also being pursued. The suspicion remains that the issue of child porn was exploited as part of a bid to gain leverage over this new, unregulated technology, in order to get things under control.

Fear and loathing in Cyberia
(on policing the internet)

In Britain, in the late summer of 1996, the Metropolitan Police told the Internet Service Providers Association (ISPA) that content on some of the newsgroups available through their services was illegal, which meant that they were breaking the law. The police had decided that service providers such as Pipex and Demon were the publishers of such materials. In a letter to the ISPA, the police wrote, 'As you will be aware the publication of obscene material is an offence.' Providers were told to monitor and filter a very extensive list of offending groups in the short term, with the long-term aim being eradication. The announcement followed a long process of discussions between the police and Pipex stretching back to the previous winter. During these discussions, the police mentioned eight usenet newsgroups that they considered to be key offenders in terms of featuring illegal images, and Pipex removed them from its newsgroup feed. When other service providers learned about this, it was suggested that the whole industry should meet with the authorities.

A week after they gathered at Scotland Yard, the police sent a letter to all service providers containing what was now a list of 132 newsgroups that they felt should be banned. Many of these were discussion groups. At least half of were from the alt.sex hierarchy, which is a usenet area primarily devoted to the discussion of sexual matters where the posting of any image file is strenuously discouraged by contributors and operators. Many of the groups listed by the police that carried image files were dedicated to adult materials. The police warning came not from the child-porn police but the vice unit responsible for patrolling adult materials. There were rumours that the Paedophile and Child Pornography Squad was displeased by the Vice Unit lumping together the problem of paedophilic imagery with adult materials legal in most parts of the Western world. The crucial distinction between illegal images and illegal acts was not made. This failure would characterise most debates concerning materials distributed on the internet in Britain.

On the back of threatened action by the police came news of the horrific series of child murders in Belgium, with allegations of the awful crimes being connected to a child porn ring. In the same month the first ever global conference on the sexual exploitation of children was convened in Sweden. A new intensity entered the discussions of paedophiles in cyberspace. Not all of the discussions were particularly well informed or helpful. The most conspicuous offender was a front-page splash in London's *Observer* from late August 1996 claiming that anonymous-remailer operator, Johan Helsingiius, and Clive Feather, associate director of Demon, a leading British internet service provider, were heavily implicated in the distribution of child pornography.[35]

Helsingiius had been operating his non-profit remailer from Finland for several years. A remailer computer system puts computer files onto the internet without any sign of their origin. This non-traceability service has many uses, from anonymous counselling, to industrial whistle-blowing, to drawing attention on a global scale to human rights abuses from within repressive states.[36] Helsingiius's service dealt with small text files. It couldn't handle large image files, and hadn't handled any image files for more than a year.

The suggestion, therefore, that Helsingiius's anon.penet service was responsible for 90 per cent of child-porn distribution made no sense. Furthermore, Finnish police officers stated that they had investigated the matter and had no issue regarding child porn with the server. They were, however, still investigating Helsingiius for his remailing of 'secret' information concerning the Church of Scientology. It was this legal wrangle with the Scientologists that caused anon.penet to be voluntarily shut down in the early autumn of 1996.

The allegations made against Demon were equally unreasonable and misleading. Demon argued for a recognition that they were not responsible for the information accessed through their host computers, or at least no more responsible than equivalent communication companies like British Telecom or the Post Office. '[Demon] is not the author of the content on the Internet as it is only a provider of connectivity. Currently it is aware of no reliable way to monitor the 2 Gigabytes of news (equivalent to 500,000,000 words) per day.'[37] This had been the position of most service providers during the previous few years: that to monitor such a volume of constantly changing traffic was more than they could do. Service providers argued for the police to do the regulating. The police said no, they didn't have the time or the resources, it was for the service providers to do this.

On a visit to the Vice and Club Unit, I was shown the computer that the police use for monitoring the internet. They said they do very little of this. On the rare occasion a member of the public complained about something they saw online, then officers would log on and check it out. Not that they felt they could really do that much. 'The images are posted and disappear so quickly,' a sergeant complains. 'It is too difficult to trace an image mostly . . . to know who posted . . . in the first place.' Following their own online experiences, the police were prepared to recognise the near impossibility of fully censoring the internet. Nevertheless, the existence of any kind of porn on the net was not something they were prepared to simply submit to. The police wanted something to be done, and their impatience with this global communications nightmare was becoming an impatience with British service providers, who, they felt sure, weren't trying hard enough. Interviewing an officer at the Vice and Clubs Unit of the Metropolitan Police on a whole range of porn matters, I noted that all lawbreakers in the unit's demonology were known as 'agents', as, for now, were also a few of the service providers.

When it was put to the community of British service providers that the way forward was self-regulation, according to the police 95 per cent of them had agreed. Laurence Blackall, MD of Global Internet, was happy to oblige: 'Our view is that anything that is obviously in this category we will drop. And if the police tell us of other newsgroups we'll drop them too. I'm not interested in any debate about them.'[38] It was the other 5 per cent, alleged to be two of the larger companies, who said it couldn't/wouldn't/shouldn't be done. Those who said this, as far as the police were concerned, had 'a vested interest in not censoring'. The police are convinced that large fortunes are being made in cyberporn, and that any unhelpful provider was too set on porn as a profit-turner to want to censor. (The idea that such providers might have an anti-censorship sensibility was not entertained.)

Now that certain internet service providers had been figured as 'agents', the police spoke of the likelihood that arrests would soon follow. The plan was for the police to launch a test case in the courts to establish whether being an internet service provider was like being a 'publisher', as described by British obscenity laws, and therefore liable for the content of the global internet. (They wanted to expand the meaning of the term as it was used in the Obscene Publications Act of 1959, where 'publish' certainly didn't cover providing access to the internet.) In effect, the police, presumably with government support, were bulldozing service providers into making an industry-wide attack upon access to porn. Through late summer and early autumn of 1996, the service provider's community was rife with rumours of impending raids. This was not simply paranoia; only quite recently the administrators of two of France's leading service providers, FranceNet and World-Net, had spent a few nights in jail. It was only a matter of time before service providers would be seen to capitulate.

It is difficult to completely eliminate offensive items on the internet – as many service providers were keen to point out. Particularly the usenet newsgroups. Anyone can create a newsgroup, and anyone can post to one. Trying to restrict materials by deleting selected newsgroups will not necessarily remove the content, and may only cause it to relocate from self-advertising groups into those that are less clearly named. In this way, offensive items become harder to monitor, and any records of illegal acts are made more difficult to track, or act upon. This could lead to such material being read unintentionally or being stumbled upon by children, the very grouping everyone wishes to protect. Sergeant Oliver Clarke of the Manchester police observed: 'Our view is that the Metropolitan Police's idea of getting UK service providers to censor newsgroups is misguided.'[39]

Following the meeting between service providers and the police, a British government statement released a challenge to the industry. 'Develop new software to come clean,' declared Ian Taylor, minister for Science and Technology. Taylor 'welcomed the inclusion of screening standards in the new version of Microsoft's Internet browser Software which can screen out unwanted and undesirable Internet material.' Apparently, Microsoft had shown the way for all to follow: 'I believe the industry has the ability to provide its own solutions – but they need to be brought to fruition urgently.'[40] It was a matter of only a few weeks, late September 1996, before such urgent fruition arrived and was ready to go public. At a London press conference the British government, the police and leading internet service providers unveiled a set of proposals for getting tough on illegal materials on Britain's piece of the internet. The first target was declared to be child pornography, but all were clear how this was just the start of things, with 'obscenity' as a target for future action.

Collectively the proposals were called 'R3 – SafetyNet'. The three Rs being Rating, Reporting and Responsibility. The announcement was the first public action of what came to be known as Internet Watch Foundation (IWF), the three-week-old industry-based organisation set up by Peter Dawe, the founder of Pipex, Britain's largest commercial internet service provider, to coordinate a unified service providers' response to the call for policing in cyberspace.

'The Internet is not a Legal Vacuum,' proclaimed IWF's launch statement. 'The law applies to activities on the Internet as it does to activity not on the Internet. If something is illegal "off-line" it will also be illegal "on-line".' With this declaration, British service providers definitively took upon themselves the role as part 'publishers' of the internet. They also accepted the job of policing account holders in the UK who were posting against domestic, terrestrial law (although the police would actually take care of law enforcement). This meant not only the posting of pictures of illegal acts, i.e. child abuse, but also pictures of legal acts, like adult sex – the usual 'obscenities' caught in the 'net' whenever any legal sweeps against 'child porn' are conducted.

Following a period of fear and paranoia, and the occasional declarations of defiance, within a matter of weeks, the British service providers had collectively buried their misgivings over censorship and fallen into line. 'The issue addressed has nothing to do with censorship ... or free speech,' Internet

Watch Foundation disingenuously announced. 'The core issue is crime.' With IWF the police and the government had got what they wanted. The protection of the young person was again to be used as an excuse to censor all adult materials.[41] This should have come as no surprise, and indeed aroused little comment. A few years earlier at a parliamentary select committee discussion on computer porn, it was revealed in passing that pointing up the issue of the young person was a way of gaining the advantage over the new technologies and pornography in general: 'The privacy argument can be defeated by appealing to the public policy of protecting the young.'[42] Two years down the line, this is exactly what had been accomplished.

IWF's plan for the policing of online materials featuring illegal acts was to involve the creation of a hot-line service to which anyone could report sightings of any offending items. This was similar to the situation in Holland, where a web site and hot-line service for online child porn had been set up as an act of self-regulation from within the Dutch internet community, which had subsequently reported the speedy removal of such items as well as the elimination of any offending posts made within the Netherlands. Apparently, once posters knew they were being watched over they weren't so keen to post.[43] Any complaints made to the IWF hot line would be checked, and then a warning shot would be sent to the original poster, as well as to service providers, requiring them to remove the material from their servers. Information would also be passed on to the police. Where anonymous remailers were concerned, IWF was especially keen to get tough: 'It is important to be able to trace the originators of child pornography and other illegal material . . . Allowing users to have truly anonymous accounts is a danger.' This danger was to be removed through requiring all UK-based remailers to keep a record of the identity of people who used the service, and to be ready to hand such details over to the police on demand.

Looking ahead, IWF made a clear commitment to developing rating systems for online materials. Beyond issues of 'illegal' items in cyberspace, they proposed to foster the classification of all 'legal' material, so making it possible for users to run PICS-like software controlling their net intake to their own custom-made levels of tolerance. Also, as PICS was slowly being made standard to major web browsers like Netscape, IWF urged service providers to install PICS into all their future software for accessing the web. In return a future internet scene in the UK was envisaged where users 'voluntarily' rated everything they placed in newsgroups and on the world wide web. IWF urged all service providers to move towards a situation where they required customers to rate their own web pages as part of the service agreement. Service providers were also to consider extending content-control systems to newsgroups, as well as a situation where newsgroup posts from anywhere in the world that contained any kind of illegal materials would be removed from the service provider's news server. (A few months earlier, when defending itself from attack by the *Observer*, Demon Internet had revealed in passing that it was working with Microsoft, among others, to develop a PICS-type rating system for usenet, where by default the system wouldn't display newsgroups deemed to contain illegal pornography.) Basically users in the UK weren't going to have a choice; from some point in the future onwards, ratings and filtration of online activities were going to be a part of the British telecommunications experience.

On the day that the CDA was rebuffed in the US Supreme Court, and Ira Magaziner, senior advisor to the Clinton administration, announced that henceforth the White House would actively push for the development of improved screening software, a few perceptive American cyber-libertarians speculated as to what this would mean abroad. 'Other governments will welcome this proposal,' observed Marc Rotenberg, director of the Electronic Privacy Information Center. 'Every government has a reason to restrict access to information they find objectionable, and the United States will now actively promote the techniques to make this possible.' Britain had already become a shining example of what Rotenberg meant. Earlier in the global internet story, the spectre of cultural imperialism found foreign governments fearing the American tradition of protecting free speech being beamed into their restrictive nation states. Now the fear was that America's anti-sex tradition was going global. 'The White House is setting itself on a dangerous course. This will come back to bite us,' said Rotenberg. 'And because it's a global plan, it's going to be a very hard battle for the civil liberties groups.'[44]

The American internet pioneer John Gilmore once observed, 'The Net interprets censorship as damage and routes around it.' With the dawn of Internet Watch Foundation in the UK there was a lot of new damage in cyberspace in need of circumventing. Although, strictly speaking, what Gilmore said remains true, such confidence seems a little misplaced in the late nineties. The internet might be censor-proof in absolute terms, but in reality the scope for restriction is considerable. Smart techno-types may well route around the road blocks, but as the internet achieves a far larger presence as a mass media, populated by the technically challenged, a degree of censorship for the many will have prevailed. Access is all, and the harder it gets, the less people care to chase after it. It's not censored, not totally; it's just too hard for too many.

Faced with the predicament of dealing with a global communications network that supposedly didn't recognise terrestrial borders, by 1997 the British government and the British police had done pretty well. Although they couldn't hope to block every last 'offensive' item, they possibly could hope for a future situation where the bulk of it won't be getting through and reaching the majority of British internet users. This was probably the best they could have hoped for. And they got it without there being any public discussion. A wider debate about pornography should have been prompted by the fact that the internet (like satellite and cable TV) provided access to adult sexual materials that are legal in most other parts of the Western world but are against the law in Britain. And, now that many more people had this chance to look at what was actually being blocked by the government, how did they feel about such restrictions. An opportunity to question the continued social acceptability of such confinement was squandered, while the British system of censorship adroitly adapted to face the latest threat to its authority.[45]

8

Future sex

Following the tale of the 'young person' in peril in cyberspace, the second leading story told about porn and new technology concerns the state of the human libido in the digital age. There are two sides to this future sex narrative. On one, there are those perplexing images of newfangled sexy gimmicks like virtual reality gropings – also known as 'teledildonics' – promising us sex such as we've never had sex before, and where we often find our carnal futures looking rather like an American science-fiction B-movie from the fifties, featuring body suits with Velcro sensors and computer cables hooked up to the groin and chest.[1] These are visions that people find simultaneously alarming and comically hard to believe in. Difficulties with presentation aside, the problem with this version of future sex is that so far our bodies haven't actually changed that much, and our conceptions of sex haven't really evolved to a point where we might meaningfully talk of new sex, if by this we mean something different happening with our bodies. Woody Allen's Orgasmatron, the ultimate sex contraption from *Sleeper*, remains an out-of-reach goal. If future sex means a truly orgasmic experience in virtual reality, then the current state of the art won't stretch to it. It's a case of come back in ten or twenty years' time, or, as Lisa Palac puts it, 'Wake me up when it's ready.'[2]

The counter-narrative to such way-out visions of future sex features a big dose of technofear, and associated misgivings voiced by theorists and artists ranging from Marshall McLuhan to David Cronenberg, concerning excess, the decline of real flesh experiences, and a dread of what happens when men and machines fall in love. The last anxiety familiarly warns of the dangers of fetishising technology, of male phallic obsessions with hard, gleaming metal machines resulting in a Freudian thrall of sexy guns and high-tech 'wargasms'. An arts tradition stretching back over a century or more gloomily ponders over the 'technology is erotic' scenario – which makes the idea of a sex machine very arousing indeed. There are the full-blown paeans to pumping erotic mechanical devices from Dadaists like Duchamp and Picabia; the souped-up sexy Cadillacs of fifties Auto-Americana; and the carnal carnage on wheels as described by Ballard in *Crash*. This tradition of simultaneously loving and loathing the machine has produced both great artworks and bad feelings.

There is a third way of thinking about future sex, however. Between rosy visions of a new age of sexual rapture in 'cyberville' and alternative, darker tales of machine alienation, there does exist another less heralded, less quantifiable tale of connectivity, a story of how in an era of convergence, where computers, televisions, phones, cables, video and compact disk technology are starting to merge in multimedia harmony, more people than ever before are gaining access through new technology to sexual materials and communities of like-minded types.

Cyberporn
(on porn in space)

The start of future sex finds an increased availability of regular porn imagery. Porn is often a key driver during the fledgling, emergent periods of new media technologies. All the porn out there in cyberspace, the soft core and hard core, pictures of porn sirens, film stars, supermodels, your next-door neighbour, all this online raunch, helped to make the internet grow, and made it sexy. In return, the hip new internet phenomenon has made porn more culturally acceptable to many more people. Much of the talk of cyberporn in the broader culture was critical and alarmist, as was to be expected, causing the shiny, brand-new new media to lose some of its lustre through the porn association. Nevertheless, a lot of people found that easy-access telecommunications changed their view on many things: politics, the world, the establishment media, and also maybe porn. Like the desktop publishing explosion in 'zines that bypassed the more conservative mainstream media – which had for so long defined porn as grubby, sleazy and dangerous – the internet was coming straight to you and enabled porn to be reconsidered and found to be not such a terrible thing after all.

Whether cyberspace is a good vehicle for porn is another issue. A lot of people think not. 'No matter how "hard" they are,' a porn fan complains in an email to the author, 'I do not find images on a computer screen particularly stimulating.' For many, however, cyberporn's possible shortcomings are secondary to the fact that it's the only porn delivery system they've got – or the only one they'll use. The convenience and anonymity of the internet makes it easier for individuals to try porn out, people who simply wouldn't go into a sex shop to buy videos, or scour their nearest red-light district looking for their hard-core magazine of choice. Singing the praises of cyberspace, a new market sector for *Hustler* magazine to trade in, publisher Larry Flynt considers the attraction of cyberporn as being about secrets: 'Guys don't want their wives to know they read magazines like *Hustler*. They're really scared, so they keep the magazine at the office or hide it at home. Now you have a guy sitting in his den at his computer. He doesn't have to go to the newsstand to buy the material, he doesn't have to worry his kids will find it, there's nothing for his wife to nag him about. It's a very private moment for him, which is why the internet has become so popular.'[3]

Porn stills online are accessed in a variety of ways. There's the private or commercial dial-up bulletin boards, with names like *Dirty Hacker*, and pay-per-view mega web sites run by large commercial porn outfits like Penthouse, Hustler, Vivid, Playboy, and Northern & Shell. There are also personal home pages on the web, or porn materials posted for free on usenet, or offered for trade via newsgroups. There's a lot of cyberporn out there (although the amounts are easily, wildly exaggerated, see Chapter 7, 'The Perils of Cyberspace'). The vast majority of the images have been taken from porn magazines, video and laser disc, and then scanned to be redistributed or resold online. This is the bulk of porn traffic.

Other materials available online may be amateur, home-made images – frequently patchy, fuzzy, or weakly lit – of part-ners posing or, less often, of couples having sex. Never before have so many husbands and wives, girlfriends and boyfriends, been posted for public consumption and accessible in a matter of seconds. Doubtless some images are being posted without the model's express permission or knowledge. However, many men and women who spoke to the author about their experi-ences as porn users also mentioned that they had taken nude pictures of themselves, and their lovers, and have been jointly posting them at appropriate web pages or newsgroups, because it was net-like and free-spirited, and because it made them feel sexy. These images were offered for free or to swap, but can also easily become part of the internet's self-organising, small-time erotic trading system, and, as previously with the lighter, low-cost video cameras, develop into another opportunity for the private production of customised porn. 'Hi my name is Ginger! You may have seen me on the internet,' reads a sales pitch. 'For the past 6 months I have been modeling on the internet by customer request. My customer's tell me what they would like to see me wear or not wear in the photos I shoot for them and what they would like to see me doing in each picture.'[4] This direct, performer-to-viewer relationship can also stretch to video productions, ordered up online but sent to customers by post. A net-poster talks of the porn stills and video he's been making with his partner: 'I posted 3 other pix . . . about a month ago to great response. We shot a short video, about a half hour just to see if we could do a decent job of it. It came out pretty good . . . solid action and very hot. Ten bucks will get you a copy.'[5]

Taking pictures of yourself, or of your lover, to then share, trade or sell to others, has been read as problematic. The anti-porn campaigner Peter Baker considers home-made adult materials as no more acceptable than commercial porn. He says he can't imagine why a woman should ever wish to feature in an amateur porn video, and therefore doubts that full consent really occurs in such situations. 'Why should people want other people to see them having sex, friends having sex. I don't understand it.' Should the arrangement be fully consenting, then Baker says he worries about the mental health of participants, wondering if these people are in need of therapy.

This would mean a lot of new business for the counselling community. Especially if there's an American university campus close by, for there's a lot of resourceful college girls out there getting in on the act. Campus Cuties, from Louisiana, is an outfit similar to Ginger's, only working with regular postal services and typewriters: 'Hi, my name is Lisa! One of the Campus Cuties! You don't know me, though some of you know what I look like through some of my rather revealing photos.' To go with these 'revealing photos', it is announced that the 'Cuties' are starting up an erotic newsletter each of which 'will highlight lovely student bodies from our group'. A photo set will cost punters five dollars. One Cutie comes in a swimsuit, another in lingerie, and a third in the nude, offering for your eyes only sights the Campus Cuties' actual college classmates 'can only dream about seeing'. Exclusively swimwear photosets of Sandy are also available, 'because you don't want any of her nude photographs out when your mother comes to visit'. The raunchier shots 'you can keep . . . under your pillow'.[6] Full-on college girl videos are also being promoted online: 'Hi, My name is Katie. I'm a college student that enjoys making amateur xxx videos to help pay my bills. Me and some of my coed friends have put together some of our best scenes on a wet and wild video. Everything's included: oral, anal, female masturbation with huge dildos . . .'[7]

Plainly, one aspect of the extended possibilities in future sex is the cashing-in that is already occurring. A fairly confident future prediction will see a lot more sex going on sale. Visiting some of alt.sex newsgroups on the usenet system has become like strolling through the cyber equivalent of a real-life red-light district, with punters being targeted, tempted and solicited in every other posting. Many direct online solicitations involve phone sex lines: 'SEXY SUSAN SAYS PLEASE,' according to susan@freelove. 'I'm 25, 5'6", busty, dirty blonde shoulder length hair, sweet voice, and people say I have a very pretty smile. Both me and a few of my closest girlfriends really enjoy open, exciting adult conversation . . . no limits . . . everything goes. . . . My toll free number is . . .' Or then there's Brandy at Fantasy Sex: 'Call me . . . I'm a showgirl at Fantasy Showbar, New Jersey's only all nude, non-alcoholic gentlemen's club. I am beautiful, kinky and ready to talk to you . . . See our Home Page for sexy details.' Full of implausible come-ons, dubious claims, and taking up valuable net space, these online sex ads cause many netizens to despair. 'Maybe . . . just maybe,' writes an angry poster, 'these ads should start reading . . . "You can call my phone sex line for $4.00 a minute, and speak to my obese sister who has a serious case of herpes" and, "Check out my home page which my 16 year old brother cooked up so we can fleece you of some of your hard-earned cash." '

Being conned or fleeced in the datasphere is a part of the future sex story all too familiar from the days before the cyber-deluge. As with any marketplace, the gullible are vulnerable to being taken for a ride, and, as usual, have few, if any, rights of redress. Sometimes a spot of techno-scepticism seems a healthy thing to have.

The intermingling dangers of sex, new science and quackery are not only considerable, they've also got a history. In the last century, in an America beleaguered by sexual stuffiness, hypochondria, and syphilis, dubious 'cure-alls' were foisted upon gullible consumers, promising to fix various sex problems. The fixes would often feature the latest technological advances. Electricity, radio waves and radioactivity were falsely credited with phenomenal powers of sexual healing. One of many phoney remedies of the time was the 'Boston Electric Belt', which was alleged to supply a mild, reviving current to any impotent or exhausted penis. In actuality the belt was doused in a chemical delivering a fiery sensation once activated by the wearer's sweat flow, tricking users into believing that something was occurring (and who knows, by this point, maybe something was).

A hundred years on, the conning and falling for it continues. In particular, too many porn fans online are letting the dream of celebrity privates get the better of them. When *Hustler* magazine printed pictures of Jackie Onassis in the early seventies, sales rocketed and Larry Flynt became a millionaire.[8] The desire for that once-in-a-lifetime celebrity exposure – could be Teri Hatcher or Sandra Bullock, Brad Pitt or Mel Gibson – can make people very credulous. From time to time, porn-related newsgroups will be inundated with rumours and requests over alleged nude celebrity action, like 'Alannis Morisette spreads her butt-cheeks for the camera' or 'lesbian action shot of Melissa Etheridge and her lover'. Often the alleged action veers towards the 'exotic', a picture of Mariah Carey having an enema maybe, or a golden showers scenario featuring Sheryl Crow . . . and then there was the one of Julia Roberts being intimate with a team of huskies. Obviously no such pictures exist. A lot of this is people having fun, and needless to say everyone is in on the joke. Or rather, not necessarily everyone. The yearning is such, the gullibility of some porners so huge, that spoof 'ads' for such far-out materials nearly always find eager takers mailing back saying, 'Gimme, gimme, gimme, I'm in!'

Another, adjoining scam with cyberporn is the booming phenomenon of pseudo-photos, where image-editing software takes a celebrity head, connects it to an image of a naked body, and manipulates the concocted image to look at least vaguely plausible. Notorious celebrity fake nudes include Jennifer Aniston, Alicia Silverstone, a grinning Mary Tyler Moore, naked and nine months pregnant, and Pam Dawber from *Mork and Mindy* doing things the real Mindy would never even have heard of. Some fakes are there simply to make you laugh, they're so egregious, and others to take you in, because maybe you like *The X Files* and have often wondered what David Duchovny or Gillian Anderson would look like with no clothes on. The spur for going to the trouble of creating fake images lies somewhere between such wishful thinking and the love of a

honour of the skill and imagination of this folk
cyber age, whole web sites are dedicated to good and
frauds that have been circulated. Mostly it's not too difficult to spot the bad joins in the fakes, the blurred pixels and
tell-tale shifts in skin tone and lighting. Legal issues of copyright abuse and the misappropriation of a celebrity's image –
depicting them in a false light – means that one of these days a
photo faker who's just too good at it, or forgets to point out
they're just offering a fantasy, could well face court action.

Getting it all at Brandy's
(on the wide range of sex for sale online)

Future sex is not always spoofs, rip-offs or porn fans being
seduced into parting with every last penny. At Brandy's Babes,
Phoenix, Arizona, 'The Worlds First Cyber-Brothel', a team of
seven 'babes' offers a wide variety of erotic performances: 'We
are here for fun to meet cool people and exchange erotic e-mail
and pictures.' The site also involves direct-access phone sex
lines, which are also available to be coordinated with erotic
photographic sessions: 'You control the camera and take the
snapshot and it gets sent right to your computer in seconds.'
The diffusion of services at Brandy's continues, 'We are getting
the vid. cam hooked up to the computer so you can request a
current still picture of the girl at the keyboard or shower.' There
is also a live video link, running 'cu-seeme software'. Techno
smart visitors to Brandy's can now 'cUm hang out' with one of
the babes, with 'viewer in one hand and your ***K in the
other . . . On line realtime sex is here.'

At present most such visual exchange systems remain image-
delayed, where the 'live' strip shows on offer are really only
semi-live, and the images very stop-go. This is changing,
however. Wide-band modems, improving software, and video-
conferencing see a future sex of real-time, high-resolution
striptease, on your computer or even your television screen,
and for your eyes only: 'Let me put on a dance tape,' suggests
an online advertisement, 'turn on my video camera, boot up
my computer, and let me dance naked for you. First, I'll start

with my clothes on . . . A short-cropped white tee-shirt that really shows off my flat, firm tummy . . . my very firm and full milky-white breasts . . . and my dark nipples that are getting really hard just thinking about this . . . when I turn around, you'll appreciate my favorite "goodluck" pair of cut-offs, how they are so fringey, and how they ride so high and delicious on my very hard dancer's ass . . . Now the fun begins . . . You've already downloaded my "personal connection" software, you've opened up the program and have hit the MAKE CALL button to call me . . . Your modem rings, my modem answers, they dance around, negotiate a connection, and, "WHAM!" You're MINE! Set up the program and call me now . . . I'm live . . . and I want to get naked for you!'

Away from the computer and modem, assorted real-life services are also on offer at Brandy's Babes with so-called 'Private Nude Dancing and Modeling. incall/outcall,' available for locals, and anybody who happens to be passing through Phoenix. The web site provides a menu of the vital statistics of each of the seven babes: 'OWNER: Brandy, 26yr, blond, blue [eyes], 5'7", 120lbs. 36–24–28. RECEPTIONIST: Trisha 19yr, blond green, 5'5" 100lbs. 38–22–32 . . . DANCER1: Ashley, 21yr, blonde blue, 5'4", 115lbs. 38–24–36 . . .' etc. And, finally getting to the heart of the matter, so as to be sure people know exactly what's occurring: 'Yes we go all the way. No we don't really dance.'

The going rate at Brandy's is '$150 for the hour in or out call', where the site takes $50, and the individual babe takes $100. 'Everyone gets Sunday and Tuesday off,' it is revealed, 'and the girls get one rotating night off.' There are new opportunities for sellers with future sex, mainly offering increased autonomy and physical security for the sex worker, and without some of the traditional drawbacks of such labour, like the police and the wrong kinds of middlemen. The changing labour markets in America and Britain during the eighties and into the nineties have seen the growing inclusion of women into the low-paid sectors of the working economy. The cyber sex industry, like its non-cyberian counterpart, draws partly from a labour pool of low-income mothers who need the money, and who appreciate the job flexibility. In advertising her pornware, Ginger also seeks new recruits for the business, looking for any would-be erotic models out there interested in doing some erotic posing. 'The site will feature a variety of models with varying modelling limits (what she will do and won't do). This will offer my large and dedicated customer base more of a selection. Models will shoot their own pictures in the comfort of their own surroundings with their own photographer, lover or friend.'[9] For some women, and men, cyber sexwork will not be the ideal job, possibly not the most rewarding work they'll ever do. And then others will find it suits them better than most other employment options on offer. Or as Ginger puts it, 'It is Great fun! Sexy!! and Very Profitable! I am confident you will find this to be as enjoyable and profitable as I have!'

At first sight, the making and selling of porn on such a cottage-industry scale appears pretty non-futurist, hardly the new sex revolution we were expecting – not a virtual reality headset in sight. In part it's this word 'revolution' that explains many of the misreadings. There is a fixation not only on hardware but on high concepts too, in preference to more matter-of-fact applications. The social impact of new technology often manifests itself through unexpected, less obvious evolutions. When video first emerged in Britain in the late seventies, the new technology, it was suggested, would revolutionise politics. A couple of decades later, green activists use lightweight video-cameras on demonstrations and sell their product to the news services and to like-minded people in alternative political net-works, and perhaps political discourse has been altered because of this. Nevertheless, nearly twenty years into the video age, and the parliamentary system shows no sign of coming apart.

In the meantime, video has radically, but also perhaps imperceptibly, altered people's concepts of time, record and memory. The VCR has also changed the shape of leisure activi-ties, and the nature of people's access to entertainment media. Video had a profound impact upon porn. The move from film to tape – from an old-fashioned film set to a one-man-and-his-camera porn production, from a cinema viewing experience in a public space to home erotic entertainments – was also a move away from the mainly out of reach, unwieldy old-style film machinery to cheaper, more user-friendly and self-processing equipment. People's intimate performances in photobooths, with Polaroids and camcorders, don't have to be developed and vetted by the local chemists. New technologies that elude such forms of regulation have therefore been adapted for ulterior purposes. (As William Gibson said, 'the street finds its own uses for things'.) Social shifts will often occur in these small ways, and in funny places, like bedrooms perhaps. They may often occur without it really being noticed – maybe not until later, when people start to reflect on the way the form of the landscape has altered. The new computer technologies provide similar opportunities. They offer not only easier access to porn materials, and alternative views on porn, but also the opportunity for forms of self-actualisation (to make your own) and self-promotion (to sell your own), also providing, therefore, a greatly enhanced opportunity for others to commission and choreograph the kind of erotic materials people desire. How this will change the precise shape of porn, or the character of people's sex lives, remains unclear for now.

Audacious (1996) is an independent film from Australia that offers a few ideas on the subject. Written and directed by Samantha Lang, it is about a woman who is bored with her love life. Her partner's not interested mostly, and when he is he's not very interesting. Instead he fiddles all the time with his new hi-8 video camera. By chance, the woman finds that the computer at the office not only connects her to the daily drudge of work but also provides access to an online customised porn service. She emails her preferred fantasy and credit card number to 'Audacious', and a husband and wife team enact her fantasy and film it for her to watch and get hot and happy with when her partner's not around. She orders up a lot of tapes. He, meanwhile, doesn't know about her burgeoning porn lusts. In time she decides she wants to perform one of her fantasies with her boyfriend. She tries tying him up, but he doesn't like it. Then, she gets herself a strap-on dildo instead and has anal sex with him for the first time ever. The next day at work he feels a bit sore, but you can tell he rather enjoyed the experience. His sex interest is renewed to those former days of glorious fervour. And then he discovers the tapes, and therefore discovers how she had prepared the way for their carnal adventure through the fantasy creations of 'Audacious'. He doesn't like this. He wants her to realise, he tells her, that he cannot be her fantasy man; he's only human, made of flesh and blood. Around the same time she realises the extent of what he has been up to with his new video camera, filming her when she's unawares, in the shower, or at night. He's a voyeur and she's a porn fantasist: technology can bring them together or it can keep them somewhat apart. Hand-in-hand, apparently reconciled, this modern couple are last seen at the end of the film heading for the bedroom, with video camera in hand, perhaps to make their own video fantasies to watch.

Chaos theory and porn
(how cyberspace could change the shape of hard core)

For the time being, the small-scale making and trading of porn in cyberspace exist alongside the far larger online commercial efforts of porn corporations such as Vivid and Penthouse. That this relatively harmonious cohabitation between porn minnows and the industrial-strength big fish will continue seems unlikely. Deep inside the debates concerning online censorship exist arguments about the future style and shape of cyberporn: will it be self-organised trading in home-made materials, or monoliths of pay-per-view fantasy beauty? It will probably be both, although that depends, in part, on which way the technology and legal interventions evolve. Should all web sites and usenet posts be required to be rated, and all online adult materials be required to be fully supported by performer records and documentation, the legal and administrative pressures to conform could reduce the levels of intimate and small-scale porn production. The conglomerates may end up making even more money than they do at present.

However, other challenges may still be up ahead for the regular porn industry. Home-made porn on the internet is partly a response to porn users' desire for new kinds of material, something different from what the adult industry has to offer. Similar processes occurred during the eighties with video, when for a few years the adult industry was in a state of panic over the new 'amateur' product that was virtually outper-forming them in the marketplace, before it had the sense to both imitate and swallow up its rival. The rapid growth of the internet during the first half of the nineties has been viewed by those of a slightly mystical disposition to be an almost organic emergence, a sort of evolutionary burst of new technology and media. This way of seeing things, mixed in with the new maths of chaos theory, figures the datasphere as resembling a kind of complex living organism. Within this centreless, unfettered, constantly evolving realm, weird and wonderful things are rumoured to happen. Small information viruses will break out, causing unexpected and unpredictable consequences, building and ultimately perhaps altering the overall shape of things. Cyberporn could be seen as one such media virus, a good idea that had to happen, and that maybe even changed the actual character of porn. 'I think the move towards amateur stuff has made porn much more interesting,' writes a woman porn fan. 'It takes a long time for the porn industry to respond to people's needs. In fact it could be argued that the entire internet growth was a result of people's needs to view por-nography not being met by providers of pornography.'[10]

The feelings and ideas behind such developments continue to thrive at web sites and newsgroups. People are speaking about porn as they've never done before. Previously such contact and candour wasn't possible. Likes and dislikes, crav-ings and disgruntlements are aired. The posters and operators of the alt.sex newsgroups treat porn as a legitimate product, not something to be ashamed about, but something to be criti-cally evaluated. It would be nice to think that the views of the users could influence the style of the commercial, hard-core product. A new connectivity could find porn becoming more responsive to what its users favour. Mainstream media doesn't talk about porn the way it talks about other kinds of entertain-ment media. There are no review pages, interviews, gossip or industry analysis. Certain groups and consumer interests are therefore not being addressed. Though some porn-related magazines like *Hustler*, *AVN* and *Video Hot Exclusif* in France, do offer some kind of review coverage, the bulk of porn magazines don't actually take porn or the readership that seriously. There is also the sense that a lot of the magazines are too close to the hard-core film industry, and disinclined therefore to champion the reader as consumer, or provide the critical perspective needed to help the product improve.

In the American gay press, newspapers and weeklies like *Frontiers*, *HomoXtra* and *The Guide* carry porn reviews. There are also the strictly review titles like *Gay Video Guide*, *Manshots* and *Adam Film World*'s annual gay porn directory, all of which maintain an independence from the industry. Consumer-oriented reviewing may have contributed to a rejuvenation in the gay porn industry. Independent-minded reviewers highlighting the porn junk made it more difficult for porn producers to carry on releasing below-average tapes onto the market with impunity. For the time being, however, the idea of the more liberal sections of the straight print media, like the style or music press, running hard-core reviews takes quite an imaginative leap, while a review of a Greg Dark movie in *The Times* or *USA Today* seems a future impossibility. Cultural and sexual values apart, in the UK there's little incentive for magazine publishers to offer coverage of hard core while the materials continue to be illegal.

Whatever transpires in the mainstream, a continued availability online of reviews of porn movies presents an opportunity for countless people to log on and find out about the recent hard-core releases. A single review posted to the alt.sex.movies or rec.arts.movies.erotica newsgroups is read by thousands of visitors, as well as possibly starting up endless discussion threads concerning stars, other films or the general state of contemporary porn. This kind of contact and communication leaves the undervalued or previously unaware porn user equipped with greater knowledge, and perhaps an increased confidence. An informed, confident consumer of porn is less likely to accept bad tapes. This doesn't mean all the porn product will immediately shift to become the way fans online would have it. The process is still only emerging. So far, porn producers seem unable to apprehend the new media as anything other than an opportunity for peddling more pornware. Online scuffles have already occurred between critics and leading industry figures like Paul Thomas. The porn producers probably think the online porn critics are no more than a small group of disgruntled geeks, and not the bulk customer. This indifference may prove foolish and ruinous for some. When the glut in straight American porn finally arrives and causes an industry shake-out (see Chapter 5, 'Not the Wild West'), at least a few of the offending companies who were repeatedly criticised online will probably go out of business, and this will partly be due to changes in the attitude of porn users caused by the internet.

The exploding CD-ROM bubble
(on the porn industry behaving badly)

With future sex the relations between porn producers and consumers have not been too encouraging as yet. The story so far of CD-ROM and porn is mainly one of rip-offs. Porn users buying disks for the new technology were often fleeced and consequently scared off, causing the CD-ROM boom to be quickly followed by its near collapse. A similar boom-bust cycle occurred with CD-ROMs in the non-pornographic mainstream, where an initial blast of enthusiasm saw the market swamped with too many second-rate disks, only to be followed by cutback and lay-offs because a lot of customers stopped buying the goods. Feeling misled by the promises of the new-tech revolution, disappointed retailers changed their tone. In France, the chain-retailer FNAC sought to win back consumer confidence by putting stickers on disks they considered to be of acceptable quality. 'Not all CD-ROMs are rubbish,' ran the chain's ad campaign, 'just three quarters of them.'[11]

The CD-ROM format offers the user a multimedia experience of image, speech, text, sound effects, music and video clips, as well as being, ideally, an interactive realm where, through simple point-and-click commands, the user can affect what is happening on screen, playing a crucial part in the way the experience unfolds. At the beginning of the penetration of the new CD-ROM technology into homes and offices, the porn sector soared. Pretty much every last scrap of porn was put out on disk. Although only a fraction of this was truly interactive or properly integrated to the new format, every disk was marketed as a radically new pornographic event. This was not an example of the porn industry behaving well. As *Adult Video News* reported in the autumn of 1996, 'The consumer has once again been burned by inferior adult product.'[12]

Three versions of the CD-ROM porn experience exist. There are photographic stills, then movies that play inside a small picture on your computer screen, and lastly there are interactive games. Compact disk technology has a tremendous lung capacity, allowing hundreds of stills or even a full-length porn movie to be stored on a single disc. The actual stills and hard-core movies may just be transfers from other formats, but they cost a lot more in CD. For instance, there is *Rainwomen*, 'when it squirts it pours'. This particular CD features fifteen all-action clips culled from the *Rainwoman* hard-core video series. Or there's *Joe Elliot's College Girls*, where the amateur film series is simply moved from video to CD-ROM. No frills, not even any stills, and certainly not interactive, just the exact same movie, at a far heftier price.

At first this obvious product weakness didn't stop people from buying hard-core CDs in large amounts. It was a new technology, and people tend to get carried away when new things are launched onto the marketplace. The rather timeless observation also holds true that some porn fanciers have more money than sense, and just can't keep their wallets in their pockets. 'Why anyone thought that people would want to watch whole adult movies on a little three-inch screen on their computers was always beyond me,' observed an editorial in *Adult Video News*. Possibly because they had nowhere else to go. Maybe the family VCR was off limits, while a compact disk is easier to hide than a videotape, as well as to access and view in secret. There were many who plumped for hard-core CDs for a while simply because they liked to watch porn at work, in the comfort of their own office, on company time.

However, if the CD-ROM was an executive toy for the mid-nineties, then the novelty soon wore off. A quick market surge was followed by endless movie transfers (many of which were misleadingly marked as interactive), much of which was rejected by the consumer, and leaving the retailer with piles of unsaleable product. Your Choice, the Dutch-based sales point for much material sold into Britain, chose the path of maximum honesty with its customer, recommending that people resisted the temptation of the CD-ROM fad: '. . . videos are cheaper'. By the autumn of 1996 *Adult Video News* announced that, 'The linear transfers of adult movies onto cd-rom . . . are, for the most part, dead.'[13]

Interactive CDs, however, were showing signs of forging a long-term position in the hard-core market. In *Space Sirens*, the player is trapped inside an alien ship, and is required to use his skills with the cursor to pleasure three onscreen sirens in order to escape. Any failure to gratify, and the sirens will kill him. Fortunately, he always has another go. 'Use your virtual reality hand, or cock,' the game's publicity boasts, and it is 'almost as good as being there'. This unconvincing claim is often made, but never true. In *Racquel Released*, Racquel Darrian, one of the so-called 'Vivid Queens' at Vivid Video, is to be seen taking a nude swim, having a 'steamy lesbian encounter' at a nightclub, and thoroughly 'indulging herself at an orgy'. Despite these carnal exertions, Racquel is still raring to go by the time she gets home, ready to 'fuck and suck her lover'. The disc is interactive in that viewers click on where you think Racquel is to be found at any given moment – could be the garage, the florists, or even somewhere described as the 'mattress shop'.

Fuckout is the porn version of the video game *Breakout*, where players need to break down walls in order to go to the next level of the game. The hard-core difference is behind every wall there's a video clip of some kind of 'live' sex action going on – a blow job, in other words. The material is lifted from assorted hard-core porn movies, the clip is slow moving and the picture is fuzzy. Then there's *Sex Castel*, a haunted house game where if the player picks the right door it leads to a sex scene. Again the video clip is slow-moving, but does seem to have been specially filmed for the game, which at least makes the game-playing experience feel more integrated. Then we have a hard-core CD-ROM game called *Fucktris*. Once there was *Tetris*, a simple yet very addictive game from the early period of Nintendo computer games, and now there's *Fucktris*! During the fifties the Ford motor company put the leading poet Marianne Moore to work over a period of several years dreaming up possible names for new models. Now in the late nineties, with vast amounts of lightweight merchandise being dispatched into the marketplace, it must have taken the German company behind *Fucktris* all of two seconds to relocate the brand name in the adult domain.

The interactive hard-core CD-ROM provides mixed returns. The images are not always crystal clear, the games are mostly rather limited, while the erotic interactive links are too silly for a lot of people to be getting on with and are quickly exhausted. Thus far there have been few major successes. This is mainly because producers don't know what they hope to achieve with the new technology beyond making a quick profit. The most successful CD-ROM erotica title is *Virtual Valerie* (I and II), and her cousin in bondage, *Donna Matrix*. Valerie is an animated, cartoon pin-up whom the player approaches and gradually persuades to relocate from the street to her love pad. Once in Valerie's boudoir, the player proceeds to use mouse and cursor, the best point-and-click arousal techniques they can muster, to bring her to a state of orgasmic bliss. Valerie was made by Mike Saenz, a man who is said to be determined to one day make animated, interactive sex as good as regular sex. The feeling and passion Saenz has for the medium and for his creations means that *Virtual Valerie* works, demonstrating the real possibilities for the new technology.

The appeal of interactive computer entertainment (apart from privacy, portability or novelty) lies possibly in it feeling less passive to many computer users. People who find mouse pad or keystroke activity to be the definition of a proper computer experience may need their future sex experience to stretch to more than just staring at an image downloaded from alt.sex.binaries, requiring, therefore, computer porn they can point and click at if it's going to work for them. The interactive CD-ROM brings the two things together. In the last few years the number of CD-ROM porn releases has greatly receded. Companies that are prepared to invest and plan for the long term – and the cost of producing decent computer porn is enormous in contrast to the usual porn investment levels – will probably, in due course, bring better-quality materials onto the market and sales may start to pick up again. Especially with the new DVD technology, with its improved capacity, speed – and hence gaming potential – becoming standard on all new PCs by the turn of the century.

Escape horizon
(how cyberporners defy the limitations of real life)

What the majority of adult CDs lack is a strong and long-lasting game-playing experience. The player's imagination is understimulated. The games need to be less mechanical and more emotionally satisfying. These qualities are often associated with the so-called online MUDs. In these multi-user domains, a group of people participate in text-based role-playing games. A gathering of users will simultaneously make believe, giving themselves names and characters and acting out scenarios in a shared environment made up of various evolving narratives. Often these concocted realms bear a resemblance to the literary inventions of J.R.R. Tolkein, or comic-book lands of princesses, wizards, castles, dungeons and dragons. Add to this erotic role-playing games, and devotees of the MUD experience claim it provides the best online sex available. Just so long as it doesn't get too serious, of course, where a person feels he or she is being molested, or pressured to perform a text-based sexual act against his or her will. In such instances, talk of cyber-rape occurs, as does the need to recognise when it's time to switch the modem off.

MUDs offer a version of sex in the head. Bulletin board service (BBS) online chat and dating facilities extend similar opportunities. Likewise the numerous *ad hoc*, private web-site sex parties, and the sex rooms and forums hosted by gated online communities like CompuServe, Prodigy, and AOL. 'Chat is the thrill. Parties and get-togethers,' says Steffani Martin, who operates the adult BBS, CyberSpice. Online sex talk at direct dial-up BBSs is as old as the new technology. For more than a decade they've been providing erotic possibilities not just for computer geeks but for assorted types with limited social skills for whom, as Mark Dery suggests, 'one night stands between discarnate individuals looks a lot like utopia'.[14] Bulletin boards can also function as a way to meet new people, to find sexual partners perhaps. 'It beats the crap out of a singles bar,' observes Steffani Martin. 'I think it is a much more humane way to meet people . . . it has liberated nerd sexuality.' In this way technology doesn't so much isolate as facilitate human contact. People without the right kind of looks, who are mostly passed up in a bar or at a club, may find it's another story in cyberspace. 'I can't wait to get online and talk to this man,' says Martin, 'not knowing he's some chubby little guy with a beard. All I know is he's clever, he's hot, he's got interesting fantasies and I enjoy spending my time with him.' Likewise, a woman, 'shy all her life, who never leaves her apartment . . . could be a sex goddess online. I may live with my vibrator, but online I'm still a sex goddess. I have the ego grati-fication that I no longer get on the street. It extends my sex life.'[15]

Intense intimacies of thought and fantasy can develop between users via phone line, keyboard and VDU screen. 'Computers and cybersex offer a whole new arena for sexual play,' writes Julie, a keen participant. 'It's the safe sex of the 90's. I've had an on-line "lover" for close to 4 months. We've had approximately 300 O's together on line. It's very fun! We send naughty pictures to each other . . . view them simul-taneously. We talk about what we find arousing about the pictures.' As well as the sharing of porn imagery, Julie's online sessions are a variation of reading and writing personalised erotic text, where the creative process is two-way and con-stantly evolving. 'We act out scenarios together. We've found ourselves on the beach, or having a food fight in front of a fire . . . All these "experiences" we've shared seem quite real. The memories are as vivid as anything in Real Space . . . the sexual encounters, as well. As we interact, creating images and sensations with words, it ceases to feel like masturbation. It's quite amazing, really . . . It transcends the medium somehow. . . the pictures contribute significantly . . . and we've at times watched porn videos "together", thousands of miles apart. The porn has given our online relationship some added longevity, I think.' Such online relationships may be one-off occurrences, or they may build and grow to something far larger: 'We've talked approximately 200 hours a month . . . the sexual talk blending in with the general conversation. I think we both have a healthy attitude about sex . . . It's playful and joyous, really. I look forward to meeting this person in Real Space. I suspect that we know each other remarkably well at this point . . . I'm not expecting a lot of surprises.'

There are also opportunities in cyberspace for new kinds of sexual betrayal. This potential is often anxiously raised in discussions of future sex. There have been stories of marital discord, real-life relationships breaking up over the 'other' person online. Whether or not sharing an orgasm via communications technology with someone you have never met, who perhaps lives an ocean away in another continent, amounts to infidelity is the kind of query that keeps moral philosophers in business. In part it depends on where individuals draw the line for acceptable conduct by a partner – will it be about thoughts, or words, or actual physical congress? It may also be a matter of how couples seek to negotiate modernity's ongoing dispute between desire and fidelity. The traditional concepts of endless, monogamous love are arguably the prison of a person's full range of desires. The ideal of romantic love shows few signs of waning in society. Despite marital failure rates, people are still booking their big day at the church. At the same time the sexualisation of culture intensifies – with men and women set upon by erotic images and signs wherever they turn, bombarded with notions of the ultimate sex experience, to replace the ultimate sex experience previously advertised. This conflict of appetite versus constancy often finds people seeking an outlet by having sexual affairs, with all the trouble and trauma they often cause. A safer, less deceitful option for many is the expanding realm of digital and onscreen sex, of vicarious pleasures and voyeuristic kicks. Future sex may well mean different kinds of promiscuity and less material cheating. Perhaps an increase in real-life monogamy shall go hand in hand with the phenomenon of more cyberian lovers.

'[Cyberspace] is a safe space in which to explore the forbidden and the taboo,' writes Carlin Meyer, professor at New York Law School. 'It offers the possibility for genuine, unembarrassed conversations about accurate as well as fantasy images of sex.' Online people are also coming out sexually, as well as making connections they could never have dreamed of before. There's the story of the balloon fetishist who knew of nobody else who felt the way he did about desire and balloons. And then he went on the internet and over time connected with more than fifty like-minded sex balloonists. There's also the gathering of tall women fanciers – really tall women – and the Tall Women video series being marketed online for interested parties to place an order, *Tall Women Parts 1, 2, 3* and *4*: 'NO FILLER, NO BULLSHIT. JUST A BUNCH OF VERY, VERY TALL SEXY WOMEN.' Each tape offers buyers in excess of fifty women, all of them at least six feet tall, and some of them as much as seven and a half. 'Our specialty is showing the height differences between these very tall girls and the much shorter people standing next to them. Ever seen a 6 10 woman standing next to 5 4 woman. You will.' Online, a woman called 'B' suggests starting a club: 'I have been contemplating the idea of putting together a pantyhose convention for all of us Pantyhose Lovers out there. Would love to get any input in the idea since we should start making plans and booking a location now for next year.' A pantyhose fan replies, 'I love the Idea . . . sounds really neat. Are you going to be there modeling? That would be worth going for.'

In truth future sex is often no more than a conversation between two people. In cyberspace people are having new kinds of discussions supplementary, in the main, to real-life social interactions, and often forging new kinds of social networks. This is ironic, as one of the key fears about new technology is that it represents the terminal decline in real communities. Associated anxieties particular to future sex concern the increased mediatisation of human desire, an alleged foreclosing of traditional eye-to-eye and bumper-to-bumper sexual communion between people. Looking at it from certain angles cyberspace does seem like a place where corporeality no longer has such a central role. Visions of a disincarnate future sex find flesh-and-sense fetishists wondering exactly how machines, cables and hard drives are ever going to replicate the full sensual experience, the perceptual nuances of sight, smell, touch, the whole sophisticated real-sex package that comes when people make a connection in non-digital space. This anxiety of superannuation is commonplace with new technology. At the moment of gaining something we fear we're losing something else. 'How completely neurotic,' observes Lisa Palac. 'First we dream up these ridiculous scenarios like the VR [virtual reality] sex suits, providing an all-you-can-eat lust buffet. Then we scare ourselves with how isolated and miserable we'd be if we actually got what we wanted.'[16]

In such a world view it might be argued that there's only one thing worse than getting what we want, and that is getting too much of it. The media theorist Marshall McLuan, the novelist J.G. Ballard and, more recently, the cybersceptic Mark Dery have variously suggested in their work a system failure intrinsic to future sex, where machines and human desire have combined to create endless titillated lust but offering no proper release. It is implied that it doesn't matter how many times you 'jack in' to 'jack off', future sex won't bring you real fulfilment, and erotic burn-out is the culture's shared destiny. As with many discussions of eroticism and porn, repetition and the replication of sameness in pleasure is seen as problematic, carrying the seeds of its own hopeless disappointment. Western societies don't know what to do with certain kinds of plenty. In *Brainstorm*, Douglas Trumbull's science-fiction film of 1983, a prototypical variation on a virtual reality headset allows the wearers to plug in to other people's recorded experiences. Typically, one poor fool rigs himself up to an endlessly repeating loop of an orgasm and consequently drives himself mad. Once again there's this fear of muchness. A residual religious guilt over non-procreative sex, perhaps, and the social disapproval of non-profitable effort, most often finds idle sexual plenitude depicted as causing harm.

Instead of damage, exhaustion and endism, we might also speak of variation, addition and extension. This leading urge of future sex, as McCluhan observed, 'to explore and enlarge the domain of sex by mechanical technique,' is captured in a way by the closing vision of Michael Ninn's high-tech porn fantasy, *Latex*. As Sunset Thomas joyfully brandishes 'her' gigantic penis extension, a rubber prosthetic of garden hose proportions, she lets loose an endless fountain of pretend ejaculate, for the biggest pop shot in porn history. With Ninn's full-on imagery resides not only the hankering for plenty, but the pornocopian belief that abundance won't necessarily make a person sad.[17]

In cyberspace, not only do people escape the limitations of the real concerning size, shape, looks, potency and endurance, or make good the lack of like-minded types in their off-line existence, but they can also perhaps elude another limitation of real life which says you really have to settle for so much, but no more, and then you must conform, accept that the promises contained within adolescent fantasies of endless carnal escapades are just that, pure dreams that do not come true. Those who tune in to porn, or those who participate in assorted sexual activities online, have perhaps found ways of defying real life's first law of lowering one's horizons. At least for a while, for an hour or so every day, or every week. In at least this sense the doomsayers of the new technology are right: future sex is partly about escape, after all. 'One day you log on,' wrote John Schwarz in the *Modern Review* in 1993, 'and you find people that never settled for the reality principle. Unabashed sybarites, they are trading dirty pictures and sharing their sexual fantasies and . . . most important they seem to be having a REALLY GOOD TIME.'[18]

9
Pornocopia

The experience of pornography is the final strand in the story of pornocopia. How does it feel watching porn? There's a silence concerning those who put porn to use. It is porn's greyest area. Studies are meagre, and too preoccupied with attaching gizmos to gonads, with measuring tumescence and blood flows, rather than subjective experiences. In discussing porn, Andrew Ross speaks of the need to pay 'attention to the voices of the exploited or unheard, in this case, sex workers and . . . consumers'. But there are no porn surveys. In part this is because it has never occurred to anyone to ask porn users what's going on. Or maybe people think they already know all there is to know about porn users: they look at dirty images, they become aroused, they're sad. 'To talk about pornography,' writes Sallie Tisdale, 'means having to talk about the millions of people who like to watch it, read it, think about it. If we talk about pornography with disdain, we have to talk about these millions of people with the same disdain.'[1]

The disdain for porn users makes for difficulties in researching the subject. To find out what people in the adult industry think, you can visit and speak with them. Porn people are mostly friendly, anxious to be understood in order to correct the myths about their line of work. The porn stigma for a performer may last, as actress Brandy Alexandre says, 'for life'. In contrast, using porn is not a similar life 'commitment'. Regular porn users see no great gain to be had from going public, and so are keeping their private pleasures to themselves.

In the mainstream media, with a few exceptions, porn users remain virtually silent.[2] Television and radio shows complain of difficulties persuading people to come on and talk positively about porn. Considering the negative cultural stereotypes of dirty, raincoated tossers, of hairy-palmed no-mates, of wastrels, lotharios, sexist dogs, misogynists (and that's just male porn users), it's really little surprise that people would rather not discuss it. The world of alternative publishing, meanwhile, of low-cost 'zine media and the internet, has provided some outlets for porn discussions. Opportunities online for anonymity and connectivity, for a kind of narrowcasting where like meets like, find an outpouring of conversations on the matter, where the porn silence becomes a hubbub.[3] However, newsgroup discussion threads or small-distribution 'zines are not particularly interested or geared to reach out and communicate to the broader culture and make people think differently about porn.

One way of thinking differently is not to look on porn as inherently problematic. Much dismissal of porn use occurs because it is felt to be a predicament, not a pleasure. There is also a general cultural difficulty with something that appeals to the love muscle rather than the thought centre. Porn has a very basic function. Though it can be educational and entertaining, the hard and soft-core truth is that arousal is porn's main event. It is important not to lose sight of this.

Unfortunately this is often precisely what happens when porn is written about in the mainstream. In the Summer of 1994, the British music journalists Miranda Sawyer and Adam Higginbotham teamed-up to test drive a wildly diverse range of adult videos in order to make sense of 'porn' for the pop magazine *Select*, and completely missed the point. This was a very peculiar event, as Miranda and Adam took some straight hard core, some gay, some lesbian, a safe sex guide, and other diverse materials, and then proceeded to watch the whole lot back-to-back, and non-stop, during a seven-hour marathon. This promiscuous choice of tapes, and a viewing situation that precluded the two viewers from acting upon any erotic stirrings, unsurprisingly rendered them puzzled, unsatisfied and 'bored'. Whatever they had in mind, Adam and Miranda appeared to have mistaken the purpose of porn, and their passing the time finding fault with the story, direction and acting only further demonstrated this. Until a brief, shared erotic frisson was recorded. 'Stop wise-cracking for the first time,' Sawyer writes. 'This is quite sexy . . . Notice that Adam has shut up too.' Adam confesses, 'Quite fancy this girl.' But before anything serious occurred, and perhaps because it couldn't, the jovial mood resumed; 'we roll about laughing'.[4] You feel the joking had to recommence, after all, where else were they going to take the beginnings of sexual arousal?

Whatever intellectual arguments there may be on the subject, the horn and porn of plenty needs to be addressed. In the autumn of 1994, *The New Yorker* reported on a major sex survey, 'Sex in America',[5] which had discovered that the most notable thing about most (American) people's sex lives, is how unremarkable they are, and that '36 percent of men aged eighteen to twenty-four had no sex with a partner in the past year or had sex just a few times'. In the same year, *Playboy* magazine gathered up a few quotes that catch a mood of carnal temperance in the nineties: 'Abstinence makes the heart grow fonder', runs a virginity ad campaign. '(You can go farther when you don't go all the way.)' Bill Lancaster, a producer for the television chat show *Geraldo* declares, 'These days, there's nothing bold or innovative about saying you sleep around. What takes a lot of guts is to say you're a virgin. Virginity has become the new sexuality.'[6] So it would seem that people in the USA are having less sex, or waiting till wedlock before they start doing it. According to the 'Sex in America' survey, the only partnered sex in a lot of peoples' lives will be with their spouse. Meanwhile, in the UK, in the autumn of 1996, the television health show *Pulse* and *Top Sante* health magazine reported that their joint 'major new survey' of British sexual habits had found increased monogamy as an emerging trend.[7]

The findings of these surveys are almost enough to make traditional moralists jump for joy. If it didn't leave you wondering how all these modest types are passing the time. Not all is pure and wholesome, for in the background lurks the dreaded solitary vice. Apart from the fact that such reports of sexual restraint might suggest a deeper moral corruption – that is, a tendency for people to lie when asked about bedroom matters – there was little doubt that masturbation is on the rise.[8] It was to America's self-loving generation that *Sky* magazine paid a visit in the summer of 1995, and found droves of young people watching piped-in cable soft core and calling it 'Wet TV'. The dull college campus life, the date-rape minefield, safe sex, the virginity push, cathode addiction and slackeritis were all cited as reasons for the boom. A 'panic' on the American nightclub scene was alleged as a consequence of a generation of youngsters lost to the porn demon. With 20 million American homes with access to pay-to-view porn channels like Spice and Playboy at $5 an hour, who needs sweaty clubs, warm beer, bad drugs? *Sky* met a college student knocking back five hours of cable porn a day, costing him a fortune, and culminating in a regular late evening rendezvous with his love-tool: 'I like to wait toward the end of the day before I actually put hand to penis.'

Typically, having used a porn story to pepper the editorial content, the magazine then seized the moral high ground, speaking of bleak addictions, dysfunction, an alienation from real life: Wet TV is 'great for sad men who'd rather sit at home and watch the boob tube than go out and pull a real woman'. To *Sky*'s predominantly late adolescent readership the word is that solo sex is for deficient types. A magazine that month-on-month assiduously courts the young male reader by featuring near-raunch glamour shots of leading female celebrities – Liv Tyler, Alicia Silverstone, the Spice Girls – proffers a righteous disapproval of a kind that would not have been out of place in the late Victorian era.[9]

Sky magazine is not alone in the continued slighting of masturbation. Celebrating the tenth birthday of *Arena* magazine, apparently the first magazine in Britain 'that looked at the world with a man's eye', Tony Parsons praises the magazine for having contributed to a cultural shift over a decade that has seen men becoming not only more familiar with the pleasures of Italian tailoring and Japanese beer, but also more in touch with their 'inner lives'. Before *Arena*, 'we could never really open up our hearts', and men were unable to be 'unashamedly male'. One thing *Arena* 'knew', and still knows, Parsons assures us, is that most men are not 'stroke merchants'. In the same issue, *Arena* pays tribute to ten great British sex symbols of our times, fashion models, singers and actresses – Louise, Elizabeth Hurley, Anna Friel, Kate Moss – and features all of them doing cheesecake poses, lips pouting, legs parted, maybe tugging at their hipster-trouser waistbands, revealing bare midriffs and heading lower with the enticing promise of some elusive celebrity privates. These pictures may be more 'tasteful' and 'arty' than gynaecological, but they are nonetheless images to contribute to a masturbator's visual repertoire, fantasy gear made for 'stroke merchants'. Clearly men getting in touch with their inner lives means never admitting to masturbation.[10]

The denial of masturbation, its roping off as a queasy state of incompleteness, and the rumoured revival of virginity and monogamy, all persist in awkward conjunction with the continuing sexualisation of mainstream culture. So many magazines, so much television, every other billboard poster campaign sells you sex, or features sex as the hook for selling other products, from holidays to motor cars, pensions and alcohol.[11] Nevertheless, masturbation is required to maintain its shadowy existence. 'Fetching come', 'flapping yourself', 'jilling', 'bashing the bishop', 'going solo', 'spanking the monkey', 'paddling your own canoe' shall not be discussed. As the science-fiction writer Brian Aldiss observes, 'people pretend to be so enlightened about sex these days, they talk happily about copulations and such subjects, about adultery and homosexuality and lesbianism and abortions. Never about masturbation though. And yet masturbation is the commonest form of sex, the cheapest and most harmless pleasure.'[12]

This is not to say it should be headline news each time a person delivers the goods single-handedly. It is more about turning thoughts of isolation to a recognition that you're not alone, of switching from images of desperation to horns of plenty, from the image of the 'hideously atrophied male genitalia' that the writer Andy Darlington found in medical text books during his adolescent years to images of better blood circulation, mental comfort, stress therapy and idle recreational abandon. 'Masturbation is not some kind of lonely, pathetic thing that happens when you're not getting laid,' writes Lisa Palac.[13] 'Everybody masturbates,' declares Audrey, 'but it's only the British and some buttoned-down yanks who deny it.'[14] And heterosexual men. When a woman masturbates it can be empowering; for a man it's just pathetic.[15] Porn movie maker Steve Perry urges a re-evaluation: 'Wanking's cool. You don't have to have anyone else there, you don't have to spend any money, you don't have to worry about driving home pissed. You can have fantasies about all these gorgeous women that you're never going to meet. That is why porn is such a wonderful commodity.'[16]

On the strange business of looking

Kate is a feminist porner. Her confessions as a porn user commence in her childhood. Before she was five, Kate started having s/m fantasies. Growing up in the countryside she couldn't wait to go horse-riding and be intimate with a leather saddle. From around the age of ten, Kate started making use of porn, masturbating to British top-shelf magazines. She does not remember the very first time she saw porn, although she remembers that her parents left such materials about the home, rather than stashed away in some out-of-reach cubbyhole.

The first view of porn can be pivotal for some, and barely memorable for others. Most of those who spoke to the author about porn had their first porn moment in their early teens with a glimpse of something mainstream. 'I discovered *Penthouse* magazine at about age 10.' Or, 'I remember finding a collection of *H&E* in my stepfather's wardrobe while looking for something else. I was about 11 or 12 at the time.'

'Well, my first experience with pornography was when my cousin showed me a *Penthouse* he had stolen from one of my uncles,' an anonymous contributor recalls. 'I was 9 or 10 at the time and I remember liking the pictures of naked women, but what really impressed me were the sexual cartoons. I spent a couple hours flipping through his collection, and I may not have looked at every photo, but I read all the cartoons. I still get equally aroused at a painting or drawing as I do at a photograph.' A gay man describes his initial view. 'My first exposure was at 6 years old. Even then the men interested me more than the women.'

The first time is not always recalled as the best time. Writing in the porn 'zine *Batteries Not Included*, Rachel James outlines an uptight Catholic upbringing, where sex education was virtually non-existent except for a guide book called *A Doctor Talks to Twelve Year Olds*, which described copulation as so: 'When a man and a woman love each other, they hold each other close in a special embrace.' James found her dad's *Playboy*s stowed away in the basement at home between *Popular Mechanics* and *Popular Science* and realised there was something about being adult and intimate that she wasn't aware of yet. Later on, still eager to find out all she could, James let her boyfriend take her to see a porn film. She was into the porn house and out again in near record time. On sitting down, first thing she saw onscreen was a woman on her knees just finishing a blow job, who then turned to face the camera, 'and let all the cum pour out of her mouth'. James recalls feeling horrified: 'I could feel my mouth drop open and I just sat there transfixed for a few minutes.' Before getting out of there fast: 'I simply was not ready to see all THAT on a wide SCREEN.'[17]

Which might have been it. But, because she liked her boyfriend, and really wanted to find out, she went again, and again. And then, one day, all the right things happened on screen for her. The right stuff came along in the shape of the actor John Leslie, like it seems to have done for several female porn converts: 'But John Leslie . . . WOW!' Brandy Alexandre similarly fell in love with the onscreen Leslie. Alexandre also found watching porn films as her most vital lead-in experience to real-life sex: 'After seeing a few adult movies in the Pussycat Theatre,' she writes at her home page on the world wide web, 'I decided I was old enough to put the knowledge I gathered into practice. WOW! Why did I wait so long? I did it three times that night.'[18]

Others remember their first time with porn as similarly positive. 'I found some porno mags when I was about 11 years old,' writes Kerri Sharp. 'I thought they were funny but wasn't upset by them. It made me realise that there was a whole subterranean psyche to grown-ups (they didn't just think about jobs and money) and it made me want to grow up fast so I could start having sex.' For one contributor, a childhood European vacation brought an unexpected revelation. 'My family was visiting Denmark and we got our car stolen. My parents were forced to stay at the hotel so they sent my brother and I (I was 10 at the time) out to see the town of Copenhagen. We went into a bookstore and I saw photographs of fellatio. I was thunderstruck and delighted. My brother (9) was disgusted. The world of sex opened up for me.' When Tuppy Owens saw her first Danish porn magazine she thought it was 'wonderful, so exciting', and was annoyed she hadn't seen it earlier. She decided to make her own, taking pictures of herself in a boat on the local river at five o'clock in the morning, 'with a doll stuck up my pussy'. Owens feels her life might have taken a different course if it hadn't been for her discovering porn, 'I'm really lucky that porn came into my life when it did.'

Into her teens, and Kate's interest in horse-riding declined, while her interest in porn grew. Her family were quite strict in many respects, she says, but not concerning sex. She thinks it likely her parents knew about her hobby, and chose to say nothing about it to her. When friends were going to London, Kate would give them money to buy porn magazines for her. She collected them all. Kate has never identified her sexuality as lesbian. She is an example of a straight woman who has regularly turned for arousal to top-shelf material made for men, predominantly featuring photo sets of naked women, and without a male member, or even a male, in sight. Julia shares similar tastes, finding the general explicitness of the photography to be the source of masturbatory excitement. Tuppy Owens says she gets turned on by the women in *Penthouse*, finding porn made for men more to her liking than the porn specifically angled at her own sex: 'The magazines made in the

UK for women are utterly dull. They are not like my sexuality at all. They're not funny enough and they're not dirty enough.'

The abundance of 'lesbian' numbers in so-called 'couples porn' is a curious thing. Clearly it isn't just straight men, or lesbian and bisexual women, who like to watch women-only scenes. (Although, many lesbians in the USA will rent not only 'dyke' porn but also the 'het' mainstream 'girl–girlers' made by people like Bruce Seven and Ona Zee.) Many heterosexual women tend to be fascinated by each other, and mostly are more open to expressing their same-sex fascinations than straight men. After all, it's women who buy all the glossy magazines like *Vogue*, *Marie Claire* and *Cosmopolitan*, filled with pictures of beautiful, barely clad women. Furthermore, in terms of viewer transference, and following the (contentious) theory that no woman knows how to give a man a blow job better than a man does, for a watching female the thought of a woman performing cunnilingus, with her presumed wiser tongue, may well prove an erotically stimulating fantasy.

These insights into diversities of taste and desire clash with the views of many male porn fans who are convinced that the makers of couples porn have got it wrong in featuring so many 'girl–girl' scenes in their upscale efforts. As far as they're concerned, girlfriends don't like watching women doing it to each other. There are repeated warnings on the internet, 'movie to be avoided at all cost if renting with your partner,' writes a male reviewer at alt.sex.movies, 'as there is an awful lot of girl–girl action in this movie'. Another reviewer advises, 'This is not, repeat NOT, suitable material for girlfriends, too many girl–girl scenes for her liking.' And yet only one woman out of the many describing their porn experiences – either to the author, or gleaned from previously published or posted materials – voiced any such distaste. Most, in fact, volunteered a fondness for such materials: 'I especially like girl–girl things,' says an anonymous straight female.

In Kate's experience, she feels she lusted over pictures of naked women in 'male' hetero porn because she found the imagery sexy in the broadest sense. Many porn users speak of being stirred just by the general 'sexiness' of simply watching other people aroused, rather than the exact bearing of the representation. In *Batteries Not Included*, a lesbian reviewer observes, 'I'm finding more and more women who love to get off on other people getting off without imagining themselves in one or the other positions. After all we are a nation of watchers.[19] Writing as a gay man who likes porn, the critic John Lyttle admits, 'The porn that truly revs my motor these days is mean dyke porn.'[20]

It is also true that many straight men confess to queer occurrences watching porn. Sure-thing heterosexuals, they thought, who've seen an erection onscreen and found themselves getting aroused by this, and wondering what that was all about. Hardly what you'd expect from the last bastion of absolutely het maleness. Inevitably the hetero male's hard-core experience involves looking at other men's penises, getting an eyeful of pumping erections. For most men it's the only place they see such things. Likewise watching men orgasm. Many find this fascinating; they want to compare it to how it works for them. Some men tell of how if they ejaculate simultaneously with the man on screen it makes the experience more complete. (Other men, however, say that they don't care about the porn stud onscreen, or his appendage.) It could be that a form of homosexual desire is going on with some men watching hetero hard core. After all, it is staring us in the face – the penis. Consider that, for the ten or fifteen years prior to video, millions of American and European males went to cinemas to sit in front of large screens and watch the male member, blown up to the size of a big log, and coming towards them. So, is the whole hetero porn thing the longest homoerotic alibi in history? Are straight men coming out to themselves as bi-men, masturbating over the sight of other hard-ons? Could be, but probably not. Meanwhile porn directors guide the situation carefully, making sure in any three-way number involving two men that the two penises shall not touch. Nevertheless, the penis is still there, taking care of business, and any analysis of the curious business of porn-watching better not forget it.

In *Sex Exposed*, Anne McClintock writes about her early days with hard core. As an innocent in early adulthood, the academic ventured into an adult book store, looking for the 'hot stuff' magazines that catered for women, only to be told there weren't any. McClintock was not so easily brushed off, however, and her porn search continued. From a state of exclusion, over time she found a way inside by tapping into feature-length hard-core movies, and by doubting the received wisdom of feminist film theory that defined the cinematic gaze as intrinsically male. In movies supposedly made for hetero men, she found a space for herself to watch, recognising that there's possibly more than one thing going on with porn. *Devil in Miss Jones* was a key moment. Watching Georgina Spelvin in a girl–girl scene, it seemed to McClintock that the presence on screen of the man and his penis was there as a fig leaf maintaining a pretence of heterosexuality. Understanding that Spelvin was 'out' as a lesbian in real life, and seeing the actress and her female co-star really 'doing' it, made the critic aware of how the 'uninvited' viewer might possibly take something from this 'men-only' porn. And this could grow: the spaces might expand depending on how legal it was, how supported it was, and how many women started getting access to porn, watching it and making it.[21]

The porn viewing experience plainly is more involved than first meets the eye; the actual imagery is sometimes less significant than the feelings, thoughts and associations going on inside the viewer's head. Though the soft-core magazines Kate used didn't directly address her sexuality, neither did they thwart or contain her own particular longings. Instead they served as a base camp building to other, more personal fantasies concerning a very different transgressive scene. The simple fact that it was porn, and explicit, and 'reprehensible', meant the commonplace soft core functioned as a 'deviant' stand-in.

These complex ways of seeing illustrate the potential for mobility in the user's point of view. An intersubjectivity that goes far beyond the reckoning of the photographer who, when asked by the author what goes on when a person looks at an erotic picture, declared, without qualification, that men always see themselves having sex with the woman.[22] This is not necessarily so. 'I generally do not place myself into a porn fantasy that I am watching or reading,' says a porn fan who goes by the alias of 'Burkman'. 'My interests are usually more voyeuristic.' Geoff is equally clear about this. 'No, I do not,' he says, 'and I don't tend to do this when I read regular fiction, either.' Then again, for others, a simple transference is indeed the way of things: 'One or more smiling beautiful girls looking straight at me while working a cock,' writes 'Demaret', from Sweden. 'By preference I like it when the girl(s) lick. I can then admire beautiful eyes and smiles close up and fantasize that the smile is an invitation for me to be there with her/them. In fact I often fantasize that I am there.' An anonymous female admits, 'I always project myself into the action, sometimes 'feeling' the enjoyment of both the male and the female.'

The obvious conclusion to be drawn is that there's no such thing as an average porn user, or 'only in the sense that there's an average height of human beings,' suggests Nicholas White. 'It's a meaningless conflation which tells us nothing about the individual subtleties and variations . . . the only thing that porn users have in common is that they all like porn.' To know the way porn works is to recognise the variety of responses a single porn work may engender. The porn viewing experience can be a distinctly personal and complex happening, involving not just the fantasy scenario on screen, but the viewer's own fantasy extracts, projections and flashbacks from their personal erotic memories. These particular brain images may leak and mix with events onscreen, or on the page, cutting and cross-cutting like a series of fast edits. A type of cross-subjectivity may occur watching porn, where viewpoints switch and change. 'Identification in porn can be multiple and shifting, bisexual and transsexual, alternately or simultaneously,' writes Anne McClintock.[23] 'While wanking over the pictures,' a long-term porner recalls, 'the meeting of my unrestrained lust and the explicit images of girls often produced an almost trance-like state in which I felt as if I were experiencing sex from the female side as well as the male.' And yet, 'This wasn't a latent homosexual desire to be penetrated, but a kind of ecstatic identification with aroused femininity.'

Desiring the porn figure so dearly, many men may also want to temporarily become that figure, because being so dearly desired is enviable. To say, therefore, that all hetero men have the same porn emotions, and they all want to be having sex with the porn woman, misses the complexity of desire. This fits with the tendency in recent times to characterise male heterosexuality as an unshakeably single-minded business. This reduction often occurs in combination with mass-communication theories that fail to take into account what audiences make of media signals within their own specific context of personal experiences, values, preferences, psychology, or simply whatever mood they happen to be in at the time. 'The variability of interpretation is the constant law of mass communications,' writes Umberto Eco; and what matters is 'not where the communication originates, but where it arrives'.[24]

In America, during 1983–84, a colossal 180 million telephone sex calls were made. In New York in the same financial year, during a twenty-four hour period, a certain pre-recorded erotic message was called up 800,000 times.[25] In *The War of Desire and Technology*, the cultural anthropologist Sandy Stone writes of the time she spent with a small community of women in the San Francisco Bay area who operated a telephone sex line. While analysing the dynamics of this all-women experience, Stone became curious about phone sex and the process of parcelling up and sending erotic arousal downline: 'The more I observed phone sex the more I realised I was observing very practical applications of data compression.' The phone-sex women were collecting the five senses, the full sensual range, and compressing them into an auditory package. In order to convey so much in such small packages, the words used by phone sex operators, the sighs, pauses, delays, giggles, amount to a highly sophisticated code, a compendium of erotic communication for the dialler to receive and decompress by adding themselves, their own detailed experiences, fantasies and predilections to the mix. 'The sex workers took an extremely complex, highly detailed set of behaviours, translated them into a single sense.' And then, 'At the other end of the line the recipient . . . reconstituted . . . a fully detailed set of images and interactions in multiple sensory mode.'[26] From this combination emerges a very elaborate, individual erotic occurrence.

Information compression is not exclusive to phone lines. I was once talking with someone about the problem of never being able to remember more than a couple of details about books that you nonetheless proclaim to love. From a 500–page biography of the writer Vladimir Nabokov, my only strong recollection concerns the image of the author as an old man taking great sensual pleasure from bath-times, and how he'd submerge his bath sponge, let it fill with water, lift it over his head and slowly squeeze out the water, letting it trickle over his head and shoulders and down his back. That's all that comes to mind when I think of this long, detailed book. This was the book's 'punctum' for me, it was suggested: a very condensed and personalised summary. In *Camera Lucida*, Roland Barthes speaks of two kinds of apprehension when looking at the photographic image. There is the *studium*, the trained, commonplace effect of a photographic composition, and then there may also be what he calls the *punctum*, the quirk within the aesthetic play that for some reason captures the viewer's eye and begins almost to stand for the whole photographic experience: 'this element which rises from the scene, shoots out of it like an arrow, and pierces me'.[27]

It's true. What appeared as a pleasant but slight detail actually contains in notation the feeling taken from the book. The impression of Nabokov as a sensualist contains also in shorthand the sensuality of experience and rapture particular to reading one of his novels. The single image of the author's bath-time was satisfactorily carrying a freight-load of meanings, memories, feelings. And so decompression isn't just something computers and modems do, or auditory erotic tokens passed down a telephone line. Like phone sex, people bring so much to porn. Porn is its own compressed delivery system. The ostensibly limited imagery contains in précis a whole range of information, erotic ideas and gestures. To it we bring our selves, and the two interrelate: like a man plunging from a plane with a small tightly packed square attached to his back, which, once the string is pulled, bursts forth into this capacious parachute, many times the size of its original container. The parachute, the punctum, the image decompressor, the pornography – so simple, and yet so densely packed.

Despite all of this mental input and output, porn continues to be seen in the main as repetitive dick fodder for dullards. Where porn and men are concerned, Catherine MacKinnon is sure that the brains and genitals aren't speaking to each other. In her demonology of the male, the mind–body split is fundamental. Referring to the Yiddish maxim, 'a stiff prick turns the mind to shit' (her rough translation), she is very clear about this: 'The common point is that having sex is antithetical to thinking.'[28] And because it does not aim for the mind, merely the lap region, porn cannot be speech, in any legally defensible sense. We are immediately aware when we look at porn that we are being communicated with, and yet some anti-porners say otherwise, that in fact we are merely being triggered like Pavlov's dog. As Drucilla Cornell observes, MacKinnon's behaviourist, mechanical version of man amounts to just another spin on the Freudian notion of anatomy as destiny: 'A man becomes his penis. He cannot help it . . . He is reduced to a prick.' Cornell doubts the use of such a crude model in seeking to explain how the body, consciousness, fantasy and desire interrelate: 'I think that men can think and have an erection at the same time.'[29]

The notion that porn use doesn't mean using your head is clearly ill-considered. 'I think that using porno is cerebral,' observes the writer Dennis Cooper. 'It's like a study. It's like a text.' In fact, if it weren't so much about the body being moved and aroused, you'd be excused for thinking that porn is really a head thing. 'I started reading porno when I was really young,' says Cooper, 'and like a lot of people I read a lot of porno before I had sex. By the time I was having sex, I expected it to be like porno. When it wasn't, I invented porno to go with my sex, because while you're doing your limited little things with your body, there's all this stuff going on in your head about what could be happening.'[30]

An online porn fan provides a small, light-hearted example of the porner's non-vegetative reach, interrupting and reconfiguring the media flow with what he describes as his *Porn Star/ Celebrity Equivalencies Handy Reference List!* Whenever he tires of formula porn, he imagines the same scenarios but featuring substitute celebrities who are porn star lookalikes: 'Nina Hartley = Goldie Hawn; Amber Lynn = Melanie Griffith; Annette Haven = Jane Seymour; Tori Welles = Raquel Welch after a big meal; Ginger Lynn = Meg Ryan; Buttman = a less-talk-more-action Seinfeld; Tom Byron = a Klingon having a bad hair day.' The porn fan as art-worker recommends additional gain through switching between porn tape and a film on television featuring one of the celebrity doubles: back and forth, back and forth, 'until the two begin to become indistinguishable in your mind!' You might even forgo sound, it is suggested, and improvise your own narrative from the joined-together mainstream and porno movie. 'Yes boys,' our fan declares, aware that he's starting to sound a little cranky, 'your Good Doctor has been snowed in a little too long!'

The perfectly 'useless' nature of such activity is as interesting as the signs of mental activity. Discussing entertainment applications for new technologies, science-fiction novelist Pat Cadigan says, 'Let's face it . . . it's not so terribly inaccurate to say that we've done some of our best work for the sake of relieving our boredom, ennui, or Weltschmerz.'[31] In this way might the alleged passivity of the porner be better grasped as a kind of socially unacceptable, non-utilitarian activity. Porners are perhaps misrepresented as slothful, idiot perverts when in fact they are *flaneurs* in a late twentieth-century setting of consoles, cathodes and couches, wastrels who feel that time spent with a close friend is time well spent indeed. So, which is it to be, porn a waste of valuable time, or porn a valuable waste of time?

The counter-accusation laid against the sex industry, of course, is that it contributes to a culture that sees sex not as idle pleasure but as hard work, requiring constant effort if it's to be any good. Where 'doing it, having it, getting it, wanting it is our duty, our task, our vocation. Boast of your idleness in other areas of your life,' writes Suzanne Moore, 'but not in this one.'[32] It's true that porn shows great athleticism and prodigious energy expenditure. Yet critics who represent this as a version of Marxist alienation from the 'natural' pleasures of the flesh are missing the most crucial point: that it's not the viewer who's doing the work, it is the well-paid porn performer. Do porn fans really absorb the porn work ethic, or do they just watch it in action? The viewer can watch, get horny, orgasm, then fall asleep.

The criticism of porn for creating a compulsiveness in viewers emerges from similar ideological terrain. Hard core's failure to wholly render the 'truth' of physical female sexual pleasure, it is suggested, means that it lacks for something, that it cannot fully deliver on its promises, and so porn viewers compulsively keep going back to try to get it all, to finally find out.[33] These fugitive pleasures – forever out of reach – make porn the ultimate Marxian commodity. Because we keep on coming back for more, porn becomes a money pit, offering easy earnings for the pornocrats. Porn, however, tends to plateau in terms of sales. Also, the approach that sees porn as compulsive is offered by critics who like to keep their distance. Unable or unwilling to get inside to the sensualities of porn, they're therefore almost bound to view repeated porn use as unsatisfactory. These observations are determined by a particular view of experience. Notions of the 'elusive' circle back to Freudian version of wants and desires, which has desire being fuelled by the person's need to find resolution, to be completed. Alternative versions might figure human longing as not a thing of lack but more concerned with replicating pleasure, of repeating loops.[34] With desire made of such 'moreness', notions of deficiency, of longing gone wrong, become less tenable. For what if porn isn't a problem after all? Beyond the arguments, perhaps it is really straightforward. You watch it, you get off, watch it again and get off; again, get off. What if, after all the bickering, it's as simple as that?

Nicholas White

(on going mental on porn)

Unfortunately it's never as simple as that, meaning that mostly the broader culture holds to the view that porn is a problem for the viewer. But does the porn user share this concern?

For ten years Nicholas White was an intense user of porn, 'to the extent that I bleakly (and in retrospect, conveniently) considered myself an "addict"'. In the last stages of this extended twist with porn, Nicholas was also contributing fantasies to the pages of various British men's magazines. His relationship with magazine porn was turbulent and complicated.

It all started in the bike sheds at school, where the adolescent black market in soft-core porn magazines took place. The associated developing interests in books, sex and adolescent rebellion coalesced for young Nicholas in the portable shape of dirty pictures. Their position within adult culture as 'hot stuff' was confirmed by an early experience at home when his secret stash was rumbled and summarily pitched into the dustbin. This parental act of cleansing passed without acknowledgement or comment. In stony-silent suburbia, Nicholas had found his teenage kicks. Made even better by the fact that unlike other teen pursuits this one was very boy's own. Girls weren't involved in porn, not in Nicholas's world. For someone already deeply troubled by his alienation from the emergent sex kittens and love goddesses down his street, owing to a serious stammer and a chronic lack of experience with any girls, this separation was just fine.

The porn bug was slow to catch on in any big way with Nicholas. Through the remainder of school years and during his time at college, porn was only on the periphery, with teachers, girls he'd seen around, and famous women providing the source materials for his masturbatory fantasies. With college failing to deliver the times of carnal excess that Nicholas had been hoping for, a self-defensive habit of detachment from women became distinctly settled in his behaviour patterns. 'After a few disastrous attempts, I more or less gave up and took refuge in what was already a well-developed erotic imagination.'

Although Nicholas's porn use was quite small and his feelings sceptical, day trips to London would invariably find him in Soho. This was the Soho of the early eighties, before the backlash on porn. Nicholas saw his first hard-core movie, but somehow this didn't work for him: 'Having learned to enjoy producing my own internal sex films in my head, I found having to passively take in a flow of alien imagery a curiously intrusive experience.' At this point the idea of full exposure didn't appeal. British-made soft-core titles like *Rustler* and *Whitehouse* sufficed, with these purchases treated more as souvenirs from the trip, for future further analysis, than urgently needed new supplies. The image Nicholas depicts is of someone holding back, dipping his toe in the water, not sure if this is what he wanted. 'To my ears the pornographer's boast of "nothing left to the imagination" sounds more like a threat than a promise.' This relaxed view, he admits, masked a deeper anxiety that in porn lay the lure of greater isolation up ahead. This was where his life seemed to be heading, but not quite yet.

Home from university after graduating, Nicholas tried and failed to get work. His stammer proved a serious obstacle in interviews. A dalliance with eastern religious faiths coupled with a continued sexual shut-out saw Nicholas become celibate for a while. 'So I stopped masturbating,' he recalls, 'took up Spanish and spent my days Not Thinking About Sex, with predictably lust-crazed results.' In due course he stopped 'giving up' and resumed masturbating. Porn use was still minimal. Two years passed without Nicholas finding work. Having gradually lost touch with friends and daily life, he made a conscious decision to cut himself off from the outside world. A while afterwards, coming home from the library one hot afternoon he stopped off at the newsagent's for a cold drink, and as he took the can out of the freezer his eyes lifted to the glossy, tempting line-up of magazines on the top shelf. Because he happened to have the money to hand, and because he was feeling lusty, on impulse Nicholas bought up half a dozen titles more or less at random. This was not how he'd previously gone

about things. Restraint and discrimination seemed to vanish. A
new age was beginning in his life. Till this point Nicholas had
bought fewer than thirty magazines in ten years. In the decade
to follow, he was to buy more than 2,000 magazines, an average
of four a week.

At first it was just a hedonistic splurge, he thought, a sensual
comedown after a prolonged exploratory bout of spiritualism.
A couple more bulk purchases occurred over the next few
months, before Nicholas decided it was time to bring his porn
blitz to a close. But he couldn't. He kept going back, buying,
disposing of, buying anew. The purchasing trips became more
frequent, weekly, bi-weekly, and more drawn out, fondly
hunting down the best raunch, a man gathered up in the thrill
of the chase. Having established what were the good time zones
for hanging out in the newsagents, and what were the rush-
hour periods to be avoided, Nicholas remembers spending long
days staring out of the window, wondering what he was doing
with his life, while waiting for his prime time at the shops to
come round again. 'I'd created a porn-shaped hole in my life
that nothing else seemed to fill.'

Finding new erotic images was paramount, as was the post-
orgasmic need to eject the magazine from out of his life and
into the nearest rubbish bin. The rate of turnover in materials
became very rapid. Sometimes things were quite absurd. One
day he bought a magazine and binned it within a few hours,
only for the next day to return to the shop and buy the same
magazine, and then throw it away again immediately after masturbating. Later, for a while, he would also cut out favourite
snaps from favourite magazines and paste them in scrapbooks,
collections that in due course were also ditched.

The collector mentality will sometimes figure in conversations on porn. A single, gay man who lives alone explains in a
letter to the author how he covers his room with images: 'I
have my bedroom walls covered with nude and semi-nude porn
posters and I look over each one every night and when I awake
in the morning. It's a kind of thrill and excitement in itself, and
gets me in a good mood for each day.' Another man records
cable and satellite services, but only the bits with big breasts,

and makes this into a kind of repeating video loop which he has running in his house all day, as a kind of ambient comfort. There's the man whose thirty-year porn story partly amounts to assembling a massive inventory of adult imagery, of cutting out, cataloguing and filing away. He's the consummate collector, who even had a compilation tape made of excerpts of shots looking up women's skirts. He was in touch briefly with the British Men and Porn counselling group, but not, it turned out, because he felt he had a problem, rather he was keen to have a look through the porn materials of other group members. Several contributors speak of computer storage problems, of squeezing their hard drives to the maximum. In his capacity as a porn fan, rather than as a professional porner, John Stagliano has his own big cache of vintage porn magazines in the garage in his home in Malibu. 'Wildchild' shows it's not just men who hoard their smut. She retains 'the more graphic stuff', she says. 'But, I never look at it.'

Collecting was a short-lived phase for Nicholas. But the ritual of giving up and disposing of the offending materials became central, as he sought to gain at least the illusion of some kind of management over his out-of-control existence. Each time he threw away only to buy anew, the plausibility of the ritual was further reduced. Once, to give it additional symbolic weight, he actually arranged the giving up to take place on a night with a full moon, as sign of a fresh start. In due course, Nicholas moved on from newsagents to second-hand market stalls where the range was greater and the costs lower. Paradoxically this just meant he bought a lot more magazines and spent greater amounts of money. Market day became the heart of his week. He would be there, ready and waiting at 8 a.m., filled with hostility towards another regular at the stall who he feared was likely to land the best issues of *Playbirds* on offer.

Nicholas was in the grip of a compulsion the end of which, he was convinced, would only come through him getting a girlfriend. But how was this going to work since, as every young man knows, girls don't go out with wankers. After four years of this, Nicholas eventually sort of fell apart. Thoughts of suicide loomed. He was in touch with the Samaritans, and then his

doctor referred him to a counsellor as well as to a speech therapist for his stammer, 'which was really the root of the whole
problem'. The porn fixation persisted but the tempestuous
stage was slowly coming to a close. The rage and self-loathing
shifted to a sense of resignation. He also started to consider his
compulsive, obsessive relationship with soft core as 'a mere
symptom of my inability (or disinclination) to communicate
well with other people'. With hindsight he considers it conceivable that what might appear as self-destructive behaviour is 'a
pre-emptive acting-out of a feared situation.' A person may
elect at some level of consciousness to stand and not flee,
becoming entangled so that they are able to find the route that
leads towards an eventual disengagement from the problem.
During his porn madness, Nicholas perhaps embraced isolation so deeply – barely seeing anyone, most days speaking
fewer than twenty words – that never again will the thought of
being alone fill him with dread.

A tentative re-emergence into the world began. And then, in
1991, things changed. Nicholas wrote to Outsiders, the self-
help group for people with disabilities who have problems
finding partners. The group was founded by Tuppy Owens.
She encouraged him to write to her about his particular situation. To be in communication with a woman who liked porn
was a revelation for Nicholas. Previously, he feels he had
accepted on a subconscious level the Dworkinite position that
all women see porn users as inadequate males who might also
be rapists.

Another development around this time found Nicholas
looking at hard-core magazines for the first time. He found this
to be less troubling than soft core. In the past the hard core in
Soho had been shrink-wrapped and costly, and the (very
realistic) fear of being ripped off and disappointed had stopped
him from taking the plunge. It is difficult, however, not to read
more into this surprisingly prolonged reluctance to 'go all the
way'. Soft-core porn provides sexual tease and alluring images
of nudity for the desiring gaze. Heterosexual hard core, meanwhile, shows men and women having sex together. There is
more going on in hard core, a mutuality and a greater oppor-

tunity perhaps to think yourself into a fantasy replica of such erotic intimacy. It is possible to argue that, if the connection is absent from the pages of soft core, so might it be absent from the fantasies of the voyeur. And though it is important to be particular and not general, and to doubt that soft core and hard core work in similar ways for everyone, nonetheless, in Nicholas's case, the suspicion grows that soft-core porn, with its potential to keep the viewer outside looking in, was a kind of vehicle for his descent into isolation, while hard core, with its sense of actual erotic activity and involvement, contained a potential route map, guiding him back from his removed stance. 'This healed much of the resentment I'd felt at being excluded from the feast – after spending so long with my nose pressed longingly to the window, I'd now at least managed to get a warmer vantage point inside.'

This transitive stage was furthered when Nicholas became involved in porn magazine production. Combining his joint loves of sex and writing, he started contributing fantasy stories, some fake 'readers' letters', too. Seeing the way the fantasy machine worked at the nuts and bolts of the mechanisms of arousal was a way to demystify, to see through, but also to harness and contextualise, using his love of arousal and turning it into something more active and less debilitating. Swearing off porn might have simply blocked him up, whereas remoulding his relations with it partially turned a problem into the start of a solution. As Nicholas emerged from his lost state, inevitably he got involved in life again. He did not join the Moonies, or a war-on-porn group, which would have been some kind of denial of himself. Instead, through a fairly circuitous route, he became an erotic dancer's chaperone. From the socially removed lone male, he turned into a stripper's escort, carrying her bags, getting her drinks, minding her discarded knickers and bras.

In due course she seduced him; they had an affair, which ran its course and ended. In the aftermath, he found that he now had a copious memory store of erotic times well spent, not just images of their couplings, but smells and the feel of touch and skin. These were now available to him as masturbatory aids, and the porn usage stopped. Dwindling for some time already, the ritual of throwing out had also ceased, until he realised it had been quite some time and that those several dozen mags he'd previously accumulated, now blanketed in dust, might feasibly be discarded. He later wondered if such a final disposal had been a little precipitate, but four years have now passed and he remains unbothered by the absence of porn in his life. Though not even 'remotely tempted to get back on the band-wagon', he does however maintain the ex-drinker's resistance to just 'one little drink' and is determined right now not to buy a porn mag again, although he can envisage a future time when he would happily share a use of porn with an enthusiastic partner.

In considering times gone by of 'self-inflicted misery' from a life position that sees him finally at ease with his own sexuality, Nicholas is convinced that soft core simply isn't good enough. He finds it indicative of 'the "giggling schoolboy" attitude to sex that pervades British popular culture.' In contrast, hard core, he feels, partly got him out of trouble, and 'had a satisfying aura of completeness and arrival'. Regarding certain feminists' objections to porn as causing male violence, he says, 'I can only say that throughout years of intense porn use, I never felt the urge to attack women.' Furthermore, 'even if it had led to sex crime, blaming porn for it would have been like blaming alcohol for the actions of a drunk driver. If porn had a positive aspect during this period, it was that it was a safe arena where I could express my rage [concerning the humiliation of long-term unemployment] without hurting anyone else.'

Users' views
(on fantasy and reality, porn and behaviour)

The 1970 US Presidential Commission on pornography included a survey that tried to establish if people felt porn was 'damaging' them. Aside from observing that there's nothing like an unloaded research question for drawing out an untainted response, it is worth noting that 24 per cent said it gave them information about sex, and 10 per cent said it improved their sex lives.[35] Contributors to *Pornocopia* were asked to comment on what influence, if any, porn has had upon their attitudes to acts and people.[36] The one thing nearly everybody agreed was that porn has influenced their sex life. 'Porn plays a significant but isolated part in my life,' writes Julie. 'It doesn't color my attitudes or behaviors outside the sexual realm. I have some conflicted feelings about porn. I consider myself a feminist . . . But I still find it arousing, and would be a hypocrite if I claimed I didn't.'

'Porn is just one small part of an extremely complex and chaotic event that we call life,' observes Burkman. 'Like anything else, it has its good points and its bad points. Certainly to a great degree it seems to serve as the vehicle for sex education in this repressed society of ours.' 'Barlow' would agree. 'I suppose [porn] made me believe that there were women who enjoyed having sex. I had been led to believe otherwise by my parents.' The educative argument is supported by Linzi Drew: 'At least porn teaches young men what a woman's body looks like . . . the sex education material we had at school was little more than diagrams – I used to think that people did it in their sleep.'[37] Several porners agree. 'Because of porn I know how to give a woman an orgasm,' writes Demaret. 'I learned more about female anatomy from one issue of *Playbirds*', says Nicholas White, 'than I did from several weeks of sex education lessons – if it weren't for girlie mags, I would never have heard of clitorises, let alone known where to find one!'

'Reading about characters' exploits have encouraged me to be more bold,' says Kerri Sharp. 'I can attribute an improvement in my sex life to when I began to read erotic literature (late teens).' An anonymous woman feels similarly positive. 'I think I am much more comfortable with my sexuality now that I know so many people share it. I have learned about many sexual activities through pornography that I might not have invented by myself.'

'Watching porno as a couple,' writes 'der Mouse', 'I have a somewhat better idea what my SO's [significant other's] sexuality responds to.' In this sense, then, porn could be said to have some influence on people. 'Yes, it can affect behaviour,' says Geoff Williams, 'in that it encourages sexual variety, teaches new techniques, etc., and I believe that it can help relieve sexual frustration . . . I have tried different sexual techniques that I have observed in videos. Watching girl/girl scenes may have helped my wife come more to grips with her bisexuality when she was first dealing with the realization of her attraction to women. I know a woman who watched videos to learn how to give better head, and it certainly seemed to have worked for her.' So the porner as pupil stands to learn a lot. 'Sure, you learn a lot,' writes 'Tresman': 'variety, things to try, and that I should have bought shares in breast implants.'

A contributor who goes by the name of 'Mr Freep' was, he admits, a late starter sexually. As a regular user he feels porn affected his attitudes in certain ways. 'I feel like I was more capable as a lover my first time out having watched porn movies,' he writes. 'It didn't help my capacity to love or care for my lover, but it helped mainly in technical ways (positions, what women may or may not like, etc.).' Did this mean, therefore, on his very first time he tried the reverse anal cowgirl position, porn's most extravagant performance piece? No, it didn't: 'Pornos are movies and as such are fake. The people don't love each other . . . they're actors. I know what the women in those movies like may not be what "real" women may like but it gives you ideas on what someone "may" like. You try things and if they don't fly at least you can say you tried, but without the pornos to show me certain moves I might never have known them even to have them try and fail . . . I am more adventurous due to porn.'

But, on a broader level, does Mr Freep notice any differences in his behaviour due to hard core? 'I pay attention to the dumbest, most insignificant things that one really does not need to remember. Ask me a math question and I am stumped. Ask me about the politics in the Nixon administration and I would have no idea. Ask me to name the cast from *The Dukes of Hazard* or ask me to recite the lyrics to the theme from *Knight Rider* and those are the kinds of stupid things I just happen to remember, those and porn stuff. Maybe because of this use of/

interest in porn I talk more openly about sex at work or among friends, etc.'

Men who use porn, according to John Jordan (a porn sceptic), are extra-sensitive to sexualised imagery in the general culture – magazine covers, television commercials, billboard ads: their sex receptors having hypertrophied through too much porning. One contributor to the author's survey describes a kind of porn circularity in his life: 'I like sex, I enjoy it, so I seek out sex-related things; this feeds back to increase the amount of time I spend thinking about sex. But the same is true of recreational mathematics, and I daresay you'd feel rather silly asking me the analogous questions about that.' It may be so that in the eyes of an intense porn user the exterior world will be more sexualised, like shapes of clouds resemble a sensimilian exhalation to a heavy dope smoker, or nearly every gesture to a Freudian may suggest a desiring subtext. But Freudians do connect with normality, to see a cigar as simply a cigar; dopers do come down; and porners in thrall to the sexualised image will more often than not masturbate or have sex, and then get on with their lives. Or, as Steve Perry puts it, 'Porn doesn't lead to rape; we all know that what porn leads to is a good wank, half a lager, a sandwich and a good night's kip.'[38]

With more compulsive attitudes to porn you need to look at other tangled issues concerning the individual's relationship with the world. It's difficult to accept porn as this uniquely toxic package. With someone who is eating too much chocolate, you don't take away his or her box of Belgian soft centres and start examining them under a microscope, rather you take the person – hopefully with that person's consent – and look at his or her story, desires and fears. In discussing his hard times on porn, Nicholas White will often reach for the analogy of alcoholism, but ultimately he dismisses the 'addiction excuse' as a denial of personal responsibility. 'The whole idea of "exploitation" is meaningless where consenting adults are concerned ... making bad choices over a long period is no one else's fault. The angst I felt at the time came from the knowledge that I was acting self-destructively and not from any sense of feeling powerless in the grip of an overwhelming force.' Mr Freep agrees, 'As I have said, I see nothing wrong with [porn] and actually find people who find it smutty to be funny. They get worked up about things we all do . . . HAVE SEX! It has not led me to see women as being cheap or easy, or as sex objects and nothing more.'

Not everybody is as sanguine as Mr Freep – at least, not always. At around the age of sixteen, Kate's long-running attachment to soft-core porn magazines started to concern her. She worried that her use of porn was negatively affecting her world view, that maybe she was seeing herself as better than the women in the pictures. These doubts coincided with a spell of seeking out a larger moral structure in her life. There followed in due course an active spell of political feminism, and then a brief but deep involvement with Christianity. Kate stopped using the magazines. She became very holy, she says. However, she remained unable to agree with what Andrea Dworkin said about porn, finding it was wrong, she says, to argue that porn represented male rage against women. Kate feels that there's much that's positive about porn for women in terms of knowledge, desire and license; it just stopped working for her for a period. Likewise, during her time of piety, she never let go of her interests in 'deviant' sex: 'I closed the door on them, but knew full well they were still there, and not wrong.' Over time, Kate gradually resurfaced from her twist with temperance to resume with porn. She also joined the fetish sex scene. These days she buys porn from time to time, and uses it with her long-term boyfriend.

Jonathan Martin is a long-time porn user. He has often wondered, he says, what porn images may have made of him, about how sexuality takes shape. 'I'm not sure that with my own make-up, that I haven't become fixated upon certain rather idealised images of women that I found in [soft-core] magazines such as *Mayfair*, which is not helpful in terms of finding sexual partners. That's not to say I think it has ruined my life,' he says, 'but neither am I saying that it was particularly helpful. And then again, when alone, porn has been extremely helpful when I needed a wank.'

A frequently made criticism of porn is that it might not only lessen respect for women in society but also render men unable to view them as anything other than sex objects. This worry derives, in part, from the second wave of feminism which offered the important insight that women were being used as sexual objects in their ordinary lives. But then some proceeded to protest against women being objectified in sex. To treat someone you work with as simply an object of sexual desire is wrong, but to be unable to see a partner as an object of sexual passion when having sex sounds like the makings of a poor erotic experience. In this sense, being sex objects is part of what sex is about, and this is also how it works with porn fantasy. 'I think folks who decry sexual objectification simultaneously decry fantasy,' writes Carol Queen, 'for the vast majority of people, men as well as women, do nothing more with their voyeuristic crushes than masturbate and fantasize.'[39]

Jonathan admits that he mostly blames porn when he's feeling down on it. 'Maybe it wasn't the *Mayfair*s, maybe it was the lingerie ads, or pictures of film stars. I'm sure it wasn't porn just itself, but it fitted into a media world where you had many idealised images of women confronting you.' And then Jonathan wonders about this as well, that maybe his erotic tastes had been fixed long before any of these images passed his way. He refers to John Money, a leading American sexologist, who posits what he calls the 'Love Map' theory, where an individual's particular reactions to erotic input are created at an early age.[40] Demaret feels sure his early, rather extraordinary sexual experiences influenced his adult sexuality: 'I think my preference for sex derives from some great blowjobs that I received from a girl when we were six years old.' In his porn life, Demaret is fond of material featuring smiling models giving blow jobs, their smiling eyes looking at him, the viewer.

In John Money's 'Love Map' paradigm, porn won't significantly refigure a person's erotic tastes. 'You can watch a hundred coprophilia films,' observes Geoff Williams, 'and still be disgusted by the whole idea.' Mr Freep describes his predilection for a particular kind of porn magazine. 'For some reason I like ones that call themselves things like *Barely Legal* or

Just Eighteen. I know they probably aren't 18 anyway (or anywhere near it) but they look young enough to pull off the bluff.
I heard once that if you don't experience sexual situations by a
certain age you seem to stall where you are for life . . . and
maybe that's why I like those mags. I didn't have sex until I was
21 and I went all through high school wanting to fuck just
about every girl, and hey if I was 15 and so were they, it didn't
make it dirty. It was puberty. So the fantasy of being able to be
with high school type girls is still there in the back of my mind.'

A contributor called 'Arcadian' writes of how he got started
with porn. 'As a single child, often on my own, I had an early,
strong curiosity about sex. Some of this was gleaned from my
peers, and mutual masturbation gave intense pleasure in my
early teens. While without company this pleasure was less satisfactory as a solitary act and I soon sought extra stimulation
with the aid of 'dirty magazines' which circulated at school. By
modern standards these were very mild,' he writes. 'Mostly
pictures of busty girls with their private parts covered or air-
brushed out. Nevertheless, they satisfied my needs for many
years – especially during my courting years when shyness/
modesty precluded any serious sexual exploration. In those
days I used to rush home, look out my cache of erotic pictures
and relieve my sexual stress. I suppose I was hooked from
teenage onwards especially as I have voyeuristic tendencies.
Whether the latter would have emerged *without* an interest in
pornography I do not know but I suspect it would because of
my curiosity about all matters sexual.' As Arcadian says, he
doesn't know for sure, he can only surmise and suspect. For, as
the child psychotherapist Adam Philips suggests, we cannot be
clear what impact early events in life may have or denote: 'We
just don't know what children experience, what it means to
them, what it will mean to them.'[41]

A related view about porn and how men are is the idea that
adult materials suggest that women are always available for sex.
More realistically, what the porn fantasy suggests is not that all
women are available for sex, but that this woman is, and only in
fantasy. 'For the vast majority of people, including myself,' a
woman contributor suggests, 'porn is a fantasy area clearly

separate from the rest of my life.' Fantasy may make people feel sexier than otherwise, but it doesn't turn them into sex pests. 'I would never try to walk into someone's house as a plumber and expect to have sex with the woman residing therein,' writes Mr Freep. 'Although sometimes I have been in situations like that . . . You're working late and a lovely woman says "I'm leaving can I do anything for you before I go" and you hear in your head the cheezy 70's wahwah pedal-guitar-type music often found in pornos and think to yourself "hmm if only in a porno."'

The separation is clearly defined by the fact that the fantasy is mediated. The woman isn't there, so why would the viewer think he can have sex with her. Porn gives viewers permission to look, and to fantasise over an image – but not permission to have real-life sex with that image, as that is a physical impossibility. Even if the man were to meet the woman he masturbated over, would he believe that she was available for sex with him? You just have to go to the trade conventions, the industry awards shindigs, the promotional appearances in video stores, and see the fans obediently waiting in line to get their $20 Polaroid snap with the porn star, to ask yourself, are these men behaving as if they think this woman is available for sex with them because they saw her naked in a magazine? 'The people who write to me don't want to seduce me,' says Linzi Drew; 'they want me to go and seduce them. That's their ultimate fantasy. It's not "I'm in charge and I'm going to take you." The typical fantasy is "I win a prize and take your photograph and as I photograph you I've got a hard-on and you come up and undo my zip." It's all about "You take charge", "You take the lead", "You be the instigator".'[42]

Any attempt to understand porn must consider the crucial role of fantasy, not least its complicated relationship with reality. A person's fantasy life may bear characteristics relating to the rest of his or her regular world. 'Fantasy is something I enjoy creating and experiencing, and it may or may not inspire my activities,' writes Barlow. 'However, I seldom fantasize outside my area of comfort anyway. For instance, I would never fantasize about rape. I would fantasize about picking up someone at the supermarket, but I might also do exactly that.'

For others, however, the fantasies they entertain work in variance to their actual lives. Your fantasy may be the last thing you'd actually wish to happen (as with people who have fantasies featuring coercive sex). Indeed the fantasy's material impossibility may often be its spur (fantasising you're having sex with a cartoon character from a Walt Disney movie).

The cultural historian Tom Englehardt remembers how as an idle schoolboy in Cold War America he'd entertain himself by dreaming the worst imaginable things. He drew a map of the world where 'Red China' conquered every last square inch of the 'free world', including the USA: 'hundreds of tiny arrows winging their way over every land mass from Greenland to Australia. To reach the United States, the Chinese invaders crossed the Bering Strait, met up with another army routed through Greenland, and swept down on my home.' He recalls, 'I found secret pleasure and entertainment then, in playing with the worst nightmare the anti-Communist mind could produce.'[43]

Several women communicated to the author a desire for a new kind of porn featuring scenarios of harsher and non-consenting sex. Not actual instances of force or sexual violence, but performances of the fantasy. 'In fact that is some of the most erotic things to me, if it is acting,' says Julia. 'Rape is part of our society and you can't play like it doesn't happen. I really don't think rapists watch movies about rape. They don't need to because they act out their own stuff.' Sallie Tisdale describes a scene from the film *Images of Desire*, where a woman is strapped in a chair and two men come into the room, holding batons which they slap against the palms of their hands. 'All unsaid, all undone, the baton never touches the woman. . . I think it is important to point out that many women are turned on by this kind of film.'[44]

'Max Hardcore' is a noted 'no-frills' American porn director whose crude middle-end videos play at being pushy. A male porn user describes his wife's 'Hardcore' predilections: 'My wife watches porn. Her favorite stars are pretty hard for most people to accept. She likes Max Hardcore because she likes to watch him "take charge". She assured me that she wouldn't like to fuck someone like Max but got very hot watching him dominate the women.' Many women, brought up to consider sex as base and a masculine preserve, something only rude girls show an interest in, are drawn to fantasy situations where the woman has sex without initiating, or being responsible (thus getting the sex while remaining 'pure'). A woman posting at alt.sex.movies describes her feelings: 'One of the fantasies I've had since high school is being taken by a couple of guys older than me. . . Women have told me they fantasise about being overwhelmed, mastered, overpowered in a soft rape scene, which may not be the same thing as a gang bang. . . I picked up *Gang Bang Girls 14* because Vanessa Chase was featured, and I was pleased to discover that her performance turned me on. . . What seems to appeal to me is the staged degradation of something pure. To me Vanessa conveys innocence, especially in this video when the men undress her and starts pawing her body, when she shifts into that special mood which suggests that she is not altogether present, an innocent girl turning fey, the reaction of a guileless, helpless coed overwhelmed by a powerful masculine force.'[45]

A lot of people are troubled on hearing such fantasies, both for their being politically incorrect and because such 'darkness' is presumed to indicate dysfunction. Fantasy is an enigmatic part of experience that has been much discussed in the psychological community, but never truly settled or understood. Because the subject is so elusive, those rather joyless tendencies in psychology will often try to pin fantasy down as being a mechanism for personal revelation (often dark revelation), as another way of finding out what we need to know about an individual. An approach that readily thinks in terms of sickness precludes the possibility of perceiving dark fantasies as indicators of a healthy state of being in the world. 'In our sexual imagination,' writes Leanne Owen, 'we can lose all control and inhibition without penalty, blame, injury or shame.'[46] A 'dark' fantasy entertained in the head may denote a good emotional state, the very opposite of pathology, in fact, as this mental exploration of the far side actually enables the person to get on and live. Ultimately, fantasy is a state of mind. 'It is a bitter

irony to me,' writes Amber Hollibaugh, 'that I was in my mid-
thirties before someone explained to me that I was not what I
dreamed, that fantasies had a reality of their own and did not
necessarily lead anywhere but back to themselves.'[47]

The idea of porn fantasies depicting non-consenting sex was
mostly turned down by male contributors. 'I don't think it is a
big fantasy for most men,' writes Geoff Williams. 'But a lot of
women find it arousing. Personally, I don't like scenes like this
at all, but should I then deny a fantasy that some women have
and might want to see?' But do men lie? 'I've always found that
some men have a hard time being honest about porn use,' says
the writer and critic Michael Bronski. 'It all gets tied up with
what they think they should like and do.'[48] A few exceptions to
an overall mood of male coyness on the matter were to be
found; they just took a bit of tracking down. In passing, an
online male reviewer mentions a viewing foible of his: 'Personally I enjoy watching Dyanna's rare anal scenes "immensely";
. . . mainly because of the perfect image she projects of mild
"discomfort".' Later he continues the thought, 'What I look for
in an anal scene . . . it's what I call the "mild domination"
factor I look for even in real life sex. Not leather or whip stuff,
and certainly *not* pain – just a slight submission. . . Since porn
is a visual medium and it's therefore very difficult to capture
these real life nuances effectively, things like apparent discomfort in anal scenes are the closest I can get to my pet
perversion.'[49]

Nicholas White describes how he used to project his own,
personally constructed fantasies of duress onto consenting situations in porn so to make it 'mean' more to him: 'The porn
stereotype of the insatiable nympho never really turned me on –
it lacked the titillating contrasts and emotional complexity of
real women. Fantasies of uncovering the whore behind the
housewife or being seduced by the 'respectable' professional
woman were more arousing. . . I liked to imagine the models as
'nice' women who'd been forced for financial reasons to
degrade themselves by posing, as the fantasised reluctance
added another dimension to what was otherwise just another
anonymous set of porno clichés.'

There is an unruliness in fantasy, an opportunity for behaving badly. This is often where the adolescent porn attitudes of *Hustler* magazine and its like comes in, with its grunt humour, gross cartoons poking fun at social taboos, and its ready stream of scatology serving as a regular affront to the bourgeois culture. These instances of bad behaviour are too easily misread as representing the 'true' nature of 'men' in all their sexist ugliness, rather than their being recognised as a type of playful regression for people who don't always want to be acting all noble and mature, cultured and responsible, but wish from time to time to revel in bad taste, to talk of bodily functions, of shit and piss, saying fuck for the sake of it, succumbing within the realm of fantasy to the 'lesser', unbridled, mental impulses. 'We must also take into account the possibility,' writes Andrew Ross, 'that a large part of porn's popularity lies in its refusal to be educated. It therefore has a large stake in celebrating delinquency and wayward or unauthorised behaviour, akin to cultural forms like heavy metal, whose definitive, utopian theme, after all, is "school's out forever".'[50] Mr Freep concurs: 'Porn doesn't need to be well behaved. It's the bastard child of the media.' Plainly not everyone is going to appreciate this kind of behaviour or find its expression to his or her liking. However, those who see it as a serious threat not only don't get the joke but also probably inspired it. 'As a feminist (not to mention a petit bourgeois and denizen of the academic classes),' writes the critic Laura Kipnis, 'I too find myself often disgusted by *Hustler*.' And, as Kipnis openly admits, 'This is *Hustler* hitting its target.'[51]

A world apart
(on porn and theories of isolation)

There is autonomy in fantasy, not only in the fantasy's specific shape or content but also in the very act of fantasising. Fantasy might serve simply to kill time: starting up while we're waiting for a bus or a train we mentally cut loose, momentarily taking flight with dreams we entertain not because we're unhappy in life, covering up for failure, or hoping to get even with this cruel world, but because daydreams give pleasure. The role of fantasy as a kind of secluded entertainment for the sake of it touches on issues of sociability and solitude. There are some for whom porn functions as this well-tended, isolated patch in their lives. It's a thing some people go in for, often men. We might call them 'garden shed' men, the kind who like to have a place to go off to every once and a while, to be alone to potter, dither, idle or mess around. Could be the computer, could be gone fishing, could literally be the garden shed, the council allotment, and then again it could be porn.

Isolation is easily misconstrued. The thing to recognise is that such isolated spaces do not represent the core of the wretched male being, that porn is not a male haven where guys become what they really are, or what they'd really like to be the rest of the time. The temptation is to link such separatist intervals to a more deep-rooted disaffection, as though a combining of solo time and probably solo sex is necessarily lethal, the slippery slope to alienation. This interpretation is forgivable if you look at the experience of someone such as Nicholas White and mistake a symptom for a condition. But the more Nicholas White reflects upon his own troubled times, and tries to make sense of what went on, the less porn figures as the key. 'The main issue was always my hypersensitivity about my stammer, and a yearning for deeper communication with people. . . Even if I'd nipped porn in the bud soon after it started, I doubt if life would have been much cosier. I would probably have found another obsession to fill the days (maybe eastern religion or writing stories).' Porn was part of a removal from regular life, 'Just a brick in the wall of my isolation', featuring music, yoga, watching sports, and a serious reading habit – all such activities determinedly pursued to fill in for the lack of human contact. There was also a deep and rather unhelpful fixation with Friedrich Nietzsche, which even stretched to learning German. 'I must say that Nietzsche was an albatross round my neck during this period, as I couldn't help thinking that Supermen shouldn't jerk off over *Fiesta* Readers' Wives!'

Nicholas White was a person cut off, who had tried and failed to get connected, and this failure suggested to him that he was better off alone. He believes that he stayed locked into porn for so long because it provided a good excuse for staying isolated. His failure to connect resulted in a no-sex situation, which made Nicholas vulnerable to the attractions of a sexualised culture, but without the outlet of a real-life partner. Therein lay the lure and utility of soft core, onto which, unfortunately, he pinned not just his need for sex, but the things porn is unable to provide. 'The fault lies not with the material,' he writes, 'but with the craving mind which demands from it a lasting satisfaction that it's not designed to deliver... Under the surface glitter, porn has one basic function – to arouse sexual desire and then help to temporarily satisfy it. I suspect that a lot of isolated men use porn not so much as a substitute for sex as (more damagingly) a substitute for intimacy.'

Though it has its solo purposes, there's no reason why porn should necessarily cause separation from the world, putting the user in a lonely place. Plenty of porn users are not isolated but leading 'regular', connected lives, and using porn when they are happy, or because it makes them happy. 'I use porn daily,' writes a contributor. 'I feel no guilt about my enjoyment of porn.' There is a distinct lack of anguish in the accounts of most of those who speak of their relations with porn. '[It] makes me very horney and makes me more sensual, and kind of serves to chill me out,' says Wildchild. 'There very much has been an improvement in my sex life due to using pornography... It has improved things in every way.' To depict porn use as somehow connected to sadness or distress would be an inaccuracy. 'Porn is a regular thing in my life,' writes Mr Freep. 'I will continue to use it sometimes as a "sleeping pill" if you will. Watching a few scenes and masturbating are better than warm milk.'

'Situational' porn use – when separated from opportunity or during times of celibacy – accounts for a share of adult sales. 'I'm very big in prisons, in the forces, and with separate people,' says Linzi Drew.[52] However, a lot also comes as part of an ongoing relationship. 'I buy a couple of magazines a month,' says a contributor. 'I use them 3 or 4 times a week for masturbation or with my partner for mutual masturbation.'[53] Another describes using porn as a fall-back, 'Mostly it fills in for actual sex when I don't feel I have the energy to be fair to my partner's needs but still feel I want to come.' Writes Mr Freep, '[Porn] *is* about arousal, masturbation (alone or with company). I use it in conjunction with being in a relationship. We use it together from time to time and I use it solo as well . . . where I didn't want to have actual sex but wanted to be satisfied.'

Porn is often characterised as a harmful presence in relationships. There are marriages where the husband has pushed for his porn fantasies to be a part of their sex life together, and his partner, feeling a distaste for such activities, has been manipulated, even bullied, into performing acts outside her own pleasure zone. Typically here porn is characterised as a demonic 'entity' irrupting inside a relationship that until then was perfectly equitable and harmonious. The situation where a husband 'forces' his porn fancies upon his wife is already abusive, and the abuse is of power, rather than porn. Porn doesn't make unreasonable demands, people do. Moreover, where there might be relationships that are hindered by porn, there are the many more troubled relationships where porn is nowhere to be seen. Where it is said that porn gets in the way of healthy relationships (whatever 'healthy' might mean), often it may be the other way around. In actuality porn can help to keep a relationship going, not only through adding extra spice to the conjugal mix, but by offering the fantasy of promiscuity. The pressures within a sexualised culture born of the contest of romance, fidelity, monogamy versus roving desire, diversity and variety are perhaps less harmfully negotiated through porn than infidelity. Porn offers multiplicity without duplicity. 'My use of erotic images and text declined during the early years of my stable marriage,' writes Arcadian. 'But in later years when sex became less satisfactory I turned to pornography more and more. It was my substitute to having an affair or seeking the services of prostitutes. Furthermore it was *safe*! As a result of my own experiences I regard pornography and erotica as a completely harmless diversion which relieves sexual stress. My marriage bond is still strong after 45 years and it has not affected that.'

The porn fleece
(on power, porn, and hard-core fraud)

The porn user may temporarily elude the limitations of the everyday through sexual fantasy. In real life we seldom earn enough, are never popular enough, and we can never be sure that the team we support will always win. Things are more amenable with porn – there's no boss, unpaid bills, or yet another sporting let-down – none of the humbling banalities, just a sovereign space where dreams come true. Porn's accommodating nature, it is suggested by critics, enables men to feel powerful. During times of social and economic upheaval, when traditional male roles are under threat, where the exact character of masculinity is said to be unstable and no longer clear, porn reassures anxious males of their continued worth and potency.

The familiar, easy conception that joins porn and hetero men in the power continuum neglects the fact that heterosexual men are not the only people who turn to adult materials. It also fails to recognise how the porn experience may actually further complicate matters of power and masculinity. Porn shows 'real men' doing it, and doing it fantastically well. But although there is a feeling that 'real men' use porn, the archetypal brick-layer or truck driver, and that using pornography can feature as a kind of rite of passage into adulthood and sexual sophistication, there is also the contradictory representation of the male porn user as a 'wanker' – some no-hoper or virgin pitiably making do with a dirty magazine. In this context, where porn mirrors and refracts the sexual paradoxes of the broader culture, as well as failing, just like the rest of society, to offer any clear resolution, male porn users are arguably under pressure. And, while the broader culture perseveres with considering porn a rather odious thing, male porn users are not of a mind to talk of any conflicting feelings they might have. The grubby silence that especially surrounds male porn use is hardly something one would associate with male supremacy.

There are also practical experiences with porn that will frequently leave a man feeling more diminished than empowered, most likely because he has been required to visit some seedy spot in the rough part of town, to land a video that turns out, once he gets it home, to be a rip-off. In these times of consumer power, where customers are used to getting what they want in the marketplace – and most certainly not getting cheated – the porn fan is mainly powerless to do anything about all the swindling that goes on. The porn stigma makes it difficult to protest the bad behaviour. If your use of porn is partly due to a low self-esteem, or if using it makes you feel like a lesser character, and then you get ripped off, this isn't going to help things much.

In this way, male porn fans are often angry fans. There are plenty of good reasons for being annoyed.[54] The anger can start with the rip-offs at point of sale, and then it spreads to the cons, to materials advertised as being something they're not: like interactive CD-ROMs that aren't interactive, or 'amateur' videos featuring a cast of professionals from the industry. For instance, there's a hard-core film called *Reel People 1*, which sells itself as 'amateur' and features on the box-cover a long critical blast against the mainstream hard-core industry. And yet this tape is put out by Vivid, the leading hard-core video company in America, and features a cast of performers who in reality have countless pro-porn movies already to their name.[55]

There is also the long-running business of box-cover fraud. Only in porn could it be accepted practice for the video box-cover photograph to show someone who isn't in the actual film. The actress Dyanna Lauren started out in porn appearing on box-covers for films she wasn't in. Later, before she was sure she was ready to go all the way on film, she often made a brief appearance in a non-sexual role, but would front the film's publicity drive as though she'd had sex with the whole cast. In the seventies, when honest hype was unheard of and blatant false advertising endemic, the German company Mike Hunter Video noticed that any titles starring the French actress Monique Carrera sold particularly well in their home market. And so they did a deal with the actress to have her name feature on the box-covers of a range of their movies, most of which didn't feature Carrera, nor had even the faintest connection with the actress.[56]

All too frequently the porn industry shows scant regard for the paying customer. Online, 'Mr Peeved' of alt.sex.movies finally bites back: 'The overall message on this VIVID effort [*Reel People*] is: YOU PEOPLE IN THE VIDEO CONSUMING PUBLIC ARE SO STUPID YOU'LL BELIEVE ANYTHING WE PUT OUT.' The American satirist H.L. Mencken once suggested that no American businessman had ever gone bankrupt through overestimating the public's gullibility. As Mr Peeved puts it, 'The honchos are counting on you to have all the blood out of your brain when it comes to video and laugh about it all the way to the bank. I get the feeling,' he continues, 'that whenever I watch an adult video I'm being sneered at behind my back and treated like a moron. I don't appreciate it.' The sex industry, he suggests, has to stop treating its customers like perverts, like 'The "raincoat crowd". . . [old guys] who can't get it up for our wives and have to get our jollies on the side. And like we're so hooked on porn that we'll buy/rent/preview anything as long as there are naked bodies in it.'[57]

From fleecing and frauds, the angry porner moves on through an extensive range of gripes concerning standards of video reproduction, of filming, photography, bad acting, a surfeit of silicone, hackneyed sex, and assorted failures of fantasy and erotics. 'Often the production values are appallingly bad,' writes 'billp', a contributor. 'The acting is seldom good,' writes another. 'The music is poorly used, the scripts are often juvenile. There is much room for improvement.' Another contributor lists her regular grievances: 'Bad lighting, no plot, corney music.' The lack of enthusiasm from performers gets one contributor particularly down and disappointed: 'What is most important in "picture" porn to me is that the person(s) in the picture appear to be actually having a good time. Almost anything else can be forgiven, but if the people are obviously faking, that usually ruins it for me.' Demaret summarises the situation from the user's perspective, 'There is such a lot of rubbish. Porn could be of better quality.'

Listomania
(on favourite things and trainspotting)

With all these complaints, one could be forgiven for thinking that nobody is having a good time with their pornware. But maybe it isn't simply that the porn is not always good enough. Maybe, like Susie Bright says, it's simply that it's a lot easier being critical with porn. To say what kind of porn you like is harder – for it is possibly more revealing. 'You can like . . . all kinds of things in a porn movie,' says Carol Queen. 'Pay attention to the things that erotically move you or interest you. You can find yourself attracted to characters, body types, the way they talk or move, their timing, the erotic roles they play . . . kind of sex they have . . . way they have it.'[58]

'You know when a really thick cock is half way out and the woman's tight flesh is stretched around it . . . I love that moment,' declares Julia. 'We freeze those pictures so I can take it in, in all its glory. I like the glossy Scandinavian hard core sex magazines for the same reason. The stills, they get right in there. The messier and muckier the better.'[59] Admits Lynne, 'I find it very arousing to watch men and women in "sexual congress". My only regret about not having a penis, is that men can watch their cocks sliding in and out . . . while women have the inferior view, especially when it's going on from the back-side.' Fortunately for Lynne, 'Videos take up the slack.'[60] Steffani Martin is similarly keen to see it all going on, 'I want to see what I can't see, because I'm not a contortionist, when I'm doing it [having sex].'[61] Likewise Abby Ehrman: 'With insertion shots. I like to see what's going on. And there's the reality: are these people screwing or making believe? You can see the same thing on NYPD Blue. I wanna know that those people are really having sex.'[62]

However, it's not all about heterosexual intercourse. Many straight women like to rent gay porn. 'I personally really get off on watching "good" gay porn,' writes 'Darklady' in a discussion thread at rec.arts.movies.erotica, 'because I enjoy watching naked men get off and if I can see two of them getting off together, then all the better.' In a similar newsgroup thread,

Tim Evanson remembers two women who shared their predilections with the gay porn critic, 'Sarah, like "Javelin", liked to watch musclemen get the hell fucked out of them. Sarah was also more interested in watching men suck cock, which she loved. Unlike fucking, which was rough and "manly," she thought sucking cock was the ultimate in "de-macho-izing" men . . . it made them MALE, not "manly."'

In another online discussion, a male fan expresses an opinion regarding 'some vintage Tiffany Million'. This is someone who knows what he likes, and it's Million's assertive onscreen performance, her 'bitchy, take-charge persona': 'I especially love the way she shoves his face into her gorgeous tits and then pulls him over to the couch when she is ready to have her pussy eaten.' Moving from the particular to the polymorphous, a contributor shares his diverse, plentiful porn fancies: 'I like gay and hetro, straight, anal, gangbang, gay leather, sm. . . I myself love hetro sex any position, gay sex, kinky sex – leather, rubber, pvc and denim worn skin tight, lots of foreplay and plenty of arousal and stimulation, rubbing sucking licking, kissing, and finally fucking to a heightened sexploding in a massive climax of super sex where the smell of sex and leather or rubber would be overwhelming.' This fan of multi-coloured preferences is like a one-man porn inventory: 'I do also love the obscene language in the mags, and videos.'

A look through the letters of contributors to this book unearths a endless list of porn fancies: 'lesbian' sets involving two or three women, especially of different races; an image of a pretty girl in various stages of dress/undress, where you may be able to see a flash of skin or panty up her skirt; long-legged models wearing high heels but no lingerie; lipstick; smoking; girls with long dark hair and medium-sized tits; men with long hair; women with hairy legs; balloons; white high heels; celebrity lookalikes; blonde women in Nazi uniforms. . . The nether region of pet fancies, chauvinisms, and lists is vast. Especially lists. Porn fans, like many hobbyists, love to catalogue. One ever-expanding list concerns the ballooning phenomenon of silicone-enhanced flesh – who's got them, who might but it's hard to tell, who's just had hers done; good fakes, bad fakes, worse fakes, and tit jobs to make a natural-lover weep – 'Rebecca Wild's man-made melons wouldn't look a bit worse if they were covered with hairy warts.'[63] Across from the fake breasts patrol is '"the list of the biggest clits": THE source for information on big clit erotica.'[64] But it's not all gynaecology and mammaries with porners; there is also much discussion of make-up. 'Shayla wears way too much makeup,' writes a net contributor; 'lots of blacks that contrast badly with her blonde hair, bright complexion and her adorable tanlines; I also hate those fake eyelashes she wears all the time.'[65]

Other lists include the top ten all-time movies, the top ten most influential hard-core movies, the ten greatest directors, the best-ever screw scenes, a list of my fifty favorite porn stars: 'How to scientifically categorise and rate a star', using the so-called 'Dunbar rating' – upon which, the inventor informs us, the distribution of ratings 'falls along a bell-curve'.[66] There is also the 'Most Personable Porn Star List', based on a fan's experiences of performers doing personal appearances at adult stores.[67] There are porn fans who will talk about their hobby all night long – 'Will Janine ever do men?' 'Did Traci Lords ever do anal?' 'Has Missy done a double penetration video yet?' 'Is Tammi Ann still in the business?' 'What went wrong with Jeff Stryker – the man of sultry good looks, but the personality of a chair?'[68] 'How come Savannah ever got to be such a big star when she always looked so bored?' 'What kind of car does Jenna Jameson drive?' 'What would it be like to date a porn star, or even marry one?' And then again, porn fans also like to talk about food, even kitchen furniture. A newcomer at alt.sex.movies posts his first ever review of an adult video and forgets himself: 'She's on her back . . . she bends over for him, they seem to get into it . . . [they] do some pretty good humpin' in a gorgeous kitchen on top of one of those islands. U know what I mean, one of those counters in the middle of a kitchen that makes better use of the space by making a little "island" in the middle. It's a nice island too, pretty tile work, two sinks, looks like it would be a great place to cook.'[69]

A book with two endings

Between the likes, the dislikes, the lists and the very particular fancies, the thing that comes across in what porn fans have to say is a near universal desire for new ideas and new things.[70] Ironically, this longing for newness is partly entwined with a sense of nostalgia for porn's golden age. With some the yearning will not cease: 'Over the last couple of nights I had the pleasure of viewing a couple classics,' writes a fan, 'Both *Pandora's Mirror* and *A Scent of Heather* were well acted and costumed, had plot lines and were hot. Anyone else like these classics?'[71] Another fan writes, 'I remember the days porn flicks had plots and good production values and were far more erotic. Am I just boring or do others also crave the high-quality "romantic" films of yore?' Then another like-minded fan wonders whatever happened to the good stuff: 'My husband and I searched at one time for sex movies that have plots. We did find one, and we really enjoyed it. Since then, we haven't found another. We enjoy movies with a story line instead of just sex, sex, sex. Any suggestions?' Though the suggested titles flood in – *Roommates, Amanda by Night, Comeback, Talk Dirty to Me, Michael Zen's Blue Movie, Firestorm, Project Ginger* – one jaundiced contributor queries the need for such frills with hard core, 'If anyone cared about the dialogue and story in skin flicks, VCR's wouldn't come without fast-forward buttons.'

The nostalgia for plots and production values persists even though lead companies in the American industry like VCA, Vivid, Wicked, and lately Ultimate and Plush are regularly turning out high-cost story-led titles, such as *Conquest, Bobby Sox, The Palace of Pleasure* and, of course, *AD 6969,* – trying to recapture some of the magic of the golden age. Furthermore, during the middle to late nineties the American adult scene has been inundated with European high-end titles, with video features from Private and Video Marc Dorcel and, most notably, the films of Joe D'Amato, who has been hailed by some as a kind of porn saviour for his line of high-gloss, shot-on-35mm, period adult movies. (From Marco Polo, through Sade, Masoch, Robin Hood (*Thief of Wives*), Casanova, Gulliver, Tarzan – no historical or literary figure is safe from the

D'Amato hard-core workover.) Though plush, well photo-graphed and featuring attractive performers cavorting enthusiastically in sumptuous outdoor locations, there is some-thing rather meagre about D'Amato's porn. As a contributor writes, 'The sex is mediocre at best. Mediocre porn with pro-duction values is still mediocre.'

So, it all boils down to sex in the end. It always does. And, as we approach the ending of this chapter and of this whole account of pornography, an ending that comes in two parts like that of a John Fowles novel, this simple truth comes once more to the fore: porn is a sex thing.

The first version of the ending has porners hoping for certain pornutopian dreams to come true. When porners dream, what does pornutopia look like? A brighter future is more well-made sex films. This requires some level of investment in higher pro-duction values, but also in time and in creative people who can think imaginatively about the erotics of porn. The impetus to change and invest confidently will take time to build, and also require better laws and a further shift in social attitudes to porn, making it a product with broader appeal and one that is more critically evaluated. This is a lot of hope about a lot of things that might not come off. Change in the direction of pornutopia, if it comes at all, will be slow.

In the meantime the hard-core film industry could be improving the quality of its current releases. With a bit of care and attention it shouldn't cost any more to make a good video than it does to make a bad one. If porn-makers are interested in what the final product feels like, they might give more thought to the lighting, framing, editing and sound. Improvement will also come through disrupting the generic flow: varying camera placements; varying the location – people in porn could screw in places other than on the settee; and varying fuck positions too. 'I bought ... *Visions*, featuring Savannah, and it was a yawn,' writes Tabatha Haasen. 'A total bore. Each sex scene played out the exact same way ... why always the same sequence of events – blow job, pussy suck, man from behind, woman on top, cum shot, cut.'[72]

The growing presence of women porn consumers may in

time cause hard core to alter. At Vivid, David Kastens says the criticisms of feminism have already had an impact: 'Hard core stopped showing women in a negative light, which was only what the rest of society was doing,' he says. 'For example, the situation with a man's hands on the back of a woman's head when she's giving a blow job not only went away for a while because of censorship threats, but because it was decided that it was degrading to women. Now, it is back, but in a more loving style.'

Steffani Martin, who's been watching porn for two decades or more, is not so sure about women causing change: 'I thought that fantasy in porn films had been dictated by the raincoat men, and being a woman of that generation, my fantasies were the same . . . that perhaps a younger woman would get turned on by a whole other thing. And that the evolution would change the fantasy. I don't think so. It seems to be the same old shit. And there are many, many women watching it now.'[73] Toni English is a woman hard-core director who, under another name, is also a highly regarded documentary film-maker. English, it is suggested, shoots porn from a woman's point of view. But watching some of her films this different perspective is hard to spot. In *Blondage*, English shoots the external ejaculations just like everybody else: it's on the breasts, belly, backside and chin.

To disrupt the generic fixity of porn might lead to re-evaluating the external ejaculation. This convention was a particular complaint for Candida Royalle in her time as a porn performer. 'I couldn't understand. . . Why there had to be come shots all the time.' Whenever she disputed the need for them, producers told Royalle they were what kept the consumer satisfied, it's what sold the product. 'I just felt, I really can't believe this.'[74] Recently, however, there's been talk in parts of the American adult industry of fewer pop shots as a possible future path. 'Vivid might go to more internal come shots, and seek to show the intensity of feeling and emotional release,' says Kastens.

When occasionally a hard-core scene closes without an ejaculation – usually because someone messed up filming – the absence is certainly noticeable. The closure it provides means it will be difficult to eliminate. The alternative is the soft-core movies of Playboy and Penthouse in which often not even the working sexual organs are present. Here men 'have sex' without erections and the faint glistening of perspiration on a woman's upper lip is the closest you will get to the visualisation of body fluids. Though potentially still erotic, such euphemistic sex is clearly unable to offer a representation of 'real' sex, in the sense not only of contact but of arousal and release. In hard core the viewer can witness bodies that are 'moved' as well as beautiful. Taking the pop shot from hard core will represent a further drift towards the visual regimes of soft core and most likely will be resisted for this reason.

Porn fans look for a kind of authenticity of fantasy. This may or may not involve copious amounts of ejaculate, but certainly means a pornutopia of more erotic tension, where film-makers work on building up the sexual anticipation. 'Directors could make their movies a little more satisfying,' writes a disgruntled viewer; 'it seems like these guys could use a few pointers on arousal technique.[75] Tabatha Haasen writes, 'So, what do I want? I want to see some erotica on tape. Explicit sex scenes with a real feel to the sex. I want to hear real moans, real groans. I want to see the guy shake and burrow his face into the woman after he's cum. Get rid of the silly plots . . . and the sex scenes, make them more clumsy and more passionate. . . Let's get some rolling around.'[76] Passion, imagination, enthusiasm, a sense of pleasure, are some of the things that make for good porn. The reason performers like Jeanna Fine, Julie Ashton, Rocco Siffredi, Laure Sainclaire, Nina Hartley, Christoph Clarke, Selena Steele, Ashlyn Gere, and their forerunners – like Annette Haven, Georgina Spelvin, Leslie Bovee, Ginger Lynn and John Leslie – are so popular, is because they're into making porn, and either having a good time, or good at making it appear that way. That's the crucial difference between just another assembly-line production and porn gold.

Alternatively

Our second ending is not another version of pornutopia, isn't something that features in an ideal world, maybe some day, but instead finds porners experiencing pornocopia now. The situation involves two people, one image, and some technology: a cybercouple in space, who have never met in real life, are getting off together for something like the two hundredth time. Here is the porn of plenty, the lure of repeating pleasures. The man and the woman are looking at the same image on their respective computer screens, talking about what they see and, in due course, becoming aroused.

The image is of a woman wearing a nurse's hat and black underwear who is having sex with a man on a hospital bed. The position is the popular reverse cowgirl, she is straddling the man, who is lying down on his back, and is facing away from him towards the camera. Her vagina is enveloping his erect penis, he is helping her lift up from his lap, and thereby maximising the visual potential. She is looking orgasmic, her eyes part closed; he is also deeply involved.

The woman who is enjoying this particular image sent the author a copy of the picture, and a saved transcript of the online erotic encounter it helped to engender, including a glossary of abbreviations. It goes like this:

gmta = great minds think alike
lol = laughing out loud
brb = be right back

David	K . . . bedtime maybe, though? You've been tired a bit this week. You need more rest.
Jane	No. . . I'm not willing!
David	lol . . . yes!
Jane	especially without an O! You can't do that to me. . .
David	oh . . . we'd have an O, of course!
Jane	:)Ohhh . . . well . . . maybe then.
David	::shakes head::
Jane	Maybe . . . after 2. . . :)
David	Maybe. . .
Jane	lol
David	Are you touchin?

Jane	Yes! You?
David	Why ask? no . . . but I will. NOW!
Jane	lol
David	::grabs HSL::
Jane	lol! Pics?
David	sure . . . which?
Jane	Nurse, maybe. . .
David	k
Jane	I think it's kinda fun. . .
David	ok!
Jane	lol
David	it is!
Jane	Remind me to get a nurse's cap. . .
David	I will. . . You may need those fake tits, too! . . . and some bigger boobs!
Jane	gmta!
David	(maybe not) Even her face looks fake . . . but I still like it!
Jane	Surely they're not fake . . . why would she have one larger than the other?
David	just the angle . . . they're fake
Jane	K . . . but wouldn't they be fun to touch?
David	yes they would! she needs to sit on that cock
Jane	She's on her way, love! Patience!
David	lol . . . k . . . is the rest of the series this nice?
Jane	I don't know. . . I'll have to go back and look. I'm imagining her moving up and down on that cock . . . mmmmm. . .!
David	me too . . . and she's liking it
Jane	Yes . . . a LOT! Bouncing and squealing. . . And he should be rubbing those tits. . .
David	yes! pulling on em
Jane	Definitely!
David	They're too big to be ignored
Jane	lol
David	They should also be fucked at some point
Jane	Yes!
David	a little oil between em. . .
Jane	Her mouth looks pretty fuckable too. . .
David	oh really? ::laughs:: Do tell
Jane	lol
David	oops . . . brb
Jane	K

David	k . . . needed something
Jane	Like what?
David	so . . . tell me about her mouth
Jane	Like what?
David	tissue ::blushes::
Jane	lol K . . . Where was it?
David	Only to blow my nose, of course
Jane	lol
David	so . . . the mouth?
Jane	Well . . . just look at it, love. . .
David	I did!
Jane	nice full lips . . . a little pouty. . .
David	mmm . . . yes
Jane	all red and suggestive. . .
David	yes indeed!
Jane	She wants it!
David	imagine a little come on 'em
Jane	:: purses her lips :: Yes. . . I am!
David	oh!
Jane	:: imagines a little come on her own ::
David	mmmm! my god. . . I can't wait to fuck your mouth!
Jane	Mmmmmm! Oh god!
David	I'll hold your head and just work my cock in and out
Jane	YES!
David	Grind all around. . .
Jane	My god, yes!
David	And you'll watch as I work . . . like it was in your pussy . . . except it will be so close
Jane	Ohhhh! You've got me there already!
David	oh my!
Jane	I'll hover. . .
David	k..! one sec. K! I'm there . . . work and come! my cock makes a final thrust between your lips!!
Jane	now! OOOOOOOOOOOOOHHHHHHHHHH!!!!!!!!!!!!!!!!!!!!!!
David	OOOOOOOOOOOOOOOOOOOOOOOOOOO!!!!!!!!!!!!!!!!!
Jane	oh my! :: clears her throat ::
David	ok!
Jane	Very nice. Thanks, love! :: smiles :: Here? . . . Tidying?
David	much better . . . you got there fast! Thanks for waiting!

The End

Afterword

When I started this book, porn as a subject of political and cultural debate was in the doldrums, stuck in a repeating loop of familiar arguments and counter-arguments, allegations and gossip. During the period of research, of drafting and writing *Pornocopia*, things have actually started to change a little on both sides of the Atlantic. The mainstream's anti-porn consensus has begun to crack, with attitudes shifting (if only tentatively, and only in parts) towards a more realistic, less condemning position on porn – as is demonstrated perhaps by the very fact of this book.

In Britain the changes are ongoing, but are also typically murky. In the summer of 1997, to mark the belated release of David Cronenberg's film *Crash*, there was a debate on film censorship at the French Institute in London. James Ferman, director of the British Board of Film and Video Classification, mentioned in passing that the Board would start giving the occasional certificates to porn movies featuring a limited amount of hard-core sex. By the end of 1997, porn videos like *The Pyramid*, *Bat Babe* and *Taboo* arrived on the British video scene sporting erections and brief glimpses of oral and penetrative sex. These films were clearly porn – they were not masquerading under the tired alibi of being 'scientific' or 'therapeutic' – and yet were granted an 18R certificate, making them legally available for purchase in the limited number of licensed sex shops across Britain. This amounts, therefore, to some kind of porn breakthrough – albeit rather lukewarm and discrete. But the very limited extent of the hard-core exposure in these films illustrates the slowness of change, due to the restrictive, outmoded sex laws in Britain. The low-key character of this 'hard core' landmark also points to the censor's fear of causing a stir. Sure enough, soon after the Labour Government criticised this mild liberalisation 'in the strongest possible terms'. The public coverage of porn can be very volatile. The wind may well change direction, and the censor's embrace of on-screen male erections could turn out to be a short-lived fling. In the absence of such a thing as a Bill of Rights, a citizen's right of access to information in Britain continues to be provisional and constantly up for review.

Meanwhile, in America, by the end of 1997 adult satellite and cable television channels such as Exxxtasy, Exotica and True Blue had started regularly transmitting full-on hard-core movies, available to subscribers in a growing number of locations across the continent. Also, Vivid Video's push for mainstream recognition, to take porn to 'new heights', found *Variety* magazine reporting the first ever Hollywood-style screening of a porn movie. Regular film critics were treated to a preview of *Bad Wives*, the latest work from Paul Thomas. In 'going Hollywood' like this and seeking to demonstrate that porn can be 'art' as well as sexy, it was suggested that Vivid craved not only a higher sales profile but also that most elusive thing of all for porners – 'respect'.[1]

In cyberspace the future for online porn remains unclear. To date the banning of online materials has chiefly been concerned with issues of child porn and materials featuring illegal acts. With hard-core porn made by and for adults, the situation in Britain appears to be on hold. At present, hard-core adult materials online continue to be readily accessible from Britain, especially for those with a credit card. So far the authorities have leaned a little on the internet industry concerning adult porn, but have pressed no further. The police, the industry and other concerned parties are waiting for the Labour government to declare itself firmly on such matters, as well as for a European parliamentary situation that could conceivably find far-reaching laws on cyberporn equivalent to British domestic laws

Notes

Quotations are from interviews with the author, or from letters or emails to the author, unless otherwise stated.

Prologue

1 Bernard Arcand, *The Jaguar and the Anteater: Pornography Degree Zero*, translated by Wayne Grady, London/New York, Verso, 1993.

2 However, in a subsequent opinion poll of 'Attitudes and Habits of Young and Middle-Aged Britons' conducted prior to Christmas 1995, only 23 per cent of the sample group admitted to having used pornography. Perhaps a key distinction is there to be drawn between 'seeing porn' and 'using porn'. Both polls were conducted by MORI.

1 Definitions

1 Lynne Hunt, 'Obscenity and the origins of modernity, 1500–1800', in Lynne Hunt (ed.) *The Invention of Pornography*, New York, Zone Books, 1993.

2 Walter Kendrick, *The Secret Museum: Pornography in Modern Culture*, New York, Viking, 1987.

3 Bernard Arcand, *The Jaguar and the Anteater: Pornography Degree Zero*, translated by Wayne Grady, London/New York, Verso, 1993.

4 Pornography is a wanton transgressor of such 'made-up' differences. Like the feminist film-maker Karyn Kay suggests, pornography is 'the disavowal of difference' (Betty Gordon and Karyn Kay, 'Look back/talk back', in Pamela Church Gibson and Roma Gibson (eds), *Dirty Looks: Women, Pornography, Power*, London, British Film Institute, 1993).

5 Hunt (see note 1).

6 Channel 4 television, Great Britain, *Red Light Zone*, spring 1995.

7 In January 1993, in Las Vegas, Nina Hartley, Patricia Kennedy, Danielle Cheeks, Lacey Rose, Beatrice Valle and several other porn women were arrested by the city vice police at a benefit performance for the Free Speech Coalition. Hartley had been giving a talk on how to make love to a woman, while two performers gave a practical demonstration on each other. The women were all charged with prostitution. Later this was changed to felony 'lesbianism'. Allegedly the case partly featured as a warning signal to the city's adult stores to watch out, as from

this moment on Las Vegas was a good, clean, family-values entertainment mecca. After a year's wrangling, and more then $100,000 in legal costs, the porn women were to plead guilty to a misdemeanour and allowed to pay a $20,000 contribution to a local charity. The porn women remained unrepentant and unquiet. 'Infamous Crimes Against Nature' was the official wording for the felony of lesbianism brought against them, and used as the title of the adult film based on the real-life events, which starred most of those who had actually been involved, including Nina Hartley, Patricia Kennedy and Beatrice Valle.

8 Hunt (see note 1).

9 Kendrick (see note 2).

10 Ibid.

11 Arcand (see note 3).

12 'Zippy', email, spring 1996.

13 Plainly, if women are not naturally, intrinsically geared towards making only erotica, then it perhaps follows that pornography is not intrinsically sexist, as argued by a certain anti-porn section within the feminist community.

14 *Modern Review*, August–September 1994.

15 Calvin Trillin, *New Yorker*, 23 September 1994.

16 Both quoted by Mandy Merck, 'From Minneapolis to Westminster', in Lynne Segal and Mary McIntosh (eds), *Sex Exposed: Sexuality and the Pornography Debate*, London, Virago, 1992.

17 Kendrick (see note 2).

18 *Adult Video News*, September 1996.

19 With help from 'Zennor', email, spring 1996.

20 Quoted by Kendrick (see note 2).

21 As described by the critic George Steiner, quoted by Al Di Lauro and Gerald Rabkin, *Dirty Movies: An Illustrated History of the Stag Movie, 1915–1970*, New York/London, Chelsea House, 1976.

22 *Details*, July 1996.

23 Email to author, spring 1996, identity withheld to spare mailer's blushes.

24 Kendrick (see note 2).

25 Early theorists of mass culture such as Theodor Adorno were Marxists opposed to the late capitalist god of consumerism, who viewed mass-cultural forms as tools for social control, manipulating the individual's will, corrupting the revolutionary desires of the proletariat. Escaping Nazi Germany, Adorno fled to California, the throbbing heart of mass culture, and didn't really like what he saw. Ironically his gloomy take on mass culture as a mind controller would feature in the Cold War America of the fifties. The right-wing McCarthyite witch-hunts found film, television, radio and comic books feared and carefully scrutinised for their message content, the urgent concern being to ensure that if the movie contained just one message and one response, if mass culture was indeed made for brainwashing, better make sure it was an imperialist capitalist doing the programming and not some lousy communist.

26 Jennifer Wicke, 'Through a gaze darkly: pornography's academic market', in *Dirty Looks* (see note 4).

27 See Allucquere Rosanne Stone, *The War of Desire and Technology at the Close of the Mechanical Age*, Cambridge, Massachusetts/London, MIT Press, 1996.

28 Carole J. Clover, Introduction to *Dirty Looks* (see note 4).

29 Quoted in *Dirty Movies* (see note 21).

30 Zak Jane Keir, interview with the author.

31 Laura Kipnis, 'She-male fantasies and the aesthetics of pornography', in *Dirty Looks* (see note 4).

32 Plainly a lot of powerful men use porn. You just have to listen to Larry Flynt, publisher of Hustler, in an interview in *Details* magazine on *Hustler* magazine's readership: 'I always felt *Hustler* was a magazine for joe lunchbox: blue-collar America. When we started doing some demographics we found out that *Hustler* readers were highly educated people – college grads and Ph.D.s.' Nevertheless it is necessary to remember how modern porn was partly defined as a proscribed pleasure once that pleasure became available to a wider constituency, both proscribed in law, but also in the broader cultural reckoning.

33 Kendrick (see note 2).

34 Ibid.

35 In actuality the embrace of pluralism may be only half-hearted at times; in other ways plurality is the prevailing myth and therefore possesses both a reality and a utility in political discussions.

36 Kendrick (see note 2).

37 Arthur and Marilouise Kroker and Chetan Bhatt respectively, both quoted by Jeffrey Weeks, *Invented Moralities: Sexual Values in an Age of Uncertainty*, Cambridge, Polity Press, 1995.

38 Quoted by Nadine Strossen, *Defending Pornography: Free Speech, Sex, and the Fight for Women's Rights*, London, Abacus, 1996.

39 Arcand (see note 3).

40 Steven Marcus, *The Other Victorians: A Study of Sexuality and Pornography in Mid-Nineteenth Century England*, New York, New American Library, 1974.

41 Kendrick (see note 2).

42 *Body Politic*, Issue 5, 1994.

43 A discussion thread at the usenet discussion group, rec.arts.movies.erotica.

44 The considerable popularity of Racquel Darrian did wane due to her only ever having sex with the dreary Derrick Lane. After all, for many the porn fantasy is about multiple-partnered sex, and most certainly does not involve an extended demonstration, movie after movie, of a loving, monogamous relationship with a bozo.

45 Steffani Martin, Creative System Operator for CyberSpice, from an interview in *Porn Free: The Porn 'Zine Dedicated to Getting You Off for Nothin'*, spring 1995.

46 Tom Eaton, *Batteries Not Included*, October 1995.

47 Walter Benjamin, 'The work of art in the age of mechanical reproduction', in Walter Benjamin (ed.), *Illuminations*, London, Jonathan Cape, 1970.

48 Interview with Tuppy Owens, *Hustler* (UK), October 1995.

2 The porn wars

1 Andrea Dworkin, *Pornography: Men Possessing Women*, London, Women's Press, 1981.

2 Quoted by Mandy Merck, 'From Minneapolis to Westminster', in Lynne Segal and Mary McIntosh (eds), *Sex Exposed: Sexuality and the Pornography Debate*, London, Virago, 1992.

3 Wendy McElroy, *XXX: A Woman's Right to Pornography*, New York, St Martin's Press, 1995.

4 Quoted by Carol S. Vance in 'More danger, more pleasure: a decade after the

Barnard sexuality conference', in Carol S. Vance (ed.) *Pleasure and Danger: Exploring Female Sexuality*, London, Pandora Press, 1992.

5 *Observer*, the 'Uncensored' magazine series, London, spring 1994.

6 See Linda Williams, on how the feminist anti-porners gifted the new right in North America and the UK a new language for their old sexist activism, 'Second thoughts on hard core: American obscenity law and the scapegoating of deviance', in Pamela Church Gibson and Roma Gibson (eds), *Dirty Looks: Women, Pornography, Power*, London, British Film Institute, 1993.

7 Quoted by Nadine Strossen, *Defending Pornography: Free Speech, Sex, and the Fight for Women's Rights*, London, Abacus, 1996.

8 Quoted by Merck (see note 2).

9 Strossen (see note 7).

10 *Libido: The Journal of Sex and Sensibility*, web site – http://www.sensualsource.com/libido/.

11 MIT web site.

12 Dworkin (see note 1). In passing it is worth mentioning that young men as a social grouping are statistically the most vulnerable to violence.

13 Ibid.

14 Susan Brownmiller, *Against Our Will: Men, Women and Rape*, Harmondsworth, Penguin, 1976.

15 Susanne Kappeler, quoted by Lynne Segal in 'Sweet sorrows, painful pleasures', in *Sex Exposed* (see note 2).

16 Susan Griffin, quoted by Lynne Segal in Introduction to *Sex Exposed* (see note 2).

17 Interview with Camille Paglia, from the *Observer* magazine series, 'Uncensored', London, spring 1994.

18 Lynne Segal, *Straight Sex: The Politics of Pleasure*, London, Virago, 1994.

19 Catharine A. MacKinnon, *Only Words*, London, HarperCollins, 1994.

20 Andrea Dworkin, *Intercourse*, London, Secker & Warburg, 1987.

21 Segal, *Straight Sex* (see note 18).

22 *Guardian*, 17 October 1996.

23 *Newsnight*, BBC television.

24 Catherine MacKinnon, 'Playboy's money', in *Feminism Unmodified: Discourses on Life and Law*, Harvard Press, 1987.

25 Quoted by Pete Hammill, 'Women on the verge of a legal breakdown', *Playboy*, January 1993.

26 Andrea Dworkin, 'Pornography: the new terrorism', *New York University Review of Law and Social Change, 1978–79*.

27 Vance (see note 4).

28 Strossen (see note 7).

29 Catherine Itzin, 'Sex and censorship: the political implications', in Gail Chester and Julienne Dickey (eds), *Feminism and Censorship: The Current Debate*, London, Prism Press, 1988.

30 Additionally such laws can be used against the interests of those whom they are supposedly there to assist. This is particularly apparent in the instances when the voicing of a radical analysis of race from a racial minority grouping has been prosecuted as racist according to the race laws.

31 Itzin (see note 29).

32 Consider in this context the British-based Campaign against Pornography and Censorship (CPC) of the late eighties: this is lobby-group nomenclature as pre-

emptive strike. By taking such a name, these feminist anti-porners tried to forestall suggestions that they were advocating censorship. Instead it was argued that it is in fact pornography that silences women. Therefore opposing the CPC actually means, in a skewed logic, that you are truly in favour of censorship and, in effect, that you support women's oppression.

33 This was one of the reasons the Ordinances were declared unconstitutional.

34 For a more detailed discussion of research into pornography and behaviour see, among others:

Larry Baron, 'Pornography and gender equality: an empirical analysis', *Journal of Sex Research*, vol. 27, no. 3, 1990.

Avedon Carol, *Nudes, Prudes and Attitudes*, Cheltenham, New Clarion Press, 1994.

Drucilla Cornell, *The Imaginary Domain: Abortion, Pornography and Sexual Harassment*, New York/London, Routledge, 1995.

Dennis Howitt and Guy Cumberbatch, *Pornography: Its Impacts and Influences, a Review of the Available Research Evidence on the Effects of Pornography*, London, HMSO, 1990, commissioned by the Home Office Research and Planning Unit, UK.

Berl Kutchinsky, 'Pornography and rape: Theory and practice? Evidence from crime data in four countries where pornography is easily available', *International Journal of Law and Society*, vol. 13, no. 4, 1990.

Thelma McCormack, 'Making sense of the research on pornography', in Valda Burstyn (ed.), *Women Against Censorship*, Vancouver, Douglas & Burstyn, 1985.

Lynne Segal, 'Does pornography cause violence? The search for evidence', in *Dirty Looks* (see note 6).

Strossen (see note 7).

35 Segal, in *Dirty Looks* (see note 34).

36 Howitt and Cumberbatch (see note 34).

37 Quoted by Strossen (see note 7).

38 John Court, testimony to new Zealand Indecent Publications Tribunal, Wellington, New Zealand, transcripts, 1990. Quoted by Avedon Carol (see note 34).

39 Quoted by Strossen (see note 7).

40 Ibid.

41 McElroy (see note 3).

42 In the autumn of 1994, the *Guardian* newspaper ran a series of anti-porn articles in the UK. They read like a bad dream of black propaganda from the late seventies, full of emotive tales but with little, if any, hard evidence, and making a case for these being representative of a whole industry. The writer Nick Davies described a woman who'd been sexually abused and who became a stripper, as if the two things were necessarily connected, and comparing her onstage performance to an amputee victim waving her stumps at the audience. All the porn women who do not feel exploited or abused, who make good livings from the sex industry, were entirely absent. A week later, long-time porner Mike Freeman wrote from jail, to query the *Guardian* on the factual accuracy of the articles: '[Davies] suggests that child pornography on video is widely distributed and easily available. This is nonsense.' Allegations from the Davies articles were reiterated soon after by the *Daily Express*, as the propaganda spread. 'I know of at least two people in TV production', wrote the journalist John Minson at the time, 'who have taken what they read as gospel. Perhaps this nonsense will appear in programmes they make too' (*Desire* magazine, issue 6).

43 There are copies of letters online from the FBI answering queries over snuff video. Readers might look at the Frequently Asked Questions digest at alt.sex.movies for an example.

44 Police interview with the author, see Chapter 4, 'An Englishman's Relish'.

45 Gayle Rubin, 'Thinking sex: notes for a radical theory of the politics of sexuality', in *Pleasure and Danger* (see note 4).

46 Pat Califia, *Public Sex: The Culture of Radical Sex*, Pittsburgh, Cleis Press, 1994.

47 Rubin (see note 45).

48 Interview with author. Mark Rose is not the person's real name.

49 MacKinnon, *Only Words* (see note 19).

50 Interview with Brittany O'Connell conducted by an anonymous poster at alt.sex.movies and archived at the alt.sex.movies web site.

51 For a more detailed discussion of such historical parallels see Cornell (note 34); McElroy (note 3); and Jeffrey Weeks, *Sex, Politics and Society: The Regulation of Sexuality since 1800*, second edition, London, Longman, 1989.

52 Cornell (see note 34).

53 Carol Queen, *Exhibitionism for the Shy*, San Francisco, Down There Press, 1995.

54 Nina Hartley, 'Reflections of a feminist porn star', *Gauntlet (exploring the limits of free expression)*, Issue 5, 1993.

55 Cornell (see note 34).

56 Hartley (see note 54).

57 When Sheldon Ranz interviewed the anti-porn 'feminist' campaigner John Stoltenberg (who lives with Andrea Dworkin) on WBAI-FM (99.5) on July 14, 1986, Stoltenberg referred to Royalle as a 'pimp'.

58 CPC policy statement, quoted by Chester and Dickey (see note 29).

59 Hartley (see note 54).

60 Andrew Ross, *No Respect: Intellectuals and Popular Culture*, New York/London, Routledge, 1989.

61 Strossen (see note 7).

62 Susan Griffin, quoted by Lynne Segal in Introduction to *Sex Exposed* (see note 2).

63 Ross (see note 60).

64 In a survey carried out by the American women's magazine *Redbook*, approximately 40 per cent of its 26,000 women spoke of using porn. Other surveys in Australia, Copenhagen, France and Germany have suggested anything between 30 per cent and 66 per cent of women use porn.

65 In the late eighties, meetings between the British MPs Clare Short and Dawn Primarolo and Andrea Dworkin and Catherine MacKinnon concerning a coordinated effort on pornography broke down due to Dworkin's refusal to discount or exempt any kind of explicit work on the basis of it having scientific, literary or artistic value. See Merck (note 2).

66 Strossen (see note 7).

67 *Ms.* magazine, January/February 1994.

68 McElroy (see note 3).

69 Jeffrey Weeks, *Sexuality*, Chichester, Ellis Harwood, 1986.

70 One thinks of the situation of women under fundmentalist Islamic law. When an American journalist was granted access behind the scenes with the Ayatollah Khomeni during the 1980s, she observed how the Islamic dress codes reminded her of Andrea Dworkin's recommended garb.

71 Correlative studies do suggest some kind of link between higher incidence of sex crimes and sexual violence and cultures, communities or families that suppress sexual information. See Baron, Kutchinsky and Carol (all note 34).

72 Strossen (see note 7).

73 McElroy (see note 3).

74 Quoted by Sallie Tisdale, *Talk Dirty To Me: An Intimate Philosophy of Sex*, London, Pan Books, 1995.

75 Tisdale, ibid.

76 *Desire* magazine, issue 14.

77 *Playboy*, May 1994.

78 Gertrud Koch, 'The body's shadow realm', in *Dirty Looks* (see note 6).

79 Anne McClintock, 'Gonad the Barbarian and the Venus Flytrap: portraying the female and male orgasm', in *Sex Exposed* (see note 2).

80 See, for example, Cherie Matrix (ed.), *Tales from the Clit*, Edinburgh/London/San Francisco, AK Press, 1996.

3 Some history

1 Linda Williams, *Hard Core: Power, Pleasure and the 'Frenzy of the Visible'*, London, Pandora Press, 1990.

2 Tom Dewe Mathews, *Censored: The Story of Film Censorship in Britain*, London, Chatto & Windus, 1994.

3 Quoted by Gertrud Koch, 'The body's shadow realm', in Pamela Church Gibson and Roma Gibson (eds), *Dirty Looks: Women, Pornography, Power*, London, British Film Institute, 1993.

4 Mathews (see note 2).

5 Koch (see note 3).

6 Al Di Lauro and Gerald Rabkin, *Dirty Movies: An Illustrated History of the Stag Movie, 1915–1970*, New York/London, Chelsea House, 1976.

7 In the early seventies, when *Deep Throat* was all the rage and making millions at the cinema box office, the movie's producer Gerard Damiano allegedly sold his handsome cash cow for a pittance – it was one of those offers – to the Gambino family of New York, who pocketed all the cash. (See Andrew Ross, *No Respect: Intellectuals and Popular Culture*, New York/London, Routledge, 1989.) Stories like the Gambino takeover helped continue the image of porn being run by the Mafia, of all its takings going to guys with vowels at the ends of their surnames. Way back when the industry wasn't legal, part of porn's reality was that somewhere down the line stag met the mafiosi; they crossed paths, transacted some kind of business. At the turn of the seventies, as porn was crawling out into the half-light of semi-legality, some of its criminal links crawled out with it and seized a share of the rich, new pickings. In the mid-eighties the journalists David Hebditch and Nick Anning had tales whispered to them from the seventies concerning a couple of German porn entrepreneurs being bullied by mobsters. There was also Atlanta's Mike Thevis, top porn man in the American southeast during the seventies, and an operator of mob-like conduct – he once blew-up a rival's peepshow-booth operation – and alleged mob backers. And during the reign of Reuben Sturman of Cleveland, the man who remade his Sovereign News newspaper-kiosk empire into a porn-distribution (even production) company for magazines, loops, movies and video booths, the FBI often sought, unsuccessfully, to connect him to the Mafia. Sturman eventually went to jail for massive tax evasion, as well as attempted jury-rigging. (Sturman died, passed away in his sleep, in the autumn of 1997.) In Britain during 1996 and 1997 it was alleged that soft-core publishers Northern & Shell had been facing some mob pressure in America (allegations flatly refuted by N & S publisher Richard Desmond, *Time Out*, 16–23 April 1997). To discuss in adequate detail the story of porn and the mob would probably require a whole book in itself. It is worth mentioning, however, that past US governments have seen

the linking of porn with the mob as a helpful way of going porn-bashing. That the FBI has rarely made allegations of mob–porn association stick suggests that they are inept, that they are faced with devilishly cunning gangsters, or that the match doesn't fit. Indeed, it would seem that during the eighties, after seismic changes within New York's Gambino family with the passing of Paul Castellano and John Gotti, as well as the precipitous collapse of profit margins in porn, the Mafia effectively lost any residual interest in distributing adult materials. If in the middle of the nineties porno is still married to the mob, then it's a long-distance relationship. Though some whisperings do continue, people actually involved in the industry, low down or higher up the rung, mostly doubt the continued veracity of such rumours.

8 Jim Holliday, *Only the Best*, Van Nuys, California, Cal Vista Direct Ltd, 1986.

9 David McGillivray suggests that all the postwar stag shown in Britain came from overseas. However, according to vintage porn aficionado Jim Holliday and veteran German porner Hans Moser, there was an active stag-productions scene in Soho during the fifties and early sixties. We're talking about a secret world that has, as far as can be established, remained mainly unrecorded and barely documented. See David McGillivray, *Doing Rude Things: The History of the British Sex Film, 1957–1981*, London, Sun Tavern Fields, 1992.

10 See Rupert Smith, *Physique, The Life of John S. Barrington*, London/New York, Serpent's Tail, 1997.

11 Interview with Richard Pacheco, *Batteries Not Included*, February 1995.

12 Interview with Camille Paglia, from the *Observer* magazine series, 'Uncensored', London, spring 1994.

13 Anthony Spinelli, interview with Richard Pacheco, *Batteries Not Included*, February 1995.

14 Williams (see note 1).

15 Interview in *Porn Free: The Porn 'Zine Dedicated to Getting You Off for Nothin'*, spring 1995.

16 The director John Stagliano suggested to the author that there have definitely been times when he got real sex from performers, but the director John Leslie claimed to author Wendy McElroy that porn women orgasm a whopping 90 per cent of the time. It's one of porn's great mysteries, and opinions differ widely. Actress Julie Rage says sometimes it's fun, and other times it's the whole works. While Chasey Lain is noncommittal, Kay Parker admitted to Robert Stoller to having a full orgasm doing a scene in *Taboo* (see Robert J. Stoller, *Porn: Myths for the Twentieth Century*, New Haven/London, Yale University Press, 1991). According to long-time porn actor Richard Pacheco, 'Most of the women I'd worked with never dreamed of having a real orgasm on camera. [They'd say] "I could never come in front of all these people!" ' (Richard Pacheco, 'A boudoir memoir', *Batteries Not Included*, April 1995). Porn actress Brandy Alexandre argues, 'Any actress who says she does, is probably only telling you what you want to hear. However much it LOOKS real, certainly does not mean it is' (see the Brandy Alexandre home page on the world wide web). In terms of faking it, in an interview with the author, Alexandre described the performer – the word is a give-away, really – exaggerating the look of pleasure: 'the roll and gaze of the eyes, the arch of the back, the stretch and curl of the fingers and toes'.

17 Though the golden age is mostly considered to have started around 1977 and been over by 1982 or 1983, a few films from further back could be said to easily meet the criteria for inclusion in the porn pantheon, as well as being its precursors, *The Opening of Misty Beethoven* and *Devil in Miss Jones* certainly being two such titles.

18 Anne McClintock, 'Gonad the Barbarian and the Venus Flytrap: portraying the

female and male orgasm', in Lybbe Segal and Mary McIntosh (eds), *Sex Exposed: Sexuality and the Pornography Debate*, London, Virago, 1992.

19 *Village Voice*, 28 May 1996.

20 Quoted by Nadine Strossen, *Defending Pornography: Free Speech, Sex, and the Fight for Women's Rights*, London, Abacus, 1996.

21 Interview with Steve Perry by Tuppy Owens, *Hustler* (UK), October 1995.

22 There is, however, one permutation, that of Silvera and Leslie, which remains untried. This is heterosexual porn, and carnal love between men seems destined never to happen.

23 At least that's my understanding of the performers' domestic relations. Maybe Lauren and Steele aren't hitched and maybe that's the first time they ever met, in which case I'm an idiot.

24 Richard Freeman, 'I love Paris', *Batteries Not Included*, June 1994.

25 McGillivray (see note 9).

26 Quoted in McGillivray (see note 9).

27 Legend has it that during the mid-sixties glamour photographers and prostitutes in Soho were making hard core and smuggling it to Denmark, where the newly deregulated film laboratories of Copenhagen were able to process and duplicate the materials legally. Hans Moser, leading German porner, alleges it was these same shorts, known as 'rollers' at the time, that were subsequently brought back into the UK from Denmark, smuggled in with all the bacon, and flogged as 'continental filth' (see David Hebditch and Nick Anning, *Porn Gold: Inside the Pornography Business*, London, Faber & Faber, 1988). Though others dispute this version of the truth, it would seem that at least some illegal hard-core loops were made in Britain during the sixties. But this hardly makes for an industry, certainly not a legitimate one.

28 Jonathan Green, *It: Sex Since the Sixties*, London, Secker & Warburg, 1993.

29 Interview with Steve Perry by Tuppy Owens, *Hustler* (UK), October 1995.

30 Cate Haste, *Rules of Desire: Sex in Britain, World War I to the Present*, London, Pimlico, 1994.

31 Hebditch and Anning, *Porn Gold* (see note 27).

32 An example of the hype sees a claim that 27 million porn magazines are sold annually in the UK. This is very hard to believe, and since only two British porn magazines are actually audited it is hard to know where such a figure could come from. There would need to be 100 monthly titles averaging a circulation of 22,000 approximately. There are plenty of soft-core titles on the domestic market, too many to keep up with, as well as some imported titles from America and South Africa. Nonetheless, there are not 100 titles, certainly not on a regular monthly basis. The largest circulation for a British monthly is inexorably slipping under 100,000. Most titles circulate at considerably lower levels. A big-name title such as *Hustler* will only claim to get 25,000 sales a month, and may actually be achieving far lower sales. Beyond all these figures, it is important to remember that it is estimated that only about 8 per cent of adult males buy soft-core magazines. A far smaller proportion of this 8 per cent will buy with any regularity. For there to be sales of 27 million this would require a hard-core group of male users consuming pornography on an inordinately compulsive basis. Which is exactly where the figure originates, in ideology and not empirically. Such a skyscraper sales figure suggests a quiet, hidden monster out of control, porn as a compulsive thing that reduces all those who come into contact with its queasy ways to the level of addicts who lose control over everything, including their purse strings.

33 Hebditch and Anning, *Porn Gold* (see note 27).

34 Ibid.

35 The Meese Commission, suggests Linda Williams, saw the passage of Robin
    Morgan's notorious conflation 'porn the theory, rape the practice' from feminist
    agitprop into the demonology of the moral majoritarian lawgiver (Williams (see
    note 1)). The fundamentalists now had some new rhetoric: porn was no longer
    the living, breathing, rutting, sweating, totally pink violation of God's law, it was
    now also violence against women; and a highly venturesome argument of a link
    between porn fantasy and real abuse was converted into a kind of Truth. A much
    repeated political rallying call became almost established fact.

36 An actual leaked memo from the Justice Department at the time included a clear
    declaration of this specific intent.

37 David Kastens, Vivid Video, interview with the author.

38 R.J. Stoller and I.S. Levine, *Coming Attractions: The Making of an X-Rated Video*,
    New Haven/London, Yale University Press, 1993.

39 For more information on this period, see Pat Califia, *Public Sex: The Culture of
    Radical Sex*, Pittsburgh, Cleis Press, 1994; Wendy McElroy, *XXX: A Woman's
    Right to Pornography*, New York, St Martin's Press, 1995; Strossen (see note 21);
    Bill Thompson, *Soft Core: Moral Crusades Against Pornography in Britain and
    America*, London/New York, Cassell, 1994.

40 The report of Howitt and Cumberbatch is a curious episode, an example of
    conspiracy by omission perhaps. The work was conscientious, meticulous and
    neutral and left no stone unturned in concluding that fears concerning
    pornography and violence remained unfounded. This made it the ideal report as
    far as the government was concerned because it required no action from them. A
    less conscientious research team, a team with a moral flavour perhaps, might have
    found trouble in porn. The government would then have been under pressure to
    act, to ban soft core, and to be seen as a party of free choice removing a whole
    mass of consumer items from the marketplace would not have been so desirable at
    that time.

41 A young woman on the thriving London fetish club scene told the author that the
    feminist debates on porn 'didn't mean a thing to her'. They were a part of history,
    from way before her time. In her early twenties, she knows about the porn wars like
    she knows about teddy boys, or the streaker craze of the seventies, a weird social
    panic specific to the past that sounds rather quaint and old-fashioned looking back
    from here in the middle to late nineties.

4 An Englishman's relish

1 Electric Blue have been releasing porn tapes in the UK for over a decade. In the
   mid-eighties individual titles in the ongoing series were hosted by leading
   performers from the American hard-core industry of the time, like Seka, Marilyn
   Chambers and Ginger Lynn, who would also feature in a soft-core scene.

2 Quoted by Bill Thompson, *Soft Core: Moral Crusades Against Pornography in Britain
   and America*, London/New York, Cassell, 1994.

3 See Tom Dewe Mathews, *Censored: The Story of Film Censorship in Britain*, London,
   Chatto & Windus, 1994; and Thompson (see note 2).

4 The Act also made it an offence to show a video, or film at a licensed sex cinema
   club, that hadn't been passed by the British Board of Film and Video
   Classification. Any cinema club that did so would also lose its local authority
   license, something it was hard-pressed to gain in the first place.

5 David Hebditch and Nick Anning, *Porn Gold: Inside the Pornography Business*,
   London, Faber & Faber, 1988.

6 In *Censored*, a history of British film censorship (see note 3), Tom Dewe Mathews
   speaks of James Ferman, top British censor, as a man preoccupied by many

things, yet with a particular twitchiness concerning kung fu weapons. So hung up was Ferman at one stage on this kung fu menace that he required that cuts be made to the family comedy thriller spoof *Dragnet*. A scene was cut in which the lead characters, Tom Hanks and Dan Akroyd, are talking and there's a film poster on the wall behind them featuring a picture of Bruce Lee holding a pair of kung fu star chainsticks. A cut was also made to the kids' movie *Mutant Ninja Turtles*, because the string of sausages around one of the turtle's necks was mistaken for a set of chainsticks by Mr Ferman.

7 Admittedly, there is the anomaly of the 18R video certificate, which will be discussed later in this chapter. Nonetheless, a prevailing feature of the response to video technology was the reconfiguring of the legal situation, which made a lack of certification the offence, with the police and prosecutors no longer being required to demonstrate obscenity to a court jury.

8 Members of the public on such mailing lists who can be proved to have bought a video through the post will be visited, questioned and possibly cautioned, and may also be used as prosecution witnesses in a future trial.

9 These police categories suggest that the 'violent' porn movies talked of whenever the police make a raid don't actually exist. Or, if they do exist, and turn up from time to time on police raids, the 'violence' being referred to is 'bondage' and 'flagellation' – that is, not violence as we would understand it, but the representation of ritualised, negotiated, consenting acts between adults.

10 Metropolitan Police Evidence Sheet.

11 *Adult Video News*, September 1996.

12 *Islington Gazette*, 15 December 1995.

13 Letter from Councillor Goodman to Councillor Jackson, 14 January 1996.

14 In the late eighties, as discussed in Chapter 2, 'The Porn Wars', Labour MP Dawn Primarolo launched her Bill into Parliament to restrict sales of all kinds of soft-core pornography (heterosexual, gay and lesbian) to licensed premises that wouldn't be permitted to sell anything else. The anti-sex-shop campaigns and new laws passed earlier in the decade had already seriously reduced the number of sex shops in Britain – the remainder of which were still being regularly picketed by anti-porn feminists and moralists seeking their closure, while also being charged a very costly license by the local council. With Primarolo, the idea was to move the porn magazines once more, to take them out of the newsagents and returning them to a now much smaller number of even more tightly regulated sex shops. The thrust of the legislation was to restrict access to porn down to the bare minimum, to virtual obsolescence for certain minorities and sexualities, and beyond this ultimately into extinction.

15 Campaign Against Censorship, undated press release.

16 This was the case not only with sex shops, but also with licensed sex cinemas, which were supposed to exhibit the 18R films, but rarely have, because local authorities have rarely granted applicants the license to run a sex cinema in the first place.

17 Quoted in Jonathan Green, *It: Sex Since the Sixties*, London, Secker & Warburg, 1993.

18 Lyn Proctor quoted in Green, ibid.

19 According to Alex Spillius, 'Who Makes the Profit', *Independent on Sunday*, 21 April, 1996.

20 See Mandy Merck, 'From Minneapolis to Westminster', in Lynne Segal and Mary McIntosh (eds), *Sex Exposed: Sexuality and the Pornography Debate*, London, Virago, 1992.

21 Green (see note 23).

22 Spencer Woodcock, interview with the author.

23 Author interview with a representative of JT Publishing, 27 September 1996.

24 The facts are revealing however. In 1992 the Obscene Publications Squad made an unsurpassed raid on a warehouse and seized 50,000 magazines. This massive haul took the year's total of magazine seizures into another dimension. It needed two months for officers to sort through the booty. A large chunk of the material consisted of British magazines and American *Penthouse*. This was not bestiality porn from Spain, featuring Blanco the Donkey, or lurid gynae-porn from Copenhagen. This was mainly high-end, low-intensity, soft-core porn held in a warehouse by a new independent wholesaler who was outside the British soft-core publishing loop. There was another such police raid on a small publisher and distributors of erotic materials in 1993. The Crown Prosecution Service gained a destruction order on the distributor's goods. Most of this material was either to be found stocked at branches of Menzies or WH Smith, including books from Virgin's Nexus imprint, or was the kind of material delivered to local newsagents by the separate, and more liberal, magazine-distribution operations run by Menzies and WH Smith.

25 HM Customs & Excise guidelines, Volume C-4, Part 34.

26 *South London Press*, 19 September 1995.

27 Pat Califia, *Public Sex: The Culture of Radical Sex*, Pittsburgh, Cleis Press, 1994.

28 Quoted in the *Independent on Sunday*, 21 April 1996.

29 Channel 4 television, *Right to Reply*, spring 1993.

30 Anonymous posting taken from usenet newsgroup UK Media, autumn 1996.

31 With a television transmission time of 10 p.m. on a Saturday night – an adult viewing slot if ever there was one.

32 Letter to Councillor Ted Goodman of the Campaign Against Censorship from London Weekend Television, 26 September 1995.

33 Mathews (see note 3).

34 BBC television news, November 1996.

35 Story offered to the author from an anonymous source.

36 Anne McClintock, 'Maid to order: commercial s/m and gender power', in Pamela Church Gibson and Roma Gibson (eds), *Dirty Looks: Women, Pornography, Power*, London, British Film Institute, 1993.

37 *Daily Sport*, 21 March 1996.
    The Whiplash trial would conclude with club manager Martin Church being found not guilty of the charge of keeping a disorderly house. The presiding judge at the trial told the jury that they should consider the trial a 'a test case' about whether in these pluralist times society wished for the police to be concerned with controlling people's private lives.

38 *Daily Mail*, 23 November 1995.

39 Letter from Ministry for National Heritage to Councillor Ted Goodman of Campaign Against Censorship, 14 November 1995.

40 Quoted by Charles Sayer, 'A Long Way From Page Three', *Spiked* magazine, January 1996.

41 This is a line of information to accompany porn magazines and videos, and also those straight-to-video erotic thrillers that clog the shelves at *Blockbusters*. These tend to come in sequel series: *Animal Instincts* I–IV, *Indecent Behaviour* I–III, *Body Chemistry* I–IV, *The Pamela Principle* I and II, and feature cult stars like Sharon Whirry, India Allen and ex-playmate Shannon Tweed, queen of the silicone-and-silk-sheets movie phenomenon.

42 A small example: in an article in *New Statesman and Society* from November 1995, concerning the decline in civil liberties during the long era of Conservative

government, there's not a single word about sexual censorship. The piece refers to employment and labour Acts, nationality Acts, secrets Acts, communications Acts, criminal evidence Acts, but not a thing about the many laws on sexual explicitness during this period.

43 Interview with William Gibson by Jack Sargeant in *Rapid Eye* 3, London, San Francisco, Creation Books, 1995.

44 And will the 'chip' always be open to customising, or will the government classification bodies do this in advance? Also, how sophisticated will the chip be? Will it just be a universal, '12', '15' and '18' adult rating, or will it be amenable to being customised so that adults who think their kids may learn about sex, but not violence, can fix things accordingly?

45 Interview with Manuel de Landa by Steve Beard and Kodo Eshun in *ID* magazine, 'The Subversive Issue'.

5 Not the Wild West: porn in the USA

1 Anthony Lane, 'Lay People', *New Yorker*, 19 December 1994.

2 Gary Andrew Poole, 'Self Love Story', *Sky* magazine, summer 1996.
   It is estimated that in 1996 Americans spent $175 million on in-house porn movie channels while staying at hotel chains such as the Hilton, Hyatt and Sheraton. This room service is quite a money-spinner for proprietors, as the hotel usually pockets a quarter of the customer's porn money up front. In the same year, Americans spent an estimated $150 million on ordering adult pay-per-view movies from their own homes. Again, such cable traffic is a highly profitable business for cable carriers like Time-Warner. (Figures from an article in *US News and World Report*, online, 28 January 1997.)

3 *Empire* film magazine, October 1996.

4 As well as featuring porn actresses in *Private Parts*, his feature film of 1997.

5 *Adult Video News*, December 1996.

6 Email to author from 'Gaetan'.

7 While *The People v Larry Flynt* was a worthy film in highlighting issues of freedom of speech concerning porn, the film pretty much skirted the issue of the content or value of porn for its own sake. The overall sense being that the film's producers rather held their nose about the fact that Flynt was a porner while they set about making a film concerned with the law and the constitution. Meanwhile *Boogie Nights*, though not entirely immune to the temptations of characterising the porn maker as dysfunctional coke-head bound to have a rough time of it, offered a mostly reasonable take on the nature of low-rent porn production during the late seventies and early eighties. In the way the world of porn was depicted as offering a kind of family structure for the outcast and misfit, Paul Thomas Anderson's film could even be said to be quite porn-positive. (*Boogie Nights* actually featured porn actresses Nina Hartley and Veronica Hart in small roles – playing the murdered nymphomaniac and a judge, respectively.) In a style rather similar to that of *Ed Wood*, Anderson's film treated with care and sympathy those aspiring folks who can't quite make the big time, but still have heart, and have their dreams and their porn lives to be going on with. Overall, *Boogie Nights* was a big step forward in the mainstream media's relationship with hard core. This was in profound contrast to the hot new film project of late 1997, *Eight Millimeter*. Written by Andrew Kevin Walker – who also wrote the deeply grim, nasty and nihilistic *Seven* – *Eight Millimeter* is a story of snuff videos and of the 'underground' American porn industry, where any kind of sordid image can be bought, if the price is right. The project was fixed to be going into production sometime in 1998 with Columbia Pictures, to be directed by Joel Schumacher, and, rather ironically, with the lead

role of Detective Tom Welles allegedly on offer to Mark Wahlberg of *Boogie Nights*.

8 Though the Japanese porn industry is large, and the only one to begin to rival the USA in terms of output, cultural differences and differences over content and censorship render it a very modest player in America and globally.

9 'Used to', because hard core was pretty much chased away from New York's 42nd Street during the mid-nineties.

10 Michael Riley, *Interview with Anne Rice*, London, Chatto & Windus, 1996.
In a report on the state of the American porn industry in early 1997, Paul Fishbein of *Adult Video News* suggested that 25,000 video stores in the USA rent or sell hard-core video tapes (*US News and World Report*, online, 28 January 1997).

11 Interview with Tuppy Owens, *Hustler* (UK), October 1995.

12 Quoted in Carol Queen, *Exhibitionism for the Shy*, San Francisco, Down There Press, 1995.

13 Susan Faludi, 'The money shot', *New Yorker*, 30 October 1995.

14 Guillermo Brown, *AD 6969*, film script (WGAw Registered).

15 *Vogue*, January 1997.

16 It's not that there were no good or interesting porn movies made. Just very few. Between notable titles like *The Grafenberg Spot*, *Taboo American Style*, *Trashy Lady*, *Beauty and the Beast* and *New Wave Hookers*, a lot of bad stuff was sloshing through the system.

17 And, as a mark of gratitude, the mainstream industry reviles amateurs for being too slack with the legalities, therefore supposedly bringing the whole porn production business into a state of further disrepute. Truly amateur performers continue to send in their tapes – like that very first husband and wife team from Nebraska who filmed their bedroom display one cold prairie night more than ten years earlier – and see them distributed to a wider audience via reputable independents like Video Enterprises. There are even the erotica videozine productions of people like Jani B, Patricia Stevens and Ugly George.

18 Ninn was to make a similar splash in the gay market with *Night Works*, which he co-directed with Gino Colbert.

19 In real life Lindemuller is bi-sexual. Separated from her construction worker husband, she was for a while intimately involved with fellow porn star Julie-Ann.

20 *Arena* magazine, February 1996. And then, in the December 1997 issue of American *Penthouse*, a photospread featuring Janine included scenes in which she appeared to perform fellatio for the first time for the camera.

21 *Batteries Not Included*, March 1995.

22 'Imperator', from the Imperial Archive, available at alt.sex.movies.

23 Wendy McElroy, *XXX: A Woman's Right to Pornography*, New York, St Martin's Press, 1995.

24 Interview with Gary Indiana, from *Let It Bleed: Essays, 1985–95*, London, Serpent's Tail, 1996.

25 'Sources close to Doll, however, have indicated that the retired performer might now be HIV-positive.' *Adult Video News*, March 1997. Tabitha Cash and Draghixa, both major European porn stars of the nineties in Europe, where condom use is equally frowned upon, were to leave the industry, they said, because of porn's continued resistance to safe sex.

26 This still only meant a safe-sex guarantee for contracted performers with Vivid in 1997.

27 Interview with Tuppy Owens, *Hustler* (UK), October 1995.

28 Taylor Wayne interview with Bill Wright, Christmas 1992, available at
alt.sex.movies web site.

29 The purported Marilyn Monroe reel from a long time ago, *Apple, Knockers, and
Coke*, is often alleged to be proof of a hard-core past. Thing is, the short is not
pornographic, merely an art nude life study; moreover, the performer is clearly
not Marilyn Monroe. Even the actual actress from the loop will avow that it is her
and not the dead screen star playing with the cola bottle.

30 Haven subsequently said she was glad about this anyway, as the script had turned
more violent after she had signed on for the project, and that she didn't wish to be
associated with such a film.

31 Interview with Gary Indiana (see note 24).

32 *Arena* magazine, winter 1995.

33 Candida Royalle interview with *Libido: The Journal of Sex and Sensibility*, web site –
http://www.sensualsource.com/libido/.

34 Interview with *Video Xcitement* online magazine, summer 1995.

35 Queen (see note 12).

36 Interview with *Video Xcitement* online magazine, spring 1995.

37 Faludi (see note 13).

38 *Arena* magazine, winter 1995.

39 This was surprising, as in *Backlash*, her book published in 1992, Faludi asserts,
contrary to the evidence, that porn had become increasingly violent as another
sign of the eighties backlash against women.

40 Jammer's suicide was due to a serious emotional instability, made worse by his
difficulties with money and with performing on camera.

41 *Desire* magazine, issue 1.

42 Richard Pacheco, 'A boudoir memoir', *Batteries Not Included*, April 1995.

43 Contrary to the continuing myth, the 'fluffers', extras employed to give secondary
head to an actor experiencing problems with wood, have long since departed from
hard-core sets. Budgets don't allow such wastage, and battle-hardened toolpackers
are supposed to make such aids unnecessary.

44 Average rates per scene for women start at around $400 and will rise as high as
$1,000. The industry average for women is about $600, the average for men is
around $400.

45 However, ex-actor Jerry Butler was rumoured for a while to be driving an
ambulance in Brooklyn. The thought of getting mouth-to-mouth resuscitation
from the star of a thousand porn movies is an interesting one.

46 Certainly in the newsgroups alt.sex.movies and rec.arts.movies.erotica.

47 Interview with Tuppy Owens, *Hustler* (UK), October 1995.

48 Interview with Matt Mranian in *Boing Boing* magazine, the 'This is Hollywood'
issue.

49 Celeste went on to have a child with Paul Norman, master of freak-show porn.
Norman's movies will feature men with python dicks and men with two dicks,
men with dicks with a double reef knot in them – all a load of prosthetics, of course.

50 Interview with *Video Xcitement* online magazine, spring 1995.

51 Royalle interview with *Libido* (see note 33).

52 Traci Lords always performed as an adult. During her time in porn she was not
making 'child porn', or even especially trying to look 'young'. After the actress
Savannah died, *Rolling Stone* magazine referred to this clearly adult person as a
'child-woman'. To which you have to say, it's really in the eye of the beholder.
Savannah was young and very freshly scrubbed. But she was legally an adult, and

clearly grown up and fronted by a silicone-enhanced, heavily articulated chest. This looking 'young', the 'barely legal' business, became a major issue at the close of the US Congress in 1996. At the eleventh hour the overall federal budget bill for the whole American government, a bill that had been held up because of wranglings between Congress and the President, was finally passed. But passed with another bill tacked on. Senator Orrin Hatch required that his moribund child pornography reform bill be passed with the budget bill, or he would withdraw his support. Nobody was going to oppose such a vital fiscal measure because it had an anti-child pornography bill attached.

This particular anti-porn law, which was immediately operative, made computer morphing of images of children into sexual situations an offence. Computer trickery that could make an event that never actually happened look 'real' was now a felony. In extending the child porn laws to include 'things' that do not actually involve children, the law also surreptitiously took in any visual depiction that 'appears' to involve under-age persons, even though it actually only involves adults. In this way, over night, a porn film featuring a pair of adults playing high-school lovers, the cheerleader and quarterback getting it on together, titled *High School Lovers*, would be deemed as child porn.

53 Quoted in R.J. Stoller and I.S. Levine, *Coming Attractions: The Making of an X-Rated Video*, New Haven/London, Yale University Press, 1993.

54 Lords has subsequently done television work, acting in small roles in shows like *Melrose Place* and *Roseanne*. (The latter actually featured a porn movie spoof with Lords.) She also sang a duet with the Manic Street Preachers. Though her porno past is the reason for her fringe success, it is a past that she disowns.

55 You may have to pay a big corporate fine, you may even go to jail.

56 These retrospective porn edits are done without acknowledgement. VCA is a company forever eager to point out to the consumer the need to be vigilant about defending a person's rights of free speech, and yet they are also readily doing the censoring themselves and not telling.

57 *Batteries Not Included*, October 1995.

58 Indiana (see note 24).

59 *Batteries Not Included*, October 1995.

60 Putting doubts and preferences aside, Stagliano conceded that the Blake package amounts to a sophisticated pornography that sells very well indeed, and he admitted to having approached Blake for him to become part of Stagliano's expanding 'evil empire'.

61 Faludi (see note 13), and Sal Volatile, 'Porno Deluxe', *Desire* magazine, issue 11.

62 Royalle interview with *Libido* (see note 33).

63 High-end porners do worry about whether this problem of 'nice porn's' detachment will be tolerated by the trad porn fans. Rumours circulate occasionally that they're concerned that their product's gone soft, and think they need to bring in some new people to rev it up a little. One wonders whether they need to worry, though – what is bland one week has a habit of looking rather classy two weeks later.

64 *Adult Video News*, September 1996.

6 Child story

1 Linda Williams, 'Second thoughts on hard core: American obscenity law and the scapegoating of deviance', in Pamela Church Gibson and Roma Gibson (eds), *Dirty Looks: Women, Pornography, Power*, London, British Film Institute, 1993.

2 David Hebditch and Nick Anning, *Porn Gold: Inside the Pornography Business*, London, Faber & Faber, 1988.

3 Recollections of such display offered to the author by legal researcher Steve King, as well as from assorted anonymous postings online.

4 *New York Times*, 22 September 1995.

5 Rumours of child-porn video production occurring in Mexico, Russia and Hong Kong do emerge from time to time. These may all be urban tales, but this would be a complacent attitude to take. To assume the worst while making every effort to support assumptions with real evidence seems the wisest policy.

6 According to interviews conducted with the Metropolitan Police, there was one case where a vendor was selling a couple of videos imported from Japan of naked children who were fourteen.

7 Author interview with the Metropolitan Police, wherein these statements were speculative and not substantiated or backed with any figures or evidence.

8 It is also true, as in the case of the British diplomat, Robert Coghlan, who was convicted in London in the summer of 1996, that in Japan video tapes featuring nude boys and girls between the ages of thirteen and sixteen are legally available and may well be smuggled into Britain and the USA, and, conceivably, passed around.

9 Both stories remain unclear at present. However the latter does suggest a very serious child-porn ring, while the former represents a quite different proposition, first and foremost the tale of the most brutal and horrible murders, which may or may not have been connected to some form of paedophile networking. Also, in late 1997, it was alleged that two other child porn rings had been uncovered, one in the Czech Republic, the other in the north of England. To date, the exact character of neither 'ring' has been demonstrated.

10 Williams (see note 1).

11 *Newsletter on Civil Liberties*, Canada, April 1996.

12 There are two possible explanations for this. First, in some cases – it would be impossible to ascertain how many – the original charge under the POCA could be 'shelved' while more serious charges such as indecent assault are pursued. Second, police cases could drop off the graph after going to the magistrates for committal hearings and being thrown out as non-cases.

13 Stephen J. King, *The Protection of Children Act (1978): A Paper* (unpublished, December 1994).

14 Quoted in the *Guardian*, 13 January 1996.

15 Ron Oliver, information supplement to *As Far as the Eye Can See*, Version 2.4, 17 January 1994 (unpublished, available to interested parties from Oliver or his photographic agent in the UK, Nicky Akehurst).

16 Letter to Councillor Ted Goodman from the Home Office, 1 December 1995.

17 *Guardian*, 6 December 1995.

18 *Amateur Photographer*, 2 December 1995.

19 For a more detailed discussion of these matters see Pat Califia, *Public Sex: The Culture of Radical Sex*, Pittsburgh, Cleis Press, 1994; Tim Tate, *Child Pornography: An Investigation*, London, Methuen, 1990; and King (see note 13).

20 Parliamentary discussions quoted by Stephen J. King (see note 13). King's research work and completed paper gave the author invaluable guidance in researching and writing parts of this chapter, particularly this portion.

21 In early 1997 all three magazines ceased to exist. No actual legal action has of yet made them illegal. However, pressure from police and child-protection groups led to a German court ruling that such titles could only go on sale if shrink-wrapped and located on the top shelf of sex shops. Previously they had been on general sale in Germany. The publishers ceased producing the magazines. In December 1997 a

police warrant was issued against Peenhill for conspiracy to publish indecent photographs.

22 According to its owner, Reginald Taylor, in conversation with Stephen J. King, Peenhill's bank would no longer support the company, because of some of the magazines it published, and so the company had to close.

23 In Holland such naturist products were in trouble towards the end of 1996 for being on sale in sex shops. An adult woman who saw an image of herself as a child in one such child naturist video sued, thus bringing the issue to public attention.

24 It is worth mentioning that possession of such materials would be an offence in cases of internet and computer porn, and that a lot of the material posted in paed-ophile newsgroups, referred to as child pornography, appears to be naturist in type.

25 Letter to Holt from The Paymaster General's Office at HM Government's Treasury, 27 April 1995.

26 Ibid.

27 Dennis Howitt, *Paedophiles and Sexual Offences Against Children*, Chichester, J. Wiley, 1995.

28 Ibid.

29 This argument has been offered by Ray Wyre, see, for example, 'Pornography and sexual violence: working with sex offenders', in Catherine Itzin (ed.), *Pornography*, Oxford, Oxford University Press, 1992. Also, author interview with Metropolitan Police.

30 Howitt (see note 27).

31 Tate (see note 19).

32 *Newsletter on Civil Liberties*, Canada, April 1996.

33 *Sunday Times*, 13 March 1994.

34 Howitt (see note 27).

35 The circulation of graphic depictions of sexual abuse in any medium or format is considered to be a continuation of the offence; the suppressing of such materials is understandably therefore pursued in order to stop this from happening.

36 *Daily Telegraph*, 11 November 1995.

37 See Sigmund Freud, 'General Theory of the Neuroses, Introductory Lectures on Psychoanalysis', part III, *The Standard Edition*, vol. xvi, translated by J. Strachey in collaboration with A. Freud, London, Chatto & Windus, 1996.

38 Quoted by Judith Levine, 'Children-who-molest', *Mojo Wired*, online magazine, spring 1996.

39 Levine, ibid.

40 Freud (see note 37).

41 Tate (see note 19).

42 *Daily Mirror*, 9 February 1996. The new law allowed for sex between consenting teenagers aged thirteen to fifteen. It maintains, however, the offence of adult males, aged sixteen and over, having sex with girls under sixteen, but not adult females having sex with boys – a sexist discrepancy partly, no doubt, the product of male fantasies of being seduced by the older woman and the patriarchal need to protect the family property, including a daughter's virginity, from adult interventions.

43 BBC television news, 14 August 1996.

44 Quoted by King (see note 13).

45 Again, gratitude is owed to Stephen J. King for his research work, and his paper (see note 13).

46 There is also a greater tradition in the figurative arts of depicting young girls. Artists

mindful of the wider context of art history may well see their portrayal as more of a challenge. Thanks are due to Nicky Akehurst, for access to materials that assisted in researching this portion of the chapter.

47 Oliver (see note 15).

48 In the autumn of 1996, the Hayward Gallery in London called in the police to assess whether any of the images in their Mapplethorpe retrospective show contravened the law. The police picked out two pictures, one an image of 'Rosie', a photo of a young girl sitting in a dress with no underwear on. Rosie herself, now an adult, who runs a café in West London, said at the time that she planned in future to hang the original, which she owns, in public view in her establishment.

49 *Amateur Photographer*, 2 December 1995.

50 Quotations from Oliver (see note 15).

51 Nor suggestive of the photographic session itself being lascivious or representing a form of indecency. The Obscene Publications Squad proceeded to investigate families of children featured in Oliver's photographs for child abuse. Though some families were contacted and interviewed by social workers, and it was confirmed that the sessions with Oliver involved no form of impropriety, for a while the police proposed to broadcast the faces of some of Oliver's subjects on national British television, on the *Crimewatch* programme, in order to obtain the identities of children from older photo work for which Oliver no longer had any records.

In the case of Cotterill, when the police interviewed the twelve-year-old girl from the original set of 'offending' pictures, she spoke of her photo sessions with Cotterill with enthusiasm. However the police interview was perhaps more disturbing for her, including questions like, *Did she sleep with her father? Had he ever had intercourse with her*, or '*fingered her front bottom or back bottom'? Had she ever seen her father with a hard penis? Had any boy or man fingered her genitals?* She was then taken into care for several weeks before being returned to her father, who himself had been threatened in no uncertain terms with being charged of allowing indecent photos to be taken of a minor. Similarly intrusive and harrowing interviews occurred during the period of the Graham Ovenden investigation. (Information on both cases sourced from the *Guardian*, 13 January 1996, and King (see note 13).)

52 Quoted in *Newsletter on Civil Liberties*, Canada, April 1996.

53 Oliver (see note 15).

54 Ironically, although Mann's family album work is the product of direction and performance, the faith that believes that what is seen is what happened has found Mann being accused of poor taste through 'overexposing' her children to the scrutiny of her camera.

55 *New Statesman and Society*, 31 March 1995.

56 Frank Lubbers, Municipal van Abbe Museum, Eindhoven, Netherlands, letter to Ron Oliver, quoted by Oliver (see note 15).

7 The perils of cyberspace

1 *Our Mutual Friend*, quoted by Walter Kendrick, *The Secret Museum: Pornography in Modern Culture*, New York, Viking, 1987.

2 Kendrick, ibid.

3 Quoted by Andrew Calcutt, 'Exposed: computer porn scandal in commons', *Living Marxism*, April 1994.

4 Elizabeth Grice, *Daily Telegraph*, quoted by Calcutt (see note 3).

5 These 'facts', never backed up with much hard evidence, would be duly reiterated in mainstream media. See, for example, *Guardian*, 27 September 1994.

6 To be engagingly entitled *The Pornographer's Handbook: How to Exploit Women, Dupe Men and Make Lots of Money.*

7 *Time*, Time Warner Magazines, 25 June 1995.

8 *Evening Standard*, 11 October 1995.

9 *SurfWatch* web site.

10 *The Times*, 13 November 1995.

11 *Time*, Time Warner Magazines, 25 June 1995. A later version of a similar product would also prevent child users from giving out personal details.

12 C-Net News.Com (a daily, online news service covering the world of information technology), 26 June 1997.

13 Ibid.

14 Once the gated online communities like CompuServe and AOL finally started providing subscribers with access to the weird and wild web, they lost the ability to supervise their subscribers, to protect them from the real cyberworld. It was time for them to take heed of what was going on – a recognition made more pressing by CompuServe's courtroom appearance in Germany at the end of 1995, when it was told by a Bavarian prosecutor to shut down its feed to usenet alt newsgroups because some of these were transmitting obscenity. Access to more than 200 internet newsgroups was suspended after being alleged as illegal under German criminal law – groups that included 'alt.gay-lesbian-bi' and many, many other similar sex-discussion groups which tend to discourage and actively flame users who posted image files in their space. By mid-February 1996, CompuServe had reinstated nearly all 200 groups, excepting five concerned with child pornography. But the Bavarian authorities would continue to make a case against CompuServe during 1997.

15 WWW Consortium PICS launch press release.

16 Standards of the Comics Code Authority for editorial matter, quoted by Les Daniels, *Comix: A History of Comic Books in America*, New York, Outerbridge & Deinstfrey, 1971.

17 Quoted at C-Net News.Com, 21 June 1996.

18 Julie, in an email to the author.

19 C-Net News.Com, 26 June 1997.

20 Ibid.

21 C-Net News.Com, 1 July 1997.

22 And where conspiracy theorists believe that black helicopters carrying federal government hit men visited the Pacific Northwest to eliminate any recalcitrant backwoodsmen.

23 Email to the author.

24 *Internet Magazine*, online, September 1996.

25 *Time*, Time Warner Magazines, 25 June 1995.

26 An anonymous contributor to a newsgroup thread on the subject of child endangerment.

27 Another nameless contributor to a newsgroup thread on the subject of child endangerment.

28 National Children's Home Action for Children Poll, 1995.

29 Tim Tate, *Child Pornography: An Investigation*, London, Methuen, 1990.

30 *Paidika*, autumn 1995.

31 Quoted in *Paidika*, autumn 1995.

32 It is important, of course, to recognise that old child-porn materials, dating back twenty to thirty years now, featured real children, now grown up, with real lives, who might well consider the availability of graphic material depicting their abuse to be a continuation of the offence. The rooting out and interdiction of the distribution of these 'antique' images for such reasons is understandable.

33 Ironically, but perhaps unsurprisingly, it is the repeated flaming and verbal abuse of paedophiles and child pornographers that amounts to a large bulk of the messages posted to such paedophile newsgroups.

34 Similarly in the USA with the Hatch Amendment to the Federal Budget Bill in late November 1996.

35 *Observer*, 25 August 1996.

36 A notorious criminal prosecution in Canada involving Paul Bernado and Karla Homulka received a government news blackout order. Helsingiius was able to remail trial reports to an electronic list service for Canadians to access.

37 Demon (UK) Limited company statement.

38 *Internet Magazine*, online, September 1996.

39 Ibid.

40 Department of Trade and Industry press release, online, September 1996.

41 The Internet Watch Foundation brought with it an all-round feelgood mood, with apparently everybody a winner. The government was now able to look executive-like; getting things fixed during the party conference season. The police were also very satisfied: having passed the burden of intelligence-gathering to the internet industry, they now simply had to wait for sightings to be reported, before they could get out there and make some arrests. (Additionally, IWF would become a management board, with directors to include representatives of the police.) Service providers, meanwhile, could look forward to the best night's sleep in ages, knowing the chance of going to jail had vastly receded.

42 Susan Edwards, quoted by Calcutt in *Living Marxism* (see note 3).

43 Reuters. In late 1997 a similar 'cybertip line' was launched in the USA.

44 C-Net News.Com, 1 July 1997.

45 European Parliamentary initiatives on policing the internet to enforce a community-wide policy that what is illegal off-line should be illegal online, which stressed the need for cooperation between member states, were unlikely to force Britain to reconsider its anomalous position on hard-core porn. Most likely the community-wide policy would find itself making exceptions for the island nation.

Alternatively, heavy British-led lobbying for a common standard on net porn might find that the European Union adopts tough British-style laws to control the internet through the community – regardless of the fact that much material proscribed online would be legal off-line in most of the territories of the community.

8 Future sex

1 Examples of such futurology include the *Observer* series of autumn 1995, also called 'Future Sex', where, on 15 October, readers were offered the cover image of a cyborgian woman wearing a suit of armour with portions of transparent latex stretched across a pair of exposed plastic breasts. Also Britain's *GQ* of spring 1996, where men were rigged up to virtual reality exoskeletons in a laboratory in Munich, or the cover of *Boing Boing* magazine's special on future sex with an image of a cyberboy and cybergirl overloaded with plug-in sex devices, floating in space.

2 *Observer*, 'Future Sex', 15 October 1995.

3 Interview with Larry Flynt in *Details* magazine, May 1996.

4 Advertising pitch online posted at usenet alt.sex.movies, and many other usenet alt.sex sites.

5 Advertising pitch online posted at usenet alt.sex.movies, and others.

6 Advertising pitch sent to the author by the Campus Cuties subscriptions office. Another example of college girl self-promotion concerns the near-celebrity figure, Jennifer Ringley. As an undergraduate studying Economics at Dickinson College in Carlisle, Pennsylvania, and later, after graduating, as a software designer in Washington, DC, Ringley rigged up a camera linked to the world wide web which features pictures of her room. Pictures are taken every three minutes and Jenni's camera never sleeps. Although mostly amounting to a detailed record of the banal – Jenni reads, Jenni talks on the phone, Jenni sleeps – the Jenni site has also featured images of Jenni naked. Indeed the Jenni site carries an archive of past images, as well as a game called 'spot the curve', where visitors to the site are supposed to guess what part of Jenni's anatomy a sample snippet of her flesh might belong to. Over time, Jenni has also occasionally proved to be a bit of an exhibitionist, performing a striptease for the camera. Inevitably this gained her some notoriety, and found grabbed images of Jenni naked posted on the usenet. Eventually her site became pay-per-view, and linked to other commercial online porn sites. In thrall to a mix of motivations – from a hunger for fame, a fascination for 'real life' soaps, as well as a post-slacker penchant for the trivial – almost in passing Jenni also remade herself as a part-time, pro-amateur porn star. (See Jennicam at www.boudoir.org.) The success of Jennicam prompted numerous imitators. The 'homecam' cult – some nude, some not; males, females, couples, or even a bunch of friends 'hanging out' – became a booming phenomenon during the second half of 1997, the number of such sites rising from a handful to well over a hundred in a matter of a few months.

7 Another advertising pitch online posted at usenet alt.sex.movies, and others.

8 Interview in *Details* magazine, May 1996.

9 Ginger's advertising pitch online posted at usenet alt.sex.movies.

10 From 'Wildchild', online porn lover and porn producer, email to the author.

11 *Guardian*, 17 October 1996.

12 *Adult Video News*, September 1996.

13 Ibid.

14 Mark Derry, *Escape Velocity*, London, Hodder & Stoughton, 1996.

15 Stefani Martin, Creative System Operator for CyberSpice, from an interview in *Porn Free: The Porn 'Zine Dedicated to Getting You Off for Nothin'*, spring 1995.

16 *Observer*, 15 October 1995.

17 Of course this closing scene from *Latex* might well have been a more mundane, ironic gesture of self-defence on the part of director Michael Ninn: a massive fake penis with its ridiculous fountain spew, which says 'I know it's fake, I am aware of what I'm doing.'

18 *Modern Review*, August/September 1993.

9 Pornocopia

All quotations from and references to the opinions of porn fans are from letters or emails to the author, unless otherwise stated.

1 Sallie Tisdale, *Talk Dirty To Me: An Intimate Philosophy of Sex*, London, Pan Books, 1995.

2 One thinks of the celebrity American radio host, Howard Stern, the British

comedian David Baddiel, *Loaded* magazine, the novelists Anne Rice and Nicholson Baker, the American writer Sallie Tisdale's *Talk Dirty To Me* – but not a lot else.

3 There are numerous 'zines concerned with or touching on porn including: *Batteries Not Included, Smut, Skin Trade, Headpress, Flesh and Blood, Velvet, The Home Front, Apaeros, Black Sheets, The Taste of Latex, Holy Titclamps, Porn Free, Pornorama, Bulk Male* (the 'zine for lovers of big, hairy men) and *Celebrate the Self,* a newsletter about solo sex, featuring masturbatory reminiscences and product evaluations. From the world of independent, alternative publishing there is also the feminist anthology *Tales from the Clit,* and the porn review work of Susie Bright.

4 *Select,* July 1994.

5 'Sex in America', University of Chicago, Harris School of Public Policy Studies.

6 *Playboy,* August 1994.

7 *Pulse/Top Sante,* autumn 1996.

8 Anthony Lane, 'Lay People', *New Yorker,* 19 December 1994.

9 Gary Andrew Poole, 'Self Love Story', *Sky* magazine, summer 1996.

10 Tony Parsons, *Arena* magazine, November 1996.

11 Over the Christmas holiday period of 1996, a London billboard poster campaign for the drink Bailey's featured a beautiful woman wearing a skimpy cardigan which barely covered her lap and provided plenty of cleavage. A drink mainly consumed by women was being sold to women through an image of seduction and sexiness usually, or supposedly, only exploited when it is men being addressed as consumers.

12 Quoted by Andy Darlington, *Desire* magazine, issue 11.

13 *Observer,* 15 October 1995.

14 *Desire* magazine, issue 5.

15 The veil of silence regarding female masturbation was at least partially raised by the women's movement of the seventies, see the book *Our Bodies Ourselves,* as well as Bettie Dodson with her 'cunt positive' guides.

16 Interview with Tuppy Owens, *Hustler* (UK), October 1995.

17 Rachel James, 'An introduction to Porno 101', *Batteries Not Included,* April 1994.

18 Brandy Alexandre, home page @ kamikaze.com.

19 Spence, *Batteries Not Included,* July 1995.

20 *Independent on Sunday,* 21 April 1996.

21 Anne McClintock, 'Gonad the Barbarian and the Venus Flytrap: portraying the female and male orgasm', in Lybbe Segal and Mary McIntosh (eds), *Sex Exposed: Sexuality and the Pornography Debate,* London, Virago, 1992.

22 The identity of photographer is best left as anonymous.

23 McClintock (see note 21).

24 Umberto Eco, 'Towards a semiological guerrilla warfare', in *Travels in Hyperreality: Essays,* translated by William Weaver, London, Picador, 1987.

25 Bernard Arcand, *The Jaguar and the Anteater: Pornography Degree Zero,* translated by Wayne Grady, London/New York, Verso, 1993.

26 Allucquere Rosanne Stone, *The War of Desire and Technology at the Close of the Mechanical Age,* Cambridge, Massachusetts/London, MIT Press, 1996.

27 Roland Barthes, *Camera Obscura,* London, Vintage, 1993.

28 Catherine A. MacKinnon, *Only Words,* London, HarperCollins, 1994.

29 Drucilla Cornell, *The Imaginary Domain: Abortion, Pornography and Sexual Harassment,* New York/London, Routledge, 1995.

30 Interview archived at Depth Probe web site.

31 *Fringeware* magazine, April 1994.

32 Suzanne Moore, *The Idler*, May–June 1995.

33 For more on male porn 'dependencies', see Linda Williams, *Hard Core: Power, Pleasure and the 'Frenzy of the Visible'*, London, Pandora Press, 1990; also Michael Kimmel (ed.), *Men Confront Pornography*, New York, Crown, 1989; as well as Alan Soble, *Pornography: Marxism, Feminism and the Future of Sexuality*, New Haven, Connecticut, Yale University Press, 1986.

34 See Leo Bersani, *Homos*, Cambridge, Massachusetts/London, Harvard University Press, 1995.

35 Cited by Lynda Nead, 'Above the pulp line: the cultural significance of erotic art', in Pamela Church Gibson and Roma Gibson (eds), *Dirty Looks: Women, Pornography, Power*, London, British Film Institute, 1993.

36 The survey was based on responses from porn users contacted through magazine ads and assorted newsgroups on usenet, and from other personal contacts – anyone with a porn view who had wanted to get in touch. It was not an attempt at a demographic cross-section of people.

37 Interview with Jonathan Green, in *It: Sex since the Sixties*, London, Secker & Warburg, 1993.

38 Ibid.

39 Carol Queen, *Exhibitionism for the Shy*, San Francisco, Down There Press, 1995.

40 John Money, *Lovemaps: Clinical Concepts of Sexual/Erotic Health and Pathology, Paraphilia, and Gender Transposition in Childhood, Adolescence, and Maturity*, New York, Irvington Publishers, 1986.

41 'Children in Crisis', *The Late Show*, BBC television, 1985.

42 *Body Politic*, Issue 5, 1994.

43 Tom Engelhardt, *The End of Victory Culture: Cold War America and the Disillusioning of a Generation*, New York, Basic Books, 1995.

44 Tisdale (see note 1).

45 Anonymous posting at alt.sex.movies, spring 1996.

46 *Desire* magazine, issue 3.

47 Amber Hollibaugh, 'Desire for the future: radical hope in passion and pleasure', in Carol S. Vance (ed.), *Pleasure and Danger: Exploring Female Sexuality*, London, Pandora Press, 1992

48 Michael Bronski, email to the author.

49 Imperator, from the Imperial Archive, available at alt.sex.movies.

50 Andrew Ross, *No Respect: Intellectuals and Popular Culture*, New York/London, Routledge, 1989.

51 Laura Kipnis, *Bound and Gagged: Pornography and the Politics of Fantasy in America*, New York, Grove Press, 1996.

52 Interview with Jonathan Green (see note 37).

53 Steve Fowle, letter to the author.

54 It is worth mentioning that many angry porners were spoken with via the modem and online. Expressing bad feelings is quite the thing in cyberspace, where some definitely luxuriate in their right as netizens to be fractious. Netheads tend to get the hump quite easily: all you need do is write something blandly controversial, like *Jesus was gay*, or, *I've just fucked my sister's puppy*, then cross-post to alt.bestiality and alt.puppy.lovers, or alt.atheism and alt.christnet and watch the flame wars begin. 'Don't use such a politically loaded (and negative word) like porn,' writes one stickler to the author. Another contributes a stern ticking off, 'If I can

contribute nothing else, let me express my contempt for the term "porn users". Would you call someone who enjoys Milton a "poetry user"? Use "erotica affectionadoe".'

Another usenet porner rebuffs the author's request for an exchange of views by sending five pages of one highly singular message, some of which goes like this: 'spam spam spam spam spam spam spam spam spam spam spam spam spam spam spam spam spam spam spam spam spam spam spam spam spam spam spam spam spam spam spam spam spam spam spam spam spam spam spam spam spam spam spam spam spam spam spam spam spam spam spam spam get the idea?'

55 There are even some interviews at the front of the tape that seek to persuade the gullible viewer that Tammi Ann, a popular actress of the mid-nineties, is in fact a 'florist' and a porn virgin who is preparing for a one-off hard-core performance for the camera.

56 See David Hebditch and Nick Anning, *Porn Gold: Inside the Pornography Business*, London, Faber & Faber, 1988.

57 'Mr Peeved' in discussion threat at alt.sex.movies, winter 1995.

58 Queen (see note 39).

59 *Desire* magazine, issue 5.

60 Ibid.

61 Interview in *Porn Free: The Porn 'Zine Dedicated to Getting You Off for Nothin'*, spring 1995.

62 Ibid.

63 Anonymous in discussion thread at alt.sex.movies, winter 1995.

64 See archive at alt.sex.movies.

65 Anonymous in discussion thread at rec.arts.movies.erotica, summer 1996.

66 Jamal Dunbar, see alt.sex.movies web site.

67 Ringthane, discussion thread at alt.sex.movies, spring 1995.

68 Discussion thread at rec.arts.movies.erotica, summer 1996.

69 Anonymous porn reviewer posting at rec.arts.movies.erotica, summer 1996.

70 This is not a newness to be defined in terms such as 'harder' or 'weirder', one that is sliding down the slippery slide to extremity. Porners do not display a tendency to be 'corrupted' in such a way.

71 These comments are edited highlights of a very long discussion thread at rec.arts.movies.erotica, autumn 1996.

72 Tabatha Haasen, *Batteries Not Included*, October 1995.

73 Steffani Martin, Creative System Operator for CyberSpice, from an interview in *Porn Free: The Porn 'Zine Dedicated to Getting You Off for Nothin'*, spring 1995.

74 Candida Royalle, from an interview with *Libido: The Journal of Sex and Sensibility*, online http://www.sensualsource.com/libido/.

75 Letter from Tom Eaton to *Batteries Not Included*, October 1995.

76 Haasen (see note 72).

Afterword

1 Reuters/Variety, 'Filmmaker wants to make porn respectable', by David Brinkerhoff, June 1997.

2 Nicholas White, letter to the author.

Select bibliography

Bernard Arcand, *The Jaguar and the Anteater: Pornography Degree Zero*, translated by Wayne Grady, London/New York, Verso, 1993.

Leo Bersani, *Homos*, Cambridge, Massachusetts/London, Harvard University Press, 1995.

Pat Califia, *Public Sex: The Culture of Radical Sex*, Pittsburgh, Cleis Press, 1994.

Avedon Carol, *Nudes, Prudes and Attitudes*, Cheltenham, New Clarion Press, 1994.

Mark Derry, *Escape Velocity*, London, Hodder & Stoughton, 1996.

Tom Dewe Mathews, *Censored: The Story of Film Censorship in Britain*, London, Chatto & Windus, 1994.

Michel Foucault, *The History of Sexuality: An Introduction*, Harmondsworth, Peregrine Books, 1984.

Pamela Church Gibson and Roma Gibson (eds), *Dirty Looks: Women, Pornography, Power*, London, British Film Institute, 1993.

David Hebditch and Nick Anning, *Porn Gold: Inside the Pornography Business*, London, Faber & Faber, 1988.

Lynne Hunt (ed.) *The Invention of Pornography*, New York, Zone Books, 1993.

Walter Kendrick, *The Secret Museum: Pornography in Modern Culture*, New York, Viking, 1987.

David Kerekes and David Slater, *Killing for Culture: An Illustrated History of Death Film from Mondo to Snuff*, London, Creation Books, 1994.

Thomas Laqueur, *The Making of Sex: Body and Gender from the*

Greeks to Freud, Cambridge, Massachusetts/London, Harvard University Press, 1992.

Wendy McElroy, *XXX: A Woman's Right to Pornography*, New York, St Martin's Press, 1995.

Dave McGillivray, *Doing Rude Things: The History of the British Sex Film, 1957–1981*, London, Sun Tavern Fields, 1992.

Jonathan Ned Katz, *The Invention of Heterosexuality*, New York, Duton, 1995.

Carol Queen, *Exhibitionism for the Shy*, San Francisco, Down There Press, 1995.

Andrew Ross, *No Respect: Intellectuals and Popular Culture*, New York/London, Routledge, 1989.

Lynne Segal and Mary McIntosh (eds), *Sex Exposed: Sexuality and the Pornography Debate*, London, Virago, 1992.

Lynne Segal, *Straight Sex: The Politics of Pleasure*, London, Virago, 1994.

Allucquere Rosanne Stone, *The War of Desire and Technology at the Close of the Mechanical Age*, Cambridge Massachusetts/London, MIT Press, 1996.

Nadine Strossen, *Defending Pornography: Free Speech, Sex, and the Fight for Women's Rights*, London, Abacus, 1996.

Sallie Tisdale, *Talk Dirty To Me: An Intimate Philosophy of Sex*, London, Pan Books, 1995.

Carol S. Vance (ed.), *Pleasure and Danger: Exploring Female Sexuality*, London, Pandora Press, 1992.

Jeffrey Weeks, *Sex, Politics and Society: The Regulation of Sexuality since 1800*, second edition, London, Longman, 1989.

Jeffrey Weeks, *Invented Moralities: Sexual Values in an Age of Uncertainty*, Cambridge, Polity Press, 1995.

Linda Williams, *Hard Core: Power, Pleasure and the 'Frenzy of the Visible'*, London, Pandora Press, 1990.

Also:

alt.sex.movies home page on the world wide web

rec.arts.movies.erotica, usenet discussion group

The Imperator Review Archive can be accessed via alt.sex.movies home page

Batteries Not Included, porn 'zine, edited by Richard Freeman (130, West Limestone Street, Yellow Springs, Ohio, 45387, USA)

Videography

Fifteen Porn Movie Classics
(in no particular order of merit)

Devil in Miss Jones (1972, Gerard Damiano, Arrow Film and Video)
Georgina Spelvin develops a carnal itch that won't be scratched in this early landmark of porn cinema. Recommended to all, except to lapsed Catholics of a nervous disposition.

Amanda By Night (1981, Robert McCallum, Caballero)
Veronica Hart and Richard Bolla team up to catch a serial killer on the loose in a porn noir almost good enough to watch without the sex. McCallum is one of the great unsung porn directors, good with the narrative as well as the sex, and technically gifted enough to have worked as Orson Welles's cinematographer.

Between Lovers (1983, Henri Pachard, Caballero)
Jessie St. James, Georgina Spelvin, John Leslie and Joey Silvera do a high-gloss erotic square dance in this tale of planes, trains and bigamists. A romantic comedy for grown-ups.

Desires Within Young Girls (1977, Ramsey Karson, Caballero)
Following an over-vigorous bout of lovemaking with her husband, Georgina Spelvin finds herself widowed and short of spending cash. Her plan to fix up her daughters, Annette Haven and Clair Dia, with rich hubbies, typically backfires when the girls take off with a pair of indigents instead. Funny, romantic, sexy – the quintessential 'couples movie'.

V – The Hot One (1978, Robert McCallum, Cal Vista)
Hard core's version of the Buñuel classic, *Belle du Jour*. Annette Haven plays the well-heeled housewife who, having been brought up to believe that 'good girls' don't like sex, becomes a part-time prostitute as a kind of therapy. The problem is, how does she keep husband John Leslie from finding out?

Sensations (1975, Lasse Braun)
An innocent American abroad makes the grand erotic tour of Europe with all the pervy trimmings. This glossy, big-budget French sex film was actually shown at the Cannes Film Festival but, for all its lusty sophistication and cocaine decadence, was a major box

office flop, causing Euro-porners to give up on porno de luxe for a generation. Worth tracking down, if only to gawp at the seventies fashion gear.

Her Name Was Lisa (1979, Richard Mahler, VCA)
Mahler was the brooding, existentialist auteur of porn's golden age. This involving film opens graveside at the funeral of fashion model Lisa. A series of flashbacks relates her downfall through drugs. Samantha Fox plays the lead (but not the same Samantha Fox as the former British page three model and pop-singing sensation).

Behind the Green Door (1972, Jim and Artie Mitchell, Mitchell Bros)
Once upon a time the fresh-faced Marilyn Chambers starred in a TV commercial for luxury soap, only to give it all up for hard core. *Green Door*, her porn debut, features the infamous sex-on-a-trapeze scene. Although sloppily filmed and politically unreconstructed, it remains a popular porn movie with women viewers.

800 Fantasy Lane (1979, Svetlana, Cal Vista)
A pair of no-hoper petrol-pump operators make believe they're millionaires looking for a luxury mansion in order to be taken care of by a glamorous all-women estate agent's. Director Svetlana was the queen of the screwball hard-core comedy. Other Svetlana movies worth looking out for: *Sex Boat* (1980, VCX), *F* (1980, Collector's Video) and *(A Little Bit of) Hanky Panky* (1984, Collector's) featuring Ginger Lynn.

Opening of Misty Beethoven (1976, Henry Paris, VCA)
Possibly the best hard-core movie ever made. Porn's *My Fair Lady*, with Jamie Gillis and Constance Money living the high life from Paris, through Rome to Manhattan, and falling in love along the way.

Wet Rainbow (1973, Duddy Kane, Arrow Film and Video)
This well-acted porn melodrama from the very early days of hard-core feature films has Harry Reems and Georgina Spelvin playing husband and wife emotionally involved in a *ménage à trois* with a footloose hippie chick.

Sex World (1978, Anthony Spinelli, Essex)
Michael Crichton's seminal sci-fi movie *Westworld* gets a memorable hard-core makeover – graphically illustrating just how much fun a futuristic holiday theme park might be. Spinelli made about a dozen or more watchable porn movies. Look out for *Talk Dirty to Me* and *Nothing to Hide*, his two-part reworking of Steinbeck's *Of Mice and Men*, as well as *The Dancers* and *Dixie Ray – Hollywood Star*.

Pandora's Mirror (1981, Warren Evans, Caballero)
This theatrical big-budget pornfest features opulent gear and film sets and Veronica Hart playing the eponymous Pandora and her highly revealing fantasy mirror.

Every Woman Has a Fantasy (1984, Edwin Durrell, VCA)
John Leslie becomes fixated on finding out what his wife and her girlfriends talk about when there aren't any men around. After assorted gambits fail, a spot of cross-dressing sees him finally get an invite to one of his wife's parties.

Little Girls Blue (1978, Joanna Williams, VCX)
Director Joanna Williams brings a routine tale of college girls sexually running amok to the boil. So much fun, she did it again five years later with *Little Girls Blue 2* (1983, VCX)

Five Titles from the Nineties

Buttman's Inferno (1991, John Stagliano, Evil Angel Video)
Stagliano's Buttman series – hand-held camera, on the hoof, so-called 'gonzo' porn – has spawned a thousand imitations. For the uninitiated, *Inferno* is an excellent way in to Stagliano's witty, teasing, erotic style, and, among other things, features Angela Summers getting personal with fans in New Zealand, and Krysti Lynn looking for fun in San Diego. (See also *Buttman versus Buttwoman*, *Ultimate Workout*, *European Vacation*, *American Buttman in London*, as well as non-Buttman movies from Stagliano like *Wild Goose Chase* and *Face Dance*.)

Steamy Windows (1993, Paul Thomas, Vivid)
Paul Thomas was a leading actor during porn's 'golden age'. As a director he continues the tradition of dramatic, feature-length films combining stories with hard-core sex. *Steamy Windows* features a strong performance from Ashlyn Gere, queen of early nineties porn, and an end-of-movie orgy scene that lasts for more than half an hour. Other couples movies from Thomas worth looking out for include *Nothing to Hide 2: Justine* (1992, Cal Vista), *Beauty and the Beast* (1988, VCA), *The Masseuse* (1990, Vivid) and *Bobby Sox* (Vivid, 1996).

Erotika (1995, Robert McCallum, Western Visuals Gold)
Samantha Strong is an exotic photographer sorting out the demons of her stormy childhood through her art. A rather so-so story is made up for by the luxury sheen of this shot-on-film, high-budget movie made on location in Los Angeles, Las Vegas, Paris and the Californian desert, and featuring sex in the dunes, by the pool and under a waterfall.

Secrets (1990, Andrew Blake, Caballero)
Blake is a key figure of the American industry during the nineties, putting the glamour back in porn. His beautifully filmed, soft-focus, 'arty' porn has brought a whole new band of viewers to hard core, including a lot of women. *Secrets* is probably the best of Blake, although *Night Trips* (1989, Caballero), *Paris Chic* (1997, Studio A Entertainment) and *Hidden Obsessions* (1992, Ultimate), with the infamous ice dildo scene, are all worth a viewing.

Latex (1995, Michael Ninn, VCA)
Nineties American hard core's journey into designer sex achieves its pinnacle with *Latex*. Jon Dough plays a 'crazy' man with a dark imagination, Tiffany Million is his nutty shrink, while Sunset Thomas goes a bundle on prosthetics. Ninn's hard-core style offers a high-speed medley of flash photography, elaborate designs and in-your-face special effects. Not everybody's all time erotic high, it's true, but a monumental piece of end-of-the-century porn nonetheless.

Other Movies and Directors of Worth

Erotic Adventures of Candy (1978, Gail Palmer, VCX)
Charli (1981, Godfrey Daniels, VCX)
Tiffany Minx (1981, Roberta Findlay, Caballero)
Cecil Howard – *Firestorm* (1984, Command) and *The Last X-Rated Movie* (1987, Command)
Alex DeRenzy – *Baby Face* (VCA) and *Pretty Peaches* (VCA)
Candida Royalle – anything from Royalle's *Femme* company if you're looking for loving, romantic sexual film fantasies.
Chuck Vincent – *Misbehavin'* (1979 Video-X-pix), *Roommates* (1982, Video-X-pix), *In Love* (1983, VCA)

Greg Dark – 'bad-ass' hard core, not for the faint-hearted, see *DMJ5: The Inferno* (VCA) and *New Wave Hookers 3* (VCA)

Cameron Grant – *Elements of Desire* (Ultimate) and *The Dinner Party* (Ultimate)

John Leslie – *Chameleons* (VCA) and porn noirs like *Dog Walker* (Evil Angel)

Toni English – for her 'Extreme Sex' series and *Hawaii* (Vivid).

Ann-Perry Rhine – *Count the Ways* (1976 Caballero) and *Teenage Sex Kitten* (1972 Caballero)

Ona Zee – the former porn actress owns a porn company especially noted for its 'all-girlers' video tapes

Tianna Collins – for her work as Buttman's nemesis, Buttwoman

Shane – see the *Shane's World* series.

Steve Perry – see his 'Ben Dover' video series for a version of Buttman in a British context.

For those who would prefer something a bit more 'continental', European film-makers of note from recent years are Marcel Ricaud, Joe D'Amato, Luca Damiano and Rocco Siffredi. European production companies such as Video Marc Dorcel, Colmax, Helen Duvall and Private tend to turn out good-quality porn. Fans of amateur hour might want to look for the freewheeling work of Becky Sunshine and Kiva, while those interested in a spot of mainstream fetishist porn might want to seek out the Red Board Video range, or the videos of Kym Wilde, Ernest Greene and Bruce Seven.

To get hold of some if not all of these videos, readers could try any of these far-flung mail-order outlets. Good Vibrations (1210 Valencia Street, San Francisco, CA, 94110) and Toys in Babeland (Seattle: (206) 328 2914) are sex shops both run by and oriented towards women. Look out for their respective web sites and online mail-order services. Likewise Blowfish, which carries a very extensive range of videos (at www.evn.com). See also the website, http://excaliburfilms.com/html/excal/hotlinks.htm. A Good Vibrations guide to adult videos is forthcoming from Down There Press during 1998. *Wise Women's Guide to Erotic Videos*, by Angela Cohen and Sarah Gardner-Fox, is published in the US by Broadway Books. Most of the recent videos mentioned above will be legally available to readers in Britain in a cut-down, soft-core variety through licensed sex shops and many high street video retailers. Alternatively there is the highly reputable Your Choice in Amsterdam (0031 20 620 4209) offering a fairly diverse list of fully hard-core titles. Video & filmudlejningen, Copenhagen, Denmark: 45 35 85 05 10, are specialists in seventies American hard core. And if you want to track down pre-seventies fringe films, from fifties 'nudies' and 'sexploitation' movies to compilation hard-core trailers (as well as a lot of other lost 'exotica'), then try Something Weird (www.somethingweird.com, or P.O. Box 33664, Seattle, WA 98133).

Index